The
African American
Encyclopedia

Second Edition

The
African American
Encyclopedia

Second Edition

Volume 2
Bla-Com

Editor, First Edition
Michael W. Williams

Consulting Editor, Supplement to First Edition
Kibibi Voloria Mack

Advisory Board, Second Edition

Barbara Bair
Duke University

Carl L. Bankston III
Tulane University

David Bradley
City University of New York

Shelley Fisher Fishkin
University of Texas, Austin

Wendy Sacket
Coast College

Managing Editor, Second Edition
R. Kent Rasmussen

Marshall Cavendish
New York • London • Toronto • Sydney

Project Editor: McCrea Adams
Production Editor: Cindy Beres
Assistant Editor: Andrea Miller
Research Supervisor: Jeffry Jensen
Photograph Editor: Philip Bader
Page Layout: William Zimmerman

Marshall Cavendish Corporation
99 White Plains Road
Tarrytown, New York 10591-9001

© 2001 Marshall Cavendish Corporation
Printed in the United States of America
09   08   07   06   05   04   03   02   01   5   4   3   2   1

Library of Congress Cataloging-in-Publication Data

The African American encyclopedia.—2nd ed. / managing editor, R. Kent Rasmussen.
      p. cm.
Includes bibliographical references and index.
1. Afro-Americans—Encyclopedias. I. Rasmussen, R. Kent.
E185 .A253   2001
973′.0496073′003—dc21
ISBN 0-7614-7208-8 (set)   00-031526
ISBN 0-7614-7210-x (volume 2)   CIP

∞ This paper meets the requirements of ANSI/NISO Z39.48-1992 (R1997)
Permanence of Paper for Publications and Documents in Libraries and Archives

Contents

Contents

The
African American
Encyclopedia

Second Edition

Black Theater Alliance: Organization of small African American commercial THEATER companies. The alliance was formed in 1971 in New York City out of the need of the companies to survive financially and to develop artistically. Its founders were Delano Stewart, Hazel Bryant, and Roger Furman; seven theater companies formed the initial membership. The alliance soon began to provide technical equipment, graphics, funds, resources, information, and touring assistance to its members. It also sponsored theater festivals, promoted its members' activities, established a newsletter, *Black Theater Alliance*, and provided the *Black Theater Resources Directory*.

Black towns: African Americans established segregated communities in the United States from the time of the AMERICAN REVOLUTION to the twentieth century. In these settlements, black Americans could escape the racism that existed in the dominant white society, could exercise political power, and, perhaps most important, could work together to establish the sense of community that comes from mutual support and cooperation among neighbors.

The majority of the black communities in the United States were settled by former slaves after the CIVIL WAR. Freed from bondage, many African Americans nevertheless faced prejudice and discrimination from their former masters and other whites. This ill treatment prompted many blacks to leave the South and migrate northward. Others chose to try to insulate themselves from white southerners by establishing black towns in such former slave states as Mississippi, Arkansas, and Texas.

The greatest number of African Americans who wanted to live in self-segregated communities, however, decided to settle in the American West. Among the black towns founded on the western frontier in the late nineteenth century were NICODEMUS, KANSAS; Blackdom, NEW MEXICO; DEARFIELD, COLORADO; and Allensworth, CALIFORNIA. Smaller black agricultural colonies existed in many parts of the American West and on the prairies of western Canada.

More black towns existed in Oklahoma than in any other U.S. jurisdiction. There the slaves of the Native Americans who had been forcibly relocated from the South were not only given freedom but also allowed to enroll as members of their respective tribes and receive land grants. Many of these freedmen pooled their resources and settled near each other, creating black communities.

The residents of black towns struggled because of a lack of economic resources. Many had to work as hired farm hands or domestic servants for wealthier (usually white) neighbors. Businesses established in black towns often failed because they had too few customers

Historical marker outside the city hall of Rentiesville, one of thirty all-black towns established in Oklahoma during the late nineteenth century. *(AP/Wide World Photos)*

with too little money to spend. Many of the towns lasted through the last years of the nineteenth century and the early decades of the twentieth but could not survive the twin crises of the 1930's—the GREAT DEPRESSION and the Dust Bowl.

The few black towns that managed to endure often owed their continued existence to a governmental agency being located within their boundaries. Such was the case of LANGSTON, OKLAHOMA, perhaps the most well known of the black towns, home of the state-supported Langston University. Correctional facilities are situated in two additional black towns in the state—Taft and BOLEY, OKLAHOMA.

—*Roger D. Hardaway*
See also: Exodusters and homesteaders; Frontier society; Mound Bayou, Mississippi.

Suggested Readings:

Crockett, Norman L. *The Black Towns.* Lawrence: Regents Press of Kansas, 1979.

Hamilton, Kenneth Marvin. *Black Towns and Profit: Promotion and Development in the Trans-Appalachian West, 1877-1915.* Urbana: University of Illinois Press, 1991.

Hardaway, Roger D. "African American Communities on the Western Frontier." In *Community in the American West*, edited by Stephen Tchudi. Reno: Nevada Humanities Committee, 1999.

Black United Front: Name of two separate CIVIL RIGHTS organizations. The first Black United Front was formed in 1968 to improve the status of African Americans during the racial turbulence of the 1960's. Its members were dissatisfied with the pace and achievements of the more established civil rights organizations such as the SOUTHERN CHRISTIAN LEADERSHIP CONFERENCE (SCLC), the NATIONAL ASSOCIATION FOR THE ADVANCEMENT OF COLORED PEOPLE (NAACP), and the NATIONAL URBAN LEAGUE. The Black United Front called for community control over police as a means of ending police violence against African Americans and of gaining black representation on police forces. Most active in the WASHINGTON, D.C., area, the organization was a mixture of moderates and militants and had on its board of directors African Americans who were officials of the DEMOCRATIC PARTY, the Washington Urban League, and the Washington City Council.

The original Black United Front was short-lived. In July, 1980, a new national civil rights group with that name was formed in Brooklyn, New York, by the Reverend Herbert Daughtry, a clergyman at the Brooklyn PENTECOSTAL Church. This group believed that many African American leaders had become puppets of the dominant power structure and had betrayed the course of development for African Americans. The Black United Front sought to develop a new national African American leadership and to build a strong grass-roots movement to combat unemployment and other problems encountered by African Americans.

The organization sprouted numerous chapters throughout the United States. Its membership included veteran social activists such as Prince Ashiel Ben Israel (ambassador from the Hebrew Israelites of Dimona, Israel), Amiri Baraka (playwright and poet), Skip Robinson (president of the United League of Mississippi), and Imari Obadele (president of the REPUBLIC OF NEW AFRICA). The fact that its membership included many African Americans experienced in civil rights struggles helped focus the organization on programs that range from quality education and housing to women's affairs, police community relations, economic development, and politics.

The group maintained contacts with liberation movements in South Africa and with Caribbean and African countries. Not only did the Black United Front begin to champion the cause of African Americans before policy makers, but it also instilled a sense of direction and discipline in African American youth as well. It participated in BLACK HISTORY MONTH by expanding the month's educational activities to include AFRICA as the origin and center of African American culture.

Blackwell, David Harold (b. April 24, 1919, Centralia, Illinois): Educator, mathematician, and statistician. Blackwell is best known for his research involving applications of time sequences that show dependence on earlier events (Markov chains). In 1965 he was the first African American mathematician to be elected to the National Academy of Sciences, and he received the prestigious Von Neumann Theory Award in mathematics in 1979. Blackwell was a professor of mathematics at

David Harold Blackwell. *(University of California, Berkeley)*

HOWARD UNIVERSITY from 1944 to 1954. He left Howard to accept a position as professor of mathematics and statistics at the University of California at Berkeley, in 1954. The author of *Basic Statistics* (1969), Blackwell also coauthored *Theory of Games and Statistical Decisions*, published in 1979.

Blake, Eubie (February 7, 1883, Baltimore, Maryland—February 12, 1983, New York, New York): Pianist and composer. Blake began playing piano in BALTIMORE clubs in 1899. He was active on the VAUDEVILLE circuit, but his career took off when he began a productive partnership with Noble Sissle in 1915. The Dixie Duo continued to perform vaudeville throughout WORLD WAR I and toured with bandleader James EUROPE. Blake took over as bandleader of the famous 369th Infantry band after Europe's death in 1919. In 1921 Blake and Sissle created music for the show *Shuffle Along*, a musical that ran continuously on Broadway until 1928. Blake wrote other revue-style shows, notably *Blackbirds of 1930* and *Swing It* (1937), but he never duplicated the success of *Shuffle Along*.

During WORLD WAR II, Blake was a featured USO performer. He went into semi-retirement after 1946, hoping to study composition formally. He reappeared in a number of RAGTIME revival shows in the 1950's and, because of his vibrancy despite an advanced age, became a regular on television talk shows of the 1960's and 1970's. His life was the basis for the 1978 Broadway show *Eubie!* Toward the end of his life, he received many honorary degrees, and in 1981 he received the Presidential Medal of Honor.

Blake's first recordings and piano rolls were made in 1917. He wrote more than three hundred songs, two of the most famous of which are "I'm Just Wild About Harry" and "Memories of You." Most of his songs used the syncopated rhythms of ragtime. His piano

Eubie Blake performing at the Newport Jazz Festival in 1979, when he was ninety-six years old. *(AP/Wide World Photos)*

playing was a direct influence on the HARLEM stride piano style of Fats WALLER and James P. JOHNSON, and his compositions were central to their repertoire. Blake was also a prime innovator in African American musical history. His late-life return to performance helped to create a resurgence of interest in and appreciation for ragtime music.

Blakey, Art (October 11, 1919, Pittsburgh, Pennsylvania—October 16, 1990, New York, New York): JAZZ drummer and bandleader. Blakey studied piano at school, and by the seventh grade, he was devoting much of his time to music. He eventually took up the drums and was greatly influenced by the driving, aggressive style of Chick WEBB. His professional career began when he joined Mary Lou WILLIAMS for a performance at Kelly's, a club in New York City. In 1943 and 1944, he traveled with Fletcher Henderson's orchestra, and from 1944 to 1947, he traveled with Billy ECKSTINE's orchestra, which was influential in nurturing many performers of modern jazz.

In 1947 Blakey formed a rehearsal band called the Seventeen Messengers, which in 1955 became an octet known as the Jazz Messengers. He took a break from music in the late 1940's and, after the death of his wife, traveled to Africa to study ISLAM. He was known briefly by the name Abdullah Ibn Buhaina. On his return to the United States in the early 1950's, he began to perform, often as a regular studio drummer for Blue Note Records, with many of the modern jazz greats, including Charlie PARKER, Miles DAVIS, Clifford Brown, and Horace Silver. His collaboration with Silver was especially productive and eventually led to the revival of the Jazz Messengers, prime innovators in the soul and funky BEBOP styles. When Silver left the group in 1956, Blakey took over its leadership. The Jazz Messengers went on to become perhaps the greatest of the hard bop bands, and the group was active until Blakey's death.

The Jazz Messengers became especially well known as an important training ground for outstanding young musicians, and Blakey earned renown as a teacher and mentor. Donald Byrd, Wayne SHORTER, Keith Jarrett, Joann Brackeen, and Wynton MARSALIS were among his most outstanding "graduates." One of Blakey's individual musical accomplishments was his adoption and insertion of African drumming devices into the jazz repertoire. Along with Max ROACH and Kenny Clarke, Blakey was among the greatest of the bebop drummers.

Bland, Bobby "Blue" (b. January 17, 1930, Rosemark, Tennessee): BLUES singer. Bland began his career as a gospel singer but went on to establish himself as a blues vocalist. He re-

Bobby "Blue" Bland (left) and B. B. King in 1982. *(AP/ Wide World Photos)*

corded more than thirty songs that reached the top thirty on the rhythm-and-blues charts, including "Turn on Your Love Light" (1961), and he performed all over the world. In 1992 Bland was inducted into the Rock and Roll Hall of Fame. He continued to perform in the 1980's and 1990's.

See also: Rhythm and blues.

Blassingame, John W. (b. March 23, 1940, Covington, Georgia): Historian. Blassingame is known as one of the leading historians of the South and of the African American experience. He earned a B.A. at Fort Valley State College, then an M.A. at Harvard University, and a Ph.D. in history at Yale in 1971. Directing his doctoral work at Yale was noted historian C. Vann WOODWARD. Blassingame also was a research associate at the University of Maryland at College Park, working on the Booker T. WASHINGTON Papers under the direction of Louis Harlan.

Blassingame's book *Black New Orleans: 1860-1880* (1973), based on his dissertation, brought him to prominence as a scholar. His most famous work, *The Slave Community: Plantation Life in the Antebellum South* (1972), is a judicious and comprehensive examination of American SLAVERY and is considered a landmark work in that field. Blassingame published or edited several volumes of slave and abolitionist testimony and worked on published writings of slaves and abolitionists. He was chosen to edit the papers of Frederick DOUGLASS and published the first volume in 1979. By 1999 five volumes of the Douglass papers had been published in a series of speeches, debates, and interviews (1979-1992) and a volume of autobiographical writings (1999).

See also: Abolitionist movement; Historiography.

Blaxploitation: Term used for certain black-themed films of the 1970's. A contraction of "black" and "exploitation," the term is usually applied to low-budget, action-oriented films. However, the blaxploitation genre has a deeper significance. Blaxploitation films were an integral part of an era, the 1970's, when Hollywood turned out an unprecedented number of films with African American themes and characters. Moreover, African American films—especially blaxploitation films—provided an essential financial boost to the Hollywood FILM industry during a time when studios were suffering from declining box office revenues.

The financial importance of blaxploitation films is illustrated best by *Shaft* (1971), directed by photographer Gordon PARKS, Sr., and starring Richard Roundtree. It was a box office hit and saved its studio, MGM, from financial disaster. Blaxploitation films played a central role in revitalizing the American film industry, gave African American audiences the chance to see an unprecedented number of films concentrating on the African American community, and gave African American film talents a chance to work in greater capacities. On the other hand, the era of blaxploitation films included negative stereotypes of African Americans. It came to a halt when Hollywood studios decided that African American films in general were no longer sure money-makers.

In examining what defines the blaxploitation genre, *Sweet Sweetback's Baadasssss Song* (1971) is critical. This Melvin Van Peebles film was an unexpected commercial success and is credited with awakening studios to the profit-making potential of films by and about African Americans. It also con-

Ron O'Neal's (left) ultracool drug dealer in *Superfly* was an archetypal blaxploitation character. *(Museum of Modern Art, Film Stills Archive)*

Actor Richard Roundtree built his reputation on his performance in the classic blaxploitation film *Shaft*. *(AP/Wide World Photos)*

tained what were to become features of the blaxploitation boom: an assertive, aggressive hero; the sexual exploits of the main character; and independent heroes or heroines, in contrast to the subservient characters played by earlier generations of African American performers. *Shaft*, *Superfly* (1972), *Coffy* (1973), and *Foxy Brown* (1974) are all representative of the aforementioned characteristics. Soon imitations and repetitions of the action-oriented blaxploitation films, often written and directed by whites, were churned out. Thus the blaxploitation genre soon became a parody of itself, a parody which is spoofed in Robert Townsend's 1987 film *Hollywood Shuffle*.

One major impact of the blaxploitation genre was that its financial success had the effect of provoking Hollywood studios' interest in and support for films with African American characters and subjects. However, the declining profits of blaxploitation films and the box office failure of the big-budget 1978 film *The Wiz*, starring Michael JACKSON and Diana Ross, led Hollywood studios to conclude that audiences were no longer interested in films about African Americans. Lack of studio interest in producing African American films persisted until well into the 1980's, largely unbroken until the success of director Spike LEE's films.

See also: Coalition Against Blaxploitation; Grier, Pam.

Blues: The blues, which originated in the survival of African musical principles, is a form of popular music that has influenced the development of American JAZZ, theatrical music, and rock and roll. As early as the 1920's, blues became a major contributor to American commercial musical development and helped win international recognition for American musicians while being imitated by artists from other countries.

The blues as a distinct genre of African American music dates from the period after the CIVIL WAR and reflects the changing lifestyle of the freed slaves. Blues songs are usually lyric poems expressing an individual's responses to everyday matters such as work and love. While many blues songs are exclusively concerned with personal joys or sorrows, others are notable for social comment that can range from subtle insinuations to militant declarations. The essential subject matter of the blues, as with African proverbs or antebellum animal fables, is advice about how to live—often presented through accounts of behavior to be avoided. Collectively, blues lyrics also record the experiences of African American people in the twentieth-century migrations from the rural South to the nation's industrial cities.

Musical Structure
As a musical and poetic form, the blues has its roots in extemporaneous folk songs. The usual twelve-bar musical structure (a "bar" is the same as a musical measure) features a stanza composed of a rhyming couplet with the first line sung twice. In the music's original, spontaneously improvised performance style, the repetition of the first line allowed the singer

time to compose a witty or otherwise appropriate rhyme:

> How long must I suffer, for one mistake I made
> How long must I suffer, for one mistake I made
> I may be mean and evil, but you know darn well I've paid.

Each line is usually interrupted by a caesura, or brief pause, in the middle: thus, the usual blues stanza can be transcribed as three lines or six. Performers can vary the routine by dropping half-lines, interpolating additional comments, or replacing singing with instrumental notes.

Birth of the Blues
William Christopher "W. C." HANDY was a popular bandleader in Memphis, Tennessee, who became widely known as "the father of the blues." Handy first heard the music sung by an itinerant musician during a trip to Mississippi. Experimenting with writing down what he remembered, he published a song entitled "The Memphis Blues" in 1912. Handy's musical accompaniment presented a twelve-bar form that could be orchestrated for standard brass bands or dance orchestras; his best-known composition, "The St. Louis Blues," was popularized by singer Ethel WATERS and sold a million copies in 1917. In 1926 Handy published the first collection of blues songs and sheet music in *Blues: An Anthology* and described how the musical setting followed the structure of the blues lyric

> As each line usually expressed a thought which, with a period after it, would still make sense, so the air [or melody] with the last syllable of each line would return to the keynote or the tonic third or fifth, so that the whole presented a period of 3 semi-independent phrases.

(continued on page 302)

Notable Blues Musicians

Blackwell, Francis "Scrapper" (Feb. 21, 1903, Syracuse, N.C.—Oct. 7, 1962, Indianapolis, Ind.). An urban blues singer, guitarist, and lyricist, Blackwell began his singing career in 1928, when he met blues pianist Leroy Carr. Carr and Blackwell helped move recorded blues toward ensemble performances and away from self-accompanied rural blues. Blackwell's hard-edged guitar style also helped raise the standard for professional guitarists.

Bland, Bobby "Blue." *See main text entry.*

Broonzy, Big Bill. *See main text entry.*

Carr, Leroy (Mar. 27, 1905, Nashville, Tenn.—Apr. 29, 1935, Indianapolis, Ind.). An urban blues singer and pianist. In 1928 Carr teamed with guitarist Francis "Scrapper" Blackwell. The duo pioneered a new urban blues style, and by 1935 Carr and Blackwell had recorded 162 songs, including the seminal "How Long, How Long Blues."

Cox, Ida. *See main text entry.*

Cray, Robert (b. Aug. 1, 1953, Columbus, Ga.). A West Coast blues singer and guitarist, Cray emerged in the mid-1980's as an innovative force in RHYTHM AND BLUES and electric blues. His recordings, including *Strong Persuader* (1986), met extensive critical and popular acclaim.

AP/Wide World Photos

Crudup, Arthur "Big Boy." *See main text entry.*

Davis, Reverend Gary (Apr. 30, 1896, Laurens County, S.C.—May 5, 1972, Hammonton, N.J.). An East Coast blues musician, Davis recorded a few songs in the 1930's, including a sampling of typically raunchy blues songs. Ordained in 1933 by the Missionary Baptist Church, Davis thereafter chose lyrics with GOSPEL themes. His playing, however, retained the qualities of traditional blues. He was one of the most influential older bluesmen of the 1960's blues revival.

Dixon, Willie. *See main text entry.*

Dorsey, Thomas A. *See main text entry.*

Guy, Buddy. *See main text entry.*

Handy, W. C. *See main text entry.*

Harpo, Slim (James Isaac Moore; Jan. 11, 1924, Lobdell, La.—Jan. 31, 1970, Baton Rouge, La.). Harmonica player Slim Harpo started his music career playing in the juke joints of rural LOUISIANA. His first single was "I'm a King Bee." Harpo's 1961 song "Rainin' in My Heart" reached the top forty. In 1966 "Baby, Scratch My Back" climbed to the top of the rhythm-and-blues charts.

Hill, Bertha "Chippie." *See main text entry.*

Hooker, John Lee. *See main text entry.*

Hopkins, Lightnin'. *See main text entry.*

House, Son (Eddie James House; Mar. 21, 1902, Riverton, Miss.—Oct. 19, 1988, Detroit, Mich.). A contemporary of Charley PATTON and an important influence on Robert JOHNSON and Muddy WATERS, country blues singer Son House made some of the first country blues recordings, including "Preaching the Blues" and "My Black Mama" for Paramount in 1930. He also recorded for the Library of Congress in 1941 and 1942. He was rediscovered in 1964 and was considered one of the most important still-living bluesmen.

Howlin' Wolf. *See main text entry.*

Hunter, Alberta. *See main text entry.*

Hurt, "Mississippi" John. *See main text entry.*

Hutto, Joseph Benjamin "J. B." (b. Apr. 26, 1926, Blackville, S.C.—June 12, 1983, Harvey, Ill.). CHICAGO blues singer and guitarist Hutto formed a trio, J. B. Hutto and the Hawks, in 1953. He assimilated the Delta blues-influenced style of Elmore James's slide guitar work. The Hawks disbanded in 1954, but Hutto resurfaced around 1965 in Chicago. Hutto met limited commercial success but enjoyed an ardent following and critical appreciation.

James, Elmore (Jan. 27, 1918, Richland, Miss.—May 24, 1963, Chicago, Ill.). Chicago blues singer and guitarist. In 1937 and 1938, James worked with Delta bluesmen Sonny Boy WILLIAMSON (Rice Miller) and Robert Johnson. In 1951 he went to Chicago, bringing with him a slide guitar lick that he played on electric guitar in the style of the Delta bottleneck guitar players. A transitional figure between the older blues style of Johnson and the modern Chicago blues of Buddy Guy, James was one of the most influential guitarists in the history of the blues.

James, Etta. *See main text entry.*

Jefferson, "Blind" Lemon. *See main text entry.*

Johnson, Lonnie. *See main text entry.*

Johnson, Robert. *See main text entry.*

King, B. B. *See main text entry.*

Leadbelly. *See main text entry.*

Little Milton (James Campbell; b. Sept. 7, 1934, Inverness, Miss.). A singer and guitarist, Little Milton recorded the hits "Blindman," "Grits Ain't Groceries," and "Sweet Sixteen" in 1964. In 1971 he released one of his finest albums, *Waiting for Little Milton*, for Stax Records, which encouraged him to cultivate his soul-drenched blues style. Unlike most blues artists after the 1960's, Little Milton appealed to an almost exclusively African American audience.

Little Walter. *See main text entry.*

McTell, Blind Willie. *See main text entry.*

Memphis Minnie. *See main text entry.*

Memphis Slim. *See main text entry.*

Milburn, Amos (Apr. 1, 1927, Houston, Tex.—Jan. 3, 1980, Houston, Tex.). Milburn was a BOOGIE-WOOGIE piano player and blues musician. His first hit single,

"Chicken Shack Boogie" (1948), sold one million copies. Many of his later recordings, including "Let's Rock Awhile" (1951) and "Rock, Rock, Rock" (1952), were precursors to rock and roll.

Muddy Waters. *See main text entry.*

Odetta. *See main text entry.*

Patton, Charley. *See main text entry.*

Professor Longhair. *See main text entry.*

Rainey, Ma. *See main text entry.*

Reed, Jimmy. *See main text entry.*

Rush, Otis (b. Apr. 29, 1934, Philadelphia, Miss.). Chicago blues singer and guitarist. In the 1950's, Rush, with Magic Sam and Buddy Guy, drove the entrenched Delta influence from Chicago blues. The new "West Side" style gave prominence to rough, wild electric guitar playing and long, improvised solos. Rush's recordings, also characterized by his intense vocals, include "All Your Love," "Double Trouble," and "Three Times a Fool."

Seals, Son (Seals, Frank; b. Aug. 13, 1942, Osceola, Ark.). Chicago blues musician. Seals was briefly a drummer for Albert King's band in the mid-1960's. He became a guitarist and vocalist, performing in the modern Chicago electric style after he moved to that city in 1966. *The Son Seals Blues Band* (1973) showcased his gruff vocals and raw guitar virtuosity. He continued to record into the 1990's.

Shines, Johnny. *See main text entry.*

Smith, Bessie. *See main text entry.*

Smith, Mamie. *See main text entry.*

Tampa Red. *See main text entry.*

Taylor, Koko. *See main text entry.*

Turner, Big Joe (Turner, Joseph Vernon; May 18, 1911, Kansas City, Mo.—Nov. 24, 1985, Inglewood, Calif.). Blues shouter Turner teamed with boogie-woogie piano player Pete Johnson in Kansas City during the 1930's and 1940's. In the 1950's he en-

(continued)

joyed a string of hits, including "Shake, Rattle and Roll" (1954) and "Corrine Corrina" (1956).

Walker, T-Bone. *See main text entry.*

Wallace, Sippie. *See main text entry.*

Wells, Junior (Amos Blackmore; Dec. 9, 1934, Memphis, Tenn.—Jan. 15, 1998, Chicago, Ill.). Chicago blues harmonica player and singer. As a teenager Wells was befriended by Muddy Waters, who acted as his "guardian" at clubs where he performed. In 1952 he took Little Walter's place in the Waters band. Between 1953 and 1955 he recorded "Eagle Rock" (1953), "Hoodoo Man" (1953), "Lawdy, Lawdy" (1954), and "So All Alone" (1954). In 1966 Wells re-leased his acclaimed *Hoodoo Man Blues*. He was increasingly influenced by soul, funk, and rhythm and blues in the 1970's and 1980's. In the 1990's his career slumped, but *Come on in This House* (1997) was critically acclaimed.

AP/Wide World Photos

Williamson, Sonny Boy. *See main text entry.*

Williamson, Sonny Boy, II. *See main text entry.*

Development of the Style

The popularity of "classic blues" as refined by Handy, Spencer Williams, Perry Bradford, and other composers was spurred by singers on vaudeville touring circuits such as the Theatre Owners Booking Association (TOBA), which included enormously popular stars such as Gertrude "Ma" RAINEY and Beulah "Sippie" WALLACE. Bessie SMITH, perhaps the most widely known and frequently recorded singer of this era, is immortalized in the Hollywood film short *St. Louis Woman*, in which, with the Hall Johnson Choir, she presents a dramatized performance of Handy's famous song. Other Hollywood and Broadway performers such as Mae West and Sophie Tucker adapted the style of the African American women with great success. Sophisticated musicians such as James P. JOHNSON and George Gershwin also utilized the blues as both motif and structural element in symphonic compositions such as Johnson's "Yamecraw" and Gershwin's renowned "Rhapsody in Blue," which premiered at Carnegie Hall with the Paul Whiteman Orchestra on Lincoln's Birthday, February 12, 1924.

The development of phonograph records as a popular medium also allowed rural blues musicians such as Mississippi's Charley PATTON and the itinerant Texas guitarist Blind Lemon JEFFERSON to be heard by a nationwide audience. Their styles, unlike the "classic

Bluesman "Mississippi" John Hurt, seen here in 1965, was virtually unknown to the public until he was in his seventies. *(Bernard Gotfryd/Archive Photos)*

blues" of vaudeville theaters, was idiosyncratic and emphasized personal virtuosity. Robert JOHNSON, a guitarist influenced by Patton, was perhaps the most extraordinary performer from this region. While he made only two recording sessions for Columbia Records, Johnson's songs such as "Crossroads" and "Dust My Broom" became standards for other blues singers and later for rock-and-roll bands.

The migration of a number of rural musicians to Los Angeles, Detroit, and Chicago during WORLD WAR II led to the development of a popular form of blues played in a small band configuration (usually guitar, harmonica or saxophone, piano, bass, and drums) with electrical amplification. Performers such as Detroit's John Lee HOOKER and Chicago's Jimmy REED and Muddy WATERS (McKinley Morganfield) exempli-

Blues singer Robert Cray performing at the Kennedy Center Summer Jazz Festival. (©*Roy Lewis Archives*)

fied this style. Waters's "I'm a Man" boasts of masculine prowess in a tone that is applicable to romance but that may also be a protest against racial discrimination. Musicians who remained in the South, such as Sam "Lightnin'" HOPKINS, not only preserved the older style of solo performance but also influenced the creation of a newer style that eventually reached a wider public through interpretations by artists such as "LITTLE RICHARD" Penniman and Ray CHARLES. A jazz-oriented blues guitar style was also pioneered by Aaron T-Bone WALKER, who influenced a generation of younger players and created the blues standard "Stormy Monday."

Variety of Styles

RHYTHM AND BLUES, the predominant popular dance form in the African American commu-

nity during the late 1940's and 1950's, was an offshoot of the blues. It was brought to great artistry and commercial success by performers such as Louis Jordan and His Tympany Five. The older style of self-accompanied singing was still presented on the concert stage by artists such as Big Bill BROONZY, Huddie "LEADBELLY" Ledbetter, Josh White, and the team of Sonny Terry and Brownie McGhee. Blues pianists such as MEMPHIS SLIM (Peter Chatman), Roosevelt Skykes, and Charles Brown also continued a style that had its roots in RAGTIME and the BOOGIE-WOOGIE style mode popular in the 1920's. Skykes's "The Night Time Is the Right Time" is among blues standards, as is Brown's "Driftin' Blues" and the perennial "Merry Christmas Baby."

As it had during the 1920's, the influence of blues-based music continued to spread beyond the African American community. While American singers such as Elvis Presley adapted songs by blues artists Arthur "Big Boy" CRUDUP and Willie Mae "Big Mama" THORNTON, young British bands such as the Beatles and the Rolling Stones were creating hits with versions of songs by HOWLIN' WOLF (Chester Burnett), Muddy Waters, and Willie DIXON. Blues music also remained popular in the rural South. Harmonica player Rice Miller, known as Sonny Boy WILLIAMSON II, won devoted fans with the old technique of creating spontaneous lyrics during his daily "King Biscuit Time" RADIO BROADCAST from Helena, Arkansas, station KFFA. The program first aired in 1942 and continued for many years.

In the 1960's and 1970's, rhythm and blues was better known as SOUL MUSIC and was performed with great vitality by artists such as Otis REDDING, Joe Tex, Aretha FRANKLIN, and the Isley Brothers; at the same time, the recordings of guitarist Jimi HENDRIX and singer Janis Joplin represented innovative adaptations of older blues styles and achieved popularity among college students as anthems of the "counterculture."

In 1990 Columbia reissued the complete recordings of Robert Johnson, and the two-CD boxed set sold more than a million copies. Throughout the 1990's, record companies and music scholars dug through archives. They found and released music that had not been available for decades, testifying to the enduring interest in the blues. Clubs such as the House of Blues and B. B. King's sprang up, providing new venues for veteran artists as well as relatively young performers. Though the audience for blues after the 1960's was mostly white, as were a number of the best-known modern blues performers, the contributions of African American musicians were not entirely diverted into other forms. A new generation of blues greats, including Robert Cray, Lonnie Shields, and Kenny Neal, entered a field in which legends such as Bobby

"Blue" BLAND, Albert Collins, B. B. KING, Buddy GUY, and Koko TAYLOR were still active and acclaimed.

—*Lorenzo Thomas,*
Updated by Janet Long
See also: African cultural transformations.

Suggested Readings:

Barlow, William. *Looking Up at Down: The Emergence of Blues Culture.* Philadelphia: Temple Unviersity Press, 1989.

Charters, Samuel B. *The Country Blues.* New York: Da Capo Press, 1975.

Davis, Angela Y. *Blues Legacies and Black Feminism: Gertrude "Ma" Rainey, Bessie Smith, and Billie Holiday.* New York: Pantheon Books, 1998.

Dixon, Robert M. W., John Godrich, and Howard Rye. *Blues & Gospel Records, 1890-1943.* 4th ed. New York: Oxford University Press, 1997.

Handy, W. C. *Blues: An Anthology.* Edited by William Ferris. New York: Da Capo Press, 1991.

Harris, Sheldon. *Blues Who's Who.* New York: Da Capo Press, 1983.

Harrison, Daphne D. *Black Pearls: Blues Queens of the 1920s.* New Brunswick, N.J.: Rutgers Unviersity Press, 1988.

Jones, LeRoi. *Blues People: Negro Music in White America.* New York: William Morrow, 1963.

Keil, Charles. *Urban Blues.* Chicago: University of Chicago Press, 1966.

Springer, Robert. *Authentic Blues: Its History and Its Themes.* Lewiston, N.Y.: Edwin Mellen Press, 1995.

Bluford, Guion Stewart, Jr. (b. November 22, 1942, Philadelphia, Pennsylvania): Astronaut. Bluford became the first African American astronaut in space when he flew as a mission specialist aboard the space shuttle *Challenger* in August, 1983, and October, 1985. Bluford was a fighter pilot in the VIETNAM WAR and an

Guion Bluford, Jr., the first African American astronaut, in 1982. (AP/Wide World Photos)

Air Force test pilot before becoming an astronaut.

See also: Aviators and astronauts.

Bluford, Lucile H.: Journalist. Bluford wrote for the *Kansas City Call* for more than forty years, beginning in the 1930's, and became the paper's managing editor in the late 1930's. She sued the University of Missouri at Columbia in 1939 for denying her admission to its journalism school. Bluford lost the case, but her efforts resulted in a journalism school being established at historically black Lincoln University in 1942.

See also: Black press; Print journalism.

Bolden, Buddy (September 6, 1877, New Orleans, Louisiana—November 4, 1931, Jackson, Louisiana): Cornetist and bandleader. Be-

cause Bolden was active as a performer before the widespread use of recording technology, information about his music is sketchy. What is repeated about his life tends toward myth and legend.

Charles Joseph "Buddy" Bolden took up music relatively late in life, even though New Orleans was a highly musical city and music of all kinds surrounded him. Bolden was born before performances of African and African-derived dance and music at Congo Square had ceased. He is said to have begun performing with a local string band in 1894. By 1895 Bolden was leading his own band, although New Orleans city records still listed his vocation as plasterer. The 1901 city directory did list Bolden as a professional musician, and he was leading a six-piece band at that time. Most of his performing took place in "Black Storyville," a district comprising a curious mixture of brothels, bars, and sanctified churches. Bolden was known as a volatile individual and performer, and as early as 1906, there were reports that he was having difficulty controlling his emotions. His difficulties with emotions and with alcohol continued. Bolden was admitted to an asylum in 1907 and stayed there until his death.

Early JAZZ and ragtime musicians' accounts of Bolden's influence tend to pay as much attention to his personality as they do to his playing. His "blues tone" is praised, as is his strong rhythmic drive, but much more often what is featured is his style of dress, his success with women, his ability to consume alcohol, his penchant for self-advertisement, and his love of competition. It is likely that Bolden's playing directly influenced Freddie Keppard, William Geary "Bunk" JOHNSON, and perhaps Louis ARMSTRONG, but it is Bolden's role in establishing jazz as a musical form somewhat outside the mainstream that is perhaps most important. Novelist Michael Ondaatje expanded the Bolden myth in his work *Coming Through Slaughter* (1976). Historian Donald Marquis attempted to demythologize and document Bolden's life in *In Search of Buddy Bolden, First Man of Jazz* (1978).

Bolden, Dorothy Lee (b. October 13, 1920, Atlanta, Georgia): Labor leader. A domestic worker herself, Bolden founded the National Domestic Workers of America and served as the union's president.

Bolden attended high school in GEORGIA before studying at the Chicago School of Dress Designers. She directed the Homemaking Skills Training Program in Atlanta. The program offered instruction in consumer rights, nutrition, child care, budgeting, cooking, and housekeeping. Bolden also directed an employment agency.

Bolden worked in a variety of government and public service positions. In 1975 she was appointed to a post in the Department of Health, Education, and Welfare. The same year, she served on the Commission on the Status of Women. Bolden was a vice president of the Black Women's Coalition of Atlanta and served on the board of directors for both the NATIONAL ASSOCIATION FOR THE ADVANCEMENT OF COLORED PEOPLE (NAACP) and the Welfare Rights Organization. She held membership in the Atlanta Legal Aid Society and the League of Women Voters. She also wrote pieces for *Ms.*, ESSENCE, and *Atlanta* magazines.
See also: Organized labor.

Bolden, J. Taber, Jr. (b. April 26, 1926, Cleveland, Ohio): Television news executive. Working for the National Broadcasting Company (NBC), Bolden was the first black director and station manager for a major network. In December, 1976, he was named as vice president for station affairs for NBC television. He held that position into the 1990's. He had previously been station manager at WRC-TV in Washington, D.C., for three years.
See also: Television industry.

Boley, Oklahoma: All-black town in OKLAHOMA's Okfuskee County. Boley was founded in September, 1904, shortly after the Fort Smith and Western Railroad laid tracks in western Okfuskee County. One of many BLACK TOWNS established in the Midwest from the 1870's to about 1910, Boley declined in proportion to the decline of railroad traffic. It survived, however, to serve as a reminder of the early separatist movement, wherein African Americans tried to withdraw from the discrimination of the white world.
See also: Frontier society; Langston, Oklahoma.

Bolin, Jane Matilda (b. April 11, 1908, Poughkeepsie, New York): Judge. Bolin graduated from Wellesley College in 1928 and re-

Jane Matilda Bolin, shortly after being sworn in as a judge in 1939. *(AP/Wide World Photos)*

ceived her law degree from Yale University Law School in 1931. She clerked in her father's law offices before passing the New York bar examination. Bolin worked as an attorney in private practice from 1931 to 1938. New York mayor Fiorello La Guardia appointed her as head of the Court of Domestic Relations in 1939, making Bolin the first African American woman judge in the United States.

After serving her first ten-year term, Bolin was reappointed to three additional terms by mayors William O'Dwyer, John Lindsay, and Robert F. Wagner, Jr. She was a member of the Harlem Lawyers' Association, the National Council of Juvenile Court Judges, and the New York State Association of Family Court Judges. During her time on the bench, Bolin served on the boards of directors of the NATIONAL ASSOCIATION FOR THE ADVANCEMENT OF COLORED PEOPLE (NAACP) and the New York Urban League. After mandatory retirement rules went into effect, Bolin stepped down from the bench in 1979.

Horace Mann Bond in 1945. *(AP/Wide World Photos)*

Bond, Horace Mann (November 8, 1904, Nashville, Tennessee—December 21, 1972, Atlanta, Georgia): Educational administrator. Bond attended LINCOLN UNIVERSITY in Pennsylvania, receiving a B.A. in 1923. He completed the master's (1926) and Ph.D. (1936) programs at the University of Chicago. While working on his advanced degrees, he served as head of the department of education at Langston University in Oklahoma (1924-1927), director of extension at Alabama State College (1927-1928), and instructor at FISK UNIVERSITY, beginning in 1928. He became the head of Fisk's department of education in 1937.

Bond's academic specialty was education, and he wrote numerous books, including statistical studies, on the subject, including *The Education of the Negro in the American Social Order* (1934). After receiving his doctorate, Bond was employed by Fort Valley State College in

Georgia as its president, taking that post in 1939. In 1945 he became the president of Lincoln University, holding that post until 1957. He then became dean of the ATLANTA UNIVERSITY school of education. In that post, which he held until 1966, he was one of the leading scholars and experts in the field of education, holding numerous consultancies and fellowships. He was named director of the Atlanta University bureau of educational and social research in 1966. He also served as chair of the board of the American Society of African Culture. His son, Julian BOND, a Georgia politician, was born in 1940.

Bond, Julian (b. January 14, 1940, Nashville, Tennessee): CIVIL RIGHTS leader and GEORGIA politician. Born Horace Julian Bond, Bond is the son of educator Horace Mann BOND; his mother, Julia (Washington) Bond, was a librarian.

Youth and Education

Julian and his younger brother, James, grew up in Lincoln, Pennsylvania, where their father served as president of LINCOLN UNIVERSITY, a HISTORICALLY BLACK COLLEGE. Both Bond brothers attended primary schools associated with the university. For his college preparatory education, Julian eventually transferred to the Quaker-directed George School, where he was the only African American student. At George School, Julian, gentle by nature, received his first lessons in the practice of nonviolence; he also suffered at least one negative awakening while at George, when a headmaster chided him for wearing his school jacket on his dates with a white girl from Philadelphia. Shocked that his headmaster was ashamed to have a black in the student body,

Julian Bond was a leading spokesperson of southern African Americans during the late 1960's. *(National Archives)*

Bond later said that he felt as though he had been slapped in the face and that, for the first time, he realized what it was to be a "negro."

In 1957 the Bond family moved to Atlanta, Georgia, where Julian again experienced white racism. Nevertheless, he continued to strive, attended Morehouse College, and graduated with a degree in English. While at Morehouse, he became friends with Martin Luther KING, Jr., from whom he took a course in philosophy. Even before his graduation, Bond gained attention for his poetry, some of which was published in various anthologies, including *New Negro Poets U.S.A.* (1964), edited by Langston HUGHES. Additionally, by the end of his senior year, Bond had become a reporter and a feature writer for a weekly African American newspaper, the *Atlanta Inquirer*; in 1963, he became the newspaper's managing editor.

At the same time, Bond became involved with the ongoing Civil Rights movement when he cofounded the Committee on Appeal for Human Rights (COHAR). The group immediately began a series of SIT-INS at Atlanta's segregated lunch counters and restaurants, whereupon Bond and other student leaders were arrested and jailed.

Activism

In April, 1960, COHAR united with other student groups across the South to form the STUDENT NONVIOLENT COORDINATING COMMITTEE (SNCC), which allied itself with King's SOUTHERN CHRISTIAN LEADERSHIP CONFERENCE (SCLC). For the next six years, Bond worked for SNCC as communications director. In general, Bond functioned as a public liaison: He facilitated the flow of information to the public, prepared news releases, and helped coordinate voter-registration drives across the South.

One of SNCC's most important early contributions to the civil rights crusade was its coordination of the growing sit-in movement. As early as 1957, the Oklahoma City activist

Clara Luper had directed sit-ins in such OKLA-HOMA cities as Tulsa, Enid, Lawton, and Oklahoma City, but she had had limited success. On February 1, 1960, four African American freshmen enrolled in North Carolina Agricultural and Technical College attracted national attention when they began a sit-in at the lunch counter of a variety store in Greensboro. Soon arrested, the students contacted civil rights organizations such as the CONGRESS OF RACIAL EQUALITY (CORE) and the SCLC. The sit-in movement soon spread, and when SNCC was created, it helped coordinate the movement, with Bond directing a most effective information and propaganda campaign.

Meanwhile, in the early 1960's, Bond also began his family. He married Alice Louise Clapton on July 28, 1961, and the two eventually had several children: Phyllis, Jane, Horace Mann, and Michael Julian. Julian and Alice were later divorced, and in March of 1990, Julian married his second wife, Pamela S. Horowitz.

Entry into Politics

Bond entered the mainstream political arena in 1965. Three years earlier, the U.S. SUPREME COURT had issued its BAKER V. CARR decision, which had ordered states to end the use of GER-RYMANDERING in legislative districts to dilute the power of the black vote; essentially, the court demanded "one man, one vote" equality at the polls. Pursuant to the ruling, the GEORGIA legislature was forced to reapportion a district in southwest Atlanta, and the black vote there became the majority vote. Bond then entered the legislative race and easily won.

By a vote of 184 to 12, however, the Georgia legislature refused to seat Bond, allegedly because he supported the SNCC decision to condemn the VIETNAM WAR as an aggressive violation of international law. In two subsequent elections, the voters of southwestern Atlanta again chose Bond; still, the legislature would not seat him until December of 1966, when the

Julian Bond (center) at the 1968 Democratic Convention, where his name was put forward as a candidate for the vice presidency. *(AP/Wide World Photos)*

U.S. Supreme Court ruled the legislature's exclusion unconstitutional. Bond then took his seat on January 9, 1967.

National Prominence

Along with another African American Georgia legislator, Ben Brown, Bond again attracted national attention when he led an insurgent delegation to the 1968 Democratic National Convention in Chicago. Bond and Brown charged that the regular DEMOCRATIC PARTY "establishment" in Georgia, headed by the racist Governor Lester Maddox, excluded meaningful African American participation. Bond and his group achieved a partial victory at the convention by being awarded one-half of Georgia's forty-two delegates. Bond delivered a rousing seconding speech in nominating peace advocate Eugene McCarthy for the presidency. In an interesting historical first, the McCarthy camp nominated Bond for the vice presidency in order to recognize the black constituency and because the nomination would give Bond a national forum to discuss the issues of the day, including civil rights, the Vietnam War, and violence then occurring in Chicago. In a series of speeches and interviews, Bond made his positions clear. Then, Bond—who according to the U.S. Constitution was too young to serve—withdrew from consideration for the nomination.

In the general elections of 1968, Bond stood for reelection to the Georgia legislature and easily won; thirteen other African Americans were also elected to the legislature. Still, the group had little power, given the overwhelming white majority in the legislature. Bond served on the Georgia house of representatives committee on education and had considerable impact, yet his calls for general economic and social reforms went largely unheeded. Nevertheless, Bond continued to serve in the Georgia house of representatives until 1975, when he won a seat in the state senate, a post he held until 1987.

Beginning in 1968, Bond stepped up his public speaking engagements, in part because his woeful legislative salary of $4,200 per year remained inadequate, in part because he loved talking to "common" people, and in part because he realized that he was newsworthy and had a national forum for his views. Particularly, Bond was loved on many of the nation's campuses, where white and black students united in showing him support. From the early 1970's into the 1990's, Bond continued his speaking tours across the country.

Honors

Because of his ongoing civic and civil rights work, Bond received many honors, including a host of honorary degrees from such schools as the University of Bridgeport, Wesleyan University, Lincoln University, HOWARD UNIVERSITY, and TUSKEGEE INSTITUTE. Additionally, he served as a visiting professor at various schools, including Drexel University (teaching classes in history and political science), Harvard University, and the University of Virginia. In 1989 he was a Pappas Fellow at the University of Pennsylvania.

Bond also served as a director of such organizations as the Southern Conference Education Fund, the Robert F. Kennedy Memorial Fund, the Highlander Research and Educational Center, the National Sharecroppers Fund, the Delta Ministry Project, the National Council of Churches, the NATIONAL ASSOCIATION FOR THE ADVANCEMENT OF COLORED PEOPLE (NAACP), the Voter Education Project, and the Southern Regional Council. For a time he directed the work of the SOUTHERN POVERTY LAW CENTER in MEMPHIS, TENNESSEE, an organization that listed him as president emeritus in the 1990's. Additionally, Bond chaired the Southern Elections Fund, which provided money and technical help to African Americans in the South who ran for public office. Such was Bond's stature that when the producers of the acclaimed television series *Eyes on the Prize* cast about for a narrator, they picked Bond to host parts one and two of the program.

In 1998 Bond was named chairman of the board of directors of the National Association for the Advancement of Colored People (NAACP), replacing Myrlie EVERS-WILLIAMS. He worked with NAACP president Kweisi MFUME in steering the organization back to a focus on fighting discrimination and supporting civil rights and affirmative action and away from an emphasis on providing services such as small business loans. Bond identified white supremacy as still "powerful, strong [and] pervasive" and vowed that the NAACP would fight it.

—*James Smallwood*
See also: Politics and government.

Suggested Readings:
Bond, Julian. "Julian Bond." Interview. *The Progressive* 62 (August, 1998): 32-35.

_____. *A Time to Speak, a Time to Act: The Movement in Politics.* New York: Simon & Schuster, 1972.

Branch, Taylor. *Parting the Waters: America in the King Years, 1954-63.* New York: Simon & Schuster, 1988.

_____. *Pillar of Fire: America in the King Years, 1963-65.* New York: Simon & Schuster, 1998.

Carson, Clayborne. *In Struggle: SNCC and the Black Awakening of the 1960s.* Cambridge, Mass.: Harvard University Press, 1981.

Forman, James. *The Making of Black Revolutionaries.* New York: Macmillan, 1972.

Neary, John. *Julian Bond: Black Rebel.* New York: William Morrow, 1971.

Powledge, Fred. *Free at Last? The Civil Rights Movement and the People Who Made It.* Boston: Little, Brown, 1991.

Barry Bonds in 1996. *(AP/Wide World Photos)*

Bonds, Barry (b. July 24, 1964, Riverside, California): Baseball player. The son of former major league ballplayer Bobby Bonds, Barry quickly established himself as one of the most exciting major league players during the late 1980's. He initially came to national attention during his years at Arizona State University, where he averaged .347 over his collegiate career, with 45 home runs and 175 runs batted in (RBIs). Known for his speed, Bonds also amassed a record of 57 stolen bases.

Bonds was selected in the first round of the major league amateur draft in June of 1985 by the Pittsburgh Pirates. He quickly became a fixture in the team's outfield. Although he batted only .233 during his first year with Pittsburgh in 1986, he led all National League rookies with his other totals: 16 home runs, 48 RBIs, 36 stolen bases, and 65 walks. In 1987 Bonds had a season record of 25 home runs. Injuries slowed him down during 1988 and 1989, but he rebounded during the 1990 season with a batting average of .301 and 33 home runs. That same year, Bonds was named to the all-star team, led the National League in slugging percentage with an average of .565, and was a key player in Pittsburgh's drive to win the Eastern Division title. With their sights set on reaching the World Series, the Pirates were disappointed after being defeated by the Cincinnati Reds in the National League championship series.

Bonds hit .292 with 25 home runs and 116 RBIs in 1991, helping lead the Pirates to another Eastern Division title. The team was defeated once again in the championship series, this time by the Atlanta Braves. In 1992 Bonds was a key factor in the team's third straight Eastern Division title. In addition to his 34 home runs, 103 RBIs, and .311 batting average, Bonds led the National League in slugging percentage (.624) and was named to the all-star team for a second time. Although Bonds and the Pirates won the Eastern Division for a third consecutive year, they were again defeated by the Atlanta Braves in the National League championship series.

Frustrated by the low salary he was offered and the seeming inability of the Pittsburgh Pirates to win important games and advance to the World Series, Bonds signed with the San Francisco Giants as a free agent in 1993. His career blossomed with the Giants, and he led the league in home runs (46) and RBIs (123). His slugging percentage of .677 was the best recorded in the National League since 1948, when Hall of Famer Stan Musial had hit .702. Bonds also was awarded his fourth consecutive Gold Glove for fielding excellence. Unfortunately his new team also missed an opportunity to compete in the World Series after being defeated by the Atlanta Braves in the National League championship series. During the strike-shortened 1994 baseball season, Bonds hit 37 home runs with a .312 batting average. In 1996 he became only the third player in history to hit at least 40 home runs and steal at least 40 bases in a single season.

In addition to his power, evidenced by more than 460 home runs in fourteen plus seasons, Bonds has shown speed and agility on the base paths with more than 460 stolen bases. A versatile player, Bonds has often been compared to Giants' great Willie MAYS. Unlike his famous godfather Mays, who was equally well known for his friendly demeanor, Bonds has occasionally displayed an arrogance that he vowed to correct in early 2000.

Bonga, George, and Stephen Bonga (George Bonga, c. 1802, near Duluth, Minnesota—1884; Stephen Bonga, c. 1820, Leech Lake, Minnesota—18??): Fur traders, interpreters, and guides. Early fur traders of African descent were welcomed into the NATIVE AMERICAN lodges as "black Frenchmen," a label reflecting their encounters with the French-speaking African Bonga clan. The Bonga family (also known as Bungo or Bonza) originated from a West Indian slave couple, Joas or Jean Bonga and Marie Jeanne, brought to MINNE-

SOTA during the late eighteenth century by Daniel Robertson, a British officer in charge of Mackinac from 1782 to 1787. The couple married in 1794 to legitimatize their children. Alexander Henry, a Canadian fur trader in charge of the Red River brigade for the North West Fur Company, purchased the couple's son Pierre in 1800.

Pierre's marriage to a Chippewa woman continued the Bonga family. On March 12, 1801, a daughter was born. In 1802 their son George was born near Duluth, Minnesota. Soon after, a second son, Jack, arrived. When Bonga's master left the company fort at the mouth of the Pembina River on extended business in January of 1803, Pierre, who spoke only French and Indian languages, carried on the business for the North West Fur Company, served as an interpreter with the Chippewas, and negotiated with fur suppliers. By 1819 Pierre had become one of the principal traders among the Chippewa (also known as Ojibwa or Ojibway).

Pierre's son, George, attended school in Montreal, became proficient in both English and French, learned the fur trade, and became a voyageur for the American Fur Company. As an interpreter, George Bonga interacted with many Native American tribes; his wife was Chippewa. He maintained the American Fur Company posts at Lac Platte, Otter Tail Lake, and Leech Lake as he reared his family: three sons—Peter, James, and Stephen—and a daughter, Marg.

In 1820 Governor Lewis Cass hired George Bonga to serve as an interpreter and to negotiate treaties with the remaining Native American tribes in the Lake Superior region of MICHIGAN territory. Listed as a licensed trader at Lac Platte in 1833-1834, George completed the Chippewa Treaty of 1837 at Fort Snelling, outside St. Paul. He became a prominent independent trader known for his manners, powerful physique, and distinctly African appearance. George settled in Leech Lake, Minnesota.

His sons followed him into the trade. By 1833 Stephen served as a clerk/voyageur for the American Fur Company guiding William Johnston in an expedition to the source of the Mississippi. By 1838 he had served as a guide and interpreter for Alfred Brunson, a missionary for the METHODIST Church. Missionaries used Stephen's influence to convince mixed-blood family members living in the Chippewa village near Elk Creek to serve as the educators for the village.

Little more is known about the family. Letters in the Minnesota and Michigan Historical Societies show a nephew, Jack Bonga, serving as a surveyor's packer in 1875. George Bonga had achieved wealth and respect by 1856, when a canoe trip brought Charles E. Flandreau, later an associate justice on the Minnesota supreme court, to his home. The judge recounted being entertained by Bonga's stories about the American Fur Company and life on the frontier. Nearly one hundred descendants lived around the Leech Lake area by 1900. Bongo Township (misspelling) in Cass County honors the Bonga family's historical role in the region.

See also: Exploration of North America; Frontier society.

Suggested Readings:

Katz, William L. *The Black West*. 3d ed. Seattle: Open Hand, 1987.

Porter, Kenneth W. *The Negro on the American Frontier*. New York: Arno Press, 1971.

Ravage, John W. *Black Pioneers: Images of the Black Experience on the North American Frontier*. Salt Lake City: University of Utah Press, 1997.

Savage, W. Sherman. *Blacks in the West*. Westport, Conn.: Greenwood Press, 1976.

Bonner, Marita (June 16, 1899, Boston, Massachusetts—December 6, 1971; Chicago, Illinois): Essayist, playwright, short-story writer, and educator. Through her sixteen years of publishing her works, Bonner made a significant contribution to African American literature.

After graduating from Radcliffe in 1922, Bonner obtained high school teaching experience in West Virginia, Washington, D.C., and Chicago, Illinois. When she was living in Washington, she joined the Round Table, a literary salon composed of several writers who convened weekly. She was influenced by several HARLEM RENAISSANCE writers, including Langston HUGHES, Countée CULLEN, Alain LOCKE, and Jean TOOMER.

Bonner's writing shows her concern for the plight of African American men and women having to cope with gender, class, and race prejudices. In 1925 she published her award-winning essay "On Being Young—a Woman—and Colored" in the magazine THE CRISIS. The essay emphasized the difficult situations that black women face in their daily lives. Bonner covers a number of themes in her short stories and plays, including racial intermixture, economic hardship, marital betrayal, and the harshness of the urban environment.

Among Bonner's short stories are "The Hands" (1925), "The Prison-Bound" (1926), "Nothing New" (1926), and "Drab Rambles" (1927). In her dramatic writings, Bonner responded to social issues in her plays *The Pot Maker: A Play to Be Read* (1927), *The Purple Flower* (1928), and *Exit, an Illusion* (1929). Bonner married William Occomy in 1930. After moving to Chicago, she continued to write fiction until 1941 and lived in Chicago until her death in 1971.

—*Nila M. Bowden*

See also: Literature; Theater.

Bontemps, Arna (October 13, 1902, Alexandria, Louisiana—June 4, 1973, Nashville, Tennessee): Author. Arna Wendell Bontemps was an influential figure in the HARLEM RENAISSANCE. To escape racial prejudice, his family moved from the South to Los ANGELES, CALIFORNIA. Bontemps graduated from Pacific Union College in 1923, then journeyed to Harlem, New York, to participate in a creative consortium of black writers, most notably Countée CULLEN, Jack Conroy, and Langston HUGHES, with whom he collaborated. To earn a living, Bontemps taught at the Harlem Academy. He completed an M.A. in library science at the University of Chicago in 1943 and worked with the Illinois Writers Project. From 1943 to 1965, he served as head librarian at FISK UNIVERSITY; in 1966, he moved to the University of Illinois to serve as curator of the James Weldon JOHNSON Collection of Negro Arts and Letters.

Paramount among Bontemps's long and short adult fiction is *God Sends Sunday* (1931),

followed by *Black Thunder* (1936), *Drums at Dusk* (1939), and *The Old South* (1973). For children he wrote *Sam Patch* (1951, with Conroy) and more than a dozen other books, some of them histories and biographies. He published poems in several African American journals, including THE CRISIS and *Opportunity*. His nonfiction, which made up most of his work during and after the 1940's, includes *They Seek a City* (1945, with Conroy), *The Story of the Negro* (1948), *Chariot in the Sky* (1951), *Frederick Douglass: Slave, Fighter, Freeman* (1959), *One Hundred Years of Negro Freedom* (1961), *Famous Negro Athletes* (1964), and *Young Booker* (1972). He also edited several noteworthy collections, including *The Poetry of the Negro* (1949), *The Book of Negro Folklore* (1958, with Hughes), *American Negro Poetry* (1963), and *Great Slave Narratives* (1969). He collaborated with W. C. HANDY to write that composer's biography, *Father of the Blues* (1941).

Respected for his literary skill and his devotion to uplifting the aims and educational level of African Americans, Bontemps earned a number of awards, including the Alexander Pushkin Award for Poetry, Jane Addams Children's Book Award, and James L. Dow Award of the Society of Midland Authors. He remained a chronicler of black achievement until his death. His best-known work is *Black Thunder*, a fictionalized account of a slave rebellion that took place in 1800.

Arna Bontemps. *(Library of Congress)*

Boogie-woogie: Musical style. This JAZZ piano style was probably first recorded in 1927 by Meade "Lux" Lewis. It became popular in the late 1930's and early 1940's, when it was performed by mainstream big bands, such as those of Tommy Dorsey and Bob Crosby. It was adapted by the Andrews Sisters and later incorporated into country and western music. Early RHYTHM AND BLUES reflects

Legendary boogie-woogie pianist Johnnie Johnson, who inspired Chuck Berry's song "Johnny B. Goode." *(AP/Wide World Photos)*

the influence of boogie-woogie, as illustrated by the piano style of Fats DOMINO.

Boston, Massachusetts: With roughly 600,000 residents as of the late 1990's, Boston was the largest city in the six New England states and the twentieth-largest city in the United States. About 70 percent of all MASSACHUSETTS residents live in the greater Boston area. Black residents make up about 25 percent of the total population of Boston, which is the state capital.

The first white settlers in the Boston area were from England. In 1630 the Puritans, a Protestant religious group, founded Boston in the hope of gaining freedom of religion. More than a hundred years later, in 1770, Americans were seeking political independence. That year a crowd of people harassed a company of British soldiers as they marched through the city; the soldiers retaliated by firing into the crowd. The first American to be killed was Crispus ATTUCKS. Born a slave, Attucks is remembered

as a fighter for freedom. Four white Americans were also killed in this incident, which soon became known as the Boston Massacre.

In the early nineteenth century, Boston became the center of the ABOLITIONIST MOVEMENT—the movement to rid the country of SLAVERY. William Lloyd GARRISON, a young white man from Boston, published the first issue of *The Liberator* there in 1831. The NEW ENGLAND ANTI-SLAVERY SOCIETY was founded in Boston in 1832. The city also provided stops on the UNDERGROUND RAILROAD (routes along which escaped slaves could find safe places to stay as they traveled to freedom). One can take a walking tour on the Black Heritage Trail through Boston's black community. Featured on the tour are abolitionist meeting places as well as stops on the Underground Railroad.

Boston's population remained of English heritage until the 1800's, when new waves of immigrants came to Boston. The largest groups were the Irish and the Italians, who brought the Roman Catholic religion with them. Though a group of Protestants had founded Boston, the Roman Catholic religion became predominant.

In the latter part of the twentieth century, a few years after the major events of the CIVIL RIGHTS movement had occurred, Boston was grappling with racial issues and segregation. In 1974 the city moved to desegregate its public schools through a program of mandatory BUSING. By busing children from one section of the city to another, officials hoped to create more equal educational opportunities and to create harmony between the races. Demonstrations, violence, and riots erupted, led by angry white parents from South Boston. Ten years later, in 1984, the busing project ended with only marginal success. Some public city schools remained segregated.

Included in Boston's cultural offerings are the Boston Ballet, the Boston Symphony Orchestra, and the Art of Black Dance and Music, a celebrated African American group. Professional sports teams in Boston include the Boston Bruins, who signed the first black ice hockey player, Canadian Willie O'Ree, in 1958. One of the most successful teams in the National Basketball Association (NBA), the Boston Celtics, has Bill RUSSELL as a major part of its history. Russell won a gold medal at the 1960 Olympics, was voted the NBA's most valuable player five times, led the Celtics to eight consecutive titles, and in 1966 was named the head coach of the Celtics, the first African American man to coach an NBA team. In politics, Thomas Atkins in 1969 was the first African American elected to the Boston city council.

—*Betsy L. Nichols*

Bowman, Sister Thea (December 29, 1937, Yazoo City, Mississippi—March 30, 1990, Canton, Mississippi): Nun, evangelist, educator, and musician. Born to Dr. Theon Bowman and Mary Esther Bowman, Bertha Bowman grew up in the Mississippi community of Canton, where her father had his medical practice. Educated in Catholic schools, she entered the community of Franciscan Sisters of Perpetual Adoration, becoming its only African American member. She received the name "Sister Thea," meaning "of God."

Sister Thea received her undergraduate degree in English from Viterbo College in La Crosse, Wisconsin, before going on to earn her master's and doctorate in English literature and linguistics from Catholic University in Washington, D.C. She distinguished herself as a scholar writing on the rhetoric of Thomas More.

The granddaughter of a slave, Sister Thea stated that she brought to the church "my black self . . . my history, my culture." Her unique mission was to celebrate racial differences. Whether telling stories or reciting poetry, she "wove together African history and memories of slavery and survival" while teaching at the Holy Child Jesus High School

in Canton. At Viterbo, as professor of English and later as department chair, she organized the Hallelujah Singers, a choir that sang spirituals throughout the United States. As a result, she was asked in 1978 to become the Director for Intercultural Awareness for the diocese of Jackson, Mississippi, and to join the faculty of Xavier University in New Orleans, where she helped found the Institute of Black Catholic Studies.

In 1984 Sister Thea was diagnosed with breast CANCER; by 1988, she was confined to a wheelchair. In spite of these physical challenges, Sister Thea continued her work. She continued to lobby for full incorporation of African American ritual, folk song, and dance into the Catholic mass and for black participation in the church's liturgy and leadership. In 1987 she even assisted in the task of organizing the Black Catholic Congress. She received national recognition by "challenging" the church's provincialism, but it was her charismatic rhetoric and her singing, "her spiritual inspiration," at lectures, workshops, and conventions for which she is most remembered. Sister Thea encouraged prelates, bishops, and others to join hands and sway together, dancing and singing the songs she identified as "the sacred heritage of African Americans." She also sang and had her audience experience the "old time religion," which "teaches us to love one another." Sister Thea edited two books, *Families: Black and Catholic, Catholic and Black* (1985) and *Ministry in Black Rural Contexts: Sharing the Good News with Blacks in the Rural South* (1987), and recorded one album, *Sister Thea: Songs of My People* (1988).

For her outstanding service, Sister Thea received many honors, including the first La Crosse Justice and Peace Award (1982), the first Sister Thea Bowman Justice Award, and the American Cancer Society's Courage Award (1990). Six days before her death, she was named the first African American recipient of the prestigious Laetare Medal of the

University of Notre Dame. The Sister Thea Bowman Black Catholic Educational Foundation was established in her honor to provide higher education scholarships.

See also: Roman Catholics.

Boxing: African Americans began dominating American boxing—particularly the heaviest weight divisions—during the late 1950's, but their involvement goes back to the very beginnings of the sport in the United States. Boxing, with its connotation of physical superiority, has always been affected by America's racial climate, and African Americans were long deprived of the right to compete fully and fairly with other ethnic groups. Nevertheless, boxing was quicker than any other American sport to allow interracial competition, and the success of black boxers helped to pave the way for African American participation in other sports.

The British Period

Modern boxing originated in eighteenth-century England and probably reached North America during the Revolution. In its early form, the sport featured bare knuckles, unlimited rounds, and wrestling throws. It seems likely that African Americans were the first American pugilists; Tom Molyneux, a former Virginia slave, claimed to be the American champion in 1809, and it is known that his father and uncles had fought before him.

England was the place where fighters could make money. Since it also provided a more liberal racial climate than the United States, it acted as a magnet for African American fighters, both during their careers and after. Molyneux and Bill Richmond, another African American expatriate, both fought memorable losing bouts to English champion Tom Cribb. Richmond went on to establish himself as a trainer, cabinetmaker, and keeper of a popular sporting house.

African American boxers continued crossing the Atlantic in pursuit of opportunity. All but forgotten in the United States, they were prominent in English ring history. The best early black boxers included Henry Sutton, Sam Robinson, Sambo (or "Massa") Sutton, Bob Smith, and Bob Travers. Sutton was a legitimate contender for the English title early in the nineteenth century. He made a great career in the 1840's and retired to teach boxing at the Cambridge University. Fighting after mid-century, Travers was an all-time great, though he lost several fights to larger men because weight classifications were undefined at the time.

Transitional Period

Irish immigration and the adoption of the Marquess of Queensberry Rules, which mandated the use of gloves and outlawed some of the more brutal tactics, transformed American boxing into a profitable and quasilegal sport, and by the 1880's, weight divisions were emerging. In the wake of emancipation, African American boxers, though facing discrimination, began asserting themselves in their native land.

At first, racist feeling warred with the sporting spirit, and separate titles for white and "colored" arose. Henry Woodson contended for the black title early in the 1880's, but soon it belonged to George Godfrey, a 175-pounder who spent most of his career vainly seeking a fight with white heavyweight champion John L. Sullivan. A recognized contender after Sullivan's temporary retirement, Godfrey lost a forty-four-round nontitle fight to Jake Kilrain in 1891.

The color line was drawn definitively against a much greater contemporary, Peter Jackson. Born in the West Indies, Jackson became a heavyweight star in Australia. He gained the English and Australian crowns, easily defeated Godfrey, and fought, while in-

(continued on page 321)

Notable Boxers

Win-loss-draw records follow names; no-decisions are not indicated here. Championship titles are followed by years in which boxers held at least one sanctioning body's title. KO = knockouts.

Ali, Muhammad (b. Jan. 17, 1942, Louisville, Ky.). 56-5-0; 37 KO; heavyweight champion, 1964-67, 1974-78, 1978-79. *See main text essay.*

Armstrong, Henry (Dec. 12, 1912, Columbus, Miss.—Oct. 24, 1988, Los Angeles, Calif.). 151-21-9; 101 KO; featherweight champion, 1937-38; lightweight champion, 1938-39; welterweight champion, 1938-40. The only boxer ever to hold world titles in three weight divisions at once, Armstrong turned pro after failing to make the 1932 Olympic team. In 1937 he won all 27 of his bouts, including 26 knockouts, and won  his first title. After retiring in 1945 he became a Baptist minister. Inducted into the International Boxing Hall of Fame (IBHOF) in 1990.

Bowe, Riddick (b. Aug. 10, 1967, Brooklyn, N.Y.). 40-1; 32 KO; heavyweight champion, 1992-93, 1995. After losing a controversial decision in the super heavyweight final of the Seoul Olympics in 1988, Bowe turned pro. He won 31 straight bouts before taking the heavyweight title from Evander Holyfield in 1992, only to lose his title in the rematch a year later. After struggling to sustain his credibility as a title contender, Bowe knocked out Holyfield in a nontitle bout in 1995.

Charles, Ezzard (July 7, 1921, Lawrenceville, Ga.—May 28, 1975, Chicago, Ill.) 96-25-1; 59 KO; heavyweight champion, 1949-51. Undefeated as an amateur, Ezzard won the AAU national middleweight title before turning pro in 1940. He beat Jersey Joe Walcott to win the vacant National Boxing Association heavyweight title in 1949. In 1950 he beat Joe Louis to become the undisputed champion, but he lost his title to Walcott in 1951. Inducted into the IBHOF in 1990.

Foreman, George (b. Jan. 10, 1949, Marshall, Tex.). 75-5-0; 68 KO; heavyweight champion, 1973-74, 1994-95. *See main text essay.*

Foster, Bob (b. Dec. 15, 1938, Albuquerque, N.Mex.). 56-8-1; 46 KO; light heavyweight champion, 1968-74). Foster held the light-heavyweight title for six years and lost only once to another light heavyweight. In 1973 he defeated Pierre Fourie in the first professional match between black and white  fighters in South Africa. Elected to *Ring*'s Boxing Hall of Fame in 1983 and to the IBHOF in 1990.

Frazier, Joe (b. Jan. 17, 1944, Beaufort, S.C.). 32-4-1; 27 KO; heavyweight champion, 1968-73. *See main text essay.*

Gans, Joe B. (Nov. 25, 1874, Baltimore, Md.—Aug. 10, 1910, Baltimore, Md.). 131-9-16; 85 KO; lightweight champion, 1902-4, 1906-8. One of the greatest lightweights of all time, Gans was the first African American to win a world title, and he defended it nine times. He continued to fight after contracting tuberculosis in 1905 and regained his title in a 42-round bout the next year. Elected to *Ring*'s Boxing Hall of Fame in 1954 and the IBHOF in 1990.

Hagler, Marvelous Marvin (b. May 23, 1954, Newark, N.J.). 62-3-2; 52 KO; middleweight champion, 1980-87. Hagler retained his title through 12 defenses, until losing a split-decision to Sugar Ray Leonard. He was the first middleweight fighter to win a one-million-dollar purse. Inducted into the IBHOF in 1993.

Hearns, Thomas (b. Oct. 18, 1958, Memphis, Tenn.). 59-4-1; 49 KO; welterweight champion, 1980-81; jr. middleweight champion, 1982-84; middleweight champion, 1987-88; light heavyweight champion,

1987, 1991. After turning pro at nineteen, Hearns won his first world title in 1980. He then worked his way up the weight divisions until he won a light heavyweight title in 1991. After losing that title to Iran Barkley the following year, he continued to fight occasionally through the rest of the 1990's.

Holmes, Larry (b. Nov. 3, 1949, Cuthbert, Ga.). 66-6-0; 43 KO; heavyweight champion, 1978-85. Muhammad Ali's sparring partner early in his career, Holmes won the heavyweight title from Ken Norton in 1978 and defended it 20 times, until losing to Michael Spinks in 1985. Until then, his record of 48-0 was second only to Rocky Marciano's 49-0 career record. Holmes continued to box occasionally as late as 1999, when he was nearly fifty years old.

Holyfield, Evander (b. Oct. 19, 1962, Atmore, Ala.). 36-4-1; 25 KO; cruiserweight champion, 1986-90; heavyweight champion, 1990-92, 1993-94, 1996-99. After winning a bronze medal as a light heavyweight in the 1984 Olympics, Holyfield turned pro. He captured a cruiserweight title in his twelfth pro fight in 1987. In 1990 he moved up to the heavyweight  division and won a title. After three successful defenses, he lost his title to Riddick Bowe in 1992, but regained it in a rematch the following year. After losing his title to Michael Moorer, he regained it by knocking out Michael Tyson in 1996. He lost the title again to British boxer Lennox Lewis in November, 1999.

Johnson, Jack (Mar. 31, 1878, Galveston, Tex.—June 10, 1946, Raleigh, N.C.). Heavyweight champion, 1908-15. *See main text essay.*

Jones, Roy, Jr. (b. Jan. 16, 1969). 41-1-0; 33 KO; middleweight champion, 1993-94; super middleweight champion, 1994-   ; light heavyweight champion, 1997-   . Jones won a silver medal in the 1988 Olympics light middleweight division. After turning pro, he won the first of three professional titles in 1993. In June, 1999, he accomplished the unusual feat of unifying three different world light heavyweight titles in a victory over Reggie Johnson. Af-

ter beating David Telesco in January, 2000, Jones suggested that he might take on heavyweight fighters.

Leonard, Sugar Ray (b. May 17, 1956, Wilmington, N.C.). 36-3-1; 25 KO; welterweight champion, 1979-80, 1980-82; jr. middleweight champion, 1981; middleweight champion, 1987; super middleweight champion, 1988-90; light heavyweight champion, 1988. After winning a gold medal in the light welterweight division at the 1976 Olympics, Leonard turned pro in 1977 and eventually became the only boxer to win world titles in five different divisions. In  1982 he underwent surgery for a detached retina and retired, only to return in 1984. After another brief retirement, he returned again in 1987, as a middleweight, and won a title fight against Marvin Hagler. After losing his challenge for the super welterweight title in 1991, he again retired. In a comeback attempt in 1997, he lost to Hector Camacho by a fifth-round TKO—the only time he ever failed to go the distance.

Liston, Sonny (May 8, 1932, near Forrest City, Ark.—Dec. 30?, 1970, Las Vegas, Nev.). 50-4-0; 39 KO; heavyweight champion, 1962-64. After winning the heavyweight title from Floyd Patterson in 1962, Liston seemed poised for a long run as champion but unexpectedly lost to Cassius Clay (later Muhammad ALI) two years later. Inducted into the IBHOF in 1991.

Louis, Joe (May 13, 1914, Lafayette, Ala.—April 12, 1981, Las Vegas, Nev.). 68-3-0; 54 KO; heavyweight champion, 1937-49. *See main text essay.*

Molyneux, Tom (1784, Washington, D.C.?—Aug. 4, 1818, Dublin, Ireland). Molyneux was not only the first African American to fight in a major championship bout, he was one of the first important American prizefighters. In 1810 he lost a bare-knuckle fight to British champion Tom Cribb in a controversial 40-round decision. After losing a rematch in 1811, he fought several more years but suffered from tuberculosis. Inducted into the *Ring* Boxing Hall of Fame in 1958 and the IBHOF in 1997.

(continued)

Moore, Archie (Dec. 13, 1913, Benoit, Miss.—Dec. 9, 1998, San Diego, Calif.). 194-26-8; 141 KO; light heavyweight champion, 1952-62. In a 27-year career, Moore knocked out more opponents than any boxer in history; he was also the only boxer to fight both Rocky Marciano and Muhammad Ali. When he finally relinquished his title in 1962, he was the oldest professional boxer to hold a world title.

AP/Wide World Photos

Norton, Ken (b. Aug. 9, 1943). 42-7-1; 33 KO; heavyweight champion, 1978. Norton turned pro in 1967 and split two matches with Muhammad Ali in 1973. After wining the World Boxing Council (WBC) title-elimination bout in 1977, he was awarded the title because of Leon Spinks's failure to defend it, but he lost the title to Larry Holmes on his first defense in 1978. He retired in 1981 and was inducted into the IBHOF in 1992. His son, Ken Norton, Jr., played linebacker for Super Bowl-winning Dallas and San Francisco football teams.

Patterson, Floyd (b. Jan. 4, 1935, Waco, N.C.). 55-8-1; 40 KO; heavyweight champion, 1956-59, 1960-62. After winning the middleweight title at the 1952 Olympics, Patterson turned pro as a light heavyweight. When Rocky Marciano retired as heavyweight champion in 1956, Patterson moved up and became the youngest heavyweight champion ever by beating Archie Moore. He lost the title to Swedish boxer Ingemar Johansson in 1959 but became the first heavyweight ever to regain his title the next year. After losing the title again, to Sonny Liston, and making several unsuccessful challenges for the title, he retired in 1972. Inducted into the IBHOF in 1991, he became boxing commissioner for New York State in 1995.

AP/Wide World Photos

Robinson, Sugar Ray (May 3, 1921, Detroit, Mich.—April 12, 1989, Culver City, Calif.). 175-19-6; 110 KO; middleweight champion, 1951, 1952-52, 1955-57, 1957, 1958-60. *See main text essay.*

Spinks, Leon (b. July 11, 1953, St. Louis, Mo.). 26-17-3; 14 KO; heavyweight champion, 1978. The brother of Michael Spinks, Leon turned pro after winning a gold medal in the heavyweight division at the 1976 Olympics. In only his eighth pro fight, he defeated Muhammad Ali for the world title, only to lose a rematch later the same year. He continued fighting with indifferent success through 1995.

Spinks, Michael (b. July 29, 1956, St. Louis, Mo.). 32-1-0; 21 KO; light heavyweight champion, 1981-85; heavyweight champion, 1985-87. After winning a gold medal in the light heavyweight division at the 1976 Olympics, Spinks turned pro and won the World Boxing Association (WBA) and WBC light heavyweight titles. In 1985 he became the first light heavyweight to win a heavyweight title when he beat previously undefeated Larry Holmes. He retired after a first-round knockout by Mike Tyson. Inducted into the IBHOF in 1994.

Tiger, Dick (Aug. 14, 1929—Dec. 14, 1971). 61-17-3; 26 KO; middleweight champion, 1962-63, 1965-66; light heavyweight champion, 1966-68. Born in Nigeria, Tiger won the British Commonwealth middleweight title before coming to United States in 1959. He took the world title from Gene Fullmer, then lost it to Joey Giardello and regained it in 1965. The next year, he won the light heavyweight championship, which he lost to Bob Foster in 1968, in the only fight he did not finish. He retired in 1970 and was inducted into the IBHOF in 1991.

Tyson, Mike (b. June 30, 1966, Brooklyn, N.Y.). 45-3-0; 39 KO; heavyweight champion, 1986-90, 1996. *See main text essay.*

Walcott, Jersey Joe (Jan. 31, 1914, Merchantville, N.J.—Feb. 25, 1994). 53-18-1; 33 KO; heavyweight champion, 1951-52. On his fifth title attempt, Walcott knocked out Ezzard Charles to become oldest heavyweight champion before George FOREMAN. He retired after being knocked out by Rocky Marciano in 1953. He later served as sheriff of Camden County, N.J., and was chairman of New Jersey's state athletic commission. Inducted into the IBHOF in 1990.

Wills, Harry (May 15, 1892, New Orleans, La.—Dec. 21, 1958, New York, N.Y.). 65-8-2; 47 KO; heavyweight (no titles). Although a top heavyweight contender during the 1920's, Wills was never allowed to fight white champion Jack Dempsey. He retired in 1932 after 110 official fights (including many no-decisions). He was elected to *Ring*'s Boxing Hall of Fame in 1970 and the IBHOF in 1992.

Wilson, Jackie (Jan. 17, 1918, Spencer, N.C.—Mar. 10, 1956). 69-19-5 (no titles). One of the great amateur boxers of his time, Wilson lost only once in 51 fights—in the 1936 Olympics, where he took the silver medal in the bantamweight division. In a 13-year pro career, he fought such legends as Sugar Ray Robinson and Jake LaMotta.

jured, a sixty-one-round no-decision contest against Jim Corbett. Jackson seemed a likely world champion until Sullivan came out of retirement and explicitly drew the color line against him. When Corbett took Sullivan's crown, he followed suit, establishing a tradition that the heavyweight title was for whites only.

The line was not drawn so rigidly in the lower weight classifications, which were less crucial to notions of white supremacy. George "Little Chocolate" Dixon was featherweight champion for most of the 1890's. Andy Bowen, lightweight "champion of the South," set the all-time endurance record for a glove fight in 1893, when he and Jack Burke fought for seven hours and nineteen minutes. Bowen fought for the lightweight crown in 1894, and his death from ring injuries nearly derailed the movement to legalize boxing nationally.

African American fighters of the second rank sometimes made a living by traveling with entertainment troupes and taking on all comers. Two of the more famous of these were Fred Morris and Billy Hill, who performed in William Muldoon's show. Hill wound up as a song-and-dance man in England. Many others were exploited in "battles royal," a perversion of the

sport in which large numbers of black fighters were herded into a ring, where they fought to the last man for a few coins.

African Americans, however, persevered. Joe Walcott took the welterweight title in 1901, and Joe Gans won the lightweight crown the following year. In 1908 Jack JOHNSON crossed the color line to become the first African American heavyweight champion. Johnson was only one of a generation of greats who were usually avoided by white fighters; Sam Langford, Sam McVey, and Joe Jeannette never held crowns, but they were among the best fighters of their time.

Johnson was, and remains, a controversial figure. He fought only one African American

Sugar Ray Robinson lands a hard right on Carman Basilio in a 1958 bout in which Robinson regained his middleweight title. *(AP/Wide World Photos)*

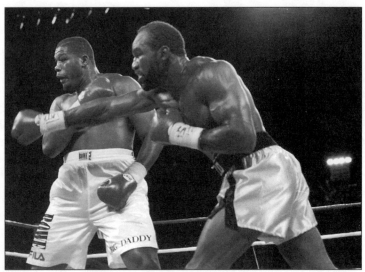

In November, 1993, Evander Holyfield (right) regained his heavyweight crown by beating Riddick Bowe (left). *(AP/Wide World Photos)*

challenger, and then only after fleeing the United States to avoid prosecution under the Mann Act. His flamboyance, extravagance, and pride made him a target for the press, while his marriage to a white society woman seemed an open challenge to racial mores. As a living affront to notions of white supremacy, he became the object of the original search for a "white hope." The best of these was former champion Jim Jeffries, who emerged from retirement in 1910 in an attempt to dethrone Johnson only to absorb a terrible beating. Feverishly promoted as a racial Armageddon, the Johnson-Jeffries fight touched off scores of racial incidents and encouraged federal officials to try to put Johnson in prison, ostensibly for crossing state lines with prostitutes. He fled to Europe, where the skills that had made him arguably the greatest of all time deteriorated. In 1915 Johnson lost to Jess Willard, a white fighter who reimposed the color line.

The Modern Era

The 1920's were a decade of frustration; neither Harry Wills nor the second George Godfrey ever fought Jack Dempsey. Yet the 1930's marked a decisive break with segrega-tion, as the great Joe Louis became the second African American to wear the heavyweight crown. Louis's spectacular one-round knockout of Max Schmeling, the unwilling representative of Nazism, made him the greatest African American hero of his time, and his electrifying power, flawless technique, and unfailing sportsmanship won the admiration of a generation. Louis was unapologetically patriotic, and his wartime service transformed him into an American icon. Louis's postwar title defenses against Jersey Joe Walcott forever abolished the color line, and his influence aided the cause of integration in other sports. It is difficult to overestimate Louis's stature in American sports history.

A contemporary, Henry Armstrong, another great talent, won acclaim for holding the featherweight, lightweight, and welterweight titles simultaneously. Sandy Saddler became the postwar featherweight king and established an all-time record of 103 knockouts. Sugar Ray Robinson, often described as pound-for-pound the greatest fighter who ever lived, dominated the postwar welterweights and was a five-time middleweight champion. As the 1950's progressed, Archie Moore established himself as one of the great light-heavyweight champions, and he twice fought for the heavyweight crown. At various times, Jersey Joe Walcott, Ezzard Charles, and Floyd Patterson reigned over the heavyweights. A golden age of African American boxing had begun.

After the retirement of Rocky Marciano in 1956, the heavyweight title became an almost exclusively African American preserve. Black heavyweight champions, through the 1990's, included Floyd Patterson, Sonny Liston, Mu-

Promoter Don King, one of the most influential and controversial figures in boxing, seen leaving a federal court building in 1998. *(AP/Wide World Photos)*

helped to revolutionize the pay scale of outstanding fighters. Don King, who promoted Ali's 1974 fight in Zaire (renamed Congo Democratic Republic in 1997), used Ali as the springboard for his own rise to the position of number-one promoter in boxing. King came virtually to control the sport and negotiated enormous fees for the best fighters.

Boxing's Drawbacks

African Americans have used the boxing ring to advance themselves and dispel the myth of white supremacy, yet there has often been a heavy price to pay. Most fighters—black and white—are treated miserably; they earn a few hundred dollars per fight in a profession so

hammad ALI, Joe FRAZIER, George FOREMAN, Larry Holmes, Mike TYSON, Evander Holyfield and Great Britain's Lennox Lewis. Bob Foster and Michael Spinks topped a list of light-heavyweight champions, while Thomas Hearns, Sugar Ray Leonard, and Marvin Hagler ruled the welterweight and middleweight divisions. Fighting in the television age, these boxers battled for purses reaching tens of millions of dollars.

Some have called Muhammad Ali the greatest heavyweight of all time. Highly controversial, Ali was, in some ways, Joe Louis in reverse. He emphatically rejected the public humility expected of fighters; his radical opinions on integration and the VIETNAM WAR cost him his title in 1967. He launched a dramatic comeback in 1970, however, and regained the crown in 1974. His behavior made him the greatest sports personality of his era and the darling of television. The attention he drew

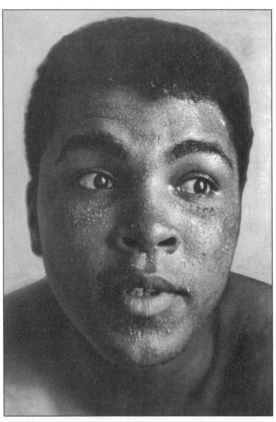

In polls taken at the end of the twentieth century, many voters ranked Muhammad Ali the greatest boxer of all time, and some ranked him the greatest athlete—regardless of sport—of the century. (*Library of Congress*)

hazardous that the American Medical Association has called for its abolition. Most boxers work without any benefits; frequently untrained, often prey to unscrupulous managers, subject to regulations that vary from state to state, victims of decisions determined by boxing politics, they face almost certain failure. Modern boxing may, in fact, be as exploitative as the old battles royal.

—*Gary K. Weiand*

Suggested Readings:

Bennett, Lerone, Jr. "Jack Johnson and the Great White Hope." *Ebony* (April, 1994): 86-92.

Douroux, Marilyn G. *Archie Moore, the Ole Mongoose: The Authorized Biography of Archie Moore, Undefeated Light Heavyweight Champion of the World.* Boston: Branden, 1991.

Frazier, Joe, and Phil Berger. *Smokin' Joe: The Autobiography of a Heavyweight Champion of the World, Smokin' Joe Frazier.* New York: Macmillan, 1996.

Hoffer, Richard. *A Savage Business: The Comeback and Comedown of Mike Tyson.* New York: Simon & Schuster, 1998.

Holmes, Larry, and Phil Berger. *Against the Odds.* New York: St. Martin's Press, 1998.

Holyfield, Evander, and Bernard Holyfield. *Holyfield: The Humble Warrior.* Nashville: Thomas Nelson, 1996.

Isenberg, Michael T. *John L. Sullivan and His America.* Chicago: University of Illinois Press, 1988.

Marqusee, Mike. *Redemption Song: Muhammad Ali and the Spirit of the Sixties.* New York: Verso Books, 1999.

Mead, Chris. *Champion: Joe Louis, Black Hero in White America.* New York: Charles Scribner's Sons, 1985.

Roberts, Randy. *Papa Jack: Jack Johnson and the Era of White Hopes.* New York: Macmillan, 1983.

Bradford, Perry "Mule" (February 14, 1893, Montgomery, Alabama—April 20, 1970, New York, New York): JAZZ pianist, composer, and producer. John Henry Perry Bradford was born in ALABAMA. When he was six years old, his family moved to Atlanta, GEORGIA. His musical career began in 1907, when he started performing with Allen's New Orleans Minstrels. He also worked as a solo pianist before getting his start as a songwriter. During his VAUDEVILLE career, Bradford performed in a musical act with a mule; that act earned him the nickname "Mule." He visited New York in 1910, touring on the theater circuit, and moved there permanently sometime before 1920.

In the summer of 1920, Bradford organized a recording session for OKeh Records featuring BLUES singer Mamie SMITH. Although legend has it that white vaudeville performer Sophie Tucker originally was slated to record Bradford's "Crazy Blues," Bradford convinced the record company to allow Smith to sing. Smith's recording sold more than one million copies and was the first single to popularize blues singing, especially among white audiences.

During the 1920's, Bradford wrote such popular songs as "Evil Blues," "That Thing Called Love," and "You Can't Keep a Good Man Down." He recorded songs with his own groups, including the Jazz Phools and Perry Bradford's Mean Four. Among his business endeavors, Bradford ran his own music publishing company and helped pioneer the use of black musicians on commercial radio. He worked with some of the top artists of early jazz in this period, including Louis ARMSTRONG and James P. JOHNSON, and worked with singers such as Alberta HUNTER and Sippie WALLACE. Among his many songs and musical comedies, Bradford wrote *The Prince of Hayti* (1916), the musical revue *Made in Harlem* (1918), the Broadway production *Put and Take* (1921), and the lyrics for *Messin' Around* (1929). His autobiography, *Born with the Blues: Perry Bradford's Own Story*, was published in 1965.

Bradley, David (b. September 7, 1950, Bedford, Pennsylvania): Novelist, essayist, and educator. The only son of David Henry Bradley, Sr., a minister and historian, and Harriette M. Bradley, David Bradley was born and reared in rural western PENNSYLVANIA. He earned a B.A. in creative writing at the University of Pennsylvania in 1972 and an M.A. in American studies from the University of London in 1974. At the University of Pennsylvania he found that his formative experiences in the country contrasted sharply with those of urban African American students. He began writing his first book, *South Street* (1975), while taking an undergraduate novel-writing course. This novel portrays a community of blacks whose stories unfold in a PHILADELPHIA bar.

During the same period, Bradley also planned his second novel, *The Chaneysville Incident* (1981). Based on a historical event that occurred near his home in Bedford County, the story centers on thirteen SLAVE RUNAWAYS who choose to take their own lives rather than face recapture and a return to SLAVERY. The novel was praised as one of the most important books by a contemporary black author and received both PEN/Faulkner and American Academy and Institute of Arts and Letters awards for literature in 1982.

Bradley worked as a book editor before teaching English at Temple University from 1976 to 1997. He also taught writing and English at San Diego State University, the Massachusetts Institute of Technology, Colgate University, the College of William and Mary, and City College of New York.

A prolific writer of essays, articles, book reviews, and screenplays, Bradley published his work in numerous journals and magazines, including *Esquire*, *The New Yorker*, and *The New York Times Book Review*. During the late 1990's, he worked on a nonfiction book exploring the origins, causes and persistence of racism in America—a theme that appears often in

David Bradley in 1981. *(AP/Wide World Photos)*

Bradley's writing. Bradley was also coeditor of *The Encyclopedia of Civil Rights in America* (1998), with Shelley Fisher Fishkin.

—*Kevin Bochynski*

See also: Literature.

Bradley, Ed (b. June 22, 1941, Philadelphia, Pennsylvania): News correspondent. Bradley was the first African American correspondent for the investigative television news program *60 Minutes*. This high-profile position capped a successful news broadcasting career.

Bradley graduated with a bachelor of science degree in education from Cheyney State College in Pennsylvania in 1961. He taught sixth grade and was a radio reporter prior to breaking into network television news as a Paris stringer for the Columbia Broadcasting System (CBS) in 1971.

Bradley followed that assignment with two years as a VIETNAM WAR correspondent. In

1974 he moved to WASHINGTON, D.C., as a White House correspondent, and he was assigned to report on the presidential campaign of Jimmy Carter in 1976. He became the principal correspondent for *CBS Reports* in 1978 and anchored the *CBS Sunday Night News* as the first black news anchor. He was also an anchorman on a number of documentaries focusing on the Far East in the late 1970's.

In 1981 Bradley received his groundbreaking assignment on *60 Minutes* when Dan Rather left to anchor the weekday evening news. Bradley's first story to air was "The Other Side of the IRA." In December, 1981, his interview with singer and actor Lena HORNE—one of his own favorites of all his interviews—was broadcast; Bradley won an Emmy award for the segment, as he did for later stories on schizophrenia and on China's

labor camps. By 1995 Bradley had reported some three hundred stories for *60 Minutes*, traveled to nearly sixty countries, and won eleven Emmy Awards.

In 1991 he became the host of a new CBS network news documentary program, *Street Stories*. Beginning in 1994, he also hosted a jazz radio program, *Jazz from Lincoln Center*, a National Public Radio program that won a Peabody Award.

Bradley's awards include numerous Emmy Awards, the Association of Black Journalists Award (1977), the George Polk Journalism Award (1980), the Pioneers of Excellence Award (1987), the Young Men's Christian Association Youth Service Award (1988), and the Robert F. Kennedy Journalism Award Grand Prize and Television First Prize (1996).
See also: Television industry.

Ed Bradley (left) on assignment in Moscow, with Diane Sawyer and Dan Rather, in 1987. *(AP/Wide World Photos)*

Bradley, Tom (December 29, 1917, Calvert, Texas—September 29, 1998, Los Angeles, California): Politician. Thomas J. Bradley was born to Lee Bradley and Crenner Hawkins, sharecroppers who had not advanced beyond the fifth grade in school. The Bradleys were a desperately poor family, and this poverty led to the early death of five of Tom's brothers and sisters. The family's only surviving female child, Willa Mae, was born in 1921, the same year the family moved to DALLAS, TEXAS. There, Lee Bradley took on odd jobs as a handyman, cook, and waiter. His wife found sporadic work as a maid. Life remained difficult, however, and the family was forced to move again, this time to the farming community of Somerton, Arizona, where relatives resided. At the age of six, Tom was enrolled in school for the first time, and Lee moved on to California in search of work. Shortly after that, the entire family followed Lee Bradley to California.

Youth and Education

The family's economic troubles continued. The Bradleys moved as many as four times in one year. The family continued to grow, with two more children born in LOS ANGELES— Ellis, who suffered from cerebral palsy, was born in 1929, and Howard was born in 1933. At the age of ten, Tom went to work selling the *Los Angeles Record*; he had already established extensive reading and study habits. Though the Bradley residence was at Fifteenth and Hooper streets in Los Angeles, Tom managed to attend one of the best high schools in the city, Polytechnic, which was far from his house. There, he competed in a number of sports; his athletic prowess was his ticket of admission to the University of California at Los Angeles (UCLA), which he entered in 1937.

In 1940 Bradley decided to leave UCLA (though he later received his degree) to join the Los Angeles Police Department (LAPD) as an officer. Shortly thereafter, he married Ethel Arnold, a beautician. Although the LAPD was one of the first departments in the country to have African Americans in uniform, in many ways it was a racist institution. Black officers were not allowed to work outside black communities, and they could not rise above the rank of sergeant. These barriers were overcome by Bradley when he was promoted to lieutenant in 1946.

Entry into Politics

At that point, Bradley began to take an interest in local DEMOCRATIC PARTY politics. In 1946 he worked on Edmund G. Brown's unsuccessful campaign for the office of state attorney general. He also worked for Ed Roybal in the latter's successful 1949 campaign for election to the Los Angeles city council and the 1962 race that led to Roybal's election to the U.S. Congress. During that period, Bradley was involved in more than a hundred clubs and organizations in Los Angeles. He utilized the leverage provided by his many contacts to continue campaigning against segregation in the LAPD.

Bradley's activism had made him well known in his community. In 1961 he retired from the police force and embarked on another career; he had managed to graduate from law school while working as an officer, and he joined the law practice of Charles Matthews. In 1963 he decided to run for election to the city council himself. He won, becoming the first African American elected to the body. Bradley quickly established a reputation as a spokesman not only for the interests of African Americans but also for Mexican Americans and others who had faced the sting of discrimination.

Bradley maintained close ties to Congressman Roybal, who was of Mexican descent, and one of Bradley's closest advisers, Maury Weiner, was Jewish. His broad support led to his being asked to run for mayor in 1969 against incumbent Sam Yorty. Despite a crowded field, on April 2, 1969, Bradley stunned many by winning 42 percent of the vote in the primary to Yorty's 26 percent. The failure to win a plurality, though, meant a runoff had to be held. At that point, controversy arose; Yorty was accused of using racist language and red-baiting to subvert the Bradley campaign. One notable piece of campaign literature—deposited anonymously on many doorsteps—showed a doctored photograph of Bradley with his arm around BLACK PANTHER PARTY leader Eldridge CLEAVER. Bradley lost the election, though he won 46.7 percent of the vote.

Campaign for Mayor

Bradley returned to the city council, where he immediately began plotting a strategy for the 1973 election. He assailed Yorty for the latter's record of excessive travel. Bradley began an extensive public-speaking effort throughout the city and engaged in a highly successful

Los Angeles mayor Tom Bradley in 1974. *(AP/Wide World Photos)*

drive to raise funds for his campaign. His strategy worked: In 1973 Bradley was elected as the first African American mayor of Los Angeles, winning 56 percent of the vote.

As mayor, one of Bradley's first efforts was an attempt to bring mass rail transit to his sprawling city of freeways. However, a rapid-transit initiative on the November, 1974, ballot did not pass. Undeterred, Bradley managed to secure federal funds for transit. Finally, in December, 1985, an appropriation for the first 4.4-mile link of a proposed 18.6-mile line connecting downtown Los Angeles, the Wilshire Boulevard corridor, Hollywood, and the San Fernando Valley was obtained. A Los Angeles-Long Beach line also was initiated.

Though mass transit helped to bring luster to Bradley's record, it also brought blemishes after a bus strike in 1974 and another in 1976. Bradley was criticized heavily for seeking to circumvent the union's leadership by taking his proposals for settlement directly to the workers. Eventually, the strike was settled, but a bitter taste was left in the mouths of many who had supported his election. He was criticized for being remote, distant, and difficult to know.

Criticism of Bradley continued after one of his two daughters was arrested repeatedly on shoplifting, drug, and traffic charges. Family woes escalated when his mother and one of his brothers died in 1973. In 1976 his top political strategist, Maury Weiner, was arrested on charges of lewd conduct and forced to leave the Bradley administration. Despite these setbacks, Bradley was reelected mayor in 1977.

Reelections and Governor's Races
During his second term, Bradley began aiming for higher goals: He began laying the foundation for bringing the 1984 Olympics to Los Angeles, and he campaigned for the office of California governor in 1982. As in his 1977 reelection bid, Bradley was dogged by the question of busing, which had become a major point of contention in the San Fernando Valley specifically and statewide generally. His Republican opponent, Attorney General George Deukmejian, raised the busing issue along with other ostensibly race-related concerns such as welfare and social programs. Perhaps in response, Bradley's African American supporters claimed that he neglected them during the campaign. Nevertheless, polls showed Bradley leading his opponent throughout the period leading up to the November election. Indeed, on the night of the election, a number of Los Angeles television stations projected Bradley as the winner. Such predictions proved to be false; Bradley lost the election by the narrow margin of 53,000 votes out of 7.7 million cast.

Bradley's effort to bring the Olympics to Los Angeles proved more effective. Despite a boycott of the games by the Soviet Union and most of its allies, the Olympics proved to be an athletic and fiscal success; a profit was generated that was used to fund youth sports pro-

Brawley, Benjamin Griffith (April 22, 1882, Columbia, South Carolina—February 1, 1939, Washington, D.C.): Clergyman, college professor, and author. Brawley earned bachelor's degrees from Morehouse College and the University of Chicago. He was also awarded a master's degree from HOWARD UNIVERSITY. Brawley taught English at Morehouse College, Shaw University, and Howard University. He is best remembered for his book *A Short History of the American Negro* (1913), a classic history of African Americans from the precolonial era.

See also: Historiography.

Braxton, Toni (b. 1968, Severn, Maryland): Singer. An elegant songstress with an earthy voice, Toni Braxton broke into the music charts with the single "Love Shoulda Brought You Home" and "Give U My Heart" from the multiplatinum sound track for the film *Boomerang* (1992), starring Eddie MURPHY. The sound track reached the top of both pop and rhythm-and-blues charts.

Braxton was the oldest of six children. Her father was a part-time preacher in the Apostolic faith, and she was not allowed to listen to popular music. Her musical influence came from her mother, who sang for a DOO-WOP group, the Vue-ettes, and was an amateur opera singer when Toni was young. Toni sang in the church choir, where she learned to play piano and began to write her own songs. She would often sneak out of the house to listen to music and watch *Soul Train*, a popular television song-and-dance show. When Braxton was fourteen, her parents converted to the less-conservative United Methodist Church and relaxed some of their religious restrictions.

Braxton and her four sisters (backup singers Traci, Towanda, Trina, and Tamar) launched their musical careers when Toni met a songwriter named Bill Pettaway. He introduced her to a producer who, in turn, ar-

Toni Braxton performing at the American Music Awards in 1994. *(AP/Wide World Photos)*

ranged a deal for the Braxton sisters at Arista Records. They recorded *The Braxtons* in 1990, but the single "The Good Life" did not sell many records. The song got the attention of Kenny "BABYFACE" Edmonds. He and his partner Antonio "L.A." Reid were starting their own record label, LaFace; they offered Toni a solo deal if she would leave the Arista label. Her family encouraged her to make the move, and her sisters also signed a deal to record for LaFace. As producers of the sound track of the 1992 film *Boomerang*, Edmonds and Reid invited Braxton to perform on the album.

Braxton's debut solo album, *Toni Braxton* (1993), conveyed an impressive range of sentiments and sold more than seven million copies by 1996. "Another Sad Love Song" showcases her deep, throaty voice. The single for "Breathe Again" conveys a sense of despair and longing. Other songs include "Love Affairs," in which a modern woman speaks her mind, and "I Belong to You." Braxton wrote and coproduced "Best Friend." Braxton earned two Soul Train Music Awards in 1994, for best female album and for best single "Breathe Again." She won Grammy Awards for best new artist and best female R&B vocal performance for "Another Sad Love Song" in 1994 and made numerous television appearances.

Her second album, *Secrets*, more varied than her first, was released in 1996, and it garnered Braxton two Grammy Awards for her singing. The album contained her number one single "You're Makin' Me High." Moving in new artistic directions, Braxton coproduced the album and cowrote four of its songs. *See also:* Rhythm and blues.

Break dancing: a popular form of DANCE associated with HIP-HOP culture in general and with RAP music in particular. Break dancing became popular in the early 1980's, and its peak year as a national craze was probably 1984. That year break dancing was featured at the ceremonies of the Los Angeles Olympic Games and was widely seen on television and in films that were quickly made to capitalize on the phenomenon. Break dancing is a hybrid of African American dance forms and includes influences ranging from VAUDEVILLE to the dance moves of soul singer James BROWN. It involves a dizzying array of techniques: distinctive headspins and backspins, flows, handglides, and windmills.

Its origins in the United States can be traced back to South Bronx street gangs and house parties, but break dancing is also similar to the Afro-Brazilian martial art/dance form *capoeira*, which has roots in African cultures. Traditionally, this martial art/dance is a competition between two participants who perform kicks, traps, sweeps, and takedowns, all to the rhythms of Afro-Brazilian music and songs. *Capoeira* is believed to have arrived in the United States with the first wave of WEST INDIES immigrants in 1916.

Break dancer Roger "Orko" Romero spins on his head during a production of *Jam on the Groove* in Los Angeles in 1996. *(AP/Wide World Photos)*

Police herd African Americans to a detention center during the 1921 Tulsa race riot that catapulted Cyril V. Briggs's African Blood Brotherhood to national fame. *(AP/Wide World Photos)*

Capoeira was often a symbolic fight, a substitute for violent conflict between two or more opposing parties. Break dancing also served this function to some extent from the early 1970's to the early 1980's. South Bronx street gangs utilized break dancing as a physical expression of argument, debate, and resolution. Break dancing therefore served a function somewhat similar to that of "the dozens"—a verbal war of wits between two combatants, often from rival gangs or neighborhoods. Just as the dozens, frequently involving the trading of rhymed insults, has been adapted into rap music, so break dancing evolved into a popular and influential form of entertainment.

—*Tyrone Williams*

See also: Dozens, the.

Briggs, Cyril V. (May 28, 1887, Chester's Park, Nevis, British West Indies—October 18, 1966): Leader of the AFRICAN BLOOD BROTHERHOOD (ABB), a militant African American organization which he founded in 1919. During its heyday, the ABB claimed thousands of members and more than a hundred branches.

Briggs advocated a black nationalist and socialist political line that rejected the anticommunist orientation of Marcus GARVEY. His ABB first rose to national prominence following a mid-1921 race riot in Tulsa, OKLAHOMA. ABB organizers assembled a force of five hundred armed African Americans and surrounded a county courthouse. Their goal was to prevent a rumored planned LYNCHING of a black shoeshine boy accused of indiscretion toward a white girl.

White mobs responded by raiding gun shops and shooting randomly at African Americans throughout the city. The African Blood Brotherhood retreated to black neighborhoods and successfully defended them until dawn the following day, when approximately two thousand whites surrounded the area and began burning down black homes, shooting those attempting to escape the confrontation. At least thirty people died in gun battles before the state militia arrived and enforced martial law, patrolling the streets with fixed bayonets and placing approximately six thousand black people in makeshift detention camps.

Both military authorities and the press later accused ABB organizers of provoking the Tulsa riot to further recruitment aims. In a statement carried in both *The New York Times* and the ABB's organ, *The Crusader,* Briggs defended his organization's actions in Tulsa as an organized effort at community self-defense. Briggs further declared that "the purpose of the African Blood Brotherhood was to instill into the mind of the negro race that it must hit back when struck or otherwise remain at the mercy of the white man." Black people could not be expected to rely upon the courts for justice, he argued.

By the mid-1920's, Briggs had begun drifting from his radical nationalist position, attracted to the possibilities offered by a class alliance with white workers in a common struggle for socialism. Linking up with militant trade unionizing efforts in the latter 1920's, Briggs dissolved the ABB at Moscow's urging and provided the American communist movement with its earliest African American cadres. *See also:* Black Nationalism; Communist Party; Race riots; Radicalism.

Briggs v. Elliott: South Carolina court case litigated from 1951 to 1954. Also known as *Harry Briggs v. R. W. Elliott,* this case challenged segregated education and the "separate but equal" doctrine handed down by the U.S. SUPREME COURT in PLESSY V. FERGUSON (1896). In 1954 *Briggs* went to the U.S. Supreme Court as a companion case to the famous BROWN V. BOARD OF EDUCATION case, wherein the Court voted unanimously to reverse *Plessy v. Ferguson.*

Brimmer, Andrew Felton (b. September 13, 1926, Newellton, Louisiana): Economist. The first African American to serve on the Federal

Andrew Felton Brimmer, after being sworn in as deputy assistant secretary of commerce in 1963. *(AP/ Wide World Photos)*

Reserve Board (1966-1974), Brimmer resigned to take a teaching position at the Harvard Graduate School of Business Administration.

While on the Federal Reserve Board, which directs the monetary policy of the United States, Brimmer pointed out that small business was declining in the country so was unlikely to be the best route for black economic development, even though government policies were promoting small business ownership for black entrepreneurs. In a paper for the American Economic Association in 1969, he noted that promotion of BLACK CAPITALISM might retard economic advancement for African Americans by discouraging them from participating in the national economy, which offered a broader set of challenges and opportunities.

In 1969 Brimmer warned that efforts to control inflation would cause unemployment. He agreed that inflation needed to be controlled, but he argued for increasing unemployment compensation and the amount of job training offered to the unemployed. Brimmer also desired some plan to provide income directly to those hit hardest by anti-inflation policies, perhaps even a guarantee of jobs with the government. He made a controversial statement calling for black bankers not to hire black employees because their relative lack of skill could put the black banks at a disadvantage.

Brimmer graduated from the University of Washington (B.A., 1950; M.A., 1951) and Harvard University (Ph.D., 1957). He did postgraduate work as a Fulbright fellow at the University of Bombay in India from 1951 to 1952. Before joining the Federal Reserve Board, he was an economist with the Federal Reserve Bank of New York City from 1955 to 1958. He taught at Michigan State University for three years, then at the Wharton School of Finance and Commerce at the University of Pennsylvania for another five years. While at the Wharton School, he served as deputy assistant secretary of commerce from 1963 to 1965 and as assistant secretary for economic affairs within the Commerce Department from 1965 to 1966. In 1976 he formed Brimmer and Company, Inc., in Washington, D.C.

Brimmer served as president of the Association for the Study of Afro-American Life and History from 1970 to 1973, then again beginning in January, 1989. He also served as cochair of the Interracial Council for Business Opportunity. At the annual dinner held in 1985 for the Joint Center for Political Studies, he said in a speech that economic progress for African Americans is hindered by their lack of education and marketable skills as well as by discrimination. Some of the problems of black people, he said, are matters of choice, such as high teenage pregnancy rates. Brimmer wrote several books about economic development and about financial markets.

Broadcast licensing: The federal government has had changing, and sometimes somewhat contradictory, policies on fostering minority ownership of broadcasting facilities such as television and radio stations. The Federal Communications Commission (FCC) is the government agency responsible for granting broadcasting licenses. The FCC stated in the mid-1960's that diversity in broadcast license ownership is "a public good." Court decisions in the 1970's pushed the FCC and Congress in the direction of providing incentives for minority ownership. In 1978, with the authorization of Congress, the FCC established the minority tax certificate program, which helped increase minority ownership. In 1995 Congress eliminated the program.

History of Tax Certificates
In 1978 the FCC instituted the minority tax certificate program. The program was intended to help increase minority ownership of radio and television stations.

It allowed station owners who sold broadcast stations or cable systems to minority owners to delay paying taxes on money made from the sale of the stations if they met certain conditions. The program resulted in significant tax savings for sellers—including, eventually, some minority broadcasters who sold interest in their broadcast properties to other minorities. The tax deferments applied if the owner sold to a company that was at minimum 50 percent minority (or female) owned.

Under the policy, the seller had to reinvest the profits within two years in other media properties, as approved by the FCC, and had to meet certain restrictions of the Internal Revenue Service (IRS). The FCC extended the tax certificate policy to include those who showed gains on investments in minority-controlled stations. In 1982 the policy was again extended, to include those who made start-up money available to minority buyers. Minority buyers were required to control the purchased station for a minimum of one year. Overall, it was found that minority buyers kept control of the stations for an average of five years.

By mid-1995, when Congress eliminated the program, 362 tax certificates had been issued to help minorities buy broadcast and cable stations. Almost 94 percent of all minority-owned television stations had been purchased through the use of tax certificates. Most of the certificates had been awarded to non-minorities. Most had also been awarded for relatively small deals: The average price for sales of the radio stations was $4 million; the average price for the television stations was $38 million.

Station Ownership

In 1976 there were thirty minority-owned radio stations and one minority-owned television station in the United States. Between 1976 and 1980, minority ownership increased to 140 radio stations and ten television stations. The rate of minority ownership began to fall off, however, from 1980 through 1992 during the Republican presidencies of Ronald Reagan and George Bush. In 1992, the final year of the Bush presidency, there were fifteen minority-owned television stations, an increase of only five stations within twelve years. Also in 1992, there were 182 minority-owned radio stations, forty-two more than in 1980. The number of broadcast outlets increased significantly during this time, but minority ownership of broadcast media did not increase in proportion.

When Bill Clinton was elected president in 1992, the rate of minority station ownership began to increase again. By 1995 African Americans owned twenty-one television stations, 172 radio stations, and ten cable systems. Minorities overall owned thirty-one television stations, 292 radio stations, and twenty-three cable systems. Although a significant improvement from figures ten or fifteen years earlier, the figures still represented less than 3 percent of all existing television stations and less than 4 percent of all radio stations.

End of the Certificate Program

In 1995 Republican efforts to eliminate AFFIRMATIVE ACTION programs throughout the nation effectively brought to a halt any major advances in minority broadcast ownership for some time. Congressional Republicans pushed bills through Congress in March and April of 1995 to abolish the tax certificate program. Despite the urging of many Democrats that he veto the bill, President Clinton signed the bill into law.

A major exception to the 1995 tax break bill stirred considerable controversy. Australian-born Rupert Murdoch, owner of the Fox television network and other media properties, was allowed a one-time tax break of $63 million for his sale of an ATLANTA, GEORGIA, television station to minorities. The exception was inserted into the bill at the request of Carol E. Moseley BRAUN, a Democrat and African American senator from Illinois. Murdoch had a signed contract to sell WATL-TV in Atlanta to Qwest, Inc., for $150 million. The Qwest company had a 55 percent minority ownership. The other 45 percent of the stations was to be owned by the Tribune Company, publishers of the *Chicago Tribune* newspaper in Moseley Braun's home state of Illinois.

Another exception to the 1995 tax certificate law allowed sellers of broadcast stations to obtain tax certificates if the terms of the basic contracts between broadcast sellers and minority buyers had been agreed upon and documented before January 17, 1995.

Role of the Courts

The FCC's 1978 action in adopting a tax certificate policy (and other policies in regard to minority ownership) had been preceded by a number of relevant court decisions since 1971. The decisions had been primarily handed down by the D.C. Circuit Court of Appeals and the U.S. SUPREME COURT on issues of diversity in broadcasting and preferential treatment of minorities in granting FCC licenses.

The court decisions through the years often conflicted with one another, particularly at the level of the D.C. Circuit Court. As presidential administrations changed, the political bent of appointees to the court also changed. To compound matters, the FCC, as a body also appointed by the president, sometimes reversed previously determined FCC actions as its membership changed.

In 1965 the FCC on its own had determined that diversity in broadcast license ownership is "a public good in a free society." Yet it was primarily the result of a 1971 D.C. Circuit Court case (*Citizens Communication Center v. Federal Communications Commission*), and appeals and related cases springing from that case up to 1978, that finally compelled the FCC to make more specific its generalized, and sometimes conflicting, policies of diversity in broadcast ownership. In the *Citizens Communication Center* case, the court rejected an FCC effort to dismantle its policies in regard to preferential minority treatment in issuing broadcast licenses. The court pointed to a linkage between diversity in ownership and diversity in program content.

In a ruling in a similar case two years later, the D.C. Circuit Court reminded the FCC of the message in its 1971 ruling that "black ownership and participation together are themselves likely to bring about programming that is responsive to the needs of the black citizenry" and that "as new interest groups and hitherto silent minorities emerge in our society they should be given [a] stake in and chance to broadcast on our radio and television frequencies."

Goaded by these decisions, the FCC began a study of major questions involved in minority ownership. The FCC concluded in its report that major financial barriers and lack of experience in broadcasting made minority entry into broadcast ownership difficult, if not impossible. As a result of these findings, the FCC established its tax certificate program and other minority ownership policies in 1978.

Of U.S. Supreme Court rulings, two cases are particularly noteworthy: *Metro Broadcasting v. Federal Communications Commission* (1990) and *Adarand Constructors v. Peña* (1995). In the *Metro Broadcasting* case, the FCC asked the Supreme Court to uphold the constitutionality of the FCC favoring minorities (and women) in issuing licenses for new stations. The FCC's position was that "the promotion of diversity in broadcast programming is a sufficiently compelling governmental interest to permit the use of a race-conscious policy."

The Supreme Court ruled in favor of the FCC in the *Metro Broadcasting* case. In its 1995 ruling in *Adarand Constructors v. Peña*, however, the Court overturned the same reasoning used by the FCC in the 1990 case. The Court stated that the FCC should have applied stricter scrutiny before making a final determination to favor a minority for a new broadcast license. According to some observers, the Court's *Adarand* decision postponed a final determination as to what the nation's legal policy was in regard to providing opportunities for minorities in broadcast licensing.

Beginning in the mid-1990's, the FCC accelerated efforts to enforce equal employment opportunity (EEO) rules, raised the level of fines on stations found guilty of violating EEO guidelines, and levied the largest EEO fine in FCC history—$121,500—against a Palm Beach cable system. Further, FCC chairman Reed Hundt, speaking to a NATIONAL URBAN LEAGUE convention, said that the FCC would be diligent in opening opportunities for minorities in developing technologies.

—*Sherrie Mazingo*

See also: Radio broadcasting; Television industry.

Suggested Readings:

Analysis of Compilation of Minority Owned Commercial Broadcast Stations in the United States.

Washington, D.C.: The Minority Telecommunications Development Program of the National Telecommunications and Information Administration, U.S. Department of Commerce, September, 1994.

Barlow, William. *Voice Over: The Making of Black Radio*. Philadelphia: Temple University Press, 1999.

Cantor, Louis. *Wheelin' on Beale: How WDIA-Memphis Became the Nation's First All-Black Radio Station and Created the Sound That Changed America*. New York: Pharos Books, 1992.

Everything You Ever Wanted to Know About Buying a Broadcast Station. Washington, D.C.: National Association of Broadcasters, 1994.

Kleiman, Howard. "Content Diversity and the FCC's Minority and Gender Licensing Policies." *Journal of Broadcasting & Electronic Media* 35 (Fall, 1991): 411-429.

Newman, Mark. *Entrepreneurs of Profit and Pride: From Black-Appeal to Radio Soul*. New York: Praeger, 1988.

Brooke, Edward W. (b. October 26, 1919, Washington, D.C.): Politician. In 1966 Brooke became the first African American since Mississippi's Blanche K. BRUCE in 1874 to win a full term in the U.S. Senate. Educated at HOWARD UNIVERSITY (B.S., 1940), Brooke served with distinction as a commando in WORLD WAR II. After the war, Brooke earned his law degree at Boston University (1948) and settled in MASSACHUSETTS, where he practiced law and participated in local REPUBLICAN PARTY politics. He became chair of the Boston Finance Commission in 1961.

In 1962 Brooke's election as attorney general of Massachusetts made him the highest-ranking African American elected state official. In 1966 he ran successfully as a Republican for Massachusetts's U.S. Senate seat, defeating the more liberal Democratic nominee, former Massachusetts governor Endicott Peabody.

Edward W. Brooke, the first African American elected to the U.S. Senate after Reconstruction. *(Archive Photos)*

In the Senate Brooke became a leader of the liberal wing of the Republican Party. He was much admired by Republican presidents Richard M. Nixon and Gerald Ford and turned down several offers of cabinet positions. He supported the VIETNAM WAR at first, but in 1971 he supported the McGovern-Hatfield Amendment calling for withdrawal of troops.

Reelected in 1972, Brooke found his influence in the Republican Party waning as the party became more conservative. After narrowly winning a hard-fought primary campaign in 1978 against a conservative Republican, Brooke, at that time the only black U.S. senator, lost the general election to his Democratic opponent, Paul Tsongas. Brooke then returned to the practice of law and worked as a lobbyist in Washington, D.C. He was made chairman of the National Low-Income Housing Coalition in 1979.

See also: Congress members; Politics and government.

Brooks, Gwendolyn (b. June 7, 1917, Topeka, Kansas): Novelist and poet, best known in American LITERATURE as the first African American writer to win a Pulitzer Prize. Her collection of poetry *Annie Allen* earned this honor in 1950. Brooks received a number of other awards, including the American Academy of Letters Award, two Guggenheim Fellowships, more than fifty honorary degrees from colleges and universities, and the designation of poet laureate of ILLINOIS.

Most of Brooks's work appears in her collections of poetry, but she also wrote a novel and an autobiography. Brooks's poetry is praised by literary critics for its technical brilliance and attention to craftsmanship. Ordinary readers, however, appreciate her portraits of such memorable characters as Satin Legs Smith, Pearl May Lee, and Lincoln West. She has also portrayed such historical figures as Emmett TILL, MALCOLM X, and Paul ROBESON.

African American people and events have been the subject of most of her poetry, which shows the influence of colloquial speech, spirituals, and blues. Her early work was expressed in conventional rhymed forms such as the ballad and sonnet. As she mastered her craft, she became more interested in writing in open forms, or free verse, and concentrated on reaching a black audience.

Throughout her long career as a writer, Brooks constantly extended her range, experimenting with new subjects and forms of poetic expression. She objected to attempts by critics to classify her poetic style or to assign her to a literary movement.

Early Life and Works

Gwendolyn Brooks was born in KANSAS but grew up in CHICAGO. Her parents were David Brooks, a custodian, and Keziah Wims Brooks, a former schoolteacher. Her family life was loving and secure, with emphasis on traditions and holidays and solid support for her literary ambitions. Gwendolyn was a shy, lonely child who showed a gift for rhyming by the age of seven. When she was eleven, she began her first poetry notebook. As a young student, she was influenced by reading the works of black poets Paul Laurence DUNBAR, Countée CULLEN, and Langston HUGHES. By the age of thirteen, she had decided to become a poet, already having published poems in local newspapers and a national magazine. As a high school student, she sent some poems to James Weldon JOHNSON and Langston Hughes, both of whom encouraged her and praised her work. At the age of sixteen, one of her protest poems was published by the CHICAGO DEFENDER, a black newspaper.

Brooks attended Wilson Junior College for two years and was active in the student group of the NATIONAL ASSOCIATION FOR THE ADVANCEMENT OF COLORED PEOPLE (NAACP). In 1939 she married Henry Blakely, with whom she had two children. In 1941 Brooks attended a series of writers' workshops conducted by Inez Cunningham Stark, a wealthy Chicago patron of the arts, and began her serious study of poetic technique. She was influenced in the development of her craft by such modernist poets as T. S. Eliot and Ezra Pound. In 1941 her work was recognized with the poetry award from the Midwestern Writers Conference.

Her first collection of poetry, *A Street in Bronzeville*, published by Harper in 1945, earned her favorable reviews from white critics. The subjects of Brooks's poems were poor and working-class blacks and street people from Chicago's South Side. Her language and use of conventional forms made her work accessible to ordinary readers and was in the traditional protest mode. She used realistic images of ordinary people and events and portrayed prejudice as a fact of life for African Americans. Her tone was ironic, often humorous, but without the outward anger that characterized her later work.

With the publication of *Annie Allen* in 1949, Brooks was acclaimed by the literary establishment and awarded the Pulitzer Prize for poetry in 1950. These poems, often described as academic and intellectual, used a more sophisticated vocabulary and symbolism, making them less accessible to the untrained reader. As Brooks said, she was experimenting with technique and becoming less dependent on conventional forms. Some black critics, however, said that though Brooks was writing about African Americans, her poetry was integrationist and directed toward winning the approval of white critics; such critics claimed that her poetry was not working toward the improvement of life for black people.

In 1953 Brooks published a novel, *Maud Martha*, the story of a young black woman growing up in Chicago: The book contains a number of autobiographical incidents and characters based on real people. Although the novel received little serious critical attention at the time of publication, later critics have ranked it with her best work as a sensitive por-

Gwendolyn Brooks during her tenure as poetry consultant to the Library of Congress in 1986. *(AP/ Wide World Photos)*

trayal of black-white relationships during the GREAT DEPRESSION and WORLD WAR II. Feminist critics describe it as an accurate portrait of the oppression of black women both by men of their own race and by the white world. *The Bean Eaters*, her collection of poems published in 1960, marked a transition in her work. Some readers found a new tone of bitterness, and Brooks herself believes that this volume alienated white critics who had previously given her favorable reviews. Certainly these poems, coming at the beginning of the CIVIL RIGHTS MOVEMENT of the 1960's, revealed a new consciousness about the oppression of African Americans by the larger society.

Later Poetry

In 1967 Brooks, who had been giving poetry readings on a number of college campuses, attended a conference at FISK UNIVERSITY and was awakened by the anger of a group of young black writers who had abandoned efforts at integration and were advocating black power. This meeting challenged her ways of thinking and forced her to question her previous belief that social problems of African Americans would be solved through faith and good will. Although Brooks's work had always expressed a realistic view of the lives of African Americans, her experience with these young, militant writers made her their ally in the Black Arts (or Black Aesthetic) movement. These writers, including Amiri BARAKA (LeRoi Jones) and Haki MADHUBUTI (Don L. Lee), believed that black artists should write and perform exclusively for black audiences. Brooks later marked this as the point when she stopped thinking of herself as a "Negro" and began to identify with her African heritage. Unlike many members of the Black Arts movement who believed that the role of the arts was political (that is, to promote black pride), Brooks adhered to her own high standards as a measure of artistic purpose and worth.

Her next collection of poems, *In the Mecca* (1968), described the tragic lives of black people in a ghetto apartment building. Some mainstream critics judged Brooks's new poetry harshly, disapproving of her revolutionary stance. She continued experimenting with new forms, publishing *Riot* in 1969 and *Family Pictures* in 1970. She also published two books of children's poetry. Acting on her belief that black publishing houses should be supported, Brooks parted from her long association with Harper and published her collections with Broadside Press in Detroit.

Report from Part One, her autobiography, was published in 1972. Two trips to Africa broadened her experience to include international subjects such as Winnie Mandela and South African martyr Steven Biko in her poetry. In 1987 she published *Blacks*, a collection of writings from her previous work originally published with Harper.

Contribution to African American Life

Like many African American writers and artists, Brooks has confronted the dilemma of writing from her own experience for a largely white reading public and literary establishment. Her early black critics, responding to her success in the white world, questioned her commitment to social activism; however, Brooks's commitment to improving the lives of African Americans was soon unquestioned. She constantly strove to refine her poetic technique and clarify her language so that her work would reach a wide reading public. She began to give financial support to a number of young writers and to give poetry awards from her own funds to schoolchildren who showed promise.

In addition to her reputation among ordinary people, Brooks has been recognized by literary critics for developing and extending common themes in African American literature. One constant theme is the black tendency to adopt white standards of beauty and reject the beauty of blackness. She wrote unblinkingly of the realities of black life, including the violence and self-destructiveness of life in the ghetto. The conviction that blacks have been denied access to the American Dream is another prominent theme in her work. Although feminists often note Brooks's portrayal of women's oppression at the hands of black men, Brooks herself said that black men and women must work side by side in the fight for survival.

Brooks's best work is marked, paradoxically, by both compassion and rage. Ultimately, she praises the strength, beauty, and resilience of African Americans. Her poetry developed from its early underlying theme of social protest expressed in conventional forms to an artistic mastery of free verse that portrays the life of African Americans in terms understandable to both black and white readers. Critics and untrained readers alike respond to the integrity of her vision and her courage in speaking the truth as she sees it.

—*Marjorie Podolsky*

Suggested Readings:

Bolden, B. J. *Urban Rage in Bronzeville: Social Commentary in the Poetry of Gwendolyn Brooks, 1945-1960*. Chicago: Third World Press, 1997.

Brooks, Gwendolyn. *Report from Part One*. Detroit: Broadside Press, 1972.

_____. *Report from Part Two*. Chicago: Third World Press, 1996.

Hawkins, B. Denise. "An Evening with Gwendolyn Brooks." *Black Issues in Higher Education* 11 (November 3, 1994): 15-19.

Hull, Gloria T., and P. Gallagher. "Update on Part One—An Interview with Gwendolyn Brooks." *CLA Journal* 21 (September, 1977): 19-40.

Kent, George E. *A Life of Gwendolyn Brooks*. Lexington: University Press of Kentucky, 1990.

Melhem, D. H. *Gwendolyn Brooks: Poetry and the Heroic Voice*. Lexington: University Press of Kentucky, 1987.

Schweik, Susan M. *A Gulf So Deeply Cut: American Women Poets and the Second World War.* Madison: University of Wisconsin Press, 1991.

Shaw, Harry B. *Gwendolyn Brooks.* Boston: Twayne, 1980.

Tate, Claudia. "Gwendolyn Brooks." In *Black Women Writers at Work.* New York: Continuum, 1989.

Broonzy, "Big Bill" (William Lee Conley; June 26, 1893, Scott, Mississippi—August 14, 1958, Chicago, Illinois): BLUES singer and guitarist. Born to former field slaves, Broonzy began his career playing country picnics with a homemade guitar fashioned from a box. In 1916 a disastrous drought in MISSISSIPPI caused Broonzy and other area farmers to seek alter-

Legendary blues guitarist "Big Bill" Broonzy. *(Frank Driggs/Archive Photos)*

native employment in the North. Broonzy settled in CHICAGO, ILLINOIS.

In Chicago Broonzy studied guitar with "Papa" Charlie Jackson while he earned money playing rent parties with contemporaries such as Sleepy John Estes and Louis Carter. In 1926 Broonzy cut four sides for Paramount Records, three of which were rejected. The one released track, "House Rent Stomp," an instrumental released in 1927 under the names of Big Bill and Thomps—John Thomas played second guitar—demonstrates young Broonzy's growth as a musician.

By the 1930's, when many musicians found it difficult to record as a result of the GREAT DEPRESSION, Broonzy continued to make records. During this period, he successfully crossed over into different styles, collaborating with jazz-influenced guitarists such as Lonnie Johnson and TAMPA RED (Hudson Whittaker) and with barrelhouse piano players "Cripple" Clarence Lofton and Georgia Tom Dorsey. He became the RCA-Bluebird label's biggest star, making his own records as well as playing on most subsequent Bluebird releases.

Broonzy's biggest break came in 1939, when promoter John Hammond hired him to play the role of the primitive bluesman at the legendary "From Spirituals to Swing" concert in Carnegie Hall. The performance garnered him tremendous acclaim. By 1941, after a series of recordings with his cousin Robert "Washboard Sam" Brown and piano player Peter "MEMPHIS SLIM" Chapman, along with other projects, Broonzy was regarded as one of Chicago's top musicians.

In the 1950's, Broonzy began a series of performances in Europe, displaying his virtuosity to adoring crowds in England, France, Denmark, and other countries. It was during one of these sojourns that he agreed to collaborate with writer Yannick Bruynoghe. The landmark *Big Bill Blues* (1955), which developed from a series of letters between the two, was Broonzy's autobiography.

Brotherhood of Sleeping Car Porters: Labor union. In the late nineteenth and first half of the twentieth century, one of the few steady jobs an African American man could get was that of a Pullman porter. Pullman porters were employed by the Pullman Company to wait on, and make and change beds for, passengers of railroad sleeping cars built by the Pullman Company and leased to long-haul passenger railroads. These jobs, although menial and paying a low wage, provided steady employment and the chance to travel for the African Americans who held them. Porters could also augment their meager wages with tips. In many black communities, Pullman porter jobs were quite prestigious.

Still, the low wages and often demeaning work conditions for Pullman porters cried out for remedies. In 1925 A. Philip RANDOLPH, a prominent black socialist magazine editor and agitator, decided to organize the Pullman porters into a labor union patterned on the railroad brotherhoods. These railroad unions, like American labor unions in general, barred African Americans from membership or segregated them into all-Negro "federal unions" with little bargaining power or recognition. The Brotherhood of Sleeping Car Porters was to be different. At first, the Pullman Company refused to recognize the union and tried to fire or blacklist its members. Randolph and the brotherhood persevered, aided by the black monopoly on this kind of work.

In 1937 the union gained recognition and a contract from the Pullman Company. As a result, conditions for Pullman porters improved considerably. The union affiliated with the American Federation of Labor, and Randolph was appointed to that body's governing board.

Ironically, just as the Brotherhood of Sleeping Car Porters gained power and benefits for its members, long-distance passenger rail travel began to decline. By the 1960's few railroads needed sleeping cars or their porters. The Pullman Company itself branched into other businesses, getting out of the sleeping car business. A decade later, Pullman porters were few and their union was moribund. The Brotherhood of Sleeping Car Porters, however, represents the first success for African Americans in the American labor movement and paved the way for later African American advances in America's labor unions.
See also: Organized labor.

Brown, Charlotte Hawkins (June 11, 1883, Henderson, North Carolina—January 11, 1961, Greensboro, North Carolina): Educator, advocate of CIVIL RIGHTS and women's rights, and founder of Palmer Memorial Institute. She was the daughter of Caroline F. Hawkins and Edmund H. Hight, both former slaves. Later, Brown's mother, with whom she lived, married a Mr. Willis. When she was five years old, a large portion of Brown's immediate and extended family moved to the BOSTON, MASSACHUSETTS, area. They settled in Cambridge, near Harvard University. The Willises earned their livelihood by operating a laundry, boarding Harvard University students, and caring for infants.

Brown graduated from Cambridge English High and Latin School. Alice Freeman Palmer, the first female president of Wellesley College, met Brown while she was a high school senior and became her mentor and benefactor. She assisted Brown in enrolling at the State Normal School in Salem, Massachusetts, to prepare for a career in teaching. After completing a year at Salem, Brown was asked to begin teaching African Americans in Sedalia, North Carolina, in the fall of 1901 by a representative of the American Missionary Association. Torn between the desire to continue her own education and the desire to educate others, she chose the latter. Because of funding problems, the school at Bethany Congregational Church in Sedalia closed after one term. Undaunted, Hawkins set out to establish her own school. She

Charlotte Hawkins Brown, founder of Palmer Memorial Institute. *(Associated Publishers, Inc.)*

Brown, Clara (1800?, Kentucky—c. 1880): Pioneer. Brown, a slave freed in Missouri, went west during the Colorado gold rush and is believed to be the first African American woman to settle in COLORADO. She opened a laundry in Central City, Colorado, hoping to earn enough money to buy her family into freedom. Brown freed some family members, and the rest were freed after the Civil War and joined her in Central City. She eventually owned several gold mines.
See also: Frontier society.

Brown, Claude (b. February 23, 1937, New York, New York): Lecturer and author. During the GREAT DEPRESSION, Brown's parents, Henry Lee Brown, a railroad worker, and Ossie Brock Brown, a domestic worker, fled the racism of the rural South for New York City, where Brown was born.

Brown was expelled from school at age eight. The next year, he was admitted to the Harlem Buccaneers, a street GANG. At age thirteen, he was shot during a burglary. He pursued street CRIME through fraud, petty theft, assault, and drug dealing, serving three terms at Wiltwyck, a New York City school for troubled youth. From age seventeen to age twenty, he worked in Greenwich Village, holding jobs in a restaurant, watch factory, shipping office, and nightclub, where he played jazz piano.

With the help of his reform school mentor, Brown abandoned crime and moved out of HARLEM. He chose a nonviolent lifestyle and earned a B.A. degree from HOWARD UNIVERSITY in 1965. He began to write about this time. Brown gained public recognition for his departure from the less strident prose of Roy WILKINS, Richard WRIGHT, and James BALDWIN, and he garnered mixed reviews for his caustic criticism of America's bigotry and oppression. His first book, *Manchild in the Promised Land*, remained unpublished for a year, until Brown's publisher found the right editor

founded the Palmer Memorial Institute, named in honor of Alice Freeman Palmer, in 1902. It operated until 1971, with Brown as president from 1902 until 1952, when she resigned.

In 1911 she married Edmund S. Brown, a Harvard graduate. The marriage was brief because of different career objectives. Brown continued to study while building Palmer. Intermittently, she studied at Harvard University, Simmons College, and Temple University. Honorary degrees were bestowed upon her by several schools, including Wilberforce University, LINCOLN UNIVERSITY in Pennsylvania, and HOWARD UNIVERSITY.

Brown was one of the organizers of the North Carolina Federation of Negro Women's Clubs and served as its second president, from 1915 to 1936. She was instrumental in founding an orphanage for African Americans in Oxford, NORTH CAROLINA, and was a founder of the Commission on Interracial Cooperation in 1919.

for the job. The book touched a nerve with both black and white readers and quickly rose to sixth place on the best-seller list. It is a psychological and sociological study of the brutality of ghetto life and is known for its dispassionate candor and raw, energetic street language, punctuated with slang and obscenities.

Brown's second book, *The Children of Ham* (1976), an equally poignant re-creation of his Harlem childhood, received scant critical attention. In addition to his novels, Brown contributed to *Esquire, Dissent*, and other periodicals. He earned the Ansfield-Wolf Award from the *Saturday Review*.

Brown, Corrine (b. November 11, 1946, Jacksonville, Florida): Florida politician and educator. Brown received her bachelor's degree from Florida A&M University in 1969 before going on to earn an Ed.S. degree from the University of Florida in 1974. She taught at Edward Waters College at the University of Florida before pursuing a career in politics. In 1983 Brown was elected to represent her state's seventeenth district in the FLORIDA state legislature. Active in Democratic politics, she served as a Florida delegate to the 1988 Democratic National Convention.

Brown decided to run for Congress and campaigned as a candidate to represent Florida's Third Congressional District. After winning election in November of 1992, Brown took office as a freshman representative in the 103d Congress in January of 1993. Upon entering the U.S. House of Representatives, she became the first African American elected to represent the state of Florida in Congress. Among her duties, Brown served on the Public Works and Transportation Committee and the Veterans Affairs Committee. Brown continued to serve in Congress through the 1990's, being re-elected in 1994, 1996, and 1998.

See also: Congress members; Politics and government.

Brown, Dorothy Lavinia (b. January 7, 1919, Philadelphia, Pennsylvania): Physician and educator. After living in an orphanage in Troy, New York, for the first twelve years of her life, Brown was placed in the foster home of Mr. and Mrs. Samuel Redmon. With help from the Redmons and a scholarship from the Troy Conference of the METHODIST Church, she attended Bennett College in Greensboro, North Carolina, and received her B.A. in 1941. She was a member of Delta Sigma Theta sorority. In 1948 she received her M.D. from MEHARRY MEDICAL SCHOOL in Nashville, TENNESSEE.

After doing her internship at Harlem Hospital in New York City, Brown became the first woman accepted for a five-year residency program in general surgery at George W. Hubbard Hospital in Nashville. When she completed her work there, she became the first African American general surgeon in the

Dorothy Lavinia Brown in 1968. *(AP/Wide World Photos)*

South. She later took the positions of clinical professor of surgery at Meharry Medical Center and chief of surgery at Riverside Hospital (1960-1983). When she adopted Lola Denise in August, 1956, she became the first single African American woman to adopt a child in TENNESSEE. Subsequently, she adopted Kevin Edward.

In 1966, running as a Democrat, she became the first African American woman to win a seat in the Tennessee legislature. During her two-year term, she introduced a bill that would permit abortion in cases of rape and incest or to save the mother's life. Her position on this issue probably contributed to her losing her bid for reelection to another term.

Brown was the first African American woman elected a Fellow of the American College of Surgeons (1959) and became a member of the Nashville Academy of Medicine, R. F. Boyd Medical Society, and NATIONAL MEDICAL ASSOCIATION. She served as director of student health services at Meharry College and at FISK UNIVERSITY in Nashville. She received an honorary doctorate (1972) from Russell Sage College in Troy, New York, and was given many other awards, including the National Sojourner Truth Award (1973).

Brown, Elaine: Social activist. Brown became a dedicated, high-ranking member of the BLACK PANTHER PARTY (BPP). As part of her political work in the BPP during the late 1960's, Brown wrote for the party newspaper, *The Black Panther*. After Eldridge CLEAVER went into self-imposed exile in 1968, Brown traveled to Algeria and other countries as part of delegations organized by the BPP's international office, headed by Cleaver. She later became highly critical of Cleaver, accusing him of being a male chauvinist who frequently beat his wife, Kathleen. This anti-Cleaver posture coincided with a split that developed in early 1971 within the Panthers, in which

Cleaver and the entire international office were expelled from the party by Huey NEWTON. Brown's criticism of Cleaver helped build her stature as a Panther dedicated to the rectification of political weaknesses, particularly the party's position on women in the struggle. This, in turn, paved the way for Brown's ascendance in the leadership of the Black Panther Party.

When Newton went into hiding in November, 1974, following his indictment for the alleged murder of a teenage prostitute, Brown became the BPP's new leader. Quickly establishing herself as a dynamic administrator, Brown sought to revive and strengthen a variety of community programs for which the Panthers originally had become known. After one year of her leadership, the party successfully had organized a number of "community survival" programs, including legal aid agencies, health clinics, community sanitation services, free food distribution to the poor, escort services for the elderly, and children's programs, including the construction of an alternative elementary school.

Although Brown had failed to win a seat on the OAKLAND, CALIFORNIA, City Council in 1973, she ran again in 1975 while retaining her leadership role in the BPP. Although she was unable to win the city council seat, she later was appointed to several city commissions and was sent to the Democratic National Convention in 1976 as a delegate pledged to Jerry Brown. Brown's participation in electoral politics symbolized the end of the BPP's insurrectionist politics and played an important role in the election of Oakland's first black mayor, Lionel Wilson.

Brown, George L. (b. July 1, 1926, Lawrence, Kansas): State legislator and business executive. Brown graduated from the University of Kansas with his B.S. degree in 1950. From 1950 to 1965, he worked as a writer and editor for the *Denver Post*. During this period, Brown pursued graduate studies at the University of Colorado and Harvard University Business School.

Brown's political career began in 1955, when he was elected to the COLORADO State House of Representatives. He later served as a state senator from 1956 to 1974. While in the state senate, Brown served as assistant director of the Denver Housing Authority from 1965 to 1969. In 1975 he was elected as lieutenant governor of Colorado, an office he held until 1979. Brown left politics in 1979 to become vice president of marketing for Grumman Ecosystems. He held a variety of executive positions before being promoted to vice president of the corporation's Washington, D.C., office in 1981.

Brown, Hallie Q. (March 10, 1845, Pittsburgh, Pennsylvania—September 16, 1949, Wilberforce, Ohio): Educator, reformer, and author. While she was still quite young, Brown's family moved to Ontario, Canada, where she received her early education. In 1873 she earned a bachelor's degree from Wilberforce University in Ohio.

Brown began her teaching career working with African American children and adults on a SOUTH CAROLINA plantation. She later conducted a school on the Sonora plantation in MISSISSIPPI. As a young teacher, Brown also worked in the public school systems of Yazoo, Mississippi, and Columbia, South Carolina. Brown's involvement with historically black institutions of higher learning began when she worked as dean at Allen University in Columbia from 1885 to 1887. She also served as "lady principal" at TUSKEGEE INSTITUTE in Alabama during the 1890's. Eventually, she returned to her alma mater as professor of education. She also worked for many years in the department of English and served as a member of Wilberforce's board of trustees.

As a reformer, Brown espoused many causes. While still a college student, she became a suffragist after listening to Susan B. Anthony speak at Wilberforce. Later, she traveled extensively, crusading on behalf of women's rights. She was an early CIVIL RIGHTS activist who demanded an end to racial discrimination in America. Brown is remembered for her condemnation of racially biased seating of African Americans who attended the All American Music Festival of the International Council of Women in Washington, D.C., in May of 1925.

Like many educated black women of her day, Brown became involved in the WOMAN'S CLUB MOVEMENT and was committed to uplifting African American women. From 1905 to 1912, she served as president of the Ohio State Federation of Colored Women's Clubs. In 1921 she became the seventh president of the NATIONAL ASSOCIATION OF COLORED WOMEN. During her tenure, she devoted serious effort to establishing a scholarship fund. As a scholar, Brown is best known for compiling and editing *Homespun Heroines and Other Women of Distinction* (1926), a tribute to black women.

Brown, Henry "Box" (1816, Richmond, Virginia—c. 1860): Escaped slave. Brown escaped from SLAVERY in 1848 in a novel way. What is known of his life and escape is found in his 1849 autobiography, *Narrative of Henry Box Brown Who Escaped from Slavery Enclosed in a Box Three Feet Long and Two Wide*. Writing about what he called "the beautiful side of the picture of slavery," Brown explained that he had been a privileged slave who wore good clothes, worked fair hours, ate adequate meals, had a good master, and was beaten only once. Brown worked as a plantation slave before being moved to his master's tobacco manufacturing firm in Richmond, Virginia.

Even with such treatment, Brown called slavery evil and insisted that so-called kind

Illustration in a contemporary antislavery publication showing how Henry Brown shipped himself to Philadelphia. *(Library of Congress)*

active on the abolitionist lecture circuit, touring with his box and with panoramas of slave scenes. After Congress enacted the FUGITIVE SLAVE LAW (1850) and two slave agents tried to return him to the South, Brown took refuge in England. He toured there for four years, lecturing against slavery, before dropping from public view.

See also: Abolitionist movement; Slave runaways.

masters did not exist. His narrative exposed the emotional persecution and "living death" of slavery, the false Christianity of slaveholders, the unrecognized status and uncertainty of slave marriages, the ubiquitous white sexual exploitation of black women, and the resultant dehumanization of formerly decent whites into brutal beasts.

Brown married a slave woman, Nancy, and had several children. After his master sold his wife and children, Brown decided to escape. Brown had aborted several escape attempts before getting a "heavenly vision" to box himself up. Samuel A. Smith, a white man, arranged for a northern ally to receive Brown, then packaged and delivered him to the Richmond office of the Adams Express Company. Twenty-seven hours later, after being transferred from wagon to train to steamboat to wagon, and after spending much of his ordeal upon his head, Brown arrived in PHILADELPHIA, PENNSYLVANIA. Local abolitionists opened the box to free him.

Antislavery groups raised money to help Brown relocate to BOSTON, MASSACHUSETTS, then to New Bedford. Soon, "Box" Brown was

Brown, H. "Rap" (b. October 4, 1943, Baton Rouge, Louisiana): Political activist. An outspoken supporter of BLACK POWER during the late 1960's and early 1970's, H. Rap Brown became a symbol of militant confrontation with the white establishment. His advocacy of armed self-defense and violent confrontation with white racists earned him the media label of "black extremist." As a result of concerted attempts by authorities to silence him, Brown would eventually serve years in prison for weapons charges and for allegedly inciting racial violence.

Early Involvement in Politics

Born Hubert Geroid Brown, Brown first became politically active in the summer of 1962, when he began working with the Nonviolent Action Group (NAG) based at HOWARD UNIVERSITY in Washington, D.C. By 1964 he was participating in voter-registration activities in Holmes County, MISSISSIPPI, and in 1965, he was elected chairman of NAG. As Brown later wrote in his book *Die, Nigger, Die!* (1969), he placed great emphasis on encouraging black college students to identify with the uneducated black masses. Brown acquired the nickname "Rap" because of his outstanding ability to converse with both uneducated blacks and college students.

In 1966 Brown joined other NAG members in working full time with the STUDENT NONVIOLENT COORDINATING COMMITTEE (SNCC). During May, 1967, the chairman of SNCC, Stokely CARMICHAEL, stepped down, and it was decided that Brown would be an able replacement.

Chairman of SNCC

As SNCC chairman, Brown quickly acquired his own notoriety. In June, 1967, a movement worker was killed in Jackson, Mississippi, by police. Angered by the death, Brown was quoted as saying, "If America chooses to play Nazis, black folks ain't going to play Jews." Just days later, Brown again attracted national attention when he arrived in ATLANTA, GEORGIA, following another police shooting of a black citizen amid racial disturbances. At a press conference, Brown declared that "we came here to blow Atlanta up."

A month later, Brown was invited to speak in Cambridge, Maryland, where racial tensions were running high. On July 25, he made a forty-five-minute speech in which he urged African Americans to arm themselves against racist attacks. He told the crowd that blacks would be taken seriously only when white-owned property was endangered, declaring that "money is their god" and that "when you tear down his store, you hit his religion." Although the demonstration ended peacefully, violence broke out scarcely an hour later. Brown himself was slightly wounded by police fire as he was walking home with several others. Angered by the heavy police presence throughout the city, blacks remained in the streets, engaging in confrontations well into the night.

By the next day, seventeen buildings had been badly damaged by fire, and Maryland governor Spiro T. Agnew sent the National Guard to Cambridge to prevent further property losses. As Agnew arrived the following day to survey the damage, he declared that H. "Rap" Brown was personally responsible for the destruction of property and should be locked up. Shortly afterward, a federal warrant was issued for Brown's arrest.

Since Brown had already left the state, the FEDERAL BUREAU OF INVESTIGATION (FBI) was brought into the case. SNCC attorney William Kunstler convinced Brown that he should surrender to authorities to avert any attempts on his life. Kunstler negotiated an agreement with the FBI for his client to present himself to authorities in New York City, but when Brown reluctantly agreed and arrived at the Washington, D.C., airport, he was arrested by waiting police before he could board a flight for New York. Brown was taken immediately to Alexandria, Virginia; the federal charges against

H. "Rap" Brown at a SNCC news conference. *(Library of Congress)*

him were dropped, and he was rearrested for extradition to Maryland. While awaiting his release on bond, Brown declared that the country was "on the eve of a black revolution" and that blacks would now "fight the enemy tit-for-tat."

Within days, additional charges were filed by officials of Dayton, Ohio, who accused Brown of inciting violence that had occurred after he made a speech there. Still more charges in New York were issued against Brown for having carried a legally registered firearm across state lines, technically an offense when the registrant is under any legal indictments. The SNCC leader had become the target of an escalating campaign of legal harassment, a tactic frequently used to immobilize black activists.

"As American as Cherry Pie"

By early 1968, Brown's name was synonymous with black extremism, an association bolstered by Brown's flair for colorful rhetoric. On one occasion, he defended his support for black armed resistance by declaring that "violence is as American as cherry pie." On February 17, 1968, Brown violated his bond restrictions by traveling to an OAKLAND, CALIFORNIA, rally sponsored by the BLACK PANTHER PARTY (BPP). During this gathering, it was unexpectedly announced that the BPP was forming an alliance with SNCC.

Cooperation notwithstanding, Brown relentlessly opposed the BPP's willingness to work with white leftist organizations, and he maintained less-than-cordial relations with Panther leader Eldridge CLEAVER. At one point, Cleaver referred to Brown as a "blippie" (black hippie). By August, the BPP had declared that it could not accept SNCC demands to repudiate its white allies, effectively ending the BPP-SNCC alliance. Brown responded by expelling Stokely Carmichael from SNCC because of his continuing collaboration with the Panthers.

On February 21, 1968, federal officers broke into Brown's New York apartment and arrested him for having violated his bond agreement when he attended the Oakland Black Panther rally. Brown was returned to New Orleans, where bond was set at $50,000. While in custody, he apparently exchanged words with a black FBI agent, who in turn accused Brown of threatening him. As a result, Brown's bond was increased to $100,000, enough to keep him in jail for more than a month awaiting trial on firearms charges. Brown remained defiant throughout, engaging in a hunger strike and preaching revolution from behind bars. Following conviction on these federal charges, he was freed on bail pending an appeal, which was delayed until March, 1970.

Embroiled in legal indictments, Brown was replaced as chairman of SNCC on June 11, 1968, by a collective leadership of veteran members. These leaders proved incapable, however, of slowing the decline of the organization's popularity. During a general SNCC meeting in mid-1969, Brown arrived with a group of supporters and demanded that the organization repudiate its stand on nonviolence and change its name. Although he prevailed, the episode resulted in the resignation of many older members. On July 22, 1969, Brown announced that he was once again in charge of SNCC, which would thenceforth be known as the Student National Coordinating Committee so as to retain the acronym "SNCC" while dropping the word "nonviolent."

Decline into Obscurity

On March 9, 1970, two of Brown's closest SNCC associates were killed as their car exploded near the Maryland courthouse where his trial was set to begin the following day. The bodies were so badly burned that Brown himself was at first reported to have been one of the victims. Investigating authorities concluded that the intended target of the bomb that destroyed the car was probably the courthouse. SNCC leaders countered with accusations that the government had resorted to an assassination plot. In any case, Brown decided to go underground rather than appear for trial, resulting in a massive FBI manhunt that placed the fugitive on the FBI's ten-most-wanted list.

Brown's whereabouts remained unknown until October 16, 1971, when he surfaced in New York City following a shootout with police. Brown and three others reportedly had attempted a robbery of drug pushers in a cocktail lounge. Wounded in the incident, Brown was immediately incarcerated and spent the following several months in the prison ward of Bellevue Hospital awaiting trial. In April, 1973, he was convicted and given a five-to-fifteen-year sentence for armed robbery and assault with a deadly weapon.

A Maryland judge later dismissed outstanding arson charges against Brown because they appeared to have been fabricated by state authorities for the purpose of bringing in the FBI; the judge also imposed on Brown a one-year sentence for firearms violations to be completed concurrently with his New York sentence. While Brown remained in prison, an appeals motion was later won after a Louisiana attorney revealed that Lansing L. Mitchell, the white judge on Brown's earlier case, had openly said at a state bar meeting that he was "going to get that nigger," referring to Brown. In reversing the earlier conviction, a federal appeals court ruled on September 24, 1976, that the judge's comment "did not comport with the appearance of justice" and ordered Brown scheduled for parole.

As Brown's parole was to begin on October 21, 1976, several firearms charges in New Orleans dating back to 1968 were dismissed because of statutory limitations. Brown was set free under terms of a ten-year probationary period; his release ended years of legal entanglement. Attorney William Kunstler indicated the desire of his client to return to society qui-

etly. Having converted to Islam while in prison, Brown took the name Jamil Abdullah Al-Amin and rejoined his wife, Lynne Brown, in Atlanta. There he operated a small grocery store, and his new life was strongly influenced by his Muslim faith. In a 1985 interview he stated, "I don't miss the '60's." Al-Amin published the book *Revolution by the Book (The Rap Is Live)* in 1993.

By the late 1990's, Brown was a well-known community leader in Atlanta's west side, which had a sizeable Muslim community. On March 17, 2000, he was believed to have been involved in a shootout near his Atlanta grocery store and allegedly killed a sheriff's deputy. In May he was put on trial on murder charges and faced a possible death penalty.

—*Richard A. Dello Buono*

Suggested Readings:

Brown, H. Rap. *Die, Nigger, Die!* New York: Dial Press, 1969.

Carson, Clayborne. *In Struggle: SNCC and the Black Awakening of the 1960's.* Cambridge, Mass.: Harvard University Press, 1981.

Forman, James. *The Making of Black Revolutionaries.* New York: Macmillan, 1972.

Lester, Julius. *Revolutionary Notes.* New York: R. W. Baron, 1969.

Sellers, Cleveland, and Robert Terrel. *The River of No Return: The Autobiography of a Black Militant and the Life and Death of SNCC.* New York: William Morrow, 1973.

Van Deburg, William L. *New Day in Babylon: The Black Power Movement and American Culture, 1965-1975.* Chicago: University of Chicago Press, 1992.

Brown, James (b. May 3, 1933, Barnwell, South Carolina): Rhythm-and-blues, SOUL, and FUNK performer and composer. James Brown grew up in Augusta, GEORGIA. He was raised by his aunts, Minnie Walker and Handsome Washington, although he remained in contact with his birth parents. His early life was difficult, as family resources were few in the segregated rural South.

Early Music Training

Most of Brown's early musical education was informal. Influenced by the GOSPEL tradition and American popular music, Brown learned by ear and by imitation, although he also picked up the rudiments of composition and piano. Louis Jordan, a pioneer of RHYTHM AND BLUES, was especially influential on the young James Brown, but he also heard and absorbed the music of Louis ARMSTRONG, Count BASIE, Wynonie Harris, Bing Crosby, Frank Sinatra, and Charles Brown, among others. He sang gospel in the church but eventually turned to singing secular music at the Lenox Theatre's amateur night to earn money to help out at home.

His musical earnings were sporadic at best, and he eventually turned to petty theft in response to the experience of poverty. He was arrested and convicted for breaking into automobiles, and, at age sixteen, was placed in the Georgia Juvenile Training Institute at Rome, GEORGIA. While in prison, he was able to continue to develop his interest in music. He formed a number of groups, although they sang mainly gospel. Most important, he met Bobby Byrd, who would become a longtime collaborator. Byrd's family eventually sponsored Brown and made it possible for him to be released after he had served three years of his eight-year sentence.

In late 1952, Brown and Byrd, along with Sylvester Keels, Doyle Oglesby, Fred Pulliam, Nash Knox, and Roy Scott, formed the group that would eventually become the FAMOUS FLAMES. Doing covers of popular rhythm-and-blues songs, they began playing gigs in Toccoa and were informally managed by a local undertaker, Barry Tremier. Their ambition and talent grew quickly, especially on trips to Greenville, South Carolina, and Atlanta to see

the biggest acts in rhythm and blues. Through auditions for promoters, and eventually by word of mouth, they began to play on a circuit of southern universities and colleges, places such as the University of Georgia, Clemson University, and the University of Tennessee.

Success

A performance by LITTLE RICHARD in Toccoa led to Brown's break. After taking the stage unannounced before Richard and putting on a dynamic performance, Brown was contacted by Richard's agent, Clint Brantly. The band relocated to Macon, Georgia, and began to play larger venues. Their solid regional reputation eventually led to their being offered a recording contract with King Records. In March, 1956, "Please, Please, Please" was released by a King subsidiary, Federal Records. Although that tune later became a James Brown standard, it (and the group) was not an immediate national success. Their gigs improved once again—the band was now playing Jacksonville, Atlanta, and Miami—but it was not until they hooked up with Ben Bart of Universal Atractions that they developed a wide following.

Bart brought the group to New York in 1957, and their records began to sell throughout the North. Bart also made the decision to begin billing the group as "James Brown and his Famous Flames," a decision that brought about the disbanding of the original members. This change did not immediately increase record sales, as "Please, Please, Please" was followed by nine unsuccessful follow-ups; King was frustrated with Brown's lack of a chart-topping hit, which he did not get until "Try Me" in late 1958.

After being re-signed by both King and Universal, Brown began to put together a new group of "Flames," including Nat Kendrick, J. C. Davis, Roscoe Patrick, and Les Buie, although the personnel often changed. It was with this group that he became known as the "hardest-working man in show business," while performing an endless series of one-nighters throughout the United States. In April of 1959, Brown performed for the first time at the APOLLO THEATER in New York, a venue with which he would become closely identified.

From 1958 to 1962, Brown's relationship with Syd Nathan at King/Federal was tense. Nathan was never quite convinced of the marketability of James Brown. This led Brown to take extraordinary steps to get his music to the people. In December of 1959, Brown went to Henry Stone of Dade Records to record "(Do the) Mashed Potatoes," which was released by the nonexistent band "Nat Kendrick and the Swans." Even after the success of that tune (which promoted a national dance craze), Nathan remained unconvinced.

Live at the Apollo

Having charted consistently but unspectacularly from 1959 to 1962, Brown got the idea—an unusual one for the time—to record a live album. He met Nathan's usual resistance, so he proceeded on his own to book the Apollo Theater for the week of October 19-25, 1962. Although the recording was temporarily shelved by Nathan, when eventually released, *The James Brown Show Live at the Apollo* would become one of the most successful and influential popular music albums of all time. Brown rode the success of the live album throughout 1963. The next year saw Brown add musicians Maceo and Melvin Parker to his now famous "James Brown Revue." Brown had hits with songs performed in a variety of styles: the gospel-influenced "Maybe the Last Time," the rock-and-rollish "Out of the Blue," the pioneering dance- and jazz-influenced "I Got You," "It's a Man's World," and "Out of Sight," and, in 1965, the anthem-like "Papa's Got a Brand New Bag." His performance in late 1964 in the T.A.M.I. show—in which he upstaged the Rolling Stones—

James Brown performing in 1964. *(Library of Congress)*

marked his entry into the highest levels of musical popularity in the United States.

In 1966 he traveled to Europe, where he had moderate success. Back in the United States, he was becoming not only a celebrity but also a prominent businessman and spokesperson, even if he was somewhat unpredictable. In that same year, with the assistance of Vice President Hubert H. Humphrey, Brown began his "Don't Be a Dropout" campaign, encouraging young people to stay in school.

Although troubled by legal disputes with record companies and the deaths of manager Ben Bart and singer Little Willie John, both friends and mentors, Brown continued to be a dominant force in American popular music in the late 1960's. The day after the assassination of Martin Luther KING, Jr., James Brown performed a televised concert intended to stem the tide of violent outrage. He also performed in Africa and for U.S. troops in Vietnam. The group that Brown took with him into the 1970's would become a large part of the foundation of funk music; in particular, Bootsy and Phelps Collins would go on to work with George Clinton and PARLIAMENT/FUNKADELIC.

In the early 1970's, Brown continued his success with "Sex Machine," "Hot Pants," and "Talkin' Loud and Sayin' Nothin'," among numerous hits. He was hurt by the tragedy of his oldest son Teddy's death in a car accident in 1973. By 1975 he was unsure of the support of his most recent record company, Polydor. His run of commercial success seemed to have come to an end. James Brown's sound was neither disco artist nor 1970's funk, the predominant styles of the period, although he had influenced both.

Comeback
Brown began a celebrated comeback in the 1980's. His performances in the feature films *The Blues Brothers* (1980) and *Rocky IV* (1985) introduced him to a new generation. "Living in America," from the *Rocky IV* sound track, marked Brown's reentry into the top regions of the music charts. Because of the strong rhythmic element of his music, his work also became the tracks of choice for RAP artists looking for interesting samples. The practice of sampling (digitally copying sounds and musical passages) became a controversial and frustrating kind of praise, as it was difficult for Brown and other performers being sampled to claim and collect royalties.

In addition to continuing to perform in the 1980's and 1990's, Brown continued to generate less favorable publicity. He was in the news in 1988 for brandishing a shotgun in an office and fleeing in his pickup truck. Apprehended, Brown was sentenced to six years in prison—a punishment of unusual severity—

for a variety of offenses related to the incident. Paroled in 1991, Brown staged a successful pay-per-view cable special that year. Brown was inducted into the Rock and Roll Hall of Fame in 1986 and was given a Grammy Award for lifetime achievement in 1992. Personal tragedy struck in 1996, when his wife died of an accidental drug overdose following surgery.

Musical and Cultural Impact
Few performers changed popular music so much and so often. While Brown and his Flames began as a rhythm-and-blues vocal act, they evolved into what could be called a "soul orchestra." Brown sang gospel, pop, rhythm and blues, rock and roll, soul, funk, disco, and rap—and, it can be argued, helped through his performances to define many of these styles. An outstanding vocalist and shouter, Brown also became one of the most influential figures in popular American DANCE, giving ideas to performers as diverse as Mick Jagger and Michael JACKSON.

As writer and composer of most of his own work, Brown was also significant, having charted with more than a hundred songs. It is not overstatement to suggest that he has been the most dynamic performer in recent American music history. His emotional and energetic performances gave clear demonstrations of the power and diversity of African American culture. While MOTOWN and Stax Records helped to define particular sounds, James Brown was always unique, an innovator who isolated the rhythmic element of popular African American music and thus helped create the foundations for funk, disco, and rap.

While his music was always first and foremost entertainment, Brown was also topical in his choice of lyrics. Most profoundly with "Say It Loud, I'm Black and I'm Proud," he was a powerful spokesperson for pride in racial and cultural heritage in the 1960's. As a pioneering African American businessman—he owned numerous radio stations—Brown promoted economic self-sufficiency. He was always his own best promoter and manager, and he exercised great control over his image and performance. Brown believed that only he could ensure that the product that he put on stage and on record was of the highest quality.

—*James C. Hall*

Suggested Readings:

Brown, Geoff. *James Brown: Doin' It to Death*. London: Omnibus Press, 1996.

Brown, James, and Bruce Tucker. *James Brown: The Godfather of Soul*. New York: Thunder's Mouth Press, 1990.

George, Nelson. *The Death of Rhythm and Blues*. New York: Pantheon Books, 1988.

Guralnick, Peter. *Sweet Soul Music: Rhythm and Blues and the Southern Dream of Freedom*. New York: Harper & Row, 1986.

Hirshey, Gerri. *Nowhere to Run: The Story of Soul Music*. London: Macmillan, 1985.

"James Brown." *Current Biography* 53 (March, 1992): 18-22.

Rose, Cynthia. *Living in America: The Soul Saga of James Brown*. London: Serpent's Tail, 1990.

Brown, Jesse (b. March 27, 1944, Detroit, Michigan): Political appointee. Reared by a single-parent mother, Brown grew up with his sister and spent his teenage years in Chicago. After graduating from high school, Brown was an honors graduate from Chicago City College. In 1963 he enlisted in the Marine Corps; he eventually served in the VIETNAM WAR. His right arm was paralyzed after he was hit by sniper fire while serving on a patrol mission near Danang in 1965. Brown received a Purple Heart and was sent home to recuperate at a veterans' hospital near Chicago. Following a year of physical therapy, Brown decided to look for employment.

Veterans Affairs secretary Jesse Brown in 1996. *(AP/Wide World Photos)*

He was offered a job with the Disabled American Veterans, a nonprofit organization that serves as an advocate for veterans' issues and benefits. After working as a national service officer with the organization's Chicago bureau, Brown was promoted to a post as supervisor of the appeals office in Washington, D.C., in 1973. Brown's skill as a lobbyist led to his appointment as the agency's first black executive director in 1988. He won widespread bipartisan support for his lobbying efforts in Congress on behalf of the agency.

In 1993 President Bill Clinton appointed Brown to become secretary of the Veterans Affairs Department, a post that had recently (in 1989) been elevated to a cabinet-level position. Brown's confirmation hearings went smoothly, and he was sworn in by President Clinton on January 22, 1993. One of Brown's first responsibilities upon taking office was serving on Hillary Rodham Clinton's commission to study health care reform. Among his other goals were to reform and revitalize the veterans health system, to provide support for homeless veterans, and to establish programs for drug-dependent veterans.

Budget cuts approved by Congress hampered the success of Brown's proposed reforms, but he generated greater attention for the situation of American veterans in need of improved medical care. He resigned as head of the Veterans Affairs Department—with more than 200,000 employees, the second-largest department of the government, after the Pentagon—in 1997.

See also: Politics and government.

Brown, Jim (b. February 17, 1936, St. Simons Island, Georgia): FOOTBALL player. Brown starred as fullback for the Cleveland Browns of the National Football League (NFL) for nine seasons. When he retired in 1965, he was the NFL's all-time leading rusher, with 12,312 yards. That record was broken by Walter Payton in 1984.

Jim Brown scoring his 106th career touchdown, then an NFL record, in a game against the Philadelphia Eagles in 1965. He went on to score two more touchdowns in that game. *(AP/Wide World Photos)*

Brown lived with his great-grandmother from infancy. When he was seven years old, his mother sent for him from Manhasset, Long Island, where she worked. By the time Brown was in Manhasset High School, he was an accomplished and versatile athlete. He earned varsity letters in baseball, football, basketball, track, and lacrosse, and he received dozens of college scholarship offers. He chose to attend Syracuse University and won All-American honors in both football and lacrosse.

When Brown graduated from Syracuse in 1957, he was drafted by the Cleveland Browns, for whom he became an immediate star. He rushed for 942 yards during his rookie year and followed with four straight one-thousand-yard seasons, while leading the league in rushing during all five seasons. More than six feet tall and weighing 230 pounds, Brown was able to bowl over the biggest defenders. His speed allowed him to outrun even the quickest defensive backs. His best season came in 1963, when he rushed for 1,863 yards, a record broken a decade later by O. J. SIMPSON, and was named the NFL's player of the year. In 1964 he led the Browns to the NFL championship.

Brown was thirty years old when he retired. Although he was free of injuries and could have played effectively for several more seasons, he left football to pursue an acting career. He recounted his experiences as an African American athlete in his 1964 autobiography, *Off My Chest*. Although he often talked of a pro football comeback, such an opportunity never materialized. He was elected to the Pro Football Hall of Fame in 1971. In later years he remained closely associated with Cleveland football and was a prominent figure when a reconstituted Browns team began playing in 1999.

Brown's success in films did not match his achievements on the gridiron. Nevertheless, he appeared in more than thirty films from 1964 through 1999. He had major roles in such early films as *Rio Conchos* (1964), *The Dirty Dozen* (1967), and *100 Rifles* (1969), and smaller rolls in later films, such as *Mars Attacks!* (1996), *He Got Game* (1998), and *On Any Given Sunday* (1999).

Brown, John (May 9, 1800, Torrington, Connecticut—December 2, 1859, Charlestown, Virginia): White abolitionist executed for leading a raid on a federal arsenal in HARPERS FERRY, Virginia (later part of WEST VIRGINIA), where he had hoped to incite slaves to rebel against their masters. Brown has since been honored by generations of African Americans for sacrificing his life to the cause of freedom.

Brown came from six generations of Connecticut farmers. After unsuccessfully trying to operate several businesses, he devoted his life to the antislavery cause. A deeply religious man, he could not abide the sin of SLAVERY. He involved his entire family, including his five sons, in the cause of freeing the slaves. He fought to keep the Kansas-Nebraska Territory a free territory barred to slaveowners, and he organized his own private army that clashed with and killed several proslavery men. Brown then took his radical mission to the South in hopes of inspiring the entire slave population to rise up against their masters.

On the night of October 16, 1859, Brown and twenty-one followers captured the federal arsenal at Harpers Ferry. The local militia, under the leadership of Colonel Robert E. Lee, attacked Brown's force, killing ten of his men and wounding Brown himself. Brown was captured; he stood trial and was executed, demonstrating dignity and serenity in the last moments of his life. In African American literature, Brown became a symbol of brotherhood and heroism, and he has often been honored as an example of the white community which rose, at its own peril, to defend the cause of freedom for all races.

—*Carl Rollyson*

Abolitionist John Brown in c. 1850. *(National Archives)*

See also: Abolitionist movement; Kansas-Nebraska Act; Slave resistance.

Brown, Les (b. February 17, 1945, Miami, Florida): Motivational speaker and author. Reared by adopted mother Mamie Brown, Leslie Calvin Brown and his twin brother, Wesley, grew up in an economically disadvantaged section of Miami. Surrounded by love and encouragement, Brown was greatly influenced by his mother and by his high school drama instructor, LeRoy Washington. Brown's lack of focus had caused him to be labeled "educably mentally retarded" in the fifth grade; Washington was the motivation behind Brown's fight to overcome and discard that label. Support from his family and mentors later helped Brown to become a successful motivational speaker.

His mind set on a career in RADIO BROAD-CASTING, Brown took cursory steps toward his goal. Employed first as a sanitation worker, Brown eventually landed a job at WMBM-AM, a Miami, FLORIDA, radio station. Although he was persistent and ambitious, Brown initially worked running errands. He soon learned about every aspect of operating a radio station, however, and his talents as a disc jockey were revealed when he filled in for another employee. Brown's improvisational skills earned him a position as a part-time and then full-time disc jockey.

In the late 1960's, Brown relocated to Columbus, Ohio, where his radio career flourished. His success with a popular radio program there afforded him the opportunity to take on extra duties as a broadcasting manager. In this capacity, Brown urged radio listeners to become socially conscious and politically active.

Brown's activism cost him his job as a broadcasting manager. Greater things were in store, however. In 1976 he won a seat in the Ohio State Legislature. Representing the state's twenty-ninth legislative district, Brown passed more legislation than any other incoming member. Remaining for three terms, Brown headed the Human Resources Committee; in 1981, he left politics and returned to Florida to care for his mother.

While in Florida, Brown's activism took on a new direction. He established a youth career training program and began speaking formally against social injustice. Under the auspices of his mentor, Mike Williams, Brown became interested in motivational speaking, encouraged by the financial rewards connected with this work. In the mid-1980's, Brown moved to Detroit to pursue yet another dream. He read books on public speaking and developed speaking skills modeled on successful speakers. Because he had limited funds, Brown lived in the office from which he worked. No matter how bleak circumstances

were, Brown persevered. Initially, he spoke to elementary students. As he gained more experience, he began addressing high school students, social clubs, and community organizations. His growing expertise earned him the Council of Peers Award for Excellence in 1989. Four years after he began his public speaking career, Brown was the first African American to receive this prestigious award.

Using his own life as an example, Brown committed himself to inspiring others to pursue their own dreams. After recording a series of motivational speech presentations for the Public Broadcasting Service (PBS) in 1990, leading companies sponsored motivational training sessions and workshops. As president of Les Brown Unlimited, Brown became a multimillion-dollar executive with specials appearing on PBS television stations. In 1992 Brown shared his idealism in his autobiographical work, *Live Your Dreams*. A year later, he hosted his own syndicated television talk show, *The Les Brown Show*, which ran until 1994. In August of 1995, Brown was married to singer Gladys KNIGHT.

Brown, Ronald Harmon (August 1, 1941, Washington, D.C.—April 3, 1996, Sveti Ivan, near Dubrovnik, Croatia): Politician. Ron H. Brown served as the chairman of the Democratic National Committee and then as secretary of commerce in the Bill Clinton administration.

Brown grew up in HARLEM and was educated in private schools. He attended Middlebury College in Vermont, where he was instrumental in integrating the fraternity system. After college, he served four years as an army officer in Germany and Korea. He then went to work for the Urban League in New York, earning a law degree (1970) at night at St. John's University. In 1973 he moved to Washington. He became the second-ranking figure in the Urban League's national office.

Early Experience in Washington
Once in Washington, Brown became deeply involved in DEMOCRATIC PARTY politics. In 1979 he joined Senator Edward Kennedy's presidential campaign as deputy manager. Kennedy appointed Brown as chief counsel to the Senate Judiciary Committee in 1980. In 1981 Brown joined the senator's staff. From 1982 to 1985, he served as deputy chairman of the Democratic National Committee (DNC).

After three years in a prestigious Washington law firm, Brown returned to full-time politics in 1988 by serving as the convention manager of Jesse Jackson's presidential campaign. Impressing many party leaders with his ability to work with people of diverse backgrounds and opinions, Brown became a candidate to succeed Paul G. Kirk as chair of the DNC. Although some were afraid that Brown's association with Jackson indicated a radicalism that might frighten moderate voters, Brown's stress on the need for party unity won him much powerful support. His 1989 election by the DNC made him the first African American to head the national organization of either major party.

As chairman, Brown downplayed racial questions and other potential sources of division, continuing to stress the need for unity. He made particular efforts to win back the so-called Reagan Democrats, conservative white voters who had left the party in the 1980's. Appearing frequently on television news programs, Brown worked hard and with some success to reconcile the various factions in the

Ronald H. Brown in 1992. *(AP/Wide World Photos)*

party. He also pressed efforts to register new Democratic voters. In 1992 he exerted himself to prevent the presidential primary campaign from leaving lasting divisions within the party. President Bill Clinton appointed Brown to serve on his cabinet as secretary of commerce in 1993.

Brown's previous work with a large Washington, D.C., lobbying firm threatened to become a stumbling block during Senate confirmation hearings. Brown, however, pledged to avoid contact with his former firm regarding his government duties.

Secretary of Commerce

After his 1993 confirmation, Brown became an important member of the Clinton cabinet and a highly regarded, if somewhat controversial, secretary of commerce. Even critics allowed that Brown might be one of the most influential and successful commerce secretaries in some time. He aggressively pursued export opportunities for U.S. businesses abroad, established an advocacy "war room" in the Commerce Department (which involved numerous government agencies in targeting opportunities for U.S. businesses abroad), and led groups of U.S. business representatives to important trade conferences all over the world.

Nevertheless, controversy followed Brown. On the eve of Clinton's inauguration, it was reported in the press that U.S. and Japanese corporations had contributed money for a Ronald Brown gala at the Kennedy Center. Following stinging criticism, the event was cancelled. Then, caught in a situation that had dogged other Clinton appointees, Brown admitted in February, 1993, that he had failed to pay Social Security taxes for his part-time cleaning employees, but he added that he had undertaken to pay the back taxes and penalties.

In August, 1993, it became known that the FEDERAL BUREAU OF INVESTIGATION (FBI) was investigating an allegation that Brown had accepted money from the government of Vietnam in exchange for a lifting of the U.S. trade embargo against that nation. Brown admitted that he had met with a Vietnamese-born U.S. businessman with ties to the Vietnamese government but denied taking any money. The Clinton administration had indeed eased the embargo against Vietnam, but Brown said that he had not been involved in those policy decisions. In February, 1994, the Justice Department announced that it had found no evidence of wrongdoing.

In May, 1995, another charge of impropriety surfaced when Attorney General Janet Reno asked for the appointment of an independent counsel to investigate Brown's personal finances. Primarily at issue were Brown's ties to former business partner Nolanda Hill and the sale by Brown to her of his share in a co-owned investment and consulting firm.

Fatal Mission

In April of 1996, Brown launched a trade mission to Bosnia and Croatia to promote peace and economic development in the war-torn region. Among the dozen American executives who accompanied him on the trip were the chairmen of two engineering firms, a manufacturer of power generators, a bank executive, and a telecommunications executive. After meeting with Bosnian representatives and U.S. peacekeeping troops in Tuzla, Brown and his delegation boarded an Air Force T-43 aircraft for Dubrovnik, Croatia. Extremely bad weather on the Adriatic Coast and limited visibility near Cilipi Airport resulted in the plane crashing into a 2,300-foot mountain known as Sveti Ivan (St. John) north of the airport. None of the thirty-three people aboard the plane survived.

—*Forest L. Grieves*

See also: Politics and government.

Brown, Ruth Weston (b. January 30, 1928, Portsmouth, Virginia): Singer and stage actor. Brown began singing hymns and spirituals in her father's AFRICAN METHODIST EPISCOPAL CHURCH choir, an experience to which she credits her early interest in the entertainment field. To the dismay of her father, Brown embarked upon a singing career. She married trumpet player Jimmy Brown and landed a short-lived spot in 1948 singing with Lucky Millinder's band. After being fired a month later as a result of the group's political infighting, she came under the guidance of manager Blanche Calloway, Cab CALLOWAY's sister, who booked her for an evening at New York's

Ruth Weston Brown performing at New York City's Carnegie Hall in 1996. *(Reuters/Peter Morgan/Archive Photos)*

biggest hit record, "Mama He Treats Your Daughter Mean." Dubbed Miss Rhythm by pop icon Frankie Laine, she became one of the biggest stars of the 1950's after she crossed over into the pop market in 1957 with "Lucky Lips."

During the 1960's, Brown re-channeled her energies into family life, raising her children on Long Island and singing sporadically in small cafés. In the early 1970's, she attempted a major comeback. With the help of friends such as comedians Redd Foxx and Nipsey Russell, Brown worked her way back into the limelight. Shortly thereafter, Brown took up acting, playing gospel great Mahalia JACKSON in the civil rights musical *Selma* and a role in the short-lived television situation comedy *Hello, Larry*. She continued her singing career as well, playing dates in Las Vegas and winning back the acclaim she had enjoyed during the 1950's. In 1989 Brown won a Tony Award for her performance in the jazz musical *Black and Blue*.

Through the early 1990's, Brown continued to perform, but the injuries she had suffered in the automobile accident in 1948 necessitated the replacement of both of her knees, severely hampering her mobility. Nevertheless, she continued to perform regularly and hosted National Public Radio's weekly broadcast of *Blues Stage*.

hallowed APOLLO THEATER. On the day of the performance, Brown was involved in a serious automobile accident that left her hospitalized for nearly ten months with injuries that included two broken legs.

Atlantic Records, which had shown a nominal interest in Brown prior to the accident, remained intrigued by her potential throughout her lengthy convalescent period. After a blistering performance at New York's Cafe Society Downtown in 1949, she soared to stardom on Atlantic with rhythm-and-blues hits such as "So Long," "I'll Get Along Somehow," "Teardrops from My Eyes," and perhaps her

Brown, Sterling A. (May 1, 1901, Washington, D.C.—January 13, 1989, Takoma Park, Maryland): Poet, literary and linguistic historian, critic, and teacher. Sterling Allen Brown

Poet Sterling A. Brown. (*©Roy Lewis Archives*)

earned fame for incorporating dialect, the rhythms of work songs, and the themes of black folk epics into his poems and for championing the black author's expression of the African American experience.

The son of Adelaide Allen and Sterling Nelson Brown, a minister and professor of religion at HOWARD UNIVERSITY, Brown was influenced by the works of W. E. B. DU BOIS, Frederick DOUGLASS, and poet Paul Laurence DUNBAR. He graduated Phi Beta Kappa from Williams College in 1921, completed an M.A. in English literature at Harvard University in 1923, and did further graduate work from 1930 to 1931. Before he finished an advanced degree, he began his teaching career at Virginia Seminary, followed by stints at FISK, LINCOLN, and HOWARD Universities. He taught at Howard from 1929 until 1969.

While continuing his editing and writing, Brown served as visiting professor at Vassar College, ATLANTA UNIVERSITY, Sarah Lawrence College, the University of Minnesota, the University of Illinois, and New York University. His dedication to teaching, along with the reluctance of publishers to advance his career, led to public neglect and severe depression that resulted in hospitalization. In 1936 he began a three-year term as Negro affairs editor for the Federal Writers' Project. For this and other scholarly work, he earned honorary doctorates, a Guggenheim Fellowship, the Lenore Marshall Poetry Prize, and membership on the staff of the Carnegie-Myrdal Study of the Negro in 1939. In 1984 he was named poet laureate of the District of Columbia.

Brown's poetry has been collected in *Southern Road* (1932), *The Last Ride of Wild Bill and*

Eleven Narrative Poems (1975), and *The Collected Poems of Sterling A. Brown* (1980, collected by Michael S. Harper). Brown also edited critical works about black poetry, drama, and fiction, including *The Negro in American Fiction* (1937), *Negro Poetry and Drama* (1937), and *The Negro Caravan* (1941). In 1966 he published a notable essay for the *Mississippi Review*, "A Century of Negro Portraiture in American Literature." Numerous poems, columns, and articles by Brown appeared in such publications as *Contempo*, *Journal of Negro Education*, *Argosy*, *Opportunity*, and *The New Republic*.

Brown, Tony (b. April 11, 1933, Charleston, West Virginia): Television broadcaster and producer. As producer and host of the long-running public affairs television show *Tony Brown's Journal*, Brown provided a forum for African Americans to define themselves and to discuss issues pertinent to their lives with some of the most prominent African American thinkers of the day. The show explored such topics as the pros and cons of Afrocentric curricula, civil rights bills, affirmative action, law enforcement, and the judicial system.

Born William Anthony Brown, Brown graduated from Wayne State University in Detroit, Michigan, in 1959 with a bachelor of arts degree. He received a master of social work degree from the University of Michigan in 1961. Although trained as a psychiatric social worker, he embarked on a career in journalistic pub-

lic affairs. In 1970 he joined the public television show *Black Journal*. He became executive producer of that program. In 1977 he founded Tony Brown Productions, and in 1978 he transformed *Black Journal* into *Tony Brown's Journal*. It was, at many times in its history, the only national black public affairs program on the air.

Brown's involvement in broadcasting crossed over into the educational arena. He was the first dean and a founder of the Howard University School of Communication. He served as dean from 1971 to 1974.

Brown was cited often for his contributions in the field of public affairs broadcasting. His awards include a National Urban League Public Service Award (1977), an International Key Women of America Award (1977), inclusion in the list of One Hundred Most Influential Black Americans (named by EBONY magazine), in-

Tony Brown in 1977. *(AP/Wide World Photos)*

clusion in the top fifty national black news-makers of the year (1974, named by the National Newspaper Publishers Association), an OPERATION PUSH (People United to Save Humanity) Communicator for Freedom Award (1973), a Frederick Douglass Liberation Award, and, in 1991, an Image Award from the National Association for the Advancement of Colored People (NAACP).

Brown ventured into film production as writer, producer, and director of the independent film *The White Girl* (1990). The film, with a preachy antidrug message, was poorly received. After twenty years of declared political independence, Brown joined the REPUBLICAN PARTY and urged other African Americans to do the same. Brown believed that the Republican Party's positions on self-help and decreased government intrusion into everyday life were compatible with the goals of African Americans.

Brown created a stir in 1994 when he stated, in a press release, that "the color of freedom is green." The following year he published his first book, *Black Lies, White Lies: The Truth According to Tony Brown*, and launched an online venture, *Tony Brown Online*.

See also: Television industry.

Brown, Willa B. (b. Glasgow, Kentucky): Pilot. Brown was instrumental in getting black pilots into the Army Air Force; he had the backing of First Lady Eleanor Roosevelt. Brown later became a lieutenant in the Civil Air Patrol and operated a flying school near Chicago, Illinois.

Brown, William Wells (1815, Lexington, Kentucky—November 6, 1884, Chelsea, Massachusetts): Author and abolitionist. Brown's novel, *Clotel: Or, the President's Daughter: A Narrative of Slave Life in the United States* (1853), although first published in England, is believed to be the first novel written by an Afri-

can American. Brown also wrote an autobiographical slave narrative in 1847 (*Narrative of William W. Brown, a Fugitive Slave, Written by Himself*) and numerous other nonfiction pamphlets and books. He also wrote at least two abolitionist plays, one of which was called *The Escape: Or, A Leap for Freedom* (1858). It is believed to be the first drama published by an African American.

In addition to his literary work, after his own 1834 escape from SLAVERY Brown worked as part of the UNDERGROUND RAILROAD, personally assisting the escapes of scores of other slaves. He took the name of Wells Brown, a Quaker who befriended him, adding it to his only given name, William. He became a lecturer and activist in the ABOLITIONIST MOVEMENT and worked as a journalist for the abolitionist cause. He also traveled abroad between 1849 and 1854, speaking to European peace activists and abolitionists. Friends in England purchased his freedom so that he could return to the United States without being subject to recapture under the FUGITIVE SLAVE LAW of 1850.

Brown's significance in the history of African American LITERATURE is based not only on his interesting stylistic blends of melodrama, documentary, abolitionist tract, and political critique, but also on his willingness to confront directly the legacy of sexual exploitation of female slaves. The story of Clotel, while fictionalized, builds on the well-known fact that many male slaveholders fathered children with their often unwilling female slaves. The novel implicates Thomas Jefferson in this practice. It extends the familiar slave narrative critique of slaveholding America into an explicitly political challenge to one of the founding fathers of the nation, and by extension it challenges the inconsistencies inherent in a Constitution that fails to protect the human rights of millions of African Americans.

Brown was able to present such a political charge in literary works that could reach a

William Wells Brown. *(Associated Publishers, Inc.)*

comparatively broad audience. The fact that the novel was not published in its original form in the United States until 1969 suggests that Brown's early literary confrontation with slavery struck a nerve.
See also: Hemings, Sally; Slave runaways.

Brown, Willie L., Jr. (b. March 20, 1934, Mineola, Texas): Politician and attorney. After growing up in Texas, Willie Brown attended Prairie View A&M College, a HISTORICALLY BLACK COLLEGE. He was asked to leave the

school before completing his degree. Brown moved to San Francisco to live with his uncle and work his way through school at San Francisco State University. After earning his undergraduate degree, Brown decided to pursue a law degree rather than be drafted to fight in the KOREAN WAR.

He was accepted at the University of California's Hastings College Law School in San Francisco in 1955 and received his degree in 1958. Brown began a storefront law practice defending the indigent. An active campaigner for DEMOCRATIC PARTY candidates, Brown also became involved in the San Francisco chapter of the NATIONAL ASSOCIATION FOR THE ADVANCEMENT OF COLORED PEOPLE (NAACP) and took part in local civil rights protests. He launched his own political career in 1962 with an unsuccessful campaign for the CALIFORNIA state assembly. He ran again in 1964 and was elected to represent a San Francisco district.

After taking office in 1965, Brown was something of a political maverick: In one session, he cast the only dissenting vote against Jesse Unruh's reappointment as speaker in the California State Assembly. Nevertheless, by building a coalition of support within the assembly through strategically orchestrated political connections, Brown began to launch his own campaign for the speaker's position. Although defeated in his 1974 bid for the speakership, Brown was successful in 1980.

He became the first black speaker of the California state legislature, while maintaining his high-profile legal practice.

Brown went on to maintain his control of the speakership for nearly fifteen years, becoming one of the longest holders of the office. As speaker, Brown wielded enormous political influence, particularly through his control of committee appointments and power over the state budget. Although he was not known as an architect of significant legislation, Brown was credited with introducing laws to compensate crime victims, to regulate health care cost to low-income families, for decriminalizing homosexuality, and for reducing costly court delays. In addition, he managed to halt many bills proposed by Republican legislators and led the fight to oppose legislation designed to establish English as the state's official language. During the course of his tenure as speaker, Brown found time to serve as national campaign chairman for Jesse JACKSON in the latter's 1988 presidential bid.

Term-limit legislation passed in California prevented Brown from running for re-election to his assembly seat in 1995. He was succeeded in the post by Republican representative Doris Allen, who secured the post with the support of Brown and the thirty-eight other Democratic representatives (Allen cast the lone Republican vote in her own favor).

Setting his sights on a different political arena, Brown announced his intention to run for mayor of San Francisco. Running against white incumbent Frank Jordan and former city supervisor and lesbian activist Roberta Achtenberg, Brown was forced into a runoff campaign after none of the candidates secured a clear majority in the November election. In a hard-fought campaign in which he appeared at numerous small events and local political rallies, Brown secured 57 percent of the votes to win a decisive victory over Frank Jordan in the December runoff election.

On January 8, 1996, Brown took the oath of office as the first African American mayor of San Francisco. He devoted his energies to projects ranging from improving the municipal railway system to revamping the city's Housing Commission to developing a new youth center.
See also: Mayors.

Brownsville incident: Racial incident that occurred August 13, 1906, in Brownsville, TEXAS, when angry whites disapproved of the arrival of the African American First Battalion of the TWENTY-FIFTH INFANTRY regiment at Fort Brown.

A rumor that a black soldier had attempted to rape a white woman incited sixteen to twenty white men to shoot randomly in Brownsville. A white civilian was killed, and a white policeman was injured. Dishonorable discharges were given to 167 black soldiers allegedly connected with the incident. In 1972 all of them were declared innocent, and their discharges were officially changed to honorable discharges.
See also: Race riots.

Brown v. Board of Education: One of the most celebrated moments in the history of American jurisprudence, a 1954 U.S. SUPREME COURT ruling that segregation in public schools is unequal and thus illegal. More fully known as *Oliver Brown et al. v. Board of Education of Topeka et al.*, this decison has been called the most significant government advancement in CIVIL RIGHTS since President Abraham Lincoln's EMANCIPATION PROCLAMATION of 1863. In its ruling, the Supreme Court struck a lethal blow against government-sanctioned racial segregation, which had been legalized by its own 1896 ruling in PLESSY V. FERGUSON. The decisions—written fifty-eight years apart—were based on different interpretations of

Linda Brown, the nine-year-old schoolgirl whose desire to attend a neighborhood school triggered a social revolution. *(AP/Wide World Photos)*

the FOURTEENTH AMENDMENT to the U.S. Constitution.

Historical Background

Following emancipation after the end of the CIVIL WAR in 1865, two amendments promising equal political status to African Americans were added to the U.S. Constitution. The FOURTEENTH AMENDMENT, ratified in 1868, extended the fundamental guarantees of the Bill of Rights to certain aspects of state and local government and thus guaranteed equality under the law for all Americans. It prohibited any state from enforcing laws that abridged

the privileges, or immunities, of American citizens; that deprived persons of life, liberty, or property without due process of law; or that denied a person living or working within its jurisdiction equal protection of U.S. law.

The FIFTEENTH AMENDMENT, ratified in 1870, guaranteed all American men the right to vote irrespective of race, color, or previous condition of servitude. That right was soon denied to African Americans, however, with the introduction of a series of regulations called JIM CROW LAWS in the 1870's. Such laws made it virtually impossible for most black people to exercise their franchise. The laws also established segregated public schools, hospitals, and other public facilities. This segregated system was upheld by the decision of the Supreme Court in *Plessy v. Ferguson*. Homer Plessy, a man who was one-eighth black and seven-eighths white, was arrested for refusing to give up his seat in a white-only section of a train, as required by LOUISIANA law. When his case eventually reached the Supreme Court, the Court ruled that segregated facilities could exist as long as they were "equal." This decision gave birth to the SEPARATE BUT EQUAL doctrine.

For almost sixty years after *Plessy v. Ferguson*, black Americans were forced to accept separate—and often unequal—treatment in many areas of their lives. In 1896, for example, the school board of Richmond County in GEORGIA voted on July 10 to terminate the prestigious Ware High School in Augusta, the only public high school for African Americans in the state. It had been established in 1880 after a long battle fought by the black community. Concluding that Ware High School was dispensable, the school board reallocated its annual budget of $845 to the hiring of four new teachers for the black elementary schools. The outrage from the black community resulted in another Supreme Court decision, CUMMING v. RICHMOND COUNTY BOARD OF EDUCATION, in 1899.

In this case, attorneys for the black plaintiffs contended that the school board had violated the law, even on the basis of *Plessy*, because high school education for blacks in the state was now nonexistent. Supreme Court Justice John Marshall Harlan circumvented the question of equality and ruled against forcing more equal allocation of education funds. He argued that the board would respond to a negative ruling from the Court by closing white high schools and that this would damage white students without helping blacks. This ruling successfully nullified the Fourteenth Amendment and perpetuated the doctrine of "separate but equal" as a pretext for government-sponsored racism.

The Brown Ruling
The battle against discrimination in education heated up in the 1950's, leading to the *Brown v. Board of Education* decision. In order to get to a black elementary school, a student named Linda Brown of Topeka, KANSAS, had to cross a railroad track and ride a bus for twenty-one blocks. There was a white school only five blocks from her house. Her plight became the basis for a new ruling on the "separate but equal" doctrine. At the trial, the defense—on the grounds of *Plessy*—argued that under the Fourteenth Amendment, the state had provided separate but equal facilities, as required by law. Thurgood MARSHALL and other legal experts representing Linda Brown challenged the Court's 1896 ruling, pointing out that the U.S. Constitution permitted "separate but equal" facilities for blacks but not for other minority groups. The attorneys forced the Court to address the question of why African Americans were singled out for different treatment.

Arguing on the basis of social scientific findings, Brown's lawyers demonstrated convincingly that separate facilities worked to the detriment of African Americans and therefore were unequal. Even if the physical facilities, equipment, and staffing were equivalent at two racially segregated schools, they argued, education would still be unequal because racial segregation deprives students of important interaction with others that enhances learning. On May 17, 1954, the Court handed down the landmark ruling requiring desegregation on the grounds that separate educational facilities are inherently unequal because they deprive minority students of equal educational opportunities essential to their success in life.

By ruling in favor of Linda Brown (the Oliver Brown of the case name was her father), the Court affirmed that education is a fundamental right that must be protected by the Fourteenth Amendment and that separate public schools for blacks violate the provision in the Constitution for equal protection of rights. It contended that education is necessary for the performance of an individual's basic civic duties and that it was doubtful whether Brown could be expected to succeed as a good citizen if she were denied access to the necessary education. The Court also ruled that when a state undertakes to provide such opportunities as education, those opportunities must be made available to all on equal terms. Chief Justice Earl Warren, who guided the Court in this decision, argued that segregating black pupils from whites of similar age and qualifications solely on the basis of their race perpetuates a feeling of black inferiority that could ruin black students' psyches in ways that were unlikely to be correctable.

The Result
This watershed ruling dealt a decisive blow to segregation in public schools, although it took

many tumultuous and difficult events—such as the LITTLE ROCK CRISIS of 1957, involving the desegregation of a Little Rock, Arkansas, high school—to establish the fact that the Court's decision truly had to be obeyed throughout the country. Ultimately the decision also led to the destruction of the legal basis for racial discrimination in many other areas of American life. It helped desegregate restaurants, parks, city buses, trains, and places of employment, and it became a platform for the 1962 BAKER V. CARR decision which ruled that the federal courts could reverse inequitable distributions of state legislative seats that historically favored whites. The *Brown* decision also influenced Congress in its passing of the VOTING RIGHTS ACT OF 1965.

Although *Brown* ended DE JURE SEGREGATION (segregation by law), desegregation in actuality did not always follow. Even after Title VI of the 1964 Civil Rights Act, which threatened to deny government funding to noncompliant states, desegregation came slowly. It had to be enforced by the 1971 Supreme Court decision in SWANN V. CHARLOTTE-MECKLENBURG BOARD OF EDUCATION, which affirmed the appropriateness of BUSING to achieve integration. It took parents in Tampa, FLORIDA, eleven years after *Brown* to win a desegregation lawsuit against local

school districts that forced black students to walk past many all-white schools to get to a black one. In New York, Chicago, Boston, Cleveland, Los Angeles, Dallas, Atlanta, and elsewhere, angry crowds violently resisted desegregation well into the late 1970's. Although progress toward desegregation was slow in many cases, it did occur.

NAACP attorneys George E. C. Hayes (left), Thurgood Marshall (center), and James M. Nabrit congratulate one another after winning the *Brown* case in May, 1954. *(AP/Wide World Photos)*

Significance

This momentous ruling drastically altered social and political life in both black and white America. By undoing the rules of exclusion, *Brown v. Board of Education* notified the nation that freedom from segregation is as much a right as freedom from slavery. It also gave African Americans hope by opening doors that historically were closed to them. Equal education promised broadened employment possibilities. By the late twentieth century, qualified blacks were much less likely to be denied a job on racial grounds than they were in 1954. Moreover, under the leadership of Chief Justices Earl Warren and Warren Burger, the Supreme Court signaled that it was tough enough and determined enough to challenge segregationist governors such as Orval Faubus of Arkansas, George Wallace of Alabama, and Ross Barnett of Mississippi.

—*N. Samuel Murrell*

See also: Constitution, U.S.; National Association for the Advancement of Colored People; Segregation and integration.

Suggested Readings:

Kluger, Richard. *Simple Justice: The History of Brown v. Board of Education and Black America's Struggle for Equality.* New York: Alfred A. Knopf, 1976.

Lagemann, Ellen C., and LaMar Miller, eds. *Brown v. Board of Education: The Challenge for Today's Schools.* New York: Teacher's College Press, 1996.

Lincoln, Charles E. *Race, Religion, and the Continuing American Dilemma.* New York: Hill & Wang, 1984.

Martin, Waldo E., ed. *Brown v. Board of Education: A Brief History with Documents.* Boston: Bedford Books, 1998.

Newby, Idus A. *The Development of Segregationist Thought.* Homewood, Ill.: Dorsey Press, 1969.

Orfield, Gary, Susan E. Eaton, and the Harvard Project on School Desegregation. *Dismantling Desegregation: The Quiet Reversal of Brown v. Board of Education.* New York: New Press, 1996.

Russo, Charles J., J. John Harris III, and Rosetta F. Sandidge. "*Brown v. Board of Education* at 40: A Legal History of Equal Educational Opportunities in American Public Education." *Journal of Negro Education* 63 (Summer, 1994): 297-309.

Stephan, Walter G., and Joe R. Feagin. *School Desegregation: Past, Present, and Future.* New York: Plenum Press, 1980.

Vasillopulos, Christopher. "Prevailing upon the American Dream: Thurgood Marshall and *Brown v. Board of Education*." *Journal of Negro Education* 63 (Summer, 1994): 289-296.

Wilson, Paul E. *A Time to Lose: Representing Kansas in Brown v. Board of Education.* Lawrence: University Press of Kansas, 1995.

Brown v. Mississippi: U.S. Supreme Court case in 1936 involving the validity of confessions. Three African American tenant farmers, Ed Brown, Yank Ellington, and Henry Shields, were arrested for murdering a white planter in Mississippi. They initially maintained that they were innocent, but white police deputies beat them savagely until they broke down and confessed to the murder.

In court the prosecution freely admitted beating and whipping the defendants. The three men were convicted on the basis of their confessions and sentenced to be hanged. Mississippi's supreme court upheld the convictions. Former Mississippi governor Earl Leroy, supported by funding from the National Association for the Advancement of Colored People (NAACP), appealed the case to the U.S. Supreme Court. In 1936 the Court overturned the convictions. The Court held that the coerced confessions had violated the men's right to due process of law, guaranteed by the Fourteenth Amendment.

Bruce, Blanche Kelso (March 1, 1841, Farmville, Virginia—March 17, 1898, Washington, D.C.): Politician. Bruce was the first African American to serve a full term as a U.S. senator. Born a slave, Bruce was raised as a companion to his owner's son and received an education from a private tutor. In 1851 his owner's family moved with their slaves to MISSOURI. Bruce escaped from slavery during the CIVIL WAR and eventually settled in Hannibal, Missouri, where he helped to set up the first school for blacks in the state. After a year at Oberlin College in Ohio, Bruce went to work as a porter on steamboats plying the Mississippi and Missouri Rivers.

Bruce sensed opportunity in the RECONSTRUCTION era, and he settled in the Mississippi Delta, where he became a successful planter. Attracted to Republican Party politics, he soon became a major figure in Bolivar County, serving simultaneously as sheriff and superintendent of schools. In 1874 the

The first African American to serve a complete term in the U.S. Senate, Blanche Kelso Bruce represented Mississippi. *(Library of Congress)*

MISSISSIPPI legislature elected Bruce to the U.S. Senate.

Bruce paid careful attention to his congressional responsibilities and became a respected senator. He strongly supported federal action to protect the voting rights of African Americans in the Reconstruction South, and he often expressed the view that American society was capable of assimilating people of all backgrounds. To this end, he opposed legislation to exclude Chinese immigrants, favored citizenship for Native Americans, and discouraged post-Reconstruction schemes that sought to persuade African Americans to emigrate. He also took a major interest in promoting river and levee improvements on the Lower Mississippi River, chairing a Senate committee on the subject.

Bruce retired from the Senate in 1881 and settled permanently in Washington, D.C. He often was rumored to be a candidate for a cabinet position, though none ever was offered. In 1881 he refused the post of ambassador to Brazil because that country still allowed slavery. He subsequently served as register of the treasury (1881-1889, 1895-1898), in which post his signature was to be found on the nation's paper currency. At his death, *The New York Times* described him as, after Frederick DOUGLASS, "the foremost man of his race." *See also:* Congress members.

Bruce, John E. (1856, Piscataway, Maryland—August 7, 1924, New York, New York): Journalist and publisher. Born of slave parents, John Edward Bruce moved to WASHINGTON, D.C., with his mother when he was a youth. He was educated at several private schools and attended HOWARD UNIVERSITY briefly in 1872. In 1874 he began a long career in journalism with *The New York Times*. Thereafter, he became a correspondent for a number of large weeklies, including the *Cherokee Advocate* and the *Progressive American*.

Bruce started his own newspaper, the *Argus*, in Washington, D.C., in 1879. He became the first African American to start a Sunday newspaper with his publication of the *Sunday Item* in 1880. It was in 1884 that Bruce began to use the pen name "Bruce Grit," by which he was primarily known through the rest of his career.

A militant figure who promoted racial pride and solidarity, Bruce supported the use of force and opposed INTERRACIAL MARRIAGE. Refusing to join any nonblack organizations, he became a member of Marcus GARVEY's black nationalist movement, the UNITED NEGRO IMPROVEMENT ASSOCIATION (UNIA), in 1918. With his established reputation as an important journalist, Bruce became a leading figure in the UNIA, which dubbed him the "duke of Uganda" in 1921 for his loyalty to the organization. Bruce was a regular contributor to the UNIA weekly newspaper, THE NEGRO WORLD, from 1920 until his health collapsed in 1923.

In addition to his other activities, Bruce served as founder and president of the Negro Society for Historical Research. One of the most significant and widely read African American journalists, he was mourned by more than five thousand people at his New York funeral. The leading eulogists were Garvey and Arthur SCHOMBURG. Afterward, Bruce's second wife and widow, Florence Bishop Bruce, who had worked closely with him in his journalism, remained a prominent figure in the *Negro World* staff.

—*Andrea E. Miller*
See also: Black press; Print journalism.

Bryan, Andrew (1737, Goose Creek, South Carolina—1812): Clergyman. Bryan emerged from SLAVERY to organize Savannah's historic First African/First Bryan Baptist Church, one of GEORGIA's first BAPTIST churches for African Americans. Ordained in

Andrew Bryan of Savannah's First Baptist Church. *(Associated Publishers, Inc.)*

1788, Bryan built an independent church and bought his own freedom. His congregation soon joined major Baptist associations and fostered daughter churches that still continue. His nephew, Andrew Marshall, succeeded him.

See also: Baptists.

Bubbles, John (John William Sublett; February 19, 1902, Louisville, Kentucky—May 18, 1986, Baldwin Hills, California): Dancer. Considered to be the father of rhythm tap dancing, Bubbles earned fame in the successful VAUDE-VILLE team of Buck and Bubbles. He helped break down racial barriers during some sixty years in the entertainment industry.

Bubbles made his stage debut at age seven, when he earned twenty-five cents a week singing at a local theater. Soon after, he teamed with Ford Lee "Buck" Washington, and the young duo became the first African Americans to dance and sing on the stage of Louisville's Mary Anderson Theatre. They performed at New York's Columbia, Palace, and Audubon Theaters before becoming 1920's headliners on the Keith Vaudeville Circuit. In 1923 Buck and Bubbles organized their own five-person revue.

A pianist, Buck was the musician in the act, and Bubbles the dancer. Buck also emulated Bubbles's syncopated tap dancing in a lazy manner between segments of piano playing; then Bubbles performed fast-paced solos. Bubbles was famous for the speed and complexity of his footwork and for the many variations he could build from one tap sequence.

Buck and Bubbles were featured in such Broadway musicals as *Weather Clear—Track Fast* (1927), *Blackbirds of 1930*, and the 1931 edition of the *Ziegfeld Follies*. Bubbles played the original character of Sportin' Life in George Gershwin's 1935 folk opera, *Porgy and Bess*, popularizing the song "It Ain't Necessarily So."

Bubbles subsequently toured Europe and performed for British royalty. He also appeared in such films as *Varsity Show* (1937), *Cabin in the Sky* (1943), *Atlantic City* (1944), and *A Song Is Born* (1948). After Buck's death in 1955, Bubbles performed solo or teamed with other entertainers. He made nightclub appearances with Danny Kaye, Judy Garland, and Anna Maria Alberghetti. During the

John Bubbles performing at the Newport Jazz Festival in 1979. *(AP/Wide World Photos)*

cision the Court ruled that a Louisville, Kentucky, segregation ordinance was unconstitutional. The Louisville ordinance, which forbade African Americans from living on the same blocks with whites, violated the equal protection clause of the FOURTEENTH AMENDMENT.

Buffalo soldiers: African American troops who, following the CIVIL WAR, fought Native Americans on the frontier. When the U.S. Army returned to peacetime status following the end of the Civil War in 1865, it enlisted African American men to serve on the frontier and help control Native Americans. Congress adopted a statute in 1866 calling for the enlistment of black volunteers. Four all-black regiments formed, two of cavalry and two of infantry. More than twelve thousand black volunteers were assigned to the West, in such present-day states as KANSAS and OKLAHOMA. The Indians called these volunteers "buffalo soldiers" because they thought the texture of their hair resembled that of the buffalo. The NINTH CAVALRY AND TENTH CAVALRY regiments are the most famous of the buffalo soldiers. The others were the TWENTY-FOURTH INFANTRY and the TWENTY-FIFTH INFANTRY.

Although modern feature films rarely portray black men fighting Indians, in actuality, it was almost exclusively buffalo soldiers who fought the Apaches. They also fought against the Sioux of Chief Crazy Horse, and it was they who captured the Apache leader Geronimo. Crazy Horse, an Oglala, commanded the

1960's, he entertained American troops in Vietnam with comedian Bob Hope and appeared on *The Tonight Show, The Lucy Show,* and other television programs. Despite suffering a stroke, Bubbles returned to the New York stage in *Black Broadway,* a 1980 tribute to the black musical comedy.

Buchanan v. Warley: U.S. SUPREME COURT decision concerning segregation. In this 1917 de-

Sioux and other Native American communities defending their land. Black soldiers thus played a central role in conquering the American West and subduing its native inhabitants. Ironically, for several years in the 1880's, buffalo soldiers were assigned to protect Indians from settlers.

The buffalo soldiers also led campaigns into present-day NEW MEXICO. They are credited with aiding in tracking down William "Billy the Kid" Bonney, who had taken refuge from the law there. One of the last engagements of the buffalo soldiers was against the Sioux at the Battle of Wounded Knee in 1890.

Little historical evidence of the various campaigns of the buffalo soldiers remains, and they receive relatively little mention in standard histories of the United States. At least one engraving, however, authenticates their work. Frederic Remington, an artist who frequently traveled with black soldiers, produced a portrait of one regiment. He depicted some of the men mounted on horses and others, dismounted, guiding their mounts down a steep hill.

See also: Frontier society; Frontier wars; Military; Native American and African American relations.

Bullard, Eugene Jacques (October 9, 1894, Columbus, Georgia—1961): Pilot. As a young man Bullard emigrated to England, then to France, in an attempt to escape discrimination in the United States. He became a professional fighter and engaged in bouts all over Europe. Bullard enlisted in the French Foreign Legion and was wounded at the front during WORLD WAR I. He then volunteered for France's newly formed aviator corps. He eventually returned to the United States. Bullard is believed to be the world's first black combat aviator.

See also: Aviators and astronauts.

Bullins, Ed (b. July 2, 1935, Philadelphia, Pennsylvania): Playwright. Bullins won the New York Drama Critics Circle Award in 1975 for his play *The Taking of Miss Janie*. In 1971 he was given an Obie Award in recognition of *The Fabulous Miss Marie* (pr. 1971, pb. 1974) and *In New England Winter* (pb. 1969, pr. 1971). Bullins is considered one of the most authentic African American writers in modern drama. Ignoring conventional techniques, his plays often feature the same characters in different

Playwright Ed Bullins in 1971. *(AP/Wide World Photos)*

times and settings; they are written for and about urban blacks. In 1995 Bullins becme a professor of theater at Northeastern University.

See also: Literature; Theater.

Bunche, Ralph J. (August 7, 1904, Detroit, Michigan—December 9, 1971, New York, New York): DIPLOMAT and CIVIL RIGHTS activist. Ralph Johnson Bunche was the son of a barber in DETROIT, MICHIGAN. Following a childhood of severe poverty, in which he was orphaned at age twelve and exposed to considerable prejudice, Bunche became the first African American to receive a Ph.D. in political science from Harvard University. Bunche became a leading U.S. statesmen and an important official of the United Nations. His many honors included the 1950 Nobel Peace Prize.

Early Life

Bunche was born amid the twenty square blocks that made up Detroit's African American ghetto. His father, Fred Bunche, ran a barbershop in the downstairs portion of the family's somewhat dilapidated home. Ralph's mother, Olive Agnes Johnson, and his maternal grandmother doted on the new baby. Ralph's grandmother became a profound influence on his personality and ethics.

At age seven, Ralph entered elementary school, where he was a natural student from the beginning. His family's economic situation worsened, however, and in time both Fred and Olive Agnes became ill. Life became so bad for the Bunches that in 1914 they had to leave Detroit. They moved to Toledo, Ohio, and stayed there for a year, until it became clear that Fred and Olive Agnes, suffering from tuberculosis and rheumatic fever, respectively, needed to live in a warmer climate. The family thus moved to Albuquerque, New Mexico. After arriving in Albuquerque, however, Bunche's parents died within three

months of each other. Ralph was twelve at the time.

Sad and almost penniless, the remnants of the family (Bunche, his grandmother, his infant sister, and two aunts) moved to LOS ANGELES, CALIFORNIA. There—with the help and sound advice of his grandmother always at his disposal—Bunche finished elementary school, graduating with awards in English composition and history. At Los Angeles's Jefferson High School, Bunche continued his work in academics, joined the debating team, and earned varsity letters in baseball, basketball, and football. In 1922 he graduated, having been named class valedictorian and won awards for debating, civics, and English composition.

The recipient of an athletic scholarship, Bunche entered the University of California at Los Angeles (UCLA) in September, 1922. Supplementing his scholarship funds with jobs as a janitor and cafeteria helper, the industrious Bunche spared no effort in his studies. In 1927 he graduated with high honors, including membership in Phi Beta Kappa, with a B.A. in international relations. One of that year's only two African American UCLA graduates, Bunche had won awards in debating, athletics, English, languages, and history.

Life's Work

Bunche's career began with a graduate fellowship at Harvard University. With the scholarship in hand, however, Bunche lacked the money to travel across the country to Harvard. The Los Angeles African American community rallied behind Bunche and raised a thousand dollars to pay his fare and provide a small nest egg. Meanwhile, however, Bunche's grandmother died, leaving him without his chief adviser and confidante.

Bunche obtained an M.A. in government from Harvard in 1928. Offered faculty jobs at many prestigious universities, Bunche took an instructorship in political science at HOWARD

UNIVERSITY in WASHINGTON, D.C. In the nation's capital Bunche saw gross discrimination against African Americans and began to consider what could be done about it. Among his answers was the establishment of a political science department at Howard. Also during that time, Bunche met Ruth Ethel Harris, one of his students, who was to become his wife.

In 1929 Bunche continued graduate study in political science at Harvard, commuting to Washington to see Ruth whenever he could. In June, 1930, they were married; they later had three children. During this time, he was also chairman of the political science department at Howard. Bunche's doctoral work at Harvard required him to travel to Africa in 1932-

Ralph J. Bunche around the time he received his Nobel Prize. *(Library of Congress)*

1933 to complete his research on French colonial rule in Togoland and Dahomey. In 1934 Bunche became the first African American to receive a Harvard doctorate in political science.

In 1936 Bunche became codirector of Pennsylvania's Swarthmore College Institute of Race Relations, where he published *A World View of Race* (1937). In his unending effort to develop useful expertise in race relations, Bunche also carried out postdoctoral research in anthropology at Northwestern University, the London School of Economics, and South Africa's Cape Town University. Another high point of his early career was his collaboration from 1938 to 1940 with Swedish sociologist Gunnar Myrdal. These efforts led to the publication of Myrdal's *An American Dilemma: The Negro Problem and Modern Democracy* (1944), a descriptive study of the basis for race prejudice in the United States. The work was based on research carried out in an extensive, and sometimes dangerous, tour of the South. Myrdal's book is still viewed as a central text on the subject.

Diplomatic Career

Bunche then returned to Howard and remained there until WORLD WAR II broke out, whereupon he began a career in public service by joining the Wartime Office of the Coordinator of Information of the National Defense Program. In charge of social science analysis for Africa and the Far East, Bunche remained with that organization for three years, during which time it became the Office of Strategic Services (OSS). In 1944 he transferred from the OSS to the State Department, where he became a specialist on Africa under Secretary of State Cordell Hull. This was another first, as Bunche was the first African American to hold an important position in the State Department.

When the war ended, Bunche again prepared to return to Howard on a full-time basis. Instead, he was named a member of the American delegation to a Washington conference that was to lay the groundwork for economic rehabilitation of the war-torn world. Immediately afterward, Bunche helped to draw up the Charter of the United Nations (U.N.). His efforts were essential to drafting the charter's trusteeship section, which provided the framework of administration and governance of the former colonies of the defeated Axis countries. So well written was this section that it was accepted virtually unchanged at the 1945 conference on the charter's adoption, testimony to Bunche's extensive knowledge of the field.

In 1946 Bunche became a member of the U.S. delegation to the U.N. General Assembly, and by 1947 he was the director of the U.N. Department of Trusteeship. During the 1948 Arab-Israeli War, Bunche was a key figure in mediation of the strife. Bunche had been assigned to accompany U.N. mediator Count Folke Bernadotte to the war zone. When Bernadotte was assassinated by terrorists, Bunche took over the job. Cajoling, mediating, and finally convincing both sides, Bunche produced an armistice.

Nobel Prize

For this effort and other contributions to world peace, Bunche won the 1950 Nobel Peace Prize. In his acceptance lecture, he discussed the paradox of a world that continually engaged in war while espousing a desire for peace. The prize and a continued involvement in the executive aspects of the United Nations were the high points of Bunche's life. Bunche dedicated the remainder of his life to the United Nations, which he saw as the greatest peace effort in history. Bunche rose in the organization until he became its undersecretary-general in 1967.

Through all of his years with the United Nations, Bunche acted as a peacemaker. His important actions included working to solve the 1956 Suez Crisis, helping to end the 1960 crisis in the Congo Democratic Republic, after it gained its independence from Belgium, and directing the 1964 peacekeeping expedition to Cyprus. In 1970 Bunche retired from the United Nations. He died in New York City the next year.

Bunche was also an active worker for equality in the United States. He urged African Americans to stand up for their rights but not to harbor bitterness. He attributed this philosophy to the teachings of his grandmother. In many instances, Bunche endorsed the fight for equality by acting passively. For example, he refused the job of assistant U.S. secretary of state in 1949 because of racism in the nation's capital. In other cases, as when he helped to lead the 1965 Selma, Alabama, civil rights march organized by Martin Luther KING, Jr., Bunche played a more active role.

—*Sanford S. Singer*
See also: American Dilemma, An; Diplomats.

Suggested Readings:

Bunche, Ralph J. *An African American in South Africa: The Travel Notes of Ralph J. Bunche, 28 September 1937-1 January 1938*. Edited by Robert R. Edgar. Athens: Ohio University Press, 1992.

Cornell, Jean G. *Ralph Bunche, Champion of Peace*. Champaign, Ill.: Garrard, 1976.

Haskins, Jim. *Ralph Bunche: A Most Reluctant Hero*. New York: Hawthorn Books, 1974.

Henry, Charles P. *Ralph Bunche: Model Negro or American Other?* New York: New York University Press, 1999.

Herzbrun, Phillip I., B. Kirk Rankin III, and Richard B. Thomas. *Ralph Bunche, World Servant*. Washington, D.C.: U.S. Information Agency, 1963.

Keppel, Ben. *The Work of Democracy: Ralph Bunche, Kenneth B. Clark, Lorraine Hansberry, and the Cultural Politics of Race*. Cambridge, Mass.: Harvard University Press, 1995.

Kugelmass, J. Alvin. *Ralph J. Bunche: Fighter for Peace*. New York: Julian Messner, 1962.

Rivlin, Benjamin, ed. *Ralph Bunche, the Man and His Times*. New York: Holmes & Meier, 1990.

Urquhart, Brian. *Ralph Bunche: An American Life*. New York: W. W. Norton, 1993.

Bureau of Colored Troops: Established by the War Department of the United States on May 22, 1863. Along with issuing the EMANCIPATION PROCLAMATION, President Abraham LINCOLN, early in 1863, issued a call for the enlistment of African Americans into the Union army to help fight against the CONFEDERACY during the CIVIL WAR (1861-1865). The new Bureau of Colored Troops was created to train black soldiers, provide economic aid, and establish schools to educate liberated freedmen.

Pennsylvania congressman John Hickman was an early proponent of the bureau. He believed that poor and uneducated whites would also benefit from the agency. With better education for poor whites, Hickman surmised, the country might even have avoided civil war. In a bill proposed on January 27, 1863, Representative Hickman supported the creation of an agency to support education, finance economic relief, increase the number of black regiments to three hundred, and provide military training. The creation of the Bureau of Colored Troops four months later brought his ideas to fruition.

By May, 1863, the War Department had increased the number of black regiments to 165, dividing them into cavalry, light and heavy artillery, infantry, and a corps of engineers. The War Department called these regiments the U.S. Colored Troops.

See also: Fifty-fourth Massachusetts Colored Infantry; Military.

Burgess, John M. (b. March 11, 1909, Grand Rapids, Michigan): First African American bishop of the EPISCOPAL Church in the United

John M. Burgess, after being elected the first black bishop in U.S. Episcopal Church history in 1969. *(AP/Wide World Photos)*

Burke, Yvonne Brathwaite (b. October 5, 1932, Los Angeles, California): Politician. The first African American woman elected to Congress from CALIFORNIA, Burke enjoyed a distinguished career as a legislator, attorney, and public servant. She was born the daughter of Lola Moore Watson, a real estate agent, and James T. Watson, a custodian. She graduated from the University of California at Los Angeles, then went to law school at the University of Southern California, from which she received her law degree in 1956. She practiced in a law firm, and in 1965, after she witnessed the WATTS RIOTS, she became a member of the McCone Commission, which investigated the causes of the uprising.

An active campaigner for Lyndon B. Johnson in the 1964 presidential election and a DEMOCRATIC PARTY activist, she ran for an assembly seat in the California legislature in 1966 and won, defeating seven male opponents. She was reelected for two more terms. As an assemblywoman, she was responsible for laws that benefited California's indigent children, residents of elderly care homes and orphanages, and the victims of governmental urban renewal and expansion projects. She was chosen vice chair, in 1972, of the Democratic National Convention in Miami, Florida. She largely presided over that tumultuous event, often charming a nationwide audience of television watchers. In that same year she won a seat in the U.S. House of Representatives. She was the first congresswoman to take a maternity leave, for the birth of her daughter, Autumn.

While a member of Congress, Burke served on a number of committees. Among the legis-

States (1970). Burgess graduated from Michigan University and Episcopal Theological Seminary in Cambridge, Massachusetts. His career included the positions of chaplain at HOWARD UNIVERSITY, canon at the Episcopal Cathedral in Washington, D.C., and superintendent of the Episcopal City Mission in Boston. Burgess retired as bishop of Massachusetts in 1976. He is noted for helping to increase minority membership in the church.

lation she sponsored were bills involving equal opportunity for such groups as displaced homemakers and construction workers on the Alaskan oil pipeline. A portion of her bill for equal opportunity for displaced homemakers was amended to the COMPREHENSIVE EMPLOYMENT AND TRAINING ACT OF 1973 (CETA). The bill provided federally funded subsidized employment and training for persons who had previously worked within the home without compensation and were economically stranded through death or divorce. The "Burke amendment" bound federal pipeline funds to affirmative action guidelines, resulting in some $312 million in contracts to women and minorities.

After six years in Congress, Burke returned to California to campaign for attorney general in 1978. She lost that election; however, her political career continued. She remained active in local Los Angeles politics. She was also a partner in a Los Angeles law firm and a fellow of Harvard University's school of government.

In 1992 Burke ran against state senator Diane Watson for the Los Angeles County supervisor's seat vacated by Kenneth Hahn. Burke was named the winner with a narrow two-thousand-vote margin. Watson alleged misconduct and fraud in the election, but in January of 1993 a judge dismissed the allegations. Burke continued to serve throughout the 1990's; in 1993-1994 and 1997-1998 she chaired the board of supervisors. *See also:* Congress members; Politics and government.

Burns, Anthony (May 31, 1834, Stafford County, Virginia—July 27, 1862, St. Catharines, Ontario, Canada): Fugitive slave. Burns was recaptured in Boston and forced to return with his master to SLAVERY in Virginia in 1854. His case was the first in MASSACHUSETTS to test the FUGITIVE SLAVE LAW of 1850. His arrest out-

Contemporary book about Anthony Burns's sensational trial. *(Library of Congress)*

raged Bostonians, a group of whom stormed the jail to free him. Later bought from slavery by black parishioners in BOSTON, he became a Baptist minister and served a congregation of freedmen in Canada.

Burroughs, Nannie Helen (1883, Washington, D.C.—1961): Activist and educator. Burroughs organized the Woman's Industrial Club to train girls in industrial skills and later raised money to open the National Training School for Girls. She was an active member in both the NATIONAL ASSOCIATION FOR THE ADVANCEMENT OF COLORED PEOPLE (NAACP) and the National Association of Colored Women's Clubs.

Bush, George Washington (c. 1791, Pennsylvania—c. 1863): Explorer. Bush fought with Andrew Jackson at the Battle of New Orleans during the WAR OF 1812, then joined the Hudson's Bay Company. He reached the Pacific Coast in 1820 while working for the company. He farmed in Missouri for about twelve years and then helped lead a group of settlers, the first in the area, to the Puget Sound in the Pacific Northwest in 1845. *See also:* Exploration of North America.

Bush administration: Although President George Bush hoped to improve the REPUBLICAN PARTY's relationship with the African American community, the majority of blacks saw his administration as continuing the policies of the Ronald REAGAN ADMINISTRATION (1981-1989), generally perceived to be anti-civil rights. Bush did manage to double Reagan's African American vote total, winning approximately 12 percent of the black vote in 1988.

On the other hand, Bush offended many by releasing a campaign advertisement that accused Democratic Party candidate Michael Dukakis of being soft on crime. The ad featured convicted black rapist Willie Horton, and many African Americans (as well as many white Americans) believed that Bush was exploiting white fears and further dividing the nation along racial lines. Thus, few blacks expected any significant gains from his administration.

As president, Bush made several gestures to African Americans. Unlike Reagan, he frequently met with key black leaders and organizations. He praised the work of Martin Luther KING, Jr. and vowed to work toward ending discrimination in housing, education, and employment. He issued the CONGRESSIONAL BLACK CAUCUS their first invitation to

President George Bush. *(Library of Congress)*

Notable African American Appointees in the Bush Administration

Louis W. Sullivan	Secretary of Health and Human Services
Jerry Curry	Director of National Highway Traffic Safety Administration
Wendell Gunn	Chief of staff for Housing and Urban Development
Stephen Glaudé	Deputy secretary of Housing and Urban Development
Jewel Lafontant	Ambassador and coordinator for refugee affairs
Constance Newman	Director of the Office of Personnel Management
Edward Perkins	U.S. Ambassador to the United Nations
Colin L. Powell	Chairman of Joint Chiefs of Staff (Defense Department)
Kristin Taylor	White House director of media relations
Joseph P. Watkins	Associate director of White House Office of Public Liaison

visit the White House in eight years. He became the first president since Jimmy Carter to address the convention of the NATIONAL URBAN LEAGUE. He met with the Black Leadership Forum, and while their comments remained guarded, many African American leaders, including Coretta Scott KING; Benjamin HOOKS, executive director of the NATIONAL ASSOCIATION FOR THE ADVANCEMENT OF COLORED PEOPLE (NAACP); Dorothy HEIGHT, president of the NATIONAL COUNCIL OF NEGRO WOMEN; and Joseph LOWERY, president of the SOUTHERN CHRISTIAN LEADERSHIP CONFERENCE (SCLC), expressed their belief that Bush was committed to fighting racism in America.

Bush proposed that Congress provide HISTORICALLY BLACK COLLEGES and institutions with matching funds to increase their endowments. For his efforts, HAMPTON University awarded Bush an honorary degree in 1991. The president also selected Army general Colin POWELL to be the first African American to serve as the chairman of the U.S. Joint Chiefs of Staff, and he nominated Clarence THOMAS for the U.S. SUPREME COURT. These efforts helped Bush achieve the highest approval rating among African Americans of any Repub-

lican president since Dwight D. Eisenhower.

Yet despite these activities, Bush gained few converts to the Republican Party. Hampton students protested Hampton's decision to grant the president an honorary degree. While Bush's appointment of Powell was considered above reproach, many viewed his Thomas appointment as an example of Uncle Tomism—in that Bush may have simply believed that, politically, he needed to replace retiring black justice Thurgood MARSHALL with another black justice, and the conservative Thomas fit the bill. Most blacks continued to believe that Bush's civil rights agenda was quite similar to Reagan's.

After the Supreme Court outlawed the use of QUOTAS in AFFIRMATIVE ACTION programs in the 1989 *Richmond v. J. A. Croson Company* case, Democratic representatives, including Senator Ted Kennedy, introduced legislation to reestablish the practice. Bush, however, vetoed a 1990 civil rights bill which would have allowed some degree of federal protection for quotas and affirmative action in employment practices. His lackluster support for the 1991 Civil Rights Act (he was essentially forced to bow to congressional pressure) also angered many African Americans.

When the conservative Supreme Court eliminated federal protection for school desegregation and voting rights in 1992, Bush remained silent. Finally, his praise for the judicial system after four white Los Angeles policemen were acquitted of beating black motorist Rodney King during a traffic stop convinced blacks that the Republican Party had little to offer the African American community. As a result, when Bush made his unsuccessful bid for reelection in 1992, fewer than 10 percent of African Americans supported his candidacy.

—*Robert D. Ubriaco, Jr.*
See also: King, Rodney, arrest and beating.

Business and commerce: A remarkable aspect of American history is the contributions of racial minorities in shaping the country. The story of the United States includes the stories of people who have survived and prospered against great adversity without losing their humanity and without forgetting the true meaning of democracy. African Americans have been instrumental in this process in their relentless drive to change America.

One of the more significant factors in the well-being of a nation and its people is the nation's economic wealth, measured in terms of its industrial base, business and commercial expertise, and human capital. The United States developed one of the most prosperous economies in history, but many Americans have not enjoyed the fruits of the nation's economic wealth, even when they made significant individual and collective contributions to it. Historically, most Americans—regardless of race or ethnicity—did not enjoy these benefits.

It was only after WORLD WAR II that the standard of living improved dramatically for most white Americans. Because of racial attitudes and policies, the African American experience has differed significantly from the experiences of white people in the economic sphere. African Americans faced the brutality of SLAVERY, the forced servitude of SHARE-CROPPING or tenant farming after the end of slavery, and constitutionally approved discrimination that severely limited economic opportunity for the vast majority of African Americans.

During the 1890's Sam Harris's Williamsburg, Virginia, "cheap store" was believed to be the largest business of its kind owned by any black entrepreneur in the United States. *(AP/Wide World Photos)*

Slavery was introduced to North America to ensure a steady supply of cheap labor, and the slave trade itself became an important industry. *(National Archives)*

The economic oppression of African Americans can reasonably be described as the United States' greatest failure as a democracy. It is only since the Civil Rights movement of the late 1950's and 1960's that African Americans and other racial minorities have moved close to equality with white citizens. Nevertheless, the contributions of African Americans to the nation's economic, commercial, and business growth have been significant.

Slavery to Freedom

Slavery was instituted to ensure that early America had a supply of free labor. Laws were enacted by the colonies, beginning around 1660, that transformed the status of black people in the colonies from free persons to slaves. These slave codes denied almost all freedoms and rights to any person of color in the colonies. Over the next decades, the slave population grew in order to meet the labor demands of the colonies, in particular the agricultural southern colonies. Between 1800 and 1860, there was a serious shortage of skilled labor; therefore, skilled African Americans were assured of work. By 1860, on the eve of the CIVIL WAR, there were approximately four million

(continued on page 388)

The Fifty Most Profitable Black-Owned Industrial and Service Businesses, 1998

1. **The Philadelphia Coca-Cola Bottling Co.** Philadelphia, Pennsylvania. Founded 1985. Soft drink bottling.

2. **Johnson Publishing Co.** Chicago, Illinois. Founded 1942. Publishing, broadcasting, TV production, cosmetics, and hair care.

3. **TLC Beatrice International Holdings Inc.** New York, New York. Founded 1987. Manufacturing and distribution of grocery products.

4. **Active Transportation.** Louisville, Kentucky. Founded 1987. Transportation services, hauling of cars and trucks to dealers.

5. **The Bing Group.** Detroit, Michigan. Founded 1980. Steel processing, steel stamping, full seat assembly.

6. **World Wide Technology Inc.** St. Louis, Missouri. Founded 1990. Distribution of information technology products and services.

7. **FUCI Metals USA Inc.** Northbrook, Illinois. Founded 1987. Raw materials importer.

8. **Granite Broadcasting Corporation.** New York, New York. Founded 1988. Selling of commercial air-time.

9. **H. J. Russell & Co.** Atlanta, Georgia. Founded 1952. Construction, property mgt., airport concessions, real estate development.

10. **Bet Holdings II Inc.** Washington, D.C. Founded 1982. Cable television programming and magazine publishing.

11. **Siméus Foods International Inc.** Mansfield, Texas. Founded 1996. Custom food manufacturing for national chain restaurants.

12. **Anderson-Dubose Co.** Solon, Ohio. Founded 1991. Food, paper products, and operating supplies distributor.

13. **Barden Companies Inc.** Detroit, Michigan. Founded 1981. Casino gaming, training, real estate, and international trade.

14. **Midwest Stamping Inc.** Bowling Green, Ohio. Founded 1993. Automotive stamping and assemblies.

15. **Exemplar Manufacturing Co.** Ypsilanti, Michigan. Founded 1977. Manufacturer of metal fasteners, electrical system supplier.

16. **Mays Chemical Co.** Indianapolis, Indiana. Founded 1980. Distributor of industrial chemicals and raw materials.

17. **Hawkins Food Group.** Detroit, Michigan. Founded 1995. Retail restaurant operations.

18. **Digital Systems International Corp.** Arlington, Virginia. Founded 1988. Information technology and marine services.

19. **Sayers Computer Source.** Mount Prospect, Illinois. Founded 1982. Computer sales and service, hardware and software, network design.

20. **Thomas Madison Inc.** Detroit, Michigan. Founded 1990. Metal fabricator and steel service center to automotive manufacturers.

21. **Essence Communications Inc.** New York, New York. Founded 1969. Magazine publishing, catalog sales, and entertainment.

22. **Spiral Inc.** Chandler, Arizona. Founded 1989. Supplies and services to groceries and amusement facilities.

23. **Dallas & Mavis Specialized Carrier Co.** Louisville, Kentucky. Founded 1994. Transportation, warehousing, logistics.

24. **Belle of Orleans DBA Bally's Casino Lakeshore Resort.** New Orleans, Louisiana. Founded 1994. Gaming entertainment.

25. **Wesley Industries Inc.** Bloomfield Hills, Michigan. Founded 1993. Coatings and castings.

26. **Pulsar Data Systems Inc.** Lanham, Maryland. Founded 1983. Provider of IT services and products.

27. **Olajuwon Holdings**. Houston, Texas. Founded 1994. Denny's Restaurants.

28. **Calhoun Enterprises**. Montgomery, Alabama. Founded 1984. Supermarkets and warehousing.

29. **The Holland Group L.L.C. DBA Workplace Integrators**. Bingham Farms, Michigan. Founded 1997. Office furniture, flooring, asset management, and design.

30. **The Bartech Group Inc.** Livonia, Michigan. Founded 1977. Contract employment and staffing services.

31. **Washington Cable Supply Inc.** Lanham, Maryland. Founded 1984. Electrical and telecommunications equipment distributor.

32. **V and J Holding Companies Inc.** Milwaukee, Wisconsin. Founded 1984. Burger King & Pizza Hut franchisee.

33. **Reliant Industries Inc.** Bedford Park, Illinois. Founded 1992. Manufacturer of fasteners and cold-formed products.

34. **Bridgeman Foods**. Louisville, Kentucky. Founded 1988. Wendy's Old Fashioned Hamburger franchisee.

35. **Specialized Packaging Group**. Hamden, Connecticut. Founded 1983. Package design, engineering, and marketing.

36. **Rush Communications**. New York, New York. Founded 1991. Music, film, television, advertising, fashion, and management.

37. **Stop Shop Save Food Markets**. Baltimore, Maryland. Founded 1978. Purchase and sale of groceries and other related products.

38. **Automotive Carrier Services**. Louisville, Kentucky. Founded 1987. Transportation and logistics.

39. **Pro-Line Corporation**. Dallas, Texas. Founded 1970. Cosmetic and hair care manufacturer and distributor.

40. **Karl Kani Infinity Inc.** Los Angeles, California. Founded 1989. Clothing design and manufacturing.

41. **Luster Products Co.** Chicago, Illinois. Founded 1957. Hair care products manufacturer and distributor.

42. **Radio One Inc./Radio One of Atlanta Inc.** Lanham, Maryland. Founded 1980. Radio broadcasting.

43. **Regal Plastics Co.** Roseville, Michigan. Founded 1985. Plastic injection-molded interior trim.

44. **Baldwin Richardson Foods Co.** Matteson, Illinois. Founded 1921. Food manufacturing sales and service.

45. **Pepsi Cola of Washington, D.C., L.P.** Forestville, Maryland. Founded 1990. Distribution of soft drinks.

46. **Surface Protection Industries Inc.** Los Angeles, California. Founded 1978. Manufacturer and distributor of paints and specialty coatings.

47. **Health Resources Inc.** Lemoyne, Pennsylvania. Founded 1983. Pharmacy and vision benefit management.

48. **Specialized Services Inc.** Southfield, Michigan. Founded 1988. Transportation, administrative and purchase support services.

49. **Wilson Office Interiors**. Carrollton, Texas. Founded 1993. Sales, service, and design of office furniture.

50. **Drew Pearson Co.** Addison, Texas. Founded 1985. Manufacturer and distributor of headwear and children's apparel.

Source: Black Enterprise magazine, June, 1999.

Note: The annual B.E. Industrial/Service 100 listing includes companies that are at least 51 percent black-owned. Not eligible for the list are real estate firms, brokerage firms, professional service firms such as accounting and legal firms, or automobile dealerships. *Black Enterprise* publishes a separate B.E. Auto Dealer 100 list.

slaves and more than half a million free African Americans in the United States. Many were skilled workers who occupied important positions in meeting the economic needs of the developing nation. Slaves, too, performed an economic function, but it was one that went unrewarded.

The Reconstruction Period

The end of the Civil War in 1865 promised great changes for African Americans. African American slaves had become essential to the economy of the southern states. Ironically, because of the availability of slaves, whites had become quite dependent on slave labor, to the extent that slaves became essential within the skilled class of workers. Many plantations were fully autonomous because slaves had learned all the skills necessary to conduct an independent economic life. Quite often, slaveholders would allow these skilled artisans to live in towns and cities, where their skills and value could be exploited. The 1865 federal census of occupations revealed that by the end of the Civil War, 100,000 of the 120,000 artisans in the South were African Americans.

The end of the Civil War produced great disruption in the economic and social systems of the South and of the nation. The agrarian-based economy of the South had been destroyed. The major task facing the nation after the Civil War was to rebuild the economic institutions of the South, basing them on free rather than slave labor. During this same time, the North was industrializing rapidly and needed cheap labor.

In 1867 Congress passed the RECONSTRUCTION Act, which enfranchised African Americans (gave them the right to vote) and established the legal basis for the nation's attempts to rebuild the South. The Thirteenth, Fourteenth, and Fifteenth Amendments and the Civil Rights Acts of 1866 and 1875, which were intended to give constitutional guarantees of full equality and protection to the newly freed

slaves, raised the hopes of African Americans that the United States was serious about including them in a true democracy on a basis of equality.

The government's failure to enforce these laws ended Reconstruction, thereby diminishing the hopes and aspirations of African Americans. Positive aspirations of the kind evoked by Reconstruction would not return for almost a century. By 1877 it had become clear that Reconstruction policies and laws had failed to relieve the plight of African Americans.

Whites in the South gained control of land redevelopment shortly after the end of the Civil War. Immediately, BLACK CODES were enacted that effectively reenslaved the freed African Americans. Scholars have noted that these black codes differed very little from earlier SLAVE CODES that had been passed with the acknowledged intent of ensuring complete subjugation of African Americans as property, with no legal standing as persons. For example, African Americans labeled as vagrants or rebellious could be arrested and forced to work on roads and levees without pay. In some states, servants were forced to work from sunrise to sunset. It was a crime for African Americans to own farmland in Mississippi.

The federal government made attempts to protect the right of freedmen to choose their own employers. These efforts failed because of the lack of political will within the federal government. Consequently, faced with severe hardships caused by the betrayal of the government, most African Americans were forced to return to work for white owners as tenant farmers or sharecroppers. Many farmers, rather than accumulating profits, would end up in greater debt to their landlords at the end of the year than at the beginning. Subsequently, this arrangement became detrimental to both groups: Many tenant farmers would not work diligently or productively, since there was nothing to be gained from the effort except greater rewards for the landowners.

Migration from the South

The unfavorable conditions of the agricultural economy of the South, along with cruelty and violence perpetuated and sanctioned by whites, compelled many African Americans to move northward or westward. Before the Civil War, the vast majority of African Americans lived in the rural South. Between 1865 and 1900, there were large-scale migrations by African Americans. Subsequent migratory waves were prompted by the need for labor in factories in the North during WORLD WAR I and again during WORLD WAR II. The pattern of the GREAT MIGRATION to the North and to urban areas in the South continued to such an extent that by 1980 the majority of African Americans lived in central cities and almost half lived outside the South. Although they often gained employment through migration, gains were sporadic and often of short duration because of the resistance of white employers and workers.

The fortunes of African Americans varied in part with the flow of white immigration. Even though there was a tremendous need for labor, white workers from Europe rather than the large labor pool of African Americans received many of the new jobs. Although African Americans represented a large source of skilled and artisan laborers, they were displaced because of fierce white opposition. For instance, prior to the end of the Civil War, the building trade industry in the South was dominated by African American labor. By the beginning of the twentieth century, African Americans had been all but forced out of the industry.

Further, in the North, with the immigration of millions of Irish during the 1860's, African American workers were fired or replaced by this new source of white labor. This pattern was to be repeated with the immigration of Italian and Jewish peasants between 1890 and 1930. African Americans were given opportunities only when there was a shortage of white labor, such as in 1914, when there was a sharp decline in the number of immigrants. During both world wars immigration was curtailed severely, causing temporary shortages of white workers. Faced with these shortages, employers again used the available source of African American labor. During these critical periods, African Americans found work in all sectors of the economy.

Unionism

Although African Americans were found in all industries, the vast majority were relegated to the two lowest-paid sectors, agriculture and domestic and personal services. For example, the 1910 census recorded that of the 5,192,535 employed African Americans, 2,881,454 were in agriculture and 1,357,598 were in domestic and personal services. Within the industrial sectors, they were employed in the least desirable jobs.

Upon the end of the Civil War, African American leaders had immediately recognized the need to join with white workers in forming labor unions and organizations. The best hope for improving economic opportunities for African Americans was through collective bargaining by strong ORGANIZED LABOR. This too was to prove to be an elusive dream, for several reasons. The effort to create an integrated union movement reflected the nation's effort to integrate American society. This effort, as described previously, was a dismal failure.

The climate for organizing workers into unions has always been hostile. Some historians have noted that the labor movement in the United States is the most violent and bloody in the history of any industrial nation in the world. America's commitment to an ideology of laissez-faire capitalism led to the concentration of power and influence in the business sectors. With this power, business interests, employing the forces of federal, state, and local governments, prevented the establishment of powerful unions for most of the period prior to the twentieth century.

The union movement's engagement in self-defeating strategies and techniques proved to be a major deterrent to the successful organization of workers. Specifically, the union movement contributed to its own failure through the adamant position taken by white workers to maintain segregated unions. The National Labor Union, formed in 1866, attempted but failed to persuade affiliates to admit African Americans into their bodies.

The Colored National Labor Union was formed in 1869 in response to this rejection, but it proved to be ineffective. The most powerful early union, the American Federation of Labor (AFL), formed in 1886. Initially, the AFL supported the principle of integrated unions, but it allowed local union affiliates to exclude African Americans. Betrayed by white unions, African Americans nevertheless formed several powerful labor organizations. In 1892 two thousand African American longshoremen conducted a successful strike in St. Louis, MISSOURI. In Galveston, TEXAS, a four-week strike by African American longshoremen had to be broken by the state militia.

The forcing of African Americans out of the labor market and union movement as equals or competitors left these workers with the alternative of working as strikebreakers, or "scabs." Several scholars have noted that from 1865 to the 1930's, African Americans were a major source of strikebreaking labor. This situation caused even greater antipathy from the white unions. The most successful unionizing effort for African Americans was conducted by A. Philip RANDOLPH, who founded the BROTHERHOOD OF SLEEPING CAR PORTERS in 1926. After a long and bitter battle, the union achieved full recognition by the Pullman Company in 1937.

By the 1930's, African Americans had become an integral part of the workforce. African Americans represented 8.5 percent of iron and steel workers, about 17 percent of the semiskilled and unskilled workers in the slaughter and packinghouse industry, 68 percent of the tobacco industry workers, and 9.2 percent of all coal miners.

WORLD WAR II proved to be a time of significant increase in black participation in unions. The number of African Americans in unions is estimated to have grown from 61,000 in 1928 to 600,000 in 1940. During the peak of World War II, this number increased to 1,250,000. By 1970 the number of African American trade unionists had grown to about 2.5 million.

Until World War II, the federal government sanctioned segregated union organizations. In 1941, however, President Franklin D. Roosevelt signed EXECUTIVE ORDER 8802, which banned discrimination in government and defense-industry hiring and created the Fair Employment Practices Commission to enforce the ban. Roosevelt signed the order under pressure: A. Philip Randolph had organized a movement to lead fifty thousand African Americans on a protest march to Washington, D.C.; the march was called off after the executive order was signed.

The president's executive order represented the first major public policy position directed to eliminate discrimination in regard to hiring, tenure, terms and conditions of employment, or union membership. The Fair Employment Practices Commission failed, however, because it did not have sufficient power to enforce its mandates. In addition, as the legal foundation for union segregation was destroyed, white unionists resorted to other means and devices to maintain their privileges and control. Nepotism-based memership policies, seniority rules, and apprenticeship programs open only to relatives and friends of union members are examples of practices and rules that effectively restricted African American membership in white unions.

African Americans were more successful in the 1960's. The Civil Rights Act of 1964 prohibited discrimination in employment, among other things, and Executive Order 11246 (1969) required equal employment clauses in all federal contracts. The nation became more serious about enforcing laws enacted to eliminate unlawful discrimination in employment and unions. The public policy reflected in these laws led to landmark decisions by the SUPREME COURT that ensured that union discrimination, whether overt or by subtle means and devices, would not be sanctioned or ignored. The irony is that just as African Americans gained greater participation in and protection from union organizations, unions began declining in size and power as a result of a weakening economy, an excess of workers, a weakening of labor laws, and a switch to more service-oriented jobs, which traditionally have not been unionized.

A State of Permanent Poverty

The most devastating impact of the American failure to eliminate discrimination is the suffering of millions of African American citizens as a result of POVERTY caused, in part, by discrimination. In the twentieth century, the American economy was affected by the growth of the international marketplace. This new competition led to massive unemployment within many major business sectors, including the automobile and steel industries. Structural changes in the American economy have caused an increase in the extent of poverty.

A U.S. Census Bureau report of August, 1992, stated that the poverty rate was 32.7 percent for African Americans, 11.3 percent for whites, 28.7 percent for Hispanic Americans, and 13.8 percent for Asian Americans. Of the 35.7 million Americans in poverty, more than 10 million were African Americans. The fact that even this high poverty rate represented an improvement in the historical economic status of African Americans is a vivid reminder of past economic deprivation.

Most African Americans lived in abject poverty from the years immediately after the Civil War until jobs created by World War I offered some respite. In the 1930's, the Great Depression was especially difficult for African Americans. Millions of Americans were incapable of self-support. In 1933 25 to 40 percent of African Americans in several large cities were on relief. In ATLANTA, GEORGIA, 65 percent of the employable African Americans were in need of public assistance, while in Norfolk, Virginia, this figure reached 80 percent.

Although poverty remains prevalent in the United States and African Americans remain disproportionately affected, the impact of poverty is different from its impact in past generations, when it was literally a life-or-death issue. Poor health and health care; deficient education, diet, housing, and living conditions; shorter life expectancy; and higher infant mortality rates—rather than actual starvation—have become typical manifestations of poverty.

Achievements

The full contribution of African Americans to the industrial development of the United States is difficult to assess. Slaves were not permitted to patent their inventions, so there is no way of knowing how many inventions actually came from the minds of slaves. The little evidence available suggests that African Americans made substantial contributions to the technical development of the United States. In 1834 Henry BLAIR received two patents for the development of corn harvesters. In 1846 Norbert RILLIEUX invented a vacuum evaporating pan that revolutionized the sugar-refining industry. Both men were free.

Benjamin Montgomery, a slave, invented a boat propeller. Jan E. Matzeliger invented the shoe-lasting machine. In 1884 John P. Parker invented a screw for tobacco presses. Elijah McCOY patented fifty different inventions, principally relating to automatic lubricators

An example of the use of Martin Luther King, Jr.'s words to promote a commercial concern. *(Martin A. Hutner)*

for machines. Granville T. WOODS made significant contributions in the fields of electricity, steam boilers, and automatic air brakes. Garrett MORGAN invented the gas mask and the automated traffic light. McKinley Jones invented portable refrigeration units. Benjamin BANNEKER has been described as the most accomplished black person in early America. He was commissioned to help define and lay out the streets of the District of Columbia.

Self-Help and Economic Development
Leaders in the African American community began as early as the 1800's to exhort a self-help philosophy encompassing the acquisition of land and reliance upon the support of African American cooperatives and merchants. This was the beginning of the historical appeal to BLACK CAPITALISM.

One of the first major business ventures organized by African Americans was the Chesapeake and Marine Railway and Dry Dock Company, established in BALTIMORE, MARYLAND, in 1865. As with most business ventures by African Americans, it went out of business, in this case in 1883. The high rate of failure resulted from a number of factors beyond the control of these early African American entrepreneurs. They lacked equal access to the marketplace and were poorly capitalized, largely because white distributors and banks did not give them an equal chance.

Black businesspeople, however, were very successful in banking, insurance, and publishing, primarily because these were areas in which white businesses would not serve black customers, leaving the markets open. The federal government chartered the Freedmen's Savings and Trust Company, which was to be controlled by African Americans, in 1865. There were thirty-four branches by 1872, but the bank was abolished in 1874. Hundreds of private savings and loan collectives, as well as LIFE INSURANCE COMPANIES, were started. Thousands of African Americans purchased land, but in the South, where African Americans constituted approximately half of the population in 1890, they owned less than one-sixth of the farms. It would not be until the 1970's that black business ownership would begin to expand greatly.

As a result of antidiscrimination laws passed beginning in the 1940's and during the CIVIL RIGHTS MOVEMENT and later, African Americans gained entry into major sectors of the private and public economy that historically had been closed to them. The number of African Americans in higher occupational categories increased significantly between 1970 and 1990. Prior to the 1970's, the vast majority of black businesses were small and primarily served the African American community. Typical businesses were barbershops, funeral homes, restaurants, and beauty salons. After the 1960's, governmental policies and capital assistance greatly expanded the types and numbers of African American businesses. Major corporations transformed their workforces to be inclusive of African Americans, allowing them to gain business experience. Major commitments and resources were devoted to the hiring and promoting of African Americans and other minorities.

—Richard Hudson

See also: National Negro Business League; Office of Minority Business Enterprise; Strikes and labor law.

Ballard, Donna. *Doing It for Ourselves: Success Stories of African American Women in Business.* New York: Berkley Books, 1997.

Butler, John S. *Entrepreneurship and Self-Help Among Black Americans: A Reconsideration of Race and Economics.* Albany: State University of New York Press, 1991.

Case, Frederick E. *Black Capitalism: Problems in Development: A Case Study of Los Angeles.* New York: Praeger, 1972.

"The Good News About Black America." *Newsweek* 133 (June 7, 1999): 28-38.

Graham, Lawrence. *Our Kind of People: Inside America's Black Upper Class.* New York: HarperCollins, 1999.

Green, Shelley, and Paul Pryde. *Black Entrepreneurship in America.* New Brunswick, N.J.: Transaction, 1990.

Herbert, James I. *Black Male Entrepreneurs and Adult Development.* New York: Praeger, 1989.

Kijakazi, Kilolo. *African-American Economic Development and Small Business Ownership.* New York: Garland, 1997.

Mandle, Jay R. *Not Slave, Not Free: The African American Economic Experience Since the Civil War.* Durham, N.C.: Duke University Press, 1992.

Todd, Gwendolyn P. *Innovation and Growth in an African American Owned Business.* New York: Garland, 1996.

Weems, R. E. *Desegregating the Dollar: African American Consumerism in the Twentieth Century.* New York: New York University Press, 1998.

Busing: Beginning in the early 1970's, the U.S. SUPREME COURT mandated that busing students to particular schools, even to schools significantly distant from their homes, was an appropriate method for remedying school segregation. Court-mandated or "forced" busing as a tool in achieving school integration has always been controversial, even among some of its supporters.

In the early 1970's, after nearly twenty years of defying the 1954 landmark BROWN V. BOARD OF EDUCATION decision that declared segregated public schools to be unconstitutional, southern schools (as well as all other U.S. school districts operating racially divided school systems) were forced to accept court-supervised busing programs as a means of achieving immediate integration. A highly controversial solution to the long-standing problem of racially separate schools, the busing remedy was upheld by the Supreme Court in the case of SWANN V. CHARLOTTE-MECKLENBURG BOARD OF EDUCATION (1971), argued successfully for the plaintiffs by Julius Chambers, lead counsel for the NATIONAL ASSOCIATION FOR THE ADVANCEMENT OF COLORED PEOPLE (NAACP) Legal Defense and Educational Fund. In a unanimous decision, the Court agreed that NORTH CAROLINA's Charlotte-Mecklenburg school district had not made good-faith progress toward desegregation. As a result, the Court affirmed a lower federal court's approval of busing both black and white schoolchildren as a constitutionally valid and expeditious method for achieving racially balanced schools.

The Origins of Busing
The adoption of busing as a court-approved tool for ending segregation in schools came about only after southern states failed to substantiate claims of progress toward school integration. Under orders since 1955, when the Supreme Court delivered its *Brown II* ruling to desegregate schools "with all deliberate speed," southern school boards instead circumvented the order by limiting desegregation plans to plans that, for the most part, preserved the status quo and produced, at best, token results.

Plans such as freedom-of-choice schools, pupil placement laws, and redrawn attendance boundaries were popular precursors of busing. In practice, such plans often consisted primarily of complicated administrative procedures designed to thwart integration. Southern federal courts regularly upheld the use of these ineffectual programs. Most influential in this respect were the opinions of Circuit Judge John A. Parker, who declared that the Constitution did not require integration but merely forbade discrimination. Parker's interpretation of the Constitution as it related to *Brown v. Board of Education* bolstered southern resistance to integration for almost twenty years.

Exasperated by the South's willful defiance of its desegregation order, the Supreme Court finally took a more active role in 1968. In the VIRGINIA case of GREEN V. COUNTY SCHOOL BOARD OF NEW KENT COUNTY, it declared that freedom-of-choice schools failed to satisfy the requirements of the *Brown* mandate and ordered school districts with racially dual systems "to come forward with a plan that promises realistically to work, and to work now!" Additionally, the Court charged the district courts with the affirmative duty to supervise the operation of desegregation plans.

It was under this order that Judge James B. McMillan, a federal district judge in Charlotte, North Carolina, found himself pressured into backing his experts' proposed busing plan for Charlotte. Although it was opposed vigorously by the Charlotte-Mecklenburg school board, the busing proposal, set in motion by the efforts of the NAACP in alliance with other local black groups, ultimately was sustained by the Supreme Court as an expedient way to end segregation in schools.

Social and Political Reactions
The order to bus schoolchildren to schools other than those nearest their homes provoked a furor across the United States. White parents in the North as well as in the South protested the decision as an infringement on their right to choose a neighborhood-school education. As a result, many fled the cities or enrolled their children in private schools, a

trend that was nicknamed WHITE FLIGHT. This situation exacerbated the problem of racial balance. Parents in South Boston, Massachusetts, stoned buses and at one point threatened to bomb a tunnel that buses used to transport children to school. All over the country, grassroots antibusing groups formed to organize against busing plans. Black children often were greeted at their new schools with taunts and other types of intimidating behavior.

For black children, busing was hardly a new mode of transportation to school. Before the *Brown v. Board of Education* decision, the precedent of PLESSY V. FERGUSON (1896) had sanctioned the practice of segregation and "separate but equal" schooling. Black children, particularly those in rural areas, customarily had been bused past white neighborhood schools to designated black schools farther away from their homes. To the NAACP and other civil rights groups that had fought in the courts for integrated schools, busing appeared to be the best recourse for abolishing the nation's segregated lifestyles. To black parents whose children had been denied an education equal to that of white children, bus rides meant that all children, by virtue of their sitting together in the same classrooms, would be educated equally.

During the 1970's, the U.S. government often reflected the confusion and emotionalism of the country over this issue. Both before and after the *Swann v. Charlotte-Mecklenburg Board of Education* decision, President Richard M.

Nearly two decades after the Supreme Court issued its *Brown v. Board of Education* decision, it ruled that busing children to schools outside their neighborhoods would be an acceptable method of achieving school integration. *(National Archives)*

Nixon actively lobbied against busing, promoting the concept of neighborhood schools. The Department of Health, Education, and Welfare reversed policy on the busing issue by first approving, then denying, then finally providing millions of dollars for desegregation plans undergirded by mandatory busing. Congress, also divided over the busing order, regularly burdened significant educational reform bills with antibusing amendments, usually resulting in delayed action on important legislation. Under pressure from their constituents, members of Congress proposed a variety of antibusing legislation as well as new laws designed to rein in what was decried as a judicially overactive Supreme Court.

Changing Views
From 1954 to *Swann*, the Supreme Court had intentionally delivered unanimous decisions in desegregation cases. Only when confronted with decades-long defiance of the *Brown* mandate had the Court felt pushed to become an enforcer of constitutional law. With the introduction of busing as a mandatory solution to segregation, however, the Court's united front began to fissure. Under the leadership of Nixon-appointed Chief Justice Warren Burger, who had replaced the liberal Chief Justice Earl Warren, architect of the *Brown* decision, the composition and ideology of the court began to shift from liberal to conservative. Consequently, decisions concerning busing became more cautious and often were split.

In MILLIKEN V. BRADLEY (1974), for example, a case involving interdistrict busing of more than 300,000 students in DETROIT, MICHIGAN, the Court, in a five-to-four decision, overturned a lower court's decision to integrate urban and suburban schools, ruling that there was no evidence proving deliberate discrimination in Detroit's school system. This decision provided an important distinction between cases involving DE JURE SEGREGATION, in which discrimination had previously

had legal sanctions, and DE FACTO SEGREGATION, most often caused by migratory shifts and housing patterns, such as those found in the North's newly black-settled urban areas.

The Supreme Court held that federal courts lack the authority to impose interdistrict—that is, involving both inner-city and suburban districts—remedies without showing an interdistrict violation of the law. This ruling, combined with changing political attitudes in the nation and the existence of numerous minority-dominated cities surrounded by white suburbs, increasingly made busing seem less feasible as an integration measure.

Some African Americans also became disenchanted with the idea of busing for the sake of integration. Starting around the mid-1970's, when the black nationalist movement began to challenge the integrationist goals of the traditional Civil Rights movement, black activists advanced the view that busing black children to predominantly white areas, away from the filial support of their communities, might actually be harming instead of helping the black students' learning and socialization processes.

In opposition to the unwavering view of the NAACP, which was adamant throughout the 1970's and 1980's in its litigious drive for busing and integration plans, leaders from such organizations as the CONGRESS OF RACIAL EQUALITY (CORE) began to lobby for schools that would be "separate, but really equal." This argument resurfaced in the 1990's, bolstered by the popularity of Afrocentric curricula and the founding, for instance, of one-race schools for black male children whose academic destinies, Afrocentrists proclaimed, were being jeopardized in indifferent, often hostile, white educational settings.

The Results of Busing
Regardless of the many problems involved, there is little doubt that busing helped move the United States toward greater racial inte-

Police officers oversee the loading of school buses in racially tense South Boston on the second day of court-ordered busing in September, 1974. *(AP/Wide World Photos)*

economic trends. In the 1990's, for example, the combined use of voluntary busing and magnet schools in urban areas often staved off the reemergence of all-black schools and limited white flight from the public school system.

As integrated schools became the norm in the nation, and as the Supreme Court became more conservative, the Court relaxed its insistence on continued mandatory busing. In the 1980's and 1990's, busing also lost support in both the executive and legislative branches. The Supreme Court made it easier during the 1990's for school districts to be released from desegregation orders, and it limited schools' responsibilities.

Court Findings in the 1990's
In 1991 the Supreme Court indicated its changing perspective by finding, in the case of Oklahoma City Board of Education v. Dowell, that despite the continued existence of

gration. According to records compiled by the National School Boards Association, forced busing was the most effective approach to integrating schools, especially in the more rural South, where mandatory busing helped make schools more integrated than they were in the North. Moreover, the use of busing challenged school administrators to come up with effective alternatives for combating the problem of resegregated schools, a problem that can occur because of changing housing patterns and

eleven all-black schools, the school district had satisfactorily complied with its desegregation plan and therefore could discontinue mandatory busing. Chief Justice William Rehnquist stated that desegregation decrees were not intended to operate "in perpetuity."

Many observers saw the decision as perhaps marking the beginning of the end of busing. The Court was careful to point out, however, that before a federal busing order could be lifted, schools must first convince courts that they have met the test of good-faith compliance and have erased all traces of past discrimination owing to segregated schooling.

The NAACP appeared to accept the decision, pointing out that this was a fairly high standard and that school systems with long histories of discrimination would be unable to prove easily that a few years of busing had ended discrimination.

Recently retired Supreme Court Justice Thurgood MARSHALL spoke out against the decision, however, arguing that the existence of one-race schools in a previously segregated district created an "inherently unequal" situation regardless of the reason. In view of the harm associated with school segregation, he believed that the offending district should be held accountable for any taint of separateness until it had been removed entirely.

In *Freeman v. Pitts* (1992), the Supreme Court stressed the importance of local control over the education of children in a case concerning DeKalb County, Georgia. Justice Anthony M. Kennedy, writing for the Court majority, said that "racial balance is not to be achieved for its own sake" but is to be achieved only where there has been de jure segregation (intentional segregation based on laws and administrative decisions by public officials that violate the Constitution). School districts were under no obligation to remedy imbalances caused by demographic factors (de facto segregation).

In *Missouri v. Jenkins* in 1995, the Supreme Court addressed a district court's requiring of funding of so-called magnet schools in Kansas City, Missouri. These well-funded schools were envisioned as one way to attract white students back from the suburbs, but the Court found this tactic to be simply an indirect way of attempting the interdistrict solutions it had previously denied. Conservative justice Clarence THOMAS, the sole black justice on the

Court, expressed the view that the lower court's remedial approach rested on an assumption that "anything predominantly black must be inferior."

The Decline of Busing

Several hundred school districts were under court-supervised integration plans in the early 1990's, but by the middle of the decade significant changes were occurring. A federal judge released Denver from court-supervised busing that had been in place for more than twenty years even though the city's schools were more segregated than ever. Norfolk, Virginia, also eliminated mandatory busing for desegregation purposes. In 1996 Minneapolis's first black mayor, Sharon Sayles Belton, spoke in favor of ending busing in the city.

By the end of the 1990's, other large school districts that had discontinued busing for desegregation included Omaha, Seattle, Cleveland, and Boston. The issue was being debated in many other cities. In 1999 the issue came to a head in the Charlotte-Mecklenburg district—the district involved in the historic 1971 Supreme Court case that had upheld mandatory busing. A group of parents brought suit against the district to end busing. A U.S. district court judge ruled in their favor, and the district decided not to appeal the ruling.

—*Tana R. McDonald*
—*Updated by Forest L. Grieves*
See also: Segregation and integration.

Suggested Readings:

Douglas, Davison M., ed. *School Busing: Constitutional and Political Developments*. New York: Garland, 1994.

Graglia, Lino A. *Disaster by Decree: The Supreme Court Decisions on Race and the Schools*. Ithaca, N.Y.: Cornell University Press, 1976.

Lukas, J. Anthony. *Common Ground: A Turbulent Decade in the Lives of Three American Families*. New York: Alfred A. Knopf, 1985.

Lupo, Alan. *Liberty's Chosen Home: The Politics of Violence in Boston.* 2d ed. Boston: Beacon Press, 1988.

McAndrews, Lawrence J. "Missing the Bus: Gerald Ford and School Desegregation." *Presidential Studies Quarterly* 27 (Fall, 1997): 791-804.

Schwartz, Bernard. *Swann's Way: The School Busing Case and the Supreme Court.* New York: Oxford University Press, 1986.

Taylor, Steven J. L. *Desegregation in Boston and Buffalo: The Influence of Local Leaders.* Albany: State University of New York Press, 1998.

Whitman, David, and Dorian Friedman. "Busing's Unheralded Legacy: The Facts Are at Odds with the Unfavorable Image of Forced Desegregation." *U.S. News and World Report* (April 13, 1992): 63-65.

Butcher, Philip (b. September 28, 1918, Washington, D.C.): Author and educator. Butcher began teaching at Morgan State University in 1947, eventually becoming a professor emeritus. He received A.B. (1942) and M.A. (1947) degrees from HOWARD UNIVERSITY and a Ph.D. (1956) from Columbia University. Butcher wrote two books about George Washington Cable and edited a book of William Stanley BRAITHWAITE readings.

Butler, Octavia E. (b. June 22, 1947, Pasadena, California): Author. Butler was the first African American woman to succeed as a writer of science fiction. She began writing at the age of ten. In 1969 and 1970 she attended classes conducted by renowned science fiction writer Harlan Ellison, who enabled her to attend the Clarion Writers Workshop, an intensive, highly respected program for beginning science fiction writers. As a result of this workshop, Butler had her first professionally published story, "Crossover," accepted for publication in the anthology *Clarion* in 1970.

Butler took various low-paying jobs while continuing to write. Her first novel, *Patternmaster*, was published in 1976. This book and four others in her Patternist series deal with racism and sexism in settings ranging from seventeenth-century Africa to alien worlds in the far future. *Kindred* (1979), one of Butler's most acclaimed novels, concerns a modern African American woman who is transported to the early nineteenth century, where she experiences SLAVERY while repeatedly rescuing a white ancestor in order to protect her own existence.

Butler went on to publish three novels in the Xenogenesis series, depicting reproduction between humans and aliens. She won the Hugo Award for her short story "Speech Sounds" in 1984, followed by the Hugo and Nebula awards for "Bloodchild" in 1985. Butler has been highly acclaimed for her novels and short stories dealing with issues of race and gender. In 1995 she won a prestigious grant of $295,000 from the MacArthur Foundation.

—*Rose Secrest*

See also: Literature.

Byas, Don (Carlos Wesley; October 21, 1912, Muskogee, Oklahoma—August 24, 1972, Amsterdam, the Netherlands): JAZZ tenor saxophonist. Byas's early musical education included the study of both violin and clarinet. He worked in various Oklahoma bands before making a name for himself leading a group at LANGSTON UNIVERSITY. After leaving OKLAHOMA in 1933, he established a reputation as a performer with a number of different bands throughout the 1930's, including those of Lionel HAMPTON, Buck Clayton, and Andy Kirk. In 1941 Count BASIE hired Byas to replace the legendary Lester YOUNG in his orchestra.

From 1943 to 1946, Byas played with a number of small groups, including those featuring Dizzy GILLESPIE and Coleman HAWKINS. Byas was unique in that he was influenced by, and performed with, the emerging "modern" players but remained comfortable with his swing and blues roots. This fact led to his being featured in many mid-1940's recordings. He established residence in Europe beginning in 1946, first in France and later in the Netherlands and Denmark. Along with many other African American musicians, he believed that he would have greater success abroad than in the United States. In the 1950's and 1960's, he was often a featured soloist at festivals throughout Europe. Although he took seriously the later musical challenges of Ornette COLEMAN, John COLTRANE, and Sonny Rollins, he did not significantly alter his own style in response to their ideas.

Although known as an accomplished imitator of Coleman Hawkins, Byas was also a crucial transitional figure in the movement from swing to BEBOP during the 1940's. Byas attempted to combine the tone of Hawkins with the musical ideas of Charlie Parker. He influenced many postswing players, including Benny Golson and Lucky Thompson.

C

Cab Calloway Jazz Institute: Organization established at Coppin State College in BALTIMORE, MARYLAND, in 1985. It built a collection centered on memorabilia and artifacts from the JAZZ career of Cab CALLOWAY. Exhibits chart Calloway's career and acknowledge his contributions as a singer, dancer, film performer, actor, composer, and outstanding bandleader.

Although initially founded as a separate institution, the institute became a part of the Peabody/Coppin Jazz Society. This merger not only strengthened the institute but also provided additional financial support for the Cab Calloway Music Academy at Douglass High School. In addition to highlighting Calloway's career, the institute began the Cab Calloway Memorial Birthday Concert, held annually in December in commemoration of Calloway's December 25, 1907, birthday.

In 1941 sculptor Max Kalish chose Cab Calloway as his model to represent popular music in an exhibition of popular arts leaders. *(AP/Wide World Photos)*

Caesar, Shirley (b. October 13, 1939, Durham, North Carolina): GOSPEL singer and evangelist. One of twelve children, Caesar developed a love of gospel from her father, Big Jim Caesar, a popular lead singer in a gospel quartet. His early death during her childhood forced her to support the family by singing gospel music during school breaks, when she was billed as Baby Shirley. After high school, she eventually turned to gospel professionally, joining the Chicago-based Caravans, a popular female gospel group, in 1958.

Early in her career with the Caravans, Caesar discovered a desire to preach. In a move that formed the spiritual framework for her entire career, she incorporated the calling of the ministry into her life, with her preaching existing alongside her music. During touring breaks, Caesar would preach at revivals and compose sermonettes, some of which she recorded. In 1966, having achieved solid acclaim as a Caravan, she resigned to pursue her own musical and spiritual interests.

The next ten years would be Caesar's most active period, as she pushed to elevate the African American gospel industry and advanced her own spirituality through evangelistic work. She attracted young consumers of RHYTHM-AND-BLUES music by updating her church-oriented style. Upbeat and rhythmic, enhanced by large choir backups, her new sound, "rock gospel," propelled gospel music to the forefront of the American music scene. Within the same period, she formed the Shirley Caesar Outreach Ministries, providing aid to needy families in Durham, her resumed home after 1966. She regularly visited hospitals and nursing homes, buying food for the less fortunate, often with her own money.

Caesar's most memorable recordings include "I'll Go" and the Grammy Award-winning "Put Your Hand in the Hand of the Man from Galilee," as well as "Let Jesus Fix It," "Reach Out and Touch," and "Don't Drive Your Mama Away." In 1976 the five-time Grammy winner, recipient of three gold albums, and featured singer on thirty albums became the first gospel singer to sign a million-dollar recording contract. Equally important to her, in 1983, she was appointed copastor of the Mount Calvary Holy Church in Winston-Salem, North Carolina.

See also: Gospel music and spirituals.

Cain, Richard Harvey (April 12, 1825, Greenbrier County, Virginia—January 18, 1887, Washington, D.C.): U.S. congressman from SOUTH CAROLINA during RECONSTRUCTION. Cain was born to free parents who moved from Virginia to Gallipolis, OHIO, in 1831. He attended school there while working on Ohio River steamboats. After moving to Missouri and entering the ministry of the AFRICAN METHODIST EPISCOPAL CHURCH, Cain was chosen to become pastor of Emmanuel Church in Charleston, South Carolina.

Richard Harvey Cain. *(Associated Publishers, Inc.)*

Cain was a delegate to South Carolina's state constitutional convention in 1868 and served in the state senate from 1868 to 1870. In 1872 he was elected in an AT-LARGE ELECTION to the U.S. House of Representatives and served on the House Committee on Agriculture. Deciding not to run for reelection after his at-large seat was eliminated in 1874, Cain returned to the ministry full-time. In 1876 he was elected to Congress as a representative from South Carolina's Second District and served on the House Committee on Private Claims. After losing the Republican nomination in 1878, Cain returned once again to the ministry and served as bishop of the AME Church for the Texas-Louisiana region and for the New Jersey region.

See also: Politics and government.

Cakewalk: DANCE form invented in the 1800's by African Americans. It probably got its name from the prizes, which traditionally were large cakes, won at plantation dance competitions and dance carnivals. The cakewalk was the first African American dance to sweep the United States. In the late 1800's, Bert Williams and George Walker made the cakewalk fashionable and appealing to the upper class. The dance itself was a strutting walk, performed to music similar to marching music.

California: In 1997 California had the second-largest African American population of any state, after NEW YORK. About 2.4 million, or 7.4 percent, of the state's population of 32.3 million were African Americans in 1997, according to U.S. Census estimates. In particular, LOS ANGELES and OAKLAND have significant African American populations.

California was admitted to the union in 1850 as a free (nonslave) state. In the nineteenth century, African Americans migrated to California both before and after the CIVIL

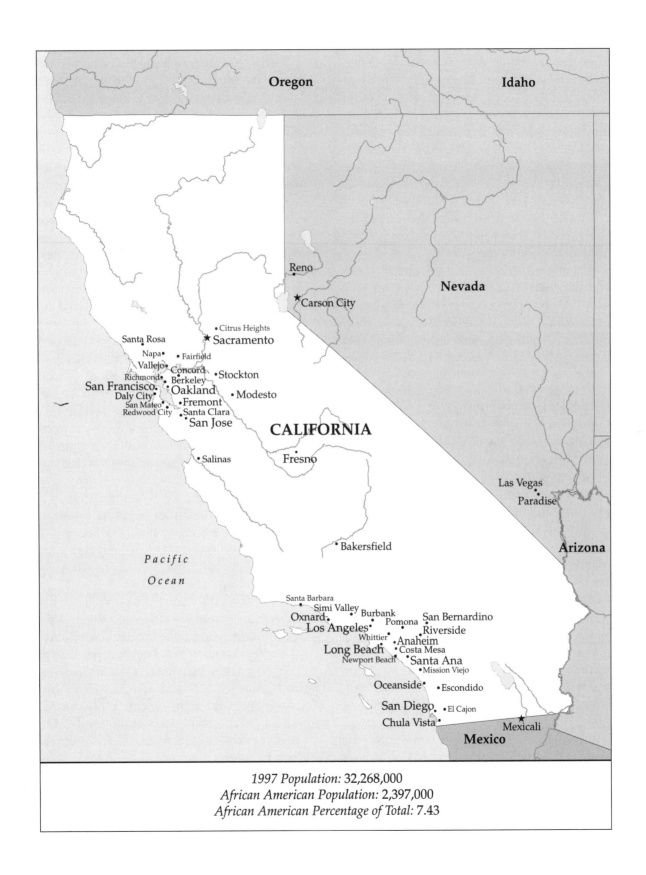

Oregon

Idaho

Nevada

Reno

★ Carson City

• Citrus Heights

Santa Rosa
• ★ Sacramento
Napa•
• Fairfield
Vallejo•
Richmond• •Concord
•Berkeley
San Francisco• •Oakland
Daly City•
San Mateo•
Redwood City• •Santa Clara
•Fremont
•San Jose

• Stockton

• Modesto

CALIFORNIA

• Salinas

• Fresno

Las Vegas
•
Paradise

Arizona

Pacific

Ocean

• Bakersfield

Santa Barbara
•
Simi Valley
Oxnard• •Burbank
Los Angeles •Pomona
•Whittier
•Anaheim
Long Beach• •Costa Mesa
Newport Beach• •Santa Ana
•Mission Viejo

San Bernardino
•Riverside

Oceanside•
• Escondido

San Diego• • El Cajon
Chula Vista•

Mexicali
★
Mexico

1997 Population: 32,268,000
African American Population: 2,397,000
African American Percentage of Total: 7.43

WAR. Some simply sought freedom; others sought opportunities to buy land and livestock, while still others arrived as part of the CALIFORNIA GOLD RUSH. By the early twentieth century, African Americans had founded communities all over California. Originally most African Americans lived in Northern California, but the black population of the San Joaquin Valley, in central California, grew as African Americans migrated there from the South; many found work in the San Joaquin Valley as cotton farmers.

Prominent African Americans in nineteenth century California included Mr. and Mrs. Alex Anderson, owners of the largest livery stable in central California, and George Smith, owner of the King's County Zoological Garden. Mary Ellen Pleasant, a bordello owner, abolitionist, and land baroness, amassed a fortune of more than a million dollars between the 1850's and 1890. Pleasant helped finance John BROWN's 1859 raid on HARPERS FERRY. She also won the right for African Americans to testify in California courts in 1863.

William Leidsdorff moved to San Francisco in 1841 and built the city's first hotel. Eventually he established its first public school. Leidsdorff launched the state's first steamship. He owned waterfront property, the largest house in San Francisco, and 35,000 acres on the south bank of the American River, land that encompassed Folsom.

In 1849 Samuel Smith, an African American, found gold at Negro Bar (later Folsom), and an all-black mining company came into being. Jeremiah B. Sanderson, an educator, opened the first black schools in San Francisco, Oakland, Sacramento, and Stockton and fought for the 1874 California law integrating schools. Muffin Wistar Gibbs helped start the state's first shoe store, established California's first black newspaper (in 1855), and was the first black judge in America's history. James BECKWOURTH found a new route over the Sierras.

Blacks were also active in MUSIC and entertainment. Sam Lucas founded an African American minstrel company. Black Patti, Bert WILLIAMS, and the HYERS SISTERS composed and performed in the California sheet music industry during the 1800's.

By 1919 about sixty thousand African Americans lived in the state. Most lived in small towns and worked in low-paying service jobs. Neighborhoods and schools were not segregated; public accommodations generally were, though not by law. In the cities, many African Americans also worked in service jobs, but some were well-paid homeowners. Los Angeles had black firemen, teachers, and city workers. San Francisco, on the other hand, had only three African Americans on the city payroll in 1940. Partly because Oakland was a major railroad hub, more African Americans originally settled there than in Los Angeles. Initially, blacks worked for the railroads as firemen and brakemen, jobs considered too dirty for whites, but when railroad workers became unionized, blacks were kept out of even those jobs.

In the first half of the twentieth century, a variety of racial attitudes could be found in California; for example, both the NATIONAL ASSOCIATION FOR THE ADVANCEMENT OF COLORED PEOPLE (NAACP) and the KU KLUX KLAN were active in the state.

The first African American politician in the state to hold statewide office was Republican Fred Roberts, who served in the California Assembly representing Los Angeles from 1918 to 1934. Augustus Hawkins, a Democrat, replaced him in 1934 and fought for African American enfranchisement. Hawkes remained in the state legislature until 1960, when he was elected to the U.S. Congress. When he retired, his seat was won by Maxine WATERS. From 1949 to 1966, W. Byron Rumford served in the California legislature. He was responsible for the Rumford Act, which outlawed discrimination in employment by companies doing business with the state. Black legislator (and subsequently mayor of San Francisco) Willie Brown became one of the state's most powerful political figures as speaker of the assembly from 1980 to 1995.

Since the 1960's, African Americans in California have frequently been at the center of controversy. The militant Black Panther Party, for example, was founded in Oakland in 1966. Activist Angela Davis was associated with the Panthers and with the Soledad Brothers. Major riots occurred in the state, including the Watts riots of 1965 and the Los Angeles riots that occurred in 1992 after the acquittal of the white police officers involved in the Rodney King arrest and beating.

Events in California have also figured in headlines involving affirmative action programs. In the Bakke case of 1978, the U.S. Supreme Court held that the affirmative action program of the University of California at Davis's medical school was unconstitutional. Seventeen years later, in 1995, the University of California regents voted to end affirmative action in its admission policies. In 1996 California voters passed Proposition 209, also known as the California Civil Rights Initiative. This heatedly debated proposition banned affirmative action programs in education and state contracts. Numerous civil rights activists protested the University of California's decision and campaigned against the Civil Rights Initiative.

—Rita Smith-Wade-El

See also: King, Rodney, arrest and beating.

California Civil Rights Initiative: Also known as Proposition 209, this state ballot measure was passed November 5, 1996. It amended California's state constitution to prohibit the use of state and local affirmative

---

Text of the California Civil Rights Initiative

(a) The state shall not discriminate against, or grant preferential treatment to, any individual or group on the basis of race, sex, color, ethnicity, or national origin in the operation of public employment, public education, or public contracting.

(b) This section shall apply only to action taken after the section's effective date.

(c) Nothing in this section shall be interpreted as prohibiting bona fide qualifications based on sex which are reasonably necessary to the normal operation of public employment, public education, or public contracting.

(d) Nothing in this section shall be interpreted as invalidating any court order or consent decree which is in force as of the effective date of this section.

(e) Nothing in this section shall be interpreted as prohibiting action which must be taken to establish or maintain eligibility for any federal program, where ineligibility would result in a loss of federal funds to the state.

(f) For the purposes of this section, "state" shall include, but not necessarily be limited to, the state itself, any city, county, city and county, public university system, including the University of California, community college district, school district, special district, or any other political subdivision or governmental instrumentality of or within the state.

(g) The remedies available for violations of this section shall be the same, regardless of the injured party's race, sex, color, ethnicity, or national origin, as are otherwise available for violations of then-existing California antidiscrimination law.

(h) This section shall be self-executing. If any part or parts of this section are found to be in conflict with federal law or the United States Constitution, the section shall be implemented to the maximum extent that federal law and the United States Constitution permit. Any provision held invalid shall be severable from the remaining portions of this section.

ACTION programs in public employment, public education, and public contracting.

The California Civil Rights Initiative (CCRI) was touted by its supporters as a vehicle to eliminate the problem of REVERSE DISCRIMINATION and to approach a "color-blind" society. The initiative's opponents argued that the measure was an attempt to destroy efforts to ensure equal opportunities for women and minorities. Despite broad-based opposition, the CCRI passed by a margin of 54 to 46 percent. A majority of white voters supported the initiative; most minority voters opposed it. Immediately following the election, a coalition of CIVIL RIGHTS groups and other organizations filed suit in a federal district court seeking to block implementation of the CCRI on the grounds that it violated the equal protection clause of the FOURTEENTH AMENDMENT. A federal judge granted a preliminary injunction against the CCRI in December of 1996, but a subsequent appeals court decision overturning the injunction was upheld by the U.S. SUPREME COURT in 1998, and the initiative went into effect.

—*Michael H. Burchett*

California gold rush: Many African Americans participated in the gold rush to the West in the late 1840's and 1850's. By 1850 a census listed more than nine hundred black residents of the state of CALIFORNIA. Most of them probably were free, but the census had no separate tally for slaves. Only two years later, the black population of the state was about two thousand, and by 1860 it exceeded four thousand. African Americans never accounted for more than 1 percent of California's population during the gold rush period.

The hope of mining gold drew tens of thousands of migrant prospectors to California. White residents of California tried to exclude African Americans and to prevent them from exercising their rights. At the state's constitutional convention in Monterey in 1849, the question of whether to exclude black migrants consumed more debate time than did any other issue. A resolution banning black migrants was rejected after some delegates reversed their positions. The issue remained contentious until about 1852, when escalating immigration by Chinese people caused the focus of racial prejudice to be placed on that group.

According to California's constitution, African Americans were not allowed to vote or to serve in the militia. African Americans were denied various rights deliberately as a way of discouraging their migration. The greatest antipathy toward African Americans came from the mining districts. Racial prejudice was widespread, as was a belief among whites that black people had some mysterious power to detect gold and would thus be more successful than the white miners.

Not all black miners were free. Some slaveowners brought their slaves to work in the mines, and others sent their slaves on their own. Some slaves were expected to earn

African American prospectors are among the hopeful patrons depicted in this contemporary engraving of a Sacramento saloon during California's mid-nineteenth-century gold rush. *(Library of Congress)*

money for their masters; others were allowed to work on their own behalf to earn enough to buy their freedom. One slave, Alvin Coffey, had earned about five thousand dollars in the gold mines by 1851. He planned to purchase his freedom, but his owner confiscated his money and sold him. Coffey convinced his new owner that he could make both of them rich, so the new owner allowed him to continue mining. By 1860 Coffey had purchased his own freedom as well as that of his wife and three children.

Black migrants formed their own churches, schools, and newspapers in response to the discrimination and segregation they faced. The Franchise League was founded in San Francisco, California, in August of 1852 to fight for the right of black people to vote in the state and for their right to be witnesses in court actions involving white people. White miners often seized claims made by African Americans or made deliberate efforts to make black miners unwelcome and to drive them away.

By 1860 most of the black settlers in California had occupations other than mining, having been discouraged from mining both by racial prejudice and by the realization (which discouraged whites and blacks alike) that there was not as much gold to be found as the prospectors had hoped. By 1860 one-third of African Americans in California lived in the counties of San Francisco and Sacramento rather than in the mining areas. African Americans began to concentrate in cities, and those remaining in mining areas took up occupations such as barbering and cooking.

Callender, Leroy Nathaniel (b. February 22, 1932, New York, New York): Civil and structural engineer. Callender graduated first in his class from Brooklyn Technical High School in 1950. He worked as a draftsman from 1950 to 1952, then designed buildings for the U.S. Army in Korea. When he returned to the

United States, he earned his bachelor's degree in civil engineering at City College of New York.

Following his graduation, Callender worked as a project engineer from 1959 to 1968. He was an engineer for the first nuclear power plant built in the East, by Consolidated Edison Company. He opened his own firm of consulting engineers in 1969 and a second company specializing in waterworks development in 1975.

See also: Engineers.

Calloway, Cab (December 25, 1907, Rochester, New York—November 18, 1994, Hockessin, Delaware): Musician and entertainer. Cabell "Cab" Calloway III was the second of six children born to Eulalia (Reed) and Cabell Calloway, Jr. His father was an attorney who also worked in the real estate business. Eight-year-old Cab was devastated when his father died, but his mother, his siblings, and his church helped him adjust.

Youth and Early Career

Calloway grew up in BALTIMORE, MARYLAND, to which his family moved when he was six. As a child, he sold newspapers to supplement the family income and became active in the Bethlehem Methodist Episcopal Church, where he performed in the choir and eventually sang solo. After he graduated from Douglass High School, Calloway considered college, for one of his father's last wishes was that Cab become an attorney. Cab, however, wanted to be an entertainer—like his older sister Blanche, whom Cab idolized because she had "made it" in Chicago as the vocalist for a big band. Blanche advised her brother, sent him railroad fare, and secured his first job for him when he reached Chicago; there, Cab began singing in a quartet.

In addition to performing with the quartet, Calloway began to study acting under

Blanche's tutelage and attended Crane College for a time. Soon, he went solo as a singer and played a circuit that included most of the clubs in the South Side of Chicago. He also performed as master of ceremonies for other acts. At a jam session in one of the clubs, he tried the drums and found that he had some natural drumming talent. He spent a year studying the drums while he worked as a relief drummer and stand-in alto saxophonist for several local clubs. In 1925 he landed the job that he said allowed his professional career to "take off": He became drummer for the house orchestra at the Sunset Cafe.

After an apprenticeship at the Sunset Cafe, Calloway organized his own orchestra, becoming its leader and vocalist. Audiences loved Calloway's performances; he had obvious star qualities. He became known for his personality on the stage; master of ceremonies and big band leader seemed to be roles that he was destined to play. His rise was relatively fast, but it was not without setbacks. He received his first recording contract in 1925 and by 1929 was leading a band known as the Alabamians in Chicago. Within six months, he and his new group were booked by the Savoy Ballroom in HARLEM, home of a continuing African American renaissance in New York City. At the Savoy, though, the band was not successful; its engagement was canceled, whereupon the crushed Calloway dissolved the band and landed himself a role in the all-black cast of a Broadway musical comedy, *Connie's Hot Chocolates*. Cab's version of "Ain't Misbehavin'" stole the show.

National Prominence

Equally important, Calloway's performance came to the attention of a Broadway manager, Irving Mills, who began to guide Calloway's career. Soon, he was fronting the Missourians; the band became nationally known with the hit "Tiger Rag—Market Street Stomp." By the time Calloway's professional career had be-

Cab Calloway in 1956. *(AP/Wide World Photos)*

gun to soar, he had met Wenonah Conacher, whom he married in 1928. They later had a daughter, Constance Wenonah.

Calloway's charisma was such that the Missourians decided to change their billing to "Cab Calloway and His Orchestra." Enjoying continued success, the group was noticed by Duke ELLINGTON, who invited them to come to the COTTON CLUB in New York City. At the club, Ellington and Calloway played alternating engagements for a decade. While at the Cotton Club, Calloway developed his style of SCAT SINGING that he and others such as Louis ARMSTRONG would make famous. Further, when Ellington played the club, Calloway toured, eventually appearing in most of the major cities of the United States; internationally, Calloway appeared in England and France.

Band Members

Calloway the bandleader was joined by a host of others in his orchestra, many of whom had special talent: Harry White, soloist on the trombone; William Blue on the clarinet; and

Walter Thomas, a tenor whose singing was a crowd pleaser. Later performers with Calloway's band included Benny CARTER, Chu Berry, Dizzy GILLESPIE, Tyree Glenn, and Jonah Jones. After the Cotton Club closed, Calloway and his band toured the United States and in 1943 accepted a contract for an extended engagement at New York's Coconut Grove. Later, other extended performances came at New Jersey's Meadowbrook and New York's Cafe Zanzibar.

Meanwhile, Calloway became active in many other entertainment media. In 1938 he published his *Hipster's Dictionary*, a pamphlet that eventually sold more than two million copies. It explained the "jive" language used by JAZZ musicians, particularly those in HARLEM. Later, New York University gave him an honorary title—"dean" of American jive.

Eventually, Cab attained such stature that many of his performances were carried live on

---

"Minnie the Moocher"

Cab Calloway developed his signature song, "Minnie the Moocher," in 1931. The song, a gimmicky mixture of "sweet" singing and the "hi-de-ho" shout, became a national rage. Early in Calloway's career, the "St. James Infirmary Blues" had been his recognition song. Soon after he opened at the Cotton Club, however, he and his manager decided that he should try to find a new and unique song. After some research, the two found nothing of interest, so early one morning they sat down to write. By the afternoon, they had composed "Minnie the Moocher." That night, Cab sang it at the club. Initially, his "hi-de-ho" had been an improvisation in another song. One night at the Cotton Club, he was introducing a new song but forgot some of the lyrics; he filled gaps by singing "skeeten, seeten, hi de ho." The audience loved it. Consequently, Calloway worked on his scat singing (singing nonsensical but rhythmic syllables) until his style was uniquely his. "Minnie the Moocher" and its "hi-de-ho" became internationally known.

---

radio. In addition to making guest appearances on regular radio shows, for a time he had his own program, *The Cab Calloway Quizzical*, a satirical look at the question-and-answer programs then popular on radio.

Film and Stage Career

In addition to his singing and bandleading career and his radio and literary efforts, Calloway also acted in various stage plays and movies. He appeared in *The Big Broadcast* in 1932, *International House* a year later, and *The Singing Kid* in 1936. He also appeared in *The Manhattan Merry-Go-Round* in 1938; in 1941's *Road Show*, he was described as being the leader in the field of "musical riot." He appeared with Lena Horne in *Stormy Weather* (1943), his role landing him an award from the Negro Actors Guild. During the war years he also appeared in *Sensations of 1945* (made in 1944).

During WORLD WAR II, Calloway served the U.S. government. Along with such white showmen as Bob Hope, he was among the first to entertain American military men and women; certainly his act could not help but boost morale, especially among African American troops who did not yet have the benefits of first-class citizenship in the country that they were fighting to defend. Calloway also toured with a road show that entertained troops in Canada's Maritime Provinces and Nova Scotia. His radio show became the first radio show broadcast from a U.S. Army camp.

Calloway led his band until 1948, when he disbanded it because of the general decline in popularity of big band music. Until the early 1950's, he frequently regrouped it to play special engagements; he then ceased to lead big bands altogether, but he still occasionally performed solo as a guest entertainer. On such occasions, he usually gave a rousing version of his signature song.

Seven years after the war's end, Cab had a chance to play the role of a lifetime. He appeared in the role of Sportin' Life in the 1952 production of *Porgy and Bess* and later toured the United States and Europe with its road company. Continuing in films, his credits included *St. Louis Blues* (1958), *The Cincinnati Kid* (1965), and *The Blues Brothers* (1980). He also appeared in numerous short films. Additionally, in the 1960's he acted with Pearl BAILEY in many performances of a Broadway version of *Hello, Dolly!* with an all-black cast. Indeed, in addition to stage and screen, Calloway eventually entertained the American public in almost every other medium, including television.

Even into the 1980's and early 1990's, Calloway was a headliner whose pleasing personality continued to charm fans. Moreover, they loved his eccentric side. Calloway, always a lover of clothes, had a performance wardrobe that included forty suits and forty pairs of shoes. When performing live, he made as many as twelve costume changes an evening; he still frequently donned the white zoot suit he had made famous in *Stormy Weather*. Certainly, Cab Calloway earned his place among the greatest of the all-around performers; he is thought of often—any time "scat" is heard, any time "Minnie the Moocher" is sung. In 1985 Coppin State College in Baltimore opened the Cab Calloway Jazz Institute with exhibits that displayed memorabilia and artifacts illustrating Calloway's versatile career as a performer. Calloway died in November of 1994, slightly more than a month before his eighty-seventh birthday.

—*James Smallwood*
—*Updated by Wendy Sacket*

Suggested Readings:

Haskins, Jim. *The Cotton Club.* New York: Random House, 1977.

Johnson, Robert E. "Nation Mourns Passing of Music Great Cab Calloway: 1907-1994." *Jet* (December 12, 1994): 58-63.

Major, Clarence. *The Cotton Club.* Detroit: Broadside Press, 1972.

Noble, Peter. *The Negro in Films.* New York: Arno Press, 1970.

Southern, Eileen. *The Music of Black Americans: A History.* New York: W. W. Norton, 1971.

Tirro, Frank. *Jazz: A History.* New York: W. W. Norton, 1977.

Cambridge, Maryland, riot: RACE RIOT that occurred in Cambridge, Maryland, on July 27, 1967. When the KU KLUX KLAN held demonstrations protesting desegregation, blacks held rallies in Cambridge protesting the Klan and segregation. Activist H. "Rap" BROWN addressed the crowd, urging it to "burn this town down" if the demands of African Americans were not met. Rioting and arson broke out later that night, and Governor Spiro Agnew ordered the National Guard to Cambridge. Brown eventually was arrested for inciting a riot, arson (the arson charges were later dropped), and disturbing the peace.

Campanella, Roy (November 19, 1921, Philadelphia, Pennsylvania—June 26, 1993, Los Angeles, California): Baseball player. Campanella was one of the first African American BASEBALL players to star in the major leagues. While in high school, he began his career in NEGRO LEAGUE BASEBALL, with the Baltimore Elite Giants. He was catching regularly while still a teenager and became one of the top stars of the Negro Leagues at a time when African Americans were excluded from the major leagues.

Campanella eventually attracted the attention of Branch Rickey, president and general manager of the Brooklyn Dodgers, who signed him in 1946. After playing for Brooklyn's minor league teams in Nashua, New Hampshire, Montreal, Canada, and St. Paul, Minnesota, from 1946 through part of the 1948 season, Campanella was called up by the Dodgers. Joining the year after Jackie ROBIN-

The Brooklyn Dodgers' starting catcher until an automobile accident ended his playing career, Roy Campanella set both offensive and defensive records for catchers. *(National Baseball Library, Cooperstown, New York)*

SON broke the color line, Campanella remained the Dodgers' regular catcher through the 1957 season.

Excelling both at bat and behind the plate, Campanella helped his team win five National League pennants and was named the National League's most valuable player in 1951, 1953, and 1955. His best season was 1953, when he hit forty-one home runs and led the league with 142 runs batted in, both major league records for a catcher. In the same year, he set a defensive record for catchers with 807 putouts. In 1951 Campanella batted .325 with thirty-three home runs and 108 runs batted in. His career was marked as well by injury-plagued seasons, in 1952 and 1954, that alternated with his greatest years.

By the end of the 1957 season, Campanella's skills had eroded somewhat, but he looked forward to a resurgence the following year in the Dodgers' new stadium in Los An-geles. An automobile accident, however, ended Campanella's career in January, 1958, leaving him a quadriplegic. Although his major league career was limited to ten years because of the ban against African American players and his career-ending injury, he accumulated 242 home runs and 856 runs batted in while batting .276. Campanella was elected to the Baseball Hall of Fame in 1969.

Campbell, "Aunt" Sally: Gold miner. Campbell mined in Deadwood, SOUTH DAKOTA, in the 1800's. She is believed to have been the first non-Native American woman to enter the Black Hills.

Campbell, Bebe Moore (b. 1950): Novelist and journalist. In various genres, Campbell's work examines issues of concern to African Americans, including the rejection of stereotypes and the need for greater love, faith, and understanding.

In her memoir *Sweet Summer: Growing Up with and Without My Dad* (1989), Campbell describes her childhood as being divided between two very different ways of life. When Bebe was ten months old, her father, George Linwood Peter Moore, was crippled in an automobile accident. After her parents' subsequent divorce, Bebe's father remained at his mother's home in Elizabeth City, North Carolina. Bebe's mother, a social worker, took her daughter back to her family home in Philadelphia. Bebe spent every school year in the extremely proper, female-dominated Philadelphia household and spent every summer in North Carolina with her high-spirited father, his brothers, and his male friends. As a result, she learned that there were quite different ways of looking at the world and, even more important, that a man who no longer lived with his wife could still be a good father to his children.

Eventually, Campbell went on to attend college and graduated summa cum laude from the University of Pittsburgh. She worked as a schoolteacher for five years, first in Atlanta and later in Washington, D.C. Like her mother, she married, had a daughter, and was later divorced. After marrying her second husband, Ellis Gordon, Jr., she acquired a stepson.

As a journalist, Campbell frequently wrote about family relationships. Her first book, *Successful Women, Angry Men: Backlash in the Two-Career Marriage*, was published in 1986. It was *Sweet Summer*, however, that established her as a writer with a distinctive point of view. Instead of perpetuating the negative picture of black men so often found in books by black women, Campbell described a father who, though imperfect, was a positive influence in his daughter's life. Campbell hoped that black men who read her book would be inspired by her father's example.

In her novels, Campbell also sought to avoid stereotypes. Although her 1992 novel *Your Blues Ain't Like Mine* was inspired by the 1955 murder of the young black boy Emmett TILL, Campbell's emphasis was not on racism but on the denial of love from his father that turned the young white character, Floyd Cox, into a heartless killer. Similarly, in *Brothers and Sisters* (1994), Campbell avoided easy answers to complex problems. Her protagonist, a successful African American woman, is torn between two compelling, yet conflicting, loyalties when a white woman friend is sexually harassed by a black male official of the bank where all three characters are employed. Campbell followed that work with the novel *Singing in the Comeback Choir*, published in 1998.

Among Campbell's honors and recognitions are the Body of Work Award from the National Association of Negro Business and Professional Women in 1978, a National Endowment for the Arts grant in 1980, and the NATIONAL ASSOCIATION FOR THE ADVANCE-

MENT OF COLORED PEOPLE (NAACP) Image Award for outstanding literary work. In appearances on National Public Radio's *Morning Edition* and television talk shows as well as in print interviews, Campbell stressed her mission: to help people of all races to understand one another and to accept their responsibilities toward their children.

See also: Autobiographies and memoirs; Print journalism.

Campbell, Bill (b. 1954, Raleigh, North Carolina): Attorney and politician. William "Bill" Campbell attended public school in Raleigh, North Carolina, and graduated as valedictorian of his high school class in 1971. He chose to attend Vanderbilt University in Tennessee, where he completed a challenging triple major in history, sociology, and political science within three years before graduating with honors in 1974. Campbell went on to pursue a law degree at Duke University Law School. After graduating with a J.D. degree in 1977, Campbell moved to ATLANTA, GEORGIA, where he was hired as a junior associate with the law firm of Kilpatrick and Cody. In 1978 he married Sharon Tapscott, a school administrator; the couple went on to have two children. From 1980 to 1981, he worked as a prosecutor for the Justice Department at its regional office in Atlanta.

Campbell launched his political career when he campaigned as a candidate for the Atlanta city council in 1981. After winning election, he served three consecutive terms on the council. In 1993 Campbell served as chair of the city council's Human Resources Committee. That same year, he became a partner in the law firm of Ellis, Funk, Goldberg, Labovitz & Campbell.

After Atlanta mayor Maynard JACKSON announced his decision not to seek reelection, Campbell declared his candidacy for mayor and won Jackson's endorsement. In striving to earn the political support of Atlanta's racially diverse population, Campbell pledged his support for improving the efficiency of city government and eliminating crime. Because he won only 49 percent of the vote in the general election, he was forced into a runoff election against Michael Lomax, his nearest rival. In spite of challenges made to his integrity and character, Campbell maintained the political support of the voters and earned 73 percent of the votes cast in the runoff election.

After taking office in January of 1994, Campbell acted on his campaign commitment to reducing crime by setting up a community policing program with miniature police precincts in the city's housing projects. He also maintained his support for AFFIRMATIVE ACTION by promoting veteran police officer Beverly Harvard to serve as the city's first female chief of police. Among his first challenges was overcoming a $30 million budget deficit. Campbell also worked hard to improve the city's facilities in preparation for hosting the 1996 Summer Olympics. The games themselves brought tragedy when a bomb exploded in Centennial Olympics Park.

Campbell was reelected in an acrimonious 1997 campaign. A year later, the FEDERAL BUREAU OF INVESTIGATION (FBI) released crime figures indicating that Atlanta's violent crime rate had dropped significantly—the total of murders for 1997 was the lowest it had been in ten years. Ten years earlier, Atlanta had been deemed the country's most dangerous city.

In 1999 Campbell reaffirmed his commitment to affirmative action when Atlanta was threatened with a lawsuit against the city's set-aside program by the conservative Southern Legal Foundation.

See also: Mayors.

Canada: Although many Americans are familiar with the role played by Canada as a destination for fugitive slaves before the outbreak of the Civil War, few are aware that the history of blacks in Canada is at least as old as their history in the United States. During a French expedition to found Port Royal in 1605, a black man named Mathieu da Costa served as an interpreter between the French and the Micmac Indians. Historical records show that the first permanent resident of African descent in Canada was a six-year-old slave owned by a privateer named David Kirke, who participated in the British invasion of Quebec in 1628. After peace was declared, Kirke sold the boy to a local French resident, and the young slave was baptized as Olivier Le Jeune. Le Jeune was freed from domestic servitude in 1638 and died in 1654.

Black slaves were uncommon during the French colony's early days, since economic dependence on the fur trade and the availability of Native American workers virtually eliminated demand for black slaves to serve as agricultural laborers or as domestic servants. By the end of the seventeenth century, however, the Company of New France had relinquished its control of the colony to the king and serious colonization efforts began to change the demands for labor. Royal governors and citizens of the colony requested and received permission to import black slaves; by the time British forces conquered Montreal in 1759, more than a thousand black slaves resided in New France, and most were employed as domestic servants. The British guaranteed the continuation of slavery in the colony as part of the conditions of the peace treaty of 1763. They had long sanctioned the use of slaves in the British colony of Nova Scotia, and many wealthy British immigrants brought black slaves with them as servants in preference to employing French Canadians.

Loyalist Influx
The most noticeable early influx of blacks to Canada came during and after the AMERICAN REVOLUTION, when Loyalist families and sol-

diers took up residence. Many wealthy Loyalists fled north to avoid personal harm and to invest their wealth in prime Canadian land. Some thirty thousand Loyalists chose to resettle in Nova Scotia and New Brunswick once the 1783 American peace treaty was signed. Among their prized possessions were black slaves who worked as personal servants and highly skilled craftsmen.

Another source of black residents came as a result of the British military policy that offered to free any slaves who joined their forces. Some of these former slaves worked as carpenters, cooks, blacksmiths, and construction workers, but others fought as soldiers with Loyalist and British regiments. One famous all-black corps was the Black Pioneers. These soldiers were promised free grants of land in Canada in exchange for their service. More than three thousand free blacks entered Nova Scotia from the port of New York as part of the withdrawal of British and Loyalist troops from the United States. Many black Loyalists formed segregated settlements near Shelburne, Halifax, and Annapolis in Nova Scotia; near Saint John and Fredericton in New Brunswick; and near Kingston, Newark, and Prescott in Upper Canada. Others settled at Sandwich and Amherstburg near Detroit.

Seeking Equality Abroad
Fewer than one-third of the black Loyalists were given the land grants promised, and most were settled on small and inferior lots left after white Loyalists received their land grants. In addition, hard economic times after the war led to outbreaks of racial violence. In 1784 a race riot broke out in Shelburne when a mob of unemployed whites attacked blacks and destroyed their houses in retaliation for black laborers' willingness to accept lower wages than those deemed acceptable to white laborers.

Confronted by the betrayal of their promised land grants and the hostility of white resi-

dents, many free blacks sought a leader who would voice their grievances to the British government. Thomas Peters, a former slave from North Carolina who had fought as a sergeant in the Black Pioneers, gathered signatures from more than two hundred black settlers in Nova Scotia and New Brunswick who had never received land or had been unfairly deprived of their grants. He sailed to England with a petition summarizing their grievances. Failing to receive sufficient promises from the government, Peters met with British abolitionists who extended an offer of free land and equality in the newly founded colony of Sierra Leone in West Africa. More than one thousand black Canadians accepted this offer and sailed to the African colony in the winter of 1791-1792.

In 1796 British transport ships brought more than 550 MAROONS, or black guerrilla fighters, from Jamaica to be settled in Halifax, Nova Scotia, where they would pose less of a threat to British colonial interests. Although they agreed to labor on military fortifications in Halifax and were settled in homes vacated by emigrants to Sierra Leone, the Maroons were dissatisfied with conditions in Canada. After lengthy negotiations with the Sierra Leone Company, the British government agreed to allow the Maroons to set sail for Sierra Leone in 1800.

The War of 1812
The next large wave of black immigrants to Canada came as a result of the WAR OF 1812. Once again, the British forces offered freedom to American slaves as a reward for military service. These slaves were encouraged by the knowledge that black Loyalists who had settled in Canada were fighting side by side with white Canadian and British troops in battles fought along the St. Lawrence River and Great Lakes border region between Upper Canada and the United States. Free black Loyalists were eager to join Canadian forces in order to

avoid the prospect of a return to slavery that might well occur if Americans invaded Canada. Among the many black soldiers who distinguished themselves during the conflict was an all-black unit known as Runchey's Company. Between 1812 and 1815, more than two thousand American slaves arrived in Nova Scotia and many others took refuge in Upper Canada. After the war ended, many American slaves continued to seek refuge in Canada.

The Underground Railroad
Although the term originated during the 1830's when steam railroads expanded throughout the United States, the UNDERGROUND RAILROAD had its origins in a network of routes developed to assist slaves to safety as early as the 1780's. While it is inaccurate to claim that the Underground Railroad was a completely secure passage to freedom, the network included routes on which sympathetic whites and free blacks were willing to extend assistance to fugitive slaves—whether in the form of active guidance and transportation or in the form of food, rest, and protection for a few days. Other routes consisted of safe trails where fugitives could travel quickly and easily across the Ohio River and on to Canada. The settlement of St. Catherines in Upper Canada near Niagara Falls was the terminus of Harriet TUBMAN's escape route. Among the fugitives who made the journey to Canada was Josiah HENSON, the alleged model for Uncle Tom in Harriet Beecher Stowe's famous novel, UNCLE TOM'S CABIN.

Legal precedents in Canada were also instrumental in encouraging fugitive slaves to make the arduous journey northward. In 1826 Canada formally refused to return fugitive slaves to the United States. The legislature of Lower Canada declared in 1829 that all slaves entering its borders would be considered free upon arrival. The British Parliament's passage of the Act of 1833 that abolished slavery throughout the British Empire in 1834 conclu-

sively established Canada as a haven for fugitive slaves, and Canadian blacks held annual celebrations on Emancipation Day, sponsoring parades and dinners to mark the anniversary of the passage of the act.

Conditions in the United States continued to worsen. In 1850 Congress passed the FUGITIVE SLAVE LAW requiring extradition of runaway slaves who had sought refuge in the North. In response, American abolitionists stepped up their efforts to transport fugitives to Canada. Black Americans such as Henry Bibb, Martin DELANY, Samuel Ringgold WARD, and Mary Ann SHADD encouraged free blacks to migrate to Canada through speeches given on the American lecture circuit, editorials in Canadian black newspapers such as the *Voice of the Fugitive* and the *Provincial Freeman*, and articles in American abolitionist newspapers. In the month after the act was signed into law, some three thousand blacks crossed the border into Canada, and it has been estimated that by 1860 nearly forty thousand more black immigrants had followed, bringing the total estimated black population to more than fifty thousand. Thriving black communities, such as the Dawn and Elgin settlements near Chatham, Canada West (present-day Ontario), were established in order to encourage refugees from the American South to progress toward self-sufficiency through education and hard work.

The Civil War and Its Aftermath
The outbreak of the CIVIL WAR in the United States did not initially stem the flow of refugees and immigrants, since the Fugitive Slave Law of 1850 remained in effect. Once the Emancipation Proclamation was issued in 1863 and the Lincoln administration began to allow the military recruitment of African Americans for the war effort, many refugees were convinced to take up arms. Military records have allowed scholars to estimate that more than thirty-five thousand Canadians

fought in the Union armies during the Civil War. Many of these Canadian recruits decided to take up permanent residence in the United States after the war ended, and their families often followed them south. By 1871 the black population of Canada had been reduced to approximately twenty thousand.

This reduction in population continued well after the RECONSTRUCTION period. Jobs in cities such as Detroit, Chicago, Boston, and New York encouraged more Canadian blacks to migrate to the United States from the turn of the century through the 1920's. Educational and professional opportunities were often greater in the United States, where segregation had encouraged the development of a wide variety of institutions to serve the black community, than in Canada, where the relative lack of segregation had not eliminated the subtle discrimination that stifled opportunities for advancement and tended to relegate blacks to second-class citizenship. Restrictive Canadian immigration policies created racial quotas that also inhibited the growth of Canada's black population.

Conditions in the Twentieth Century

Black Canadians shared many of the same experiences as their counterparts in the United States during the early twentieth century. The KU KLUX KLAN spread its reign of terror into Canada during the 1920's and 1930's and thrived well into the 1950's. Black military units distinguished themselves during WORLD WAR I and WORLD WAR II despite segregation and harassment from white soldiers abroad and white mobs at home. Some Canadian cities prohibited blacks from using public facilities, such as parks, swimming pools, and theaters, and other communities forced blacks to maintain segregated cemeteries. Black workers were prohibited from joining white unions.

Gradually, black communities in Canada fought against these forms of discrimination.

A. Philip RANDOLPH, head of the BROTHERHOOD OF SLEEPING CAR PORTERS, extended his efforts during the 1940's to unionize black porters and railway attendants working on Canadian railroads. Randolph also helped organize the Alberta branch of the ASSOCIATION FOR THE ADVANCEMENT OF COLORED PEOPLES (AACP). Other chapters of the AACP were founded throughout the Canadian provinces. In 1969 these AACP chapters and other black organizations formed the National Black Coalition to oversee all civil rights activities on behalf of black Canadians. Although discriminatory laws have been eliminated, black Canadians have fewer legal mechanisms and government programs designed to alleviate the persistent effects of racial discrimination than those available to blacks in the United States.

Immigrant Influx

The population of African Canadians grew in the early 1960's because of an influx of black African and West Indian immigrants. Canada's elimination of quotas through immigration reforms in 1962 and 1966, combined with new restrictions in the United States and Great Britain, created encouraging conditions for

West Indian Canadians singing at a Seventh-day Adventist gathering in Toronto. *(Dick Hemingway)*

West Indians and Africans. By the late 1970's, researchers estimated that Canadians of West Indian descent composed nearly 80 percent of the black Canadian population. These new black Canadians were accustomed to societies in which the black majority population had significant political power, and they were more willing to use the Canadian legal system to fight against the effects of racism and discrimination. The immigrants also infused black Canadian society with their rich cultural heritage in music, sports, food, and the arts.

—*Ellyn West*

See also: Immigration and ethnic origins of African Canadians.

Suggested Readings:

Alexander, Ken, and Avis Glaze. *Towards Freedom: The African-Canadian Experience.* Toronto: Umbrella Press, 1996.

Brathwaite, Keren S., and Carle E. James. *Educating African Canadians.* Toronto: James Lorimer, 1996.

Clarke, Austin. *Public Enemies: Police Violence and Black Youth.* Toronto: HarperCollins, 1992.

Elgersman, Maureen G. *Unyielding Spirits: Black Women and Slavery in Early Canada and Jamaica.* New York: Garland, 1999.

Foster, Cecil. *A Place Called Heaven: The Meaning of Being Black in Canada.* Toronto: HarperCollins, 1996.

Hill, Daniel G. *The Freedom-Seekers: Blacks in Early Canada.* Agincourt, Canada: The Book Society of Canada, 1981.

Identity: The Black Experience in Canada. Toronto, Canada: Gage Educational Publishing, 1979.

Killiam, Crawford. *Go Do Some Great Thing: The Black Pioneers of British Columbia.* Vancouver, Canada: Douglas & McIntyre, 1978.

Quamina, Odida T. *All Things Considered: Can We Live Together.* Toronto: Exile Editions, 1996.

Ruggles, Clifton, and Olivia Rovinescu. *Outsider Blues: A Voice from the Shadows.* Halifax, N.S.: Fernwood, 1996.

Walker, James W. St. G. *The Black Loyalists: The Search for a Promised Land in Nova Scotia and Sierra Leone, 1783-1870.* New York: Africana, 1973.

Winks, Robin W. *The Blacks in Canada: A History.* 2d ed. Montreal; Kingston: McGill-Queen's University Press, 1997.

Canady, Hortense (b. August 18, 1927, Chicago, Illinois): Educational administrator. Best known as a former president of Delta Sigma Theta sorority, Canady was born to a pharmacist father and a mother employed as a social worker. She grew up in the rigidly segregated environment of Jackson, TENNESSEE, where the family moved after her father's death. Although Jackson's schools, buses, and theaters still were segregated in her youth, Canady took advantage of cultural and educational programs at Lane College in the city's black community. She developed her earliest business and organizational skills when her mother entrusted her with knowledge about the family's property, insurance, bank accounts, and other assets that would finance Canady's college education.

Canady graduated from FISK UNIVERSITY in Nashville in 1947 and was director of a community nursery school from 1947 to 1948. In the ensuing years, she served on the Education Committee of the NATIONAL ASSOCIATION FOR THE ADVANCEMENT OF COLORED PEOPLE (NAACP) and on the board of directors of the UNITED NEGRO COLLEGE FUND. In 1968 she was awarded the Sojourner Truth Award by the Negro Business and Professional Women's Association. Canady was named to the Michigan State Women's Commission in 1969 and was elected to the Board of Education in Lansing the same year. She helped develop a desegregation plan for Lansing's public schools in the 1970's.

After receiving her master's degree from Michigan State University in 1977, Canady served two terms as the president of Delta Sigma Theta, an African American women's sorority stressing public service, leadership, and scholarship. Under her guidance from 1983 to 1988, the organization focused on the issues of illiteracy, international human rights, single parenting, drug abuse, and ACQUIRED IMMUNODEFICIENCY SYNDROME (AIDS).

Canady convened Delta Sigma Theta conferences throughout the world, promoting the causes of African American women and earning a reputation for professionalism under pressure. Nationally, she promoted Delta Sigma Theta's academic achievement programs and urged members of the African American middle class to serve as role models and surrogate families to youth in the black community. The achievements of Delta Sigma Theta sorority under her administration show that programs pooling women's ideas, resources, and talents can achieve positive results.

See also: College fraternities and sororities; Fraternal societies.

Cancer: One of the most fear-provoking diseases of the twentieth century, cancer is a disorder in which normal cells become abnormal and multiply rapidly. These cells eventually may spread to different organs of the body (metastasize) and prevent them from functioning. Although cancer strikes persons of all ages, older persons are more at risk for most types of cancer. Since the 1950's, the death rate from cancer has increased among all segments of the population, with an alarming increase in cancer deaths among African Americans.

Early Cancer Data
Cancer statistics from the nineteenth century are fragmentary, and their reliability is open to argument. Records of vital statistics and the writings of physicians and surgeons about cancer prior to the twentieth century suggest some disagreement regarding the incidence of cancer among African Americans. Physicians generally agreed that women were more likely to develop the disease than were men and that the genital system was the most common site for cancer among women. Many surgeons and physicians believed that black people were physiologically different from whites and that race was a factor affecting the incidence of cancer and other disorders.

Alexander J. C. Skene, in his *Treatise on the Diseases of Women* (1888), wrote that certain individuals might be at greater risk for cancer than others, but he doubted whether race was a significant factor in making one more or less susceptible to cancer. Writing in 1894, Edward P. Ballock, a member of the HOWARD UNIVERSITY medical faculty, observed that African Americans exhibited a remarkable immunity from malignant diseases. Samuel Jean Pozzi, in his *Treatise on Gynæcology, Medical and Surgical* (1891-1892), stated that cancer occurred more frequently in women and that race, heredity, age, and environment were other factors affecting the incidence of the disease. He believed that race was an important factor and noted that information from the United States indicated that uterine cancer was extremely rare among blacks. Frederick L. Hoffman, cancer researcher and statistician for the Prudential Insurance Company of America, rejected the notion that black women were immune from uterine cancer and offered statistical data in support.

Although statistics are incomplete or even totally lacking in some areas, there are a few examples of statistics that provide additional information on the incidence of cancer in the nineteenth century. WASHINGTON, D.C., for example, had a large black population that increased significantly during the CIVIL WAR era. Moreover, the district had a significant black medical community and a teaching hospital that primarily served African Americans. From 1879 to 1899, the reports of the health officer listed deaths as a result of cancer under the heading of "constitutional diseases," or disorders affecting the whole body. In 1879, 89 cancer deaths were reported, 27 among blacks, 24 of whom were women. The health officer commented on uterine cancer, noting that 11 of the 20 women who died of that disease were black. The following year, cancer accounted for 71 deaths, 21 of them African Americans. Uterine cancer accounted for 68 percent of the cancer mortality among white women and 31 percent among blacks.

In 1891 the number of cancer deaths reported was 100, uterine cancer having claimed the lives of 22 white and 5 black people. From 1883 through 1888, cancer deaths in Washington, D.C., increased, and there was a disproportionate number of white decedents. In the 1887 annual report, the health officer noted that 1,066 persons had died of cancer and that a remarkable difference in racial susceptibility was apparent, since whites accounted for 707 of the deaths.

Records of admissions and deaths at historically black Freedmen's Hospital (later Howard University) indicate that between 1886 and 1899, 111 black people diagnosed with cancer received treatment in the hospital and at its dispensary. During the same period, 37 African Americans admitted to Freedmen's Hospital died from cancer, some diagnosed with uterine cancer.

Cancer as a Health Threat

Vital statistics and hospital records indicate that at least in Washington, D.C., cancer did account for a degree of morbidity and mortality in the black community. However, the disease was not considered a serious health threat to black Americans at that time. In 1896 and 1897, historically black ATLANTA UNIVERSITY organized conferences dealing with the survival of African Americans. Both confer-

ences examined the causes of excessive black mortality across the United States, especially among urban residents. Neither the physicians nor the reformers present at the conferences mentioned cancer as a cause for concern; they did identify TUBERCULOSIS as a major threat to blacks. Similarly, participants in race conferences held at Hampton Institute in Virginia in 1898 and 1899 looked at widespread morbidity and mortality among blacks and indicated that tuberculosis and INFANT MORTALITY were the primary health concerns at that time. They also failed to mention cancer.

During the early decades of the twentieth century, black mortality rates continued to be higher than those for whites, primarily because of tuberculosis. An upward trend in can-

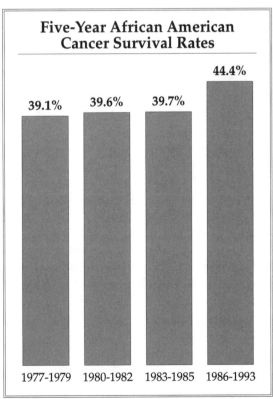

Five-Year African American Cancer Survival Rates

1977-1979	1980-1982	1983-1985	1986-1993
39.1%	39.6%	39.7%	44.4%

Source: U.S. National Institutes of Health, National Cancer Institute.

Note: Average rate for all types of cancer combined. Five-year survival rate represents the likelihood that a person will not die from causes directly related to his or her cancer within 5 years.

cer mortality rates, however, was becoming evident for all Americans. Statistics from the South, home to the majority of African Americans at that time, indicate that in eight major cities of the region, the cancer death rate (1911-1915) was 93.8 per 100,000 of the white population and 72.3 per 100,000 for blacks. Charleston, South Carolina, had the lowest number of black deaths from the disease, and New Orleans had the highest. In fact, African Americans in New Orleans had a higher cancer death rate than did whites. No reason was known for the increased incidence of cancer morbidity and mortality among blacks except that it was part of a national or even worldwide trend.

Charles S. Johnson's Findings

During the 1920's, black sociologist Charles S. JOHNSON of FISK UNIVERSITY in Nashville, Tennessee, noted in his studies of black mortality that cancer was not a major cause of death among blacks. Generally, the disease occurred less frequently among blacks than among whites. However, more black than white women between the ages of fifteen and forty-five died of cancer. Black women also appeared to be more at risk for cancer in the genital area than did whites. Black men, on the other hand, were found to have a lower cancer mortality rate than whites at all ages.

Johnson later assisted with a 1928 report on black mortality in the state of Tennessee. This study indicated that blacks generally died as a result of cancer at an earlier age than did

whites. Blacks appeared more at risk for cancer in the genital site but were less at risk for cancer of the skin and mouth. Finally, in every category except for cancer of the reproductive organs, there were fewer black deaths. This study suggested that syphilitic or gonococcic infections plus poor obstetrical treatment might account for the higher incidence of black cancer morbidity and mortality in this site. Significantly, the Tennessee study suggested that improper diagnosis and underreporting might distort findings with regard to the disorder among African Americans.

Newer Patterns of Cancer Mortality

Until the mid-1950's, cancer mortality figures reflected a lower death rate for blacks of both sexes (except for the reproductive site in women). By the middle of the 1950's, a different pattern had emerged: The highest rate of cancer deaths was occurring among black men. Many experts, including researchers at Howard University's cancer center who gathered extensive data on blacks, believed that better diagnosis and reporting alone did not account for the increased incidence of cancer. Rather, they believed, these figures represented a true increase in cancer deaths.

During the post-World War II era, a significant migration from the rural South to the urban North occurred among African Americans. One important result of this population shift was increased exposure to environmental factors known to be associated with cancer. Black men have been placed at greater risk for

Cancer Deaths per 100,000 people, 1995						
			Age			
Race and Sex	1-4	5-14	15-24	25-44	45-64	65+
Black males	3.2	3.3	5.4	35.4	468.2	1,933.5
White males	3.7	3.1	5.9	23.2	275.7	1,437.8
Black females	3.4	2.5	4.2	39.6	296.8	981.0
White females	2.9	2.5	3.9	27.0	231.0	911.9

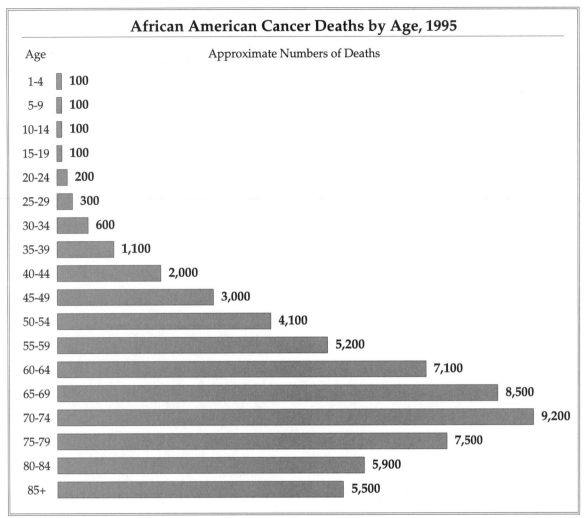

African American Cancer Deaths by Age, 1995

Age	Approximate Numbers of Deaths
1-4	100
5-9	100
10-14	100
15-19	100
20-24	200
25-29	300
30-34	600
35-39	1,100
40-44	2,000
45-49	3,000
50-54	4,100
55-59	5,200
60-64	7,100
65-69	8,500
70-74	9,200
75-79	7,500
80-84	5,900
85+	5,500

Source: U.S. National Center for Health Statistics.

the disease as a result of changes in employment than have black women.

This trend continued into the 1960's and 1970's. Researchers at Howard University studied cancer statistics in the ten Standard Metropolitan Statistical Areas (SMSAs) with the largest black populations in the United States. They found that African Americans in Washington, D.C., had the highest age-adjusted cancer death rate. BALTIMORE, MARYLAND, had the second-highest rate. Cancer mortality rates in all the SMSAs were higher than the national average for Americans. Moreover, death rates for black men were ris-

ing more rapidly than were those for white men. The rates for black women had remained constant, while those for white women had declined. In 1975 for example, male African American cancer mortality rates were 27 percent higher than those for whites. Rates for black women were 11 percent higher than those for white women.

In 1991 cancer was cited as the second leading cause of death among black Americans. The major cancer sites in black men have been identified as the lung, prostate, colon and rectum, esophagus, and pancreas. For women, the major sites are the breast, lung, colon and rectum, uterus, and pancreas. Higher cancer deaths among both black men and women as compared with their white counterparts have been attributed to several factors, including later diagnosis and lower survival rates. Evidence suggests that the causes of increased cancer morbidity and mortality among African Americans are related more to POVERTY, lower educational levels, and lesser access to medical care than to any inherent racial characteristics or peculiarities.

—*Betty L. Plummer*

See also: Health; Women's health.

Suggested Readings:

Cancer Facts and Figures for Minority Americans. New York: American Cancer Society, 1983.

"Do Blacks Need to Protect Themselves from the Sun?" *Jet* (June 2, 1997): 14-17.

U.S. Department of Human Services, Task Force on Black and Minority Health. *Report on the Secretary's Task Force on Black and Minority Health.* 8 vols. Washington, D.C.: U.S. Government Printing Office, 1990.

U.S. House of Representatives, Committee on Energy and Commerce, Subcommittee on Health and the Environment. *Health Problems Confronting Blacks and Other Minorities: A Legislative Forum of the National Medical Association.* Washington, D.C.: U.S. Government Printing Office, 1985.

U.S. Public Health Service. *Healthy People 2000: National Health Promotion and Disease Prevention Objectives.* Washington, D.C.: U.S. Government Printing Office, 1990.

White, Jack. *Cancer in Non-White Americans.* Chicago: Year Book Medical Publications, 1980.

Wingo, Phyllis A., et al. "Cancer Statistics for African Americans, 1996." *Ca* 46 (March/April, 1996): 113-125.

Canon formation: The development of a canon (a group of works recognized as having particular merit) in the African American literary tradition began during the early history of black people in colonial America. African slaves were separated forcibly from their cultures, and their African languages were suppressed. Slaves therefore began to use English not only to communicate routine matters but also to express a wide array of feelings and remembrances in stories and songs recognized today as authentic American FOLKLORE. The folklore produced by plantation slaves was first preserved in the oral tradition and later became a rich source of material, both substantive and structural, for literary works.

Eighteenth and Nineteenth Centuries

It was against formidable odds that some slaves and former slaves became literate, since the education of black people was against the law in many areas of the South and only limited opportunities for schooling were available to them in the North. This was true even after 1830, when most northern blacks had been freed. Nevertheless, some blacks beat the odds in order to tell their stories, a fact attested to by a large body of SLAVE NARRATIVES, autobiographical accounts of the trials and sufferings of bondage. These writings show the extreme perseverance and determination of antebellum blacks to prove their humanity and intelligence to a mainstream white society that largely refused to acknowledge either. The slave narrative laid the foundation for the African American literary canon.

The true beginning of the African American canon is often set at 1746, the year when the first poem written by a young slave woman, Lucy TERRY, was written down by a second party. The verse was called "Bars Flight," and it gave an account of an Indian raid on a white settlement. In 1760 Jupiter Hammon became the first black person in America to have a poem published. It was an eighty-eight-line religious poem printed as a broadside, entitled "An Evening Thought:

Salvation by Christ, with Penitential Cries." Also in 1760, Briton Hammon (no relation to Jupiter) published the earliest African American prose of record, *A Narrative of the Uncommon Suffering and Surprising Deliverance of Briton Hammon, a Negro Man.* In 1773 Phillis WHEATLEY, a young slave woman living in Boston, Massachusetts, had a 124-page volume of verse printed in London.

After the CIVIL WAR, African Americans became better equipped, through increased educational opportunities, to develop their literary talents. The RECONSTRUCTION period and the following decades produced such writers as Charles W. CHESNUTT, Frances E. W. HARPER, Ida B. WELLS, and Paul Laurence DUNBAR.

Twentieth Century

The early 1900's were a period of artistic burgeoning in the black community, with the center of activity being HARLEM, New York. This period of heightened creativity has been called the HARLEM RENAISSANCE. Literary luminaries such as W. E. B. Du BOIS, James Weldon JOHNSON, Countée CULLEN, Claude McKay, and Langston HUGHES dominated the movement, although two black female novelists of note, Nella LARSEN and Jessie Redmon FAUSET, were acclaimed critically for their works. Zora Neale HURSTON, recognized as the first modern black woman writer, and Richard WRIGHT, who has been called the dean of black novelists, wrote during the waning days of the Harlem Renaissance.

Some black writers began to find wider acceptance in literary circles, although the marketplace remained less hospitable to them than to their white counterparts. Since 1928, when Claude McKay's *Home to Harlem* (1928) became the first book written by a black American to be placed on a national best-seller list, black writers have produced works that have, at one time or another, won most of the major annual literary prizes offered in the United States. It is no longer rare to see works of merit written by black writers achieving best-seller status.

With the greater inclusion of black writers in mainstream literary circles since the 1960's, it became debatable whether African American LITERATURE still should be viewed as having a separate canon. Many scholars pointed to the fact that black writers were being placed in anthologies and school texts alongside white writers. They argued that the African American experience is an American experience comparable to those of any other racial or ethnic group. Other scholars, however, maintained that because of years of neglect of black writers, a focus on African American literature as a field unto itself should be continued, at least until the reclamation of underrated and lesser-known black writers is more complete.

See also: Autobiographies and memoirs.

Cape Verde Islanders: The Cape Verde Islands (the main islands are São Tiago, Santo Antão, São Vicente, Fogo, São Nicolau, Boa Vista, Sal, Maio, Brava, and Santa Luzia) are located 385 miles off the west coast of Africa. They were uninhabited when they were discovered by the Portuguese in 1456. Toward the end of the sixteenth century, the islands were settled by the Portuguese. Slaves from Portuguese Guinea, a Portuguese colony in Africa, were brought to the islands to work the land. A cotton-based slave economy developed, and the islands' slave population grew. There was also a substantial influx of Genoese and Spanish immigrants. Some slaves were brought to the islands with the intent of shipping them across the Atlantic. Some were left on the islands when the SLAVE TRADE was abolished in the nineteenth century. Their descendants still populate the islands.

The Republic of Cape Verde became independent of Portugal on July 5, 1975. The islands have seen steady emigration to Brazil, Africa, Portugal, and the United States. In spite of emigration, the islands' population has increased steadily, reaching almost 450,000 by 1999. More than 60 percent of the islands' inhabitants are of mixed African and European descent.

Capital Press Club: Organization of African American communications professionals. The Capital Press Club was founded in 1944 with headquarters in WASHINGTON, D.C. Its primary goal was to expand opportunities for minorities within the communications industry. It established scholarships for minority journalism students and sponsored employment seminars; it also began a tradition of acting as a forum for the exchange of new concepts in the communications industry.

See also: Black press; Print journalism.

Capital punishment: In 1791 the Fifth Amendment to the U.S. Constitution authorized the federal government to put convicted criminals to death, as long as the conviction and sentencing resulted from "due process of law." The FOURTEENTH AMENDMENT extended this authorization to the states in 1868. Therefore, both state and federal government may employ capital punishment—the death

penalty. Its use or nonuse, while authorized by the Constitution, is determined by elected officials of each state. Not all states have the death penalty. Several states followed the lead of Michigan, which became the first state to abolish capital punishment in 1846.

Although controversy surrounded executions since they were first authorized, it became more intense in the 1960's, when public support for capital punishment declined. Some opponents argued that the Eighth Amendment, which forbids "cruel and unusual punishment," makes the death penalty unconstitutional. However, the usual view of legal scholars has been that executions are neither cruel nor unusual if they are carried out in a relatively quick and painless manner.

Complaints were also voiced about the discriminatory application of the death sentence. Prosecutors and juries were relatively free to determine which convicted criminals deserved to die. This situation resulted in discrepancies in capital sentencing based on race, gender, social class, and age. Disproportionately larger numbers of blacks and other minorities were on death rows compared with whites who had committed the same crimes. Death sentences were sometimes imposed on blacks for crimes such as rape, armed robbery, and nighttime burglaries of occupied dwellings.

These factors were duly noted by the U.S. SUPREME COURT in the 1972 case *Furman v.*

Executions for Murder and Rape, 1930-1967

Period	Executed for Murder			Executed for Rape		
	Total*	White	Black	Total*	White	Black
	3,591	1,820	1,734	455	48	405
1930 to 1939	1,514	803	687	125	10	115
1940 to 1949	1,064	458	595	200	19	179
1950 to 1959	601	316	280	102	13	89
1960 to 1967	155	87	68	28	6	22

Source: U.S. Law Enforcement Assistance Administration.
*Includes races other than white and black.

Executions, 1984-1994			
Year	Total*	White	Black
1984	21	13	8
1985	18	11	7
1986	18	11	7
1987	25	13	12
1988	11	6	5
1989	16	8	8
1990	23	16	7
1991	14	7	7
1992	31	19	11
1993	38	23	14
1994	31	20	11

Source: U.S. Bureau of Justice Statistics.
*Includes races other than black and white.

Georgia, in which the Court ruled that the death penalty as it was then administered constituted cruel and unusual punishment and violated the Eighth Amendment because of its racially discriminatory application. Also noted was the capricious and arbitrary manner in which it was imposed and the fact that possible mitigating circumstances were not always considered. The Court nullified the death penalty statutes in all forty states that provided for capital punishment at that time. Executions themselves were not declared unconstitutional, but limitations were placed on their capricious application. The death penalty was also declared inappropriate punishment for some crimes, such as rape, because it was disproportionate to the crime.

Then, in 1976, the Supreme Court approved the newly written death-penalty statutes of Georgia, Florida, and Texas. They were quickly copied by other states. Questions of RACIAL DISCRIMINATION in the application of the death penalty continued. Earlier studies showed that blacks were not only more likely to be executed than whites but also executed for less serious crimes, at younger ages, and more often without appeals.

Subsequent studies indicated that the race of the victim is an important factor in the de-termination of who receives the death penalty. The Supreme Court heard data presented in the 1987 case *McCleskey v. Kemp* indicating that murderers of whites are four times more likely to be sentenced to death than are murderers of blacks. In this case the Court ruled that although there is some risk of jury prejudice, apparent disparities in sentencing are an inevitable part of the American criminal justice system.

—*Philip E. Lampe*
See also: Crime and the criminal justice system.

Suggested Readings:

Bedau, Hugo Adam, ed. *The Death Penalty in America.* New York: Oxford University Press, 1997.
Jackson, Jesse. *Legal Lynching.* New York: Marlowe, 1996.

Cardozo, Francis Louis (February 1, 1837, Charleston, South Carolina—July 22, 1903, Washington, D.C.): RECONSTRUCTION statesman. Born free, Cardozo apprenticed as a car-

Francis Louis Cardozo. *(Library of Congress)*

penter. He later studied at the University of Glasgow in Scotland and at seminaries in London and Edinburgh. During the Reconstruction era (1865-1877), he served as a member of the SOUTH CAROLINA constitutional convention and as secretary of state for South Carolina. His 1868 appointment as secretary of state marked the first time that an African American had been appointed to a cabinet post at the state level. He later served as state treasurer. He was one of the best-educated African Americans of the period. Cardozo was noted for his integrity during a time of widespread political corruption.

See also: Politics and government.

Carey, Archibald J., Jr. (b. February 29, 1908, Chicago, Illinois): Chicago-area politician and political appointee. Carey was educated at Lewis Institute and received his bachelor of science degree in 1929. He received his J.D. law degree from Kent College in 1935. Carey served as pastor of the Woodlawn AFRICAN METHODIST EPISCOPAL CHURCH in CHICAGO, ILLINOIS, from 1930 to 1949 and was an attorney in private practice from 1939 to 1966. He was elected as alderman from Chicago's Third Ward for two terms, from 1947 to 1955. In recognition of Carey's political support, President Dwight D. Eisenhower appointed him as alternate delegate to the United Nations from 1953 to 1956 and later as vice chairman of the President's Committee on Governmental Employment Policy. Carey became judge of the Cook County Circuit Court in 1977 and was appointed to serve as judge on ILLINOIS's supreme court in 1989.

See also: Judges; Politics and government.

Carey, Lott (also spelled Cary; 1780?, Charles City County, Virginia—November 10, 1828, Cape Mesurado, Liberia): Early African American colonist. Carey was born into SLAV-ERY but purchased his freedom in 1813. He became an ordained BAPTIST minister. Carey is especially significant for his involvement in independent black missionary efforts in AFRICA. In 1815 he was a founding member of the Richmond (Virginia) Baptist Missionary Society, and he carried his commitment to autonomous black organizing (religious and otherwise) to Africa in 1821. Carey worked under the auspices of the controversial AMERICAN COLONIZATION SOCIETY, but once in Africa he led efforts to create strong African American leadership in the new colony. Despite poor financial backing from white Baptist churches in the United States, Carey was able to found and build several congregations in Africa, including the first Baptist church in LIBERIA. He was also involved in the political life of emerging Liberia, serving as both vice governor and acting governor of the colony.

As a leader of the COLONIZATION MOVEMENT, Carey had to deal with the dubious motivations of some white colonization advocates who supported colonization as a means of eliminating black activists and, indeed, whole black communities from the American landscape. Carey had long and ongoing conflicts with white leaders of the American Colonization Society as well as white members of the colony of Liberia. He tried unsuccessfully to establish a black leadership of the colony. Ironically, given the nature of African American history, he also had to confront the resistance of African peoples themselves, who fought against the early American-led settlements on their shores.

Carey arrived in Africa motivated by evangelical Christianity and a nationalist political commitment to building an African American colony. These motivations led to complications as the colonists encountered the indigenous African population. After working to secure the colony and build a strong missionary presence, Carey was killed during an armed confrontation with Africans.

Carey, Mariah (b. March 27, 1970, New York, N.Y.): Singer. The most commercially successful female American pop singer of the 1990's, Mariah Carey enjoyed phenomenal record sales and a string of hits that topped those of such superstars as Madonna and Whitney HOUSTON during the decade.

When Carey was a child, her strongest influence was her Irish mother, Patricia, a professional opera singer. Patricia's marriage to Alfred Carey—of Hispanic and African descent—ended soon after Mariah's birth. Consequently, Carey grew up in a single-parent, financially strapped family. She had only limited contact with her father. Her mother gave her singing lessons and encouraged her to develop her musical talent.

Upon graduating from high school in 1987, Carey settled in Manhattan and pursued a singing career. Her break came in November of 1988 when Tommy Mottola, president of Columbia Records, heard a demo tape of her singing. He signed her to a contract and care-

Mariah Carey performing at 1997 Nobel Peace Prize concert in Oslo, Norway. *(AP/Wide World Photos)*

fully nurtured her early career, beginning with the album *Mariah Carey* in 1990. The two also became romantically involved. Carey and Mottola were married in 1993; they divorced in 1998.

Carey's songs contain elements of several musical genres. Her early tunes were often gospel-flavored ballads and upbeat dance numbers. Toward the end of the 1990's, however, she moved more toward RHYTHM AND BLUES and HIP-HOP music. She also developed an interest in acting, appearing in the film *The Bachelor* in 1999. Throughout the decade, Carey played a direct role in her career development; she cowrote most of her songs and arranged and produced several of them.

—*Roger D. Hardaway*

See also: Music.

Carmichael, Stokely (Kwame Toure; June 29, 1941, Port of Spain, Trinidad—November 15, 1998, Conakry, Guinea): Political activist who came to prominence as a militant student activist during the CIVIL RIGHTS MOVEMENT. In the late 1960's he was a leading figure of the BLACK POWER MOVEMENT; subsequently, Carmichael emerged as a spokesman for PAN-AFRICANISM.

Education

Stokely Carmichael spent his early childhood in TRINIDAD, but when he was ten, his family of eight immigrated to NEW YORK CITY in search of better economic conditions. They lived in a one-bedroom apartment in the Bronx, surrounded by crime-infested streets. Carmichael later attended the prestigious Bronx High School of Science. He graduated in 1960 and entered HOWARD UNIVERSITY in Washington, D.C., where he majored in philosophy. At the time he entered college, he had already been greatly influenced by the fervor of BLACK NATIONALISM in New York City and was politically astute. At Howard, he first began to discuss the ideals of pan-Africanism. Carmichael graduated from Howard in 1964 with honors.

Early Civil Rights Work

While a student at Howard, Carmichael became active in the Civil Rights movement. He first participated in a multiracial protest demonstration against the House Committee on Un-American Activities. Afterward, he joined and worked actively with the Nonviolent Action Group (NAG), an affiliate organization of the STUDENT NONVIOLENT COORDINATING COMMITTEE (SNCC), and later participated in the FREEDOM RIDES.

During his first year in college, Carmichael had become a member of SNCC. While organizing in the South, he was repeatedly arrested. He was beaten on several occasions and witnessed the deaths of several of his coworkers. Six years later, he became chairman of SNCC. As leader of SNCC, he worked directly with other CIVIL RIGHTS activists, including Martin Luther KING, Jr., in the fight to desegregate the South. The SNCC worked with King's SOUTHERN CHRISTIAN LEADERSHIP CONFERENCE (SCLC) and James FARMER's CONGRESS OF RACIAL EQUALITY (CORE). The organizations combined their efforts to win political, economic, educational, and social rights for African Americans in the rural South and the urban ghettos in the North.

Carmichael walked from door to door in the rural South registering African Americans to vote. He helped to organize the MISSISSIPPI FREEDOM DEMOCRATIC PARTY (MFDP) in 1964, working with activist Fannie Lou HAMER. In 1965 he was instrumental in organizing the Lowndes County Democratic Freedom Organization in Alabama, a party responsible for electing the first southern African American sheriff since Reconstruction.

As police continued to use water hoses, riot batons, dogs, and other physical constraints on nonviolent activists during sit-ins and marches, however, Carmichael and other young activists became dissatisfied with the nonviolent tactics and goals of the older civil rights leaders. These differences led to internal divisions within the movement.

Rise of the Black Power Movement

During the summer of 1966, Carmichael, Martin Luther King, Jr., and other civil rights leaders organized a protest march from MEMPHIS, TENNESSEE, to Jackson, Mississippi. During this event, major internal divisions became publicly known, changing the direction of the Civil Rights movement. Carmichael, strongly influenced by the ideas of MALCOLM X and other radical political leaders, became internationally known during this march for espousing the black power ideology.

The Black Power movement demanded that African Americans be given political, economic, and social power immediately or they would take it by force. The movement asserted racial and cultural pride and simultaneously denounced integration as a means of preventing the development of this self-pride. SNCC began publicly criticizing white support for African American organizations, arguing that this support would lead to white control of such organizations. Because coalitions between African Americans and whites were seen as being historically controlled by the white left, the Black Power movement was opposed to working with organizations that were not formed and controlled by African American activists. Moreover, black power activists no longer advocated nonviolence as a response to violence. These changes were a radical departure from the methods of the interracial, nonviolent Civil Rights movement that had graced the early 1960's. The cry for black power became the slogan for youth during the late 1960's.

SNCC, under Carmichael's leadership, criticized the United States' role in Vietnam and denounced the VIETNAM WAR. SNCC also

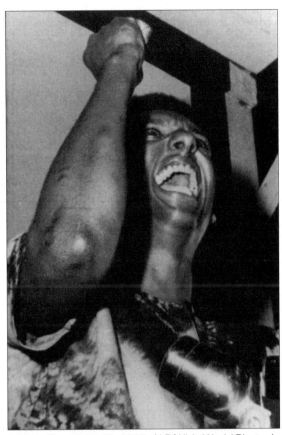

Stokely Carmichael in 1967. *(AP/Wide World Photos)*

became the first national organization to publicly denounce Zionism during the 1967 Arab-Israeli War. Carmichael's work expanded to include the organizing of migrant laborers during the lettuce and grape boycotts of the 1960's and the supporting of Native Americans in their work to reclaim their lands. Carmichael's ideas had become so radical and influential that members of the U.S. Congress were beginning to discuss the possibility of deporting him.

In 1967 Carmichael traveled extensively as a SNCC activist, visiting Puerto Rico and North Vietnam, where he met and conferred with Ho Chi Minh. Carmichael visited Europe, the Middle East, Africa, and Cuba. In Cuba, he attended and addressed the First Conference of the Organization of Latin American Solidarity and afterward was invited to the Republic of Guinea by its president, Sékou Touré; in Guinea, he met the former president of Ghana, Kwame Nkrumah. Carmichael also attended the congress of the Guinean Democratic Party in Conakry, Guinea.

Pan-African Activism

While in Guinea, Carmichael engaged in numerous lengthy discussions with the pan-Africanist Nkrumah regarding the political and economic problems of peoples of African descent, the Black Power movement in the United States, colonialism, and communism. Nkrumah discussed the importance of building an international pan-African political party that would include all peoples of African descent, a party he called the ALL-AFRICAN PEOPLE'S REVOLUTIONARY PARTY (A-APRP).

Influenced greatly by the two pan-African giants in Africa, Touré and Nkrumah, Carmichael strongly embraced the idea of pan-Africanism. Like Marcus GARVEY and Malcolm X before him, he had come to believe that the problems of peoples of African descent throughout the world were inextricably linked. Like Touré and Nkrumah, Carmichael believed that these problems could be solved only with the unification of Africa under a single strong, socialist government. As a pan-Africanist, he saw Africa as the true homeland for African Americans.

When Carmichael returned to the United States in December, 1967, his passport was immediately seized. He continued his political work by calling for the formation of the first Black United Front organization in the United States. He argued that capitalism and imperialism were the true oppressors of peoples of African descent, and he called for African Americans to unite and become a part of a world struggle to eliminate these social systems. Carmichael continued to denounce the inclusion of leftist white activists in African American organizations, arguing the need for African Americans to lead themselves.

In February, 1968, Carmichael was invited by BLACK PANTHER PARTY leaders Huey NEW-TON, Bobby SEALE, and Eldridge CLEAVER to serve as the organization's prime minister and to help organize more Black Panther chapters around the world. In April, he was deeply affected by the assassination of Martin Luther King, Jr., which reminded him of the dangers to his own life created by his radical stance. Shortly afterward, he married South African singer Miriam Makeba.

In August, 1968, Carmichael was fired from SNCC for disregarding certain decisions made by its executive body. At the time, he seriously entertained Nkrumah's idea of an international pan-African political party and began to discuss plans of building a chapter of the A-APRP in the United States with other militant activists. His passport was returned to him in October, and a few months later, Carmichael and Makeba moved to Guinea. Carmichael lived primarily in Guinea for the rest of his life.

The 1970's and After

While in Guinea, Carmichael studied and conferred with Touré and Nkrumah and taught university courses. In 1969 he decided to resign from the Black Panther Party over differences in ideas and objectives. By 1971 Carmichael, traveling as an ambassador from Guinea, decided to return to the United States to begin building a new organization. In 1972 he made the formal announcement of the creation of Nkrumah's A-APRP.

Unlike SNCC and other civil rights organizations of the 1960's, the A-APRP focused on the problems of Africa and the peoples of African descent. The A-APRP would not attempt to organize protests, marches, sit-ins, or boycotts, but would instead focus on finding permanent solutions to the problems of African Americans.

Carmichael was constantly traveling and away from home, and he and Makeba were di-vorced in 1979. Carmichael then married a Guinean woman, Marietou, and had a son; they were divorced in 1992. Carmichael changed his name to Kwame Toure in commemoration of the pan-African contributions made by his mentors, Kwame Nkrumah and Sékou Touré. He remained critical of Zionism and became an organizer for the Anti-Zionist Front.

—Kibibi Mack-Williams
See also: Africa and African American activism.

Suggested Readings:

Berry, Mary F., and John W. Blassingame. *Long Memory: The Black Experience in America.* New York: Oxford University Press, 1982.

Carmichael, Stokely. *Stokely Speaks.* New York: Random House, 1971.

Carmichael, Stokely, and Charles V. Hamilton. *Black Power: The Politics of Liberation in America.* New York: Vintage Books, 1967.

Carson, Clayborne. *In Struggle: SNCC and the Black Awakening of the 1960s.* Cambridge, Mass.: Harvard University Press, 1981.

Cobb, Charlie. "Revolution: From Stokely Carmichael to Kwame Ture." *The Black Scholar* 27 (Fall/Winter 1997): 32-38.

Stewart, Charles J. "The Evolution of a Revolution: Stokely Carmichael and the Rhetoric of Black Power." *The Quarterly Journal of Speech* 84 (November, 1997): 429-446.

Carney, William H. (1840, Norfolk, Virginia—December 9, 1908, Boston, Massachusetts): MILITARY hero. At the July 18, 1863, battle of Fort Wagner, South Carolina, during the CIVIL WAR, Sergeant Carney, a Union soldier, took the regimental flag from his company's color bearer, who had been wounded mortally. Carney made it to the fort, which then was attacked by Confederate troops. Carney was wounded three times before he made it back to his company, but he never let the flag touch the ground. He won the Medal of Honor for his

Sergeant William H. Carney, the first African American to receive the Congressional Medal of Honor during the Civil War. (Associated Publishers, Inc.)

bravery and was the first of twenty black soldiers to be so decorated during the Civil War. He was discharged on June 30, 1864, because of disability from his wounds. He eventually settled in New Bedford, Massachusetts, and worked as a mail carrier for more than thirty years.

Carroll, Diahann (Carol Diahann Johnson; b. July 17, 1935, New York, New York): Singer and actor. Carroll was born the daughter of a subway conductor, John Johnson, and a nurse, Mabel Faulk. As a teenager, she dropped out of New York University's sociology program to pursue a career as a nightclub singer. In the theater, she won acclaim for a supporting role in the Broadway musical *House of Flowers* (1954). Impressed by her talents, famed composer Richard Rodgers created the musical *No Strings* as a vehicle for Carroll. Her performance in the lead role of a model involved in

an interracial romance won a Tony Award for Carroll.

Carroll's screen credits include a variety of roles in such films as *Carmen Jones* (1954), *Porgy and Bess* (1959), *Paris Blues* (1961), *Hurry Sundown* (1967), and *The Five Heartbeats* (1991). Her most notable portrayal came in the film *Claudine* (1974), in which she plays a single mother who falls in love with a garbage man. For this performance, she earned an Academy Award nomination and an IMAGE AWARD from the NATIONAL ASSOCIATION FOR THE ADVANCEMENT OF COLORED PEOPLE (NAACP).

Carroll garnered two Emmy nominations, as a guest star in the *Naked City* series (1961) and then for her starring role as a widowed nurse raising her young son in *Julia* (1968-

Diahann Carroll polishes her new star on the Hollywood "Walk of Fame" in 1990. (AP/Wide World Photos)

1971). *Julia* was distinguished by the fact that not since AMOS 'N' ANDY (1951-1953) had there been a situation comedy starring an African American who was not playing a domestic. Both Carroll and the series gained considerable attention when it went on the air. A frequent guest on talk and variety shows, Carroll also hosted a summer series, *The Diahann Carroll Show* (1976), and starred in such made-for-television films as *Roots: The Next Generations* (1979), *I Know Why the Caged Bird Sings* (1979), and *Sister, Sister* (1982). In the 1980's, Carroll took on the role of Dominique Devereaux in the dramatic series *Dynasty* (1984-1987). As the affluent half sister of the patriarch of the powerful Carrington family, she portrayed one of the few recurring African American characters on a prime-time soap opera.
See also: Film; Television industry; Television series.

Carson, Benjamin Solomon (b. September 18, 1951, Detroit, Michigan): Neurosurgeon. In 1985 Carson was named director of pediatric neurosurgery at The Johns Hopkins Hospital in Baltimore, Maryland. He was that hospital's first African American neurosurgical resident, from 1978 to 1982. Carson performed a famous operation in 1987, separating West German conjoined twins who were attached at the backs of their heads.
See also: Medicine.

Carson, Clayborne (b. 1944, New York, New York): Scholar. Carter earned his B.A., M.A., and Ph.D. at the University of California at Los Angeles, where African American and U.S. history were his major fields of study. Among his numerous writings on the African American experience is a study of the STUDENT NONVIOLENT COORDINATING COMMITTEE (SNCC) entitled *In Struggle: SNCC and the Black Awak-*

ening of the 1960's (1981). He also edited a volume about MALCOLM X and was given the task of editing the papers of Martin Luther KING, Jr.

Carter, Benny (b. August 8, 1907, New York, New York): JAZZ saxophonist, composer, arranger, and orchestra leader. A multi-instrumentalist, Carter performed on tenor and alto saxophones, clarinet, and trumpet. Although he studied piano with his mother, he can be considered a self-taught musician influenced by trumpeters Bubber Miley and Cuban Bennett, his cousin. Carter wrote such jazz standards as "When Lights Are Low" (1936) and "Blues in My Heart" (1931).

Born Bennett Lester Carter, Carter began performing in 1923, working briefly with Duke ELLINGTON, Charles Johnson, June Clark, and Earl "Fatha" HINES. He attended Wilberforce University in 1925 and joined Horace Henderson's Wilberforce Collegians. He worked with Fletcher Henderson from 1930 to 1931 and produced such arrangements as "Keep a Song in Your Soul" (1930), "Lonesome Nights" (1934), and "Symphony in Riffs" (1935). After serving as music director of McKinney's Cotton Pickers, Carter formed

Saxophonist Benny Carter in 1997. *(AP/Wide World Photos)*

his own successful orchestra in New York in 1932. His orchestra included saxophonist Ben WEBSTER and pianist Teddy WILSON. Carter migrated in 1934 to London, where he became a staff arranger for the dance orchestra of the British Broadcasting Corporation, and led his own orchestra in the Netherlands in 1937.

Back in the United States, Carter formed a sextet in 1941 that included Jimmy Hamilton and Dizzy GILLESPIE. He relocated to Los Angeles in 1942 and concentrated on studio recording and arranging for Hollywood films. He wrote the television sound track for *M Squad* and sound tracks for such films as *Stormy Weather* (1943), *The Gene Krupa Story* (1959), and *An American in Paris* (1951).

Carter also wrote arrangements for such legends as Sarah VAUGHAN, Ella FITZGERALD, and Ray CHARLES. During the 1960's, he recorded *Further Definitions* (1961), and in 1985 he recorded *Benny Carter: A Gentleman and His Music* (1985). In the 1980's, Carter continued to arrange and lead orchestras. *Benny Carter: A Life in American Music* by Morroe Berger, et al. (1982) documents Carter's life. Carter premiered his "Harlem Renaissance Suite" in 1992.

Carter, Betty (May 16, 1930, Flint, Michigan—September 26, 1998, Brooklyn, New York): Singer and composer. Known as one of the great JAZZ singers, Carter always sought to present jazz in its purest form. She is often called a pure jazz singer, and her musical style and voice were keenly original. She not only made her own way in the business but also helped pave the way for many younger musicians.

Carter was born Lillie Mac Jones and grew up during difficult times; her family struggled throughout the Depression. When her father found employment in Detroit, she received piano training at the Detroit Conservatory of Music, becoming interested in jazz while attending Northwestern High School in Detroit. She sang with Lionel HAMPTON's band at a local dance in Detroit and was later hired as Hampton's vocalist. Hampton nicknamed her "Betty Bebop," and Betty Carter became her stage name.

In 1948 Carter began performing regularly with Hampton's band, with engagements at prominent jazz clubs throughout the United States. While singing with Hampton, Carter started doing her own musical arrangements. In 1951 she began performing on her own in New York, and by 1960 she was touring with Ray CHARLES. Their biggest hits were "Georgia on My Mind" and "Baby, It's Cold Outside." In 1969 Carter started her own record company, Bet-Car Productions, and in 1970 she released her first album on her own label. After the 1970's, Carter mentored some of the best and brightest young musicians in the world of jazz. She received a Grammy Award in 1989 for her album *Look What I Got!*

—*Alvin K. Benson*

See also: Music.

Carter, Ron (b. May 4, 1937, Ferndale, Michigan): JAZZ bassist. Ronald Levin Carter grew up in a musical family—all seven of his brothers and sisters played musical instruments. At age ten, he began studying cello. When his family moved to Detroit, however, he realized that career opportunities for African American cello players were limited. It was after Carter switched to the double bass that he developed an interest in jazz music. Dedicated practice and study earned Carter a scholarship to the Eastman School of Music in Rochester, NEW YORK, where he earned his bachelor's degree in 1959. He played in the school's symphony orchestra, but he also honed his jazz skills in his own group on weekends. After a brief stint in 1959 with the Chico Hamilton Quintet, Carter attended the Manhattan School of Music in NEW YORK CITY. He re-

Bassist Ron Carter in 1976. *(AP/Wide World Photos)*

ceived his master's degree in 1961.

In New York, Carter earned a reputation as a gifted bass player. He began a career as a freelance bassist, touring and recording with noted musicians such as guitarist Wes Montgomery and saxophonist Julian "Cannonball" ADDERLEY. In 1963 Carter joined the Art Farmer group, but he left almost immediately when offered a position with renowned trumpeter Miles DAVIS.

Considered by many critics and enthusiasts to be one of the greatest jazz bands of all time, the Miles Davis Quintet of the 1960's provided Carter with an intensely creative setting. Davis was known for allowing his sidemen a great deal of artistic freedom, and Carter worked well with creative young drummer Tony Williams. Carter played on critically acclaimed albums such as *Miles Smiles* (1967) and *Nefertiti* (1968); on his final album with Davis, *Filles de Kilimanjaro* (1969),

Carter played electric bass, an instrument he believed to be less expressive than the acoustic bass. Weary of constant touring, he stopped traveling with the band in 1968. He returned to New York and concentrated on recording and playing club dates in New York.

Throughout the 1970's, Carter led his own jazz group, recorded as a studio musician, and occasionally toured with groups composed of some of jazz's leading musicians. The most renowned of these groups was V.S.O.P., led by a former Davis band member, pianist Herbie HANCOCK. It also included saxophonist Wayne SHORTER and drummer Tony Williams. In his own quartet, Carter was accompanied by a drummer, a pianist, and an additional bass player, which allowed Carter the freedom to solo on the double bass or on the piccolo bass, a cross between the traditional bass and the cello. Carter also played in duos with a pianist or a guitarist. In solo performances, he played not only jazz but also pieces composed for him by modern classical musicians.

Carter's playing earned him numerous musical awards and the admiration of his peers. In January of 1995, a host of jazz musicians ranging from veterans Milt Hinton and Milt Jackson to newcomer Christian McBride paid tribute to Carter at a celebration concert held in New York's Merkin Concert Hall. Always in demand as a performer and recording sideman, Carter had probably played on more than one thousand jazz and soul albums by the late 1990's. Carter also authored his own instructional guide to jazz bass playing. Albums under his own name include *All Blues* (1973), *Piccolo* (1977), *Telephone* (1984), *Duets* (1990), and *Bass and I* (1997).

Carter, Rubin "Hurricane" (b. May 15, 1937, Clifton, New Jersey): Middleweight boxer convicted of murder but later released. Carter was sentenced to two consecutive life terms for the murders of three whites in a Paterson, NEW

JERSEY, bar in 1966. At the time of his arrest, he was a contender for the world middleweight BOXING championship and was awaiting a rematch with title holder Dick Tiger.

On June 17, 1966, at the Lafayette Grill, two people were killed and two others were wounded, one fatally. Witnesses indicated that two African Americans in a white car were involved. Carter and his companion, John Artis, were picked up, questioned, and presented to the two survivors (one of whom died later). These witnesses could not identify Carter and Artis. The two men were released, but four months later they were charged with three murders. Two small-time criminals, Alfred P. Bello and Arthur Bradley, said they had seen Carter and Artis with guns. A bullet of the caliber used in the murders was found in Carter's car. Carter and Artis were found guilty by an all-white jury.

Numerous complexities plagued the case. After they could no longer be prosecuted for perjury, Bello and Bradley, who had failed to identify Carter and his companion on the night of the murder, changed their story and claimed that their testimony was an effort to gain leniency in unrelated criminal charges

Rubin "Hurricane" Carter testifying before the House subcommittee on Civil and Constitutional Rights in 1993. *(AP/Wide World Photos)*

against them. Carter and Artis were released on bail and scheduled for a new trial in 1976. At that trial, Bello, but not Bradley, claimed that a reporter for *The New York Times* and two others had paid him to recant his testimony against Carter and Artis. Witnesses who had provided alibis for Carter previously now said that they had perjured themselves. Once again, Carter and Artis were convicted.

A model prisoner, Artis was paroled in 1981. Carter and his lawyer continued to fight. Finally, in November of 1985, federal judge H. Lee Sarokin overturned Carter's conviction, stating that the 1976 jury had been racially biased and that the prosecution had withheld evidence. In 1987 a Philadelphia federal appeals judge denied the efforts of the prosecution to reinstate the conviction.

In 1999 actor Denzel Washington, Jr., played Carter, and Garland Whitt played Artis, in *The Hurricane*—a big-budget film about Carter's legal struggles directed by Norman Jewison.

See also: Jury selection.

Carter, Stephen L. (b. 1954, Washington, D.C.): Educator, lawyer, and author. Carter is considered an important member of a group of black authors and thinkers called by one critic the "new intellectuals." One of five children born to Lisle Carter, the first president of the University of the District of Columbia, and Emily Carter, an assistant to the head of the National Urban Coalition, Stephen Carter grew up in Washington, D.C. When he was thirteen, his father took a teaching post at Cornell University and moved the family to Ithaca, New York. Carter remained in Washington, living with a Jewish family while he finished school. He later attributed that experience to helping him see the way religion can permeate the lives of people. It also influenced Carter's decision to study history and religion as an undergraduate at Stanford University.

After completing his bachelor's degree, Carter went on to attend Yale Law School before working as a legal clerk for U.S. SUPREME COURT justice Thurgood MARSHALL. Carter eventually joined the faculty of Yale University, where he was appointed William Nelson Cromwell Professor of Law. He became recognized as a leading expert on American constitutional law.

Carter's 1993 book *The Culture of Disbelief: How American Law and Politics Trivialize Religion* demonstrates his ongoing interest in history and religion. The work examines the ways in which American politics, the courts, universities, and the press have sought to banish religion from public discourse. Carter argues that American democracy suffers when its citizens resort to religious stereotyping.

In his controversial first book, *Reflections of an Affirmative Action Baby* (1991), Carter explored the dangers of racial stereotyping and what he considered the misuse of AFFIRMATIVE ACTION to correct past racial inequities. In his memoir, Carter describes the way in which affirmative action policies affected him personally, compelling him to attend law school at Yale University rather than Harvard University. (Although his application to Harvard Law School was initially rejected, Carter later received a letter of acceptance once the school's officials realized that he was black.)

Throughout the memoir, Carter uses himself as an example of what can happen when affirmative action goes awry. In the life experiences of Carter and others who are "affirmative action babies," those who have grown up in socially and economically advantaged households have overwhelmingly received preferential treatment, while others who lack those advantages have continued to fall through the cracks and have failed to receive assistance from affirmative action efforts. Carter notes that many proponents of affirmative action incorrectly assume that being black automatically means that an individual is underprivileged. Critiquing the evolution of affirmative action policies, Carter argues that many well-meaning efforts not only have missed truly disadvantaged minorities who need such help but also have exposed American society's preference for cheap or expedient solutions to the complex problem of racial justice.

Defying the efforts of others to describe his position along the political spectrum, Carter attempted to establish a moderate position capable of bridging the gap between the views of the mainstream black leadership and black CONSERVATIVES. This elusive intellectual position places Carter outside the ranks of the political and racial ideologues and presents a forceful argument for tolerance of diverse views within the black community. His 1994 book *The Confirmation Mess: Cleaning Up the Federal Appointments Process* pleads eloquently for rules that will apply fairly to all appointees. In an interview published by *Choice* magazine, Carter said his book was likely to be the only one "to defend both Robert Bork and Lani GUINIER." In 1998 Carter published *The Dissent of the Governed: A Meditation on Law, Religion, and Loyalty* and *Civility: Manners, Morals, and the Etiquette of Democracy*.
See also: Intellectuals and scholars.

Carter administration: As governor of GEORGIA between 1971 and 1975, Jimmy Carter strongly denounced RACIAL DISCRIMINATION. Partly because of this stand, his 1976 presidential campaign received strong support from African American leaders such as Maynard JACKSON, Martin Luther KING, Sr., and Andrew YOUNG. In Carter's November victory over Gerald Ford, 94 percent of black voters backed Carter. They turned the tide in several states, most notably Mississippi and Louisiana.

President Carter's first major African American appointment was Young, whom he named U.S. Permanent Representative to the

Notable African American Appointees in the Carter Administration

Patricia R. Harris	Secretary of Housing and Urban Development; secretary of Health, Education, Welfare
Andrew Young	U.S. ambassador to the United Nations (cabinet post under Carter)
Clifford L. Alexander	Secretary of the Army
Mary Frances Berry	Assistant secretary of Health, Education, and Welfare
Preston Davis	Director of small business affairs (Agriculture Department)
Ernest G. Green	Assistant secretary at Labor Department
Alexis N. Herman	Director of women's bureau (Labor Department)
Donald F. McHenry	U.S. ambassador to the United Nations (succeeded Andrew Young)
Wade McCree	Solicitor general
Eleanor Holmes Norton	Chair of Equal Employment Opportunity Commission
Erna H. Poston	Commissioner of the U.S. Civil Service Commission
Emmett J. Rice	Member of Federal Reserve Board
Barbara M. Watson	Assistant secretary of state; ambassador to Malaysia

United Nations in December. Carter then selected Patricia HARRIS to head the Department of Housing and Urban Development and chose Eleanor NORTON to lead the EQUAL EMPLOYMENT OPPORTUNITY COMMISSION (EEOC). Drew Days, a lawyer for the NATIONAL ASSOCIATION FOR THE ADVANCEMENT OF COLORED PEOPLE (NAACP), became Carter's assistant attorney general for CIVIL RIGHTS. Wade MCCREE, an appeals judge, was named U.S. solicitor general. In 1978 Carter brought Louis Martin, a long-time power in the DEMOCRATIC PARTY, into the White House to serve as a special contact to African American groups. Overall, 12 percent of Carter's appointments were African Americans. (Only about 4 percent of President Ronald Reagan's, who followed Carter, would be.)

The Carter administration actively supported AFFIRMATIVE ACTION regarding businesses, forbidding government contracts to nine companies that resisted hiring minorities and setting aside 15 percent of contracts in public construction projects for minority contractors. Regarding school admissions, the administration's position was less clear. Debate raged within the administration over the famous 1978 Allan Bakke "REVERSE DISCRIMINATION" case against the University of California

President Jimmy Carter. *(White House Historical Association)*

(*Regents of the University of California v. Allan Bakke*). This ambiguity weakened Carter's reputation among African American leaders.

Carter and his administration certainly achieved some successes in the eyes of African Americans. Carter recognized the heroic all-black 761st Tank Battalion, whose WORLD WAR II exploits had previously been ignored by the

U.S. government. He sent his daughter Amy to an integrated public school in the District of Columbia. He hosted many prominent black African leaders at the White House, including Tanzania's President Julius Nyerere and Zimbabwe's President Robert Mugabe. In more concrete terms, his appointee Norton reorganized the EEOC and made significant headway in reducing the backlog of discrimination cases.

At the United Nations, Young's record was mixed. His numerous controversial statements sometimes drew censure from Carter himself. On the other hand, he made a strong contribution to a peace settlement in Zimbabwe and to that country's eventual independence, and he gained respect and friendship from the leaders of many nations. In 1979 Young met unofficially with a representative of the Palestine Liberation Organization, violating U.S. policy. As a result, he was fired by Carter.

The firing of Young sparked widespread criticism of Carter by African Americans, led by Jesse JACKSON and Vernon JORDAN. It was only one aspect of the general sense of disappointment with Carter among blacks. Despite Carter's impressive record of African American appointments, his powerful symbolic efforts, and the gains orchestrated by officials such as Norton, Carter was not as popular among African Americans in the 1980 election as he had been in 1976. This shift was one of many reasons for Carter's 1980 loss to Ronald Reagan.

—Andy DeRoche

See also: Bakke case.

Suggested Readings:

Dumbrell, John. *The Carter Presidency: A Reevaluation*. 2d ed. Manchester: Manchester University Press, 1995.

Jones, Bartlett C. *Flawed Triumphs: Andy Young at the United Nations*. Lanham, Md.: University Press of America, 1996.

Carver, George Washington (July 12, 1861(?), near Diamond Grove, Missouri—January 5, 1943, Tuskegee, Alabama): Scientist and educator. Carver was the son of Mary, a slave belonging to Moses and Susan Carver. His father was reported to have been a slave on a nearby farm who was accidentally killed before George's birth. Early in Carter's infancy, his mother disappeared, reputedly captured by slave raiders. Carter and his older brother, James, were then reared by the childless Carvers on their small, self-sufficient farm.

Youth and Education

While George was still young, the Carvers and their neighbors became aware that he was an exceptional child. Racism overcame the community's awe of his abilities, however, and George was not allowed to attend the local school because of his color. The Carvers sought to teach him and hired a tutor, but Carver left home at an early age to seek more education. By the time he was twelve, he moved in with a black family in nearby Neosho to attend the black school there. After discovering that his teacher knew little more than he did, Carver hitched a ride to Fort Scott, KANSAS. The move began for Carver more than a decade of wandering around the Midwest in search of elusive educational opportunities. He supported himself by laundering, cooking, and, at one point, homesteading in Kansas.

Rejected by Highland College when officials learned he was black, Carver finally enrolled in Simpson College at Indianola, IOWA, in 1890. An art major, he was the only African American enrolled. His art teacher recognized both his talents and the obstacles he faced as a black artist; she convinced him to transfer to Iowa State University to study horticulture.

Arriving at Iowa State in 1891, Carver won the affection of the all-white student body and the respect of the all-white faculty. He participated in many campus activities and compiled an impressive academic record. He was especially gifted in plant hybridization and mycology—the study of fungi. His talents led the faculty to ask him to remain as a postgraduate student while taking care of the greenhouse and teaching freshman biology. After he received his master's degree in AGRICULTURE in 1896, Carver could have remained at Iowa, but he decided instead to accept Booker T. WASHINGTON's offer to head the agricultural department at Tuskegee Normal and Industrial Institute—widely known simply as TUSKEGEE INSTITUTE—in Tuskegee, Alabama.

Career at Tuskegee Institute

Believing that he had a duty to share his knowledge with other blacks, Carver went to Tuskegee in 1896 expecting to stay only a few years before pursuing his artwork or a doctorate in botany. Instead, he remained there until his death in 1943. During his first years, he was swamped with administrative and teaching duties but still managed to open and operate the only agricultural experiment station staffed entirely by African Americans.

George Washington Carver during his early years at Tuskegee. *(Library of Congress)*

The Tuskegee station received a mere fifteen-hundred-dollar annual appropriation to cover its operation and the publication of agricultural bulletins. Carver conducted research similar to that done at white-operated stations, but his constituency and low funding led him to focus on inexpensive ways to improve farmers' productivity and standard of living. Most Alabama farmers were landless tenants and SHARECROPPERS who were trapped in a vicious cycle of debt and POVERTY. Carver sought alternatives to store-bought supplies to decrease their debt burden.

Carver advocated natural fertilization methods instead of the extensive use of expensive fertilizers. He also tried to improve the daily lives and diets of sharecroppers by encouraging them to grow crops and to use available resources to meet more of their needs. He taught farmers how to turn native clays into paint. Peanuts, which later became his major source of recognition, were chosen as a cheap source of protein that would not deplete soil as much as cotton. To encourage peanut planting as well as the planting of such crops as potatoes and cowpeas, Carver published bulletins with recipes for peanut use.

To get the word out to illiterate and busy farmers, Carver used such standard educational outreach programs as institutes, fairs, and short courses. He was also an early pioneer in taking instruction directly to farmers through the Jesup Wagon, a movable school that traveled around the countryside, giving agricultural lessons at the end of cotton rows.

Rise to Fame

When Booker T. Washington died in 1915, Carver was respected by fellow agricultural researchers, loved by his students, and a favorite speaker at black agricultural conferences all over the South, but he was barely known by the general public. Several events soon increased his fame. In 1916 he was invited to join the Royal Society for the Arts.

Peanut growers' associations then discovered his usefulness, paying his way to testify at congressional tariff hearings in 1921. His natural showmanship fascinated both committee members and the press. Soon afterward, some Atlanta businessmen founded the Carver Products Company to market his products. He also won the coveted SPINGARN MEDAL of the National Association for the Advancement of Colored People (NAACP). The company never accomplished anything more than helping Carver to get his only patent, which was never used. Nevertheless, the publicity helped propel Carver into national prominence as the Peanut Man.

Although Carver's "cookstove chemistry," as he called it, had been aimed at replacing commercial goods, he was seduced into making commercial claims for his products—not for money but for recognition. He became known more and more for the sheer quantity of his peanut products. Fame might have eluded him but for his compelling personality and endearing eccentricities as well as the appeal of his life story. Publicists wrote of the flowers in his lapel, of his rambles in the woods, and of his rise from SLAVERY.

Group after group began to use Carver as a symbol of their causes. For New South boosters, he epitomized the dawning of a more industrial future for the region. Religious leaders of all denominations related to his nonsectarian but devout faith in their battles against the materialism of the scientific age. During the GREAT DEPRESSION, Carver became a rags-to-riches example of opportunity in America. Advocates of racial justice pointed to his genius as proof of African American ability. At the same time, apologists for slavery and segregation hailed Carver as an ex-

ample of the essential rightness of both.

Carver's circle of friends included share-croppers, senators, and such famous people as Henry Ford. Few came into contact with Carver without feeling they had a special relationship with him. His magnetic personality inspired countless Tuskegee students, many of whom remained in contact with the professor until his death. Beginning in the 1920's, his inspirational powers were directed at white college students as well. The Commission on Interracial Cooperation and the Young Men's Christian Association sent Carver on speaking tours at white campuses. He insisted on meeting informally with students and for dozens became a confidant and father figure. Because he never married or had children, Carver cre-

George Washington Carver in early 1942. *(Library of Congress)*

ated an unofficial family of Tuskegee students. Soon, whites also became adopted "children."

Legacy

Carver died on January 5, 1943, leaving a mixed legacy. His refusal to take a public stand on political or racial issues, combined with his outwardly humble demeanor, probably did reinforce some destructive white ideas about African Americans. On the other hand, both the man and the myth inspired young and old, black and white, in positive ways as well. In addition, his early work in agricultural research and education enriched the lives of countless poor farmers and sharecroppers. He became one of the nation's most effective popularizers of scientific agriculture and crop diversification. His frugal lifestyle also enabled him to contribute sixty thousand dollars to establish the George Washington Carver Foundation, an agency that still funds research at Tuskegee Institute. Had he been given the same opportunities as white scientists, his genius would probably have led him to make more significant scientific contributions in either mycology or plant hybridization—and he would have likely died virtually unknown.

—*Linda O. McMurry*

See also: Science and technology; Sharecropping.

Suggested Readings:

Elliott, Lawrence. *George Washington Carver: The Man Who Overcame.* Englewood Cliffs, N.J.: Prentice-Hall, 1966.

Holt, Rackham. *George Washington Carver: An American Biography.* Garden City, N.Y.: Doubleday, Doran, 1943.

Jenkins, Edward S. *To Fathom More: African American Scientists and Inventors.* Lanham, Md.: University Press of America, 1996.

Kremer, Gary R. *George Washington Carver in His Own Words.* Columbia: University of Missouri Press, 1987.

McMurry, Linda O. *George Washington Carver: Scientist and Symbol.* New York: Oxford University Press, 1981.

Cary, Lorene (b. November 29, 1956, Philadelphia, Pennsylvania): Writer, educator, and journalist. Cary's first book, *Black Ice* (1991), is an autobiographical account of her experiences as one of the first African American students at an exclusive New England prep school: St. Paul's School in Concord, NEW HAMPSHIRE. Entering St. Paul's as a high school sophomore in 1972, Cary was torn between the world of her Philadelphia family and that of her wealthy white classmates. The book reveals her ambitions to further the CIVIL RIGHTS struggle, her fears of losing her blackness, and her lack of self-esteem caused by the subtle racism of the school. It can be read as a response to the black power philosophy articulated in Eldridge CLEAVER's memoir *Soul on Ice* (1968). A deep undercurrent of the book is a struggle for religious faith, for Cary is torn between the God of the black church and the God worshiped in the chapel at St. Paul's School.

Cary becomes a student leader and succeeds academically, and she returns to the school as a teacher and trustee. Nevertheless, in a concluding chapter about her return to St. Paul's for her fifteenth reunion in 1989, she acknowledges the painful struggles of people like herself who were among the first to enter schools and jobs previously reserved for whites. *Black Ice* belongs in the company of classic African American stories and memoirs about education and coming of age, including books written by Booker T. WASHINGTON, James BALDWIN, Maya ANGELOU, and Anne Moody.

Upon graduation from St. Paul's in 1974, Cary attended the University of Pennsylvania and graduated with bachelor's and master's degrees in 1978. In the early 1980's, she was a writer for *Time* and an associate editor at *TV*

Guide. As a contributing editor at *Newsweek* in 1992, she published "A Children's Crusade," an article about the pressures on children of color who were caught up in educational reform movements.

Cary's first novel, *The Price of a Child* (1995), was published to enthusiastic reviews. Based on the historical case of an escaped slave named Jane Johnson as told by William Still in *The Underground Railroad* (1872), the novel opens in 1855 when Ginnie and her two eldest children are traveling with their master Jackson Pryor, a Virginia planter-diplomat who is journeying to Nicaragua. Stranded in Philadelphia after the group misses their steamboat, Ginnie secretly contacts agents of the UNDERGROUND RAILROAD and makes her escape, knowing that her baby son will be left in SLAVERY in Virginia. She enters the thriving world of black Philadelphia abolitionists, changes her name to Mercer Gray, and becomes a lecturer in the ABOLITIONIST MOVEMENT. In a stunning scene, Gray risks her freedom to confront Jackson in court over his claims that she was coerced to leave him. Besides telling a gripping tale of the Underground Railroad and race relations in Philadelphia in the years before the CIVIL WAR, Cary plumbs the emotional depths of Mercer Gray as a woman and a mother. As Toni MORRISON did in *Beloved* (1987), Cary created a heroine who liberates herself by giving voice to the experiences of slavery and freedom. Cary publisher her next novel, *Pride*, in 1998.

See also: Autobiographies and memoirs; Literature; Print journalism.

Cary, William Sterling (b. August 10, 1927, Plainfield, New Jersey): Clergyman and political activist. Cary was pastor of Grace Congregational Church in NEW YORK CITY from 1958 to 1968 before becoming the first African American president of the National Council of Churches in 1972. During his three-year term,

William Sterling Cary. *(Illinois Conference, United Church of Christ)*

he advanced the concerns of African Americans and the poor by advocating welfare reform, low-income housing, and strict enforcement of fair employment laws.

Catlett, Elizabeth (b. April 15, 1915 or 1919, Washington, D.C.): Sculptor and printmaker. Catlett is best recognized for her monumental carvings of African American mothers and children and prints depicting black female laborers, artists, and farm workers. She was the first student to receive a master of fine arts degree from the University of Iowa and taught at several American colleges before moving to MEXICO in 1946. Her art brought public attention to black women's struggles and to the economic, social, and political issues affecting African Americans.

See also: Painters and illustrators; Sculptors; Visual arts.

Cato: SLAVE RESISTANCE leader. Cato, who had recently been brought to the colony of SOUTH

Carolina from Angola, led the Stono rebellion at Stono River in September of 1739. The first major slave insurrection, it was prompted by Spain's promise to set free any slaves from South Carolina who managed to reach St. Augustine, Florida. Cato—who is known only by that name—led a group of about one hundred slaves. They broke into a storehouse to obtain weapons and killed more than twenty white people as they attempted to make their way south. The group was overtaken within several hours, and many of the slaves were executed.

Cemeteries and funeral customs: While death is a universal human event, religious beliefs, social conditions, and cultural forces affect how it is experienced and understood. They also influence how burial customs are carried out. African Americans' funeral customs reflect both their history of enslavement and their enduring African heritage.

Belief System

African slaves arrived in North America from many different regions of Africa. Nevertheless, some generalities about their belief systems can be made. These include the dominant African belief in the duality of life—that is, the idea that there is a physical world that humans inhabit and know on a conscious level and a spiritual world that, although unseen, is as real and active as the physical world. To die is not to end one's existence but to transfer it into the spiritual world. The death of a loved one, therefore, does not remove him or her from the community's daily activity. Instead, the deceased becomes an active spirit-world being who continues to interact with the living, sometimes providing assistance and comfort, sometimes hardship and grief. Proper burial is important not to provide a permanent resting place for the soul, but to make sure it is comfortable, satisfied, and well-equipped for life as a spirit, thus encouraging more assistance and less grief.

Under Slavery

On the plantations of colonial America, the harsh conditions of slavery made death all too common for the transplanted Africans. Funerals took place within the slave community; activities included the preparation of the body, which was frequently done by women, and the digging of the grave, a task sometimes assigned to children. Services did not always coincide with the actual burial of the deceased. If an individual died during a busy harvest season, for example, the body would be taken care of but the funeral itself would wait until the plantation's business had been completed. Then the slaves would assemble for a long, free-spirited ceremony marked by song, dance, and drumming (if permitted by the slaveowner), a celebration of passage from the hardships

Funeral procession during the Reconstruction years. *(Associated Publishers, Inc.)*

443

of the physical world to the ease and grace of the spirit world.

Because of the African emphasis on the spirit world as a destination, the grave was seen as only a temporary resting place. It was therefore unnecessary to construct elaborate or enduring markers. Graves were simple affairs, adorned perhaps with a wooden pole or sign bearing the name of the deceased. More typical would have been a collection of objects belonging to the deceased, often intentionally broken to symbolize departure from the physical world.

The placing of personal possessions on a grave is a custom going back to the era of slavery. *(Library of Congress)*

Plants were also used to mark gravesites. Slave burial grounds were located away from the main plantation cemetery; thus the plantation owner could ensure a permanent separation between blacks and whites.

After the Civil War

The ending of slavery after the CIVIL WAR did little to change this pattern. Blacks were still buried by blacks, and whites by whites. This fact created a demand for undertakers in the African American community. Since few other professional trades were open to blacks at this time, the individuals who filled these positions were highly regarded, enjoying prominence and status in the African American community. They often served as spokespeople and as community leaders.

Cemeteries also continued to be segregated, particularly in the South. Well into the twentieth century, blacks were buried in graveyards attached to African American churches, in private cemeteries owned by African American organizations, or in "colored" sections of public cemeteries. Many of these burial grounds, and especially the earlier slave cemeteries attached to plantations, were lost along the way to time and neglect, but their reclamation and restoration has since become a priority for historical preservation groups.

Modern Trends

Despite the fact that cemeteries eventually became officially desegregated, the funeral industry has largely remained racially divided in practice. Mortuary professionals attribute this division to a combination of cultural, social, and economic factors. Economically, blacks are far more likely to pay for funeral expenses with burial insurance, a situation which means that the funeral home must wait longer for payment. Black-owned mortuaries are more accommodating of this fact than white-owned mortuaries. Socially, because a mortuary or funeral home tends to serve multiple members and even multiple generations of a single family, there are no strong shifts in clientele; both black and white families are likely to patronize the same funeral home year after year. Culturally, black funeral homes serve the black community well because they understand how to; they know and share African American burial customs, which continue to bear a degree of African influence.

The African American attitude toward death is somewhat more holistic than that of the general U.S. population. Blacks see death as a form of passage, often speaking of "passing" or "homegoing" instead of dying. At some African American funerals, a baby is passed over the casket to symbolize the ebb and flow of life in this world. Because of the importance of friends and family gathering to bid farewell to the deceased, African American funerals are frequently held on weekends, when attendance is highest.

—*Regina Howard Yaroch*

See also: Segregation and integration; Slave religions.

Suggested Readings:

Nichols, Elaine. *The Last Miles of the Way: African-American Homegoing Traditions 1890-Present*. Columbia: South Carolina State Museum, 1989.

Raboteau, Albert J. *Slave Religion*. Oxford, England: Oxford University Press, 1978.

Trinkley, Michael. *Grave Matters: The Preservation of African-American Cemeteries*. Columbia, S.C.: Chicora Foundation, 1996.

Wright, Roberta Hughes, and Wilbur B. Hughes. *Lay Down Body: Living History in African-American Cemeteries*. Detroit: Gale Research, 1995.

Census of the United States: Representation of African Americans in the U.S. Census has been a subject of frequent and sometimes heated political debate. Issues such as minority undercounting and racial classification have called into question the validity of census data and even the motives of census officials.

History

The gathering of census data on African Americans has carried political implications since the completion of the first U.S. Census in 1790. Various individuals and groups have sought to use census data relating to blacks to gain political influence, shape public policy, and incite racial tensions. For example, the apportionment of congressional representatives—based on census population figures—was of particular interest in southern states with large black populations.

Early censuses treated slaves primarily as property, and thus they yielded few details on the lives of slaves. Free persons of color were included in the regular rolls but were often undercounted; arbitrary and inconsistent methods of racial classification further muddled data on blacks and other minorities. Yet despite these inconsistencies, early census records have provided a viable means of illustrating general trends in population, DEMOGRAPHY, and migratory patterns of minority groups in the United States.

Undercounting

One of the more frequent criticisms of the U.S. Census is the charge that it underrepresents population figures for African Americans and other minority groups. Historical evidence indicates that free African Americans were inadvertently undercounted in early censuses. The precarious status of free blacks in the antebellum United States prompted many blacks to avoid census officials for fear that they would be enslaved, returned to SLAVERY, or at minimum subjected to white harassment. In addition, many light-skinned free blacks were able to "pass" as white or Native American and were classified as such by census officials. Following the CIVIL WAR, geographical mobility and mistrust of white officials continued to render the counting of African Americans difficult; later government estimates indicate that the 1870 census may have undercounted blacks by nearly 8 percent.

Critics of the U.S. Census have argued that the undercounting of black Americans continued through the twentieth century, partly because significant numbers of transient and homeless blacks in urban areas may not have been counted. Some minority activists accused the Census Bureau of OVERT RACISM in the undercounting of blacks, but evidence generally seems to implicate technical and logistical problems as the primary causes of undercounting. Proposals to correct undercounting in the 1980 and 2000 censuses through statistical sampling (rather than direct counting) were rejected by the U.S. SUPREME COURT.

Racial Classification

Methods of classifying persons by race and ethnicity in the census have also been a source of controversy. Racial classifications in early censuses were usually based on local custom, and therefore they varied from locality to locality. American Indians and dark-skinned immigrants were often counted as black, and some light-skinned blacks passed as whites. These phenomena continued into the twentieth century even as census criteria for racial classification became more standardized.

In the 1970's, minority groups seeking greater recognition began to push for expansion of the list of racial and ethnic classifications included in the census questionnaire. Conflicting political agendas quickly became a part of the debate. On one hand, many sought freedom from outdated and limited racial classifications. On the other hand, many leaders of various minority groups feared that expansion of racial categories would lead to a statistical reduction in their numbers and therefore would dilute their political influence. For this reason, proposals to include a "multiracial" category or to allow respondents to choose more than one racial category in the 2000 census were met with opposition from some minority leaders. The Census Bureau did not include such a category, but it decided to allow people to choose more than one racial category to describe themselves if they wished.

—Michael H. Burchett
See also: Biracial and mixed-race children; Passing.

Suggested Readings:

Anderson, Margo J. *The American Census: A Social History.* New Haven, Conn.: Yale University Press, 1988.

Ashabranner, Melissa. *Counting America: The Story of the United States Census.* New York: Putnam, 1989.

Lee, Anne S. *The Development of the United States Census.* Washington, Conn.: Center for Information on America, 1975.

In 1990 the U.S. Census Bureau hired extra workers to ensure that homeless persons were counted. *(AP/Wide World Photos)*

U.S. Bureau of the Census. *1990 Census of Population: Characteristics of the Black Population.* Washington, D.C.: U.S. Government Printing Office, 1994.

U.S. Bureau of the Census. *Statistical Abstract of the United States.* Washington, D.C.: U.S. Government Printing Office, published annually.

Central America: Definitions of "Central America" vary. The people of the region themselves regard Guatemala, Honduras, El Salvador, Nicaragua, and Costa Rica as Central American nations. Outsiders often consider Panama, after it gained independence in 1903, and Belize (formerly British Honduras), to be part of Central America.

Early Colonial Era

Central America was explored and settled by Spaniards from MEXICO and Panama beginning in 1510, but it remained largely undeveloped until the last half of the nineteenth century. Few precious metals were found, and the area was isolated and cut off from Europe by the low-lying, tropical coast.

Placer gold mines and the Indian SLAVE TRADE were the first sources of wealth exploited. Large numbers of Indian slaves, perhaps as many as 200,000, were sold to Peru between 1520 and 1550. Consequently a labor shortage developed that led to *encomenderos* (Spanish settlers who had the use of Indian labor) opposing exportation of Indian slaves and to attempts by the Spanish crown to prohibit the enslavement of Indians.

After the decline of the Indian slave trade, cacao became the export crop of Central America. The cacao plantations were located primarily along the Pacific coast of Guatemala and El Salvador. Indians furnished most of the labor on the cacao plantations. Only a few wealthy planters used black slaves: They were very expensive, and the supply was limited.

All told, a total of 10,000 to 24,000 African slaves were imported into Central America before Central American independence in 1823.

Importation of Slaves

The first black slaves were introduced in 1543 at San Pedro, in Honduras, in the amount of 150 *piezas* (a pieza was the equivalent of the labor of one adult man). By royal decree they were to serve in the mines, in factories, and on indigo and sugar plantations. The largest African population during the colonial period was located in El Salvador, along the Pacific coast.

When cacao production declined as a result of a decrease in Indian labor and competition from Venezuela, indigo became the chief export in the Pacific coastal region. The reduced labor required by indigo could at first be provided by Indians. However, the continued devastating toll of European diseases on the Indian population led to plantation owners petitioning the Spanish king in the 1580's to allow the importation of African slaves at the king's expense. Because of concerns about security and the numbers of African slaves already in the area, local governments opposed the request. The king did not have the money or interest to answer the petition.

African slaves were introduced to other parts of Central America during the same period. In Panama a small number of African slaves were used in the transit trade. Black slaves were brought to Belize and the Caribbean coast by English loggers and merchants in the 1660's. Guatemala used few black slaves because of the continued availability of Indian labor.

Escaped slaves mixed with the Moskito Indians along the Caribbean coast from Honduras to Costa Rica. Spain was never able to control this area. The Zambo Moskito population not only controlled the low-lying coastal area but also raided the Spanish-controlled uplands. Spanish authorities settled free blacks

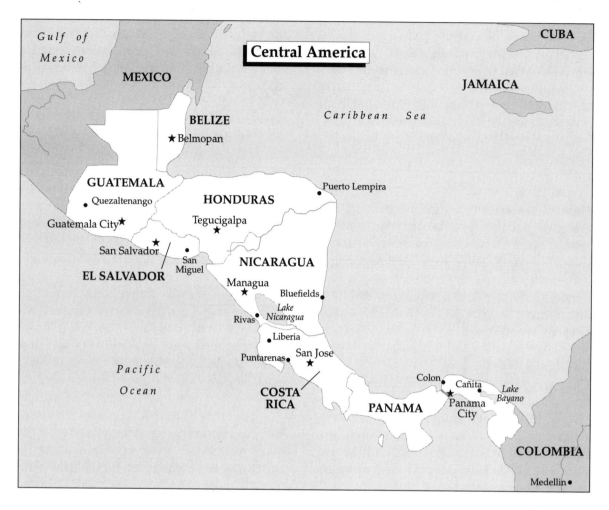

and mulattoes in the border area in an attempt to prevent the raids. These blacks were given authority over the area and over the local Indians. Some were successful and achieved prominent political and social positions. Throughout Central America, Africans were gradually becoming assimilated and blending with the region's other ethnicities. By the 1820's, the time of independence, no clear-cut racial or cultural divisions were visible.

The largest slaveowners in Central America during the colonial period were two religious orders, the Dominicans and Jesuits. These orders owned the largest sugar plantations and mills and used perhaps as many as nine hundred black slaves. Toward the end of the eighteenth century, planters turned to con-scripted rural peasants, mixed-bloods, and Indians for labor. Conscripted labor was cheaper than maintaining an enslaved labor force, and it proved to be as reliable. Planters often freed their slaves as a cost-cutting measure.

After Independence

When the Central American Confederation (consisting of Guatemala, Honduras, El Salvador, Nicaragua, and Costa Rica) became independent in 1823, Liberals controlled the government. They abolished SLAVERY even before the official adoption of the Constitution of 1825, which included emancipation. By that time, assimilation of the Africans was virtually complete.

In the last half of the nineteenth century, the

Central American nations sought economic development and granted numerous concessions to native and foreign investors. In 1871 Costa Rica granted a railroad concession to the North American railroad builder Henry Meiggs. Meiggs developed banana plantations to provide revenue for his railroad. Banana production became a major industry and expanded along the Caribbean coast. A labor shortage developed because the upland population would not move to the hot and disease-ridden coast. Blacks from Jamaica and other Caribbean Islands were brought in, creating a substantially different racial composition. Social tensions emerged.

Blacks from the WEST INDIES also came to the coastal areas of the other Central American nations, with the same results. In Panama blacks were imported to work on the canal. Most did not return home when the canal was completed, and already existing resentment in Panama increased.

At first, when native labor did not want jobs in the coastal area, West Indian blacks were welcomed. As their population increased and jobs became scarcer, however, resentment against the immigrant blacks grew. West Indians continued to speak English and were Protestant—in contrast to the Spanish-speaking and Roman Catholic culture of Central America—causing additional opposition. Charges of discrimination became numerous. In the second and third decades of the twentieth century, laws were passed to limit or prohibit migration from the West Indies, but they were not always enforced.

Modern Era

After WORLD WAR II, when nationalism increased, attempts to force the use of the Spanish language and other measures designed to promote assimilation led to ill will, rioting, and attacks on blacks. Even though attempts to assimilate blacks were only partially successful, the disorders had ended by the 1970's,

to be replaced by leftist reform movements.

In the post-World War II years, blacks were largely assimilated into the population except in Belize and Panama. Blacks constitute about 5 percent of the population, and the mixture of black and Indian about 1 percent. Both groups are concentrated along the Caribbean coast. Guatemala and El Salvador have small black populations. There is little difference between the economic position of blacks and the rest of the poor population in the area.

—*Robert D. Talbott*

Suggested Readings:

Bowser, Frederick. "The African in Colonial Spanish America." *Latin American Research Review* 7, no. 1 (1972): 77-94.

Dostert, Pierre E. *Latin America, 1995*. Harpers Ferry, W.Va.: Stryker-Post, 1995.

Edmonston, Barry, and Jeffrey S. Passel, eds. *Immigration and Ethnicity: The Integration of America's Newest Arrivals*. Washington, D.C.: Urban Institute Press, 1994.

Golden, Reny. *Hour of the Poor, Hour of Women*. New York: Crossroad, 1991.

Goodman, Louis W., William Leo Grande, and Johanna Mendelson Forman. *Political Parties and Democracy in Central America*. Boulder, Colo.: Westview, 1992.

Klien, Herbert S. *Slavery in Latin America and the Caribbean*. New York: Oxford University Press, 1968.

Chamberlain, Wilt (August 21, 1936, Philadelphia, Pennsylvania—October 12, 1999, Los Angeles, California): BASKETBALL player. Chamberlain played fourteen seasons in the National Basketball Association (NBA), 1959-1973, and set impressive scoring records.

Chamberlain was born into a large family. After a standout career at Overbrook High School, he accepted a scholarship from the University of Kansas, where he won All-America honors. He left Kansas after his junior year and played the 1958-1959 basketball season with the HARLEM GLOBETROTTERS. By this time, he had grown to seven feet, one inch, and NBA teams were vying for his services.

Chamberlain was drafted by his hometown PHILADELPHIA Warriors in 1959, and he became an immediate superstar. At that time, the NBA had few seven-footers, and Chamberlain was able to dominate the game as few others have done. He led the NBA in scoring during his first seven seasons. In the 1961-1962 season, he scored a record 4,029 points, 50.4 points per game. On March 2, 1962, he made NBA history by scoring 100 points in a single game; he hit 36 field goals and 28 foul shots, both single-game records.

Despite Chamberlain's individual efforts—he won most valuable player awards four times—his teams repeatedly were denied the NBA title by Bill RUSSELL's Boston Celtics. Only in 1967 did Chamberlain's Philadelphia 76ers stop Russell's team. Later in his career, after he had been traded to the Los Angeles Lakers, Chamberlain again played with a winner. The 1971-1972 Lakers won a record thirty-three straight games at midseason and swept through the playoffs to the NBA title. By this time, Chamberlain had ceased being an explosive scorer, but his rebounding and stalwart defense earned him the most valuable player award for the NBA finals.

By the time Chamberlain retired in 1973, he had scored a record 31,419 career points, with an average of 30.1 points per game. Five years after he retired, he was inducted into the Naismith Memorial Basketball Hall of Fame. By 1996, when a panel named him one of the fifty greatest players of the NBA's first half century, the Philadelphia 76ers, Golden State Warriors, and Los Angeles Lakers had retired his jersey numbers.

Wilt Chamberlain floats up to the basket in a playoff game against the Boston Celtics during his rookie season. *(AP/Wide World Photos)*

Chamberlain's career scoring record was surpassed by Kareem ABDUL-JABBAR during the 1980's. However, by the time of his death, in 1999, Chamberlain still held scores of league records. These included most points in a game (100 in 1962), most points in a season (4,029 in 1961-1962), most consecutive seasons leading league in scoring (7), most games 50 or more points (58), most rebounds in a game (55 in 1960), most rebounds in a season (2,149 in 1960-1961), most career rebounds (23,924), and most seasons leading league in rebounding (11).

After his basketball career ended, Chamberlain devoted much of his time to volleyball. He also acted in films. His experiences are recorded in two autobiographies, *Wilt: Just Like Any Other Seven-Foot Black Millionaire Who Lives Next Door* (1973) and *A View from Above* (1991).

Chambers v. Florida: U.S. SUPREME COURT case involving confessions. In this 1940 ruling, the Court held that confessions extracted through some forms of stressful interrogation were unconstitutional even if no physical abuse had occurred. The case grew out of a FLORIDA incident in which an elderly white man had been killed. Police brought in and questioned more than twenty-five black men. Isaiah Chambers and three others were kept in isolation and interrogated almost continuously for five days and nights. They confessed on the fifth day. Law enforcement officers were accused of using force, but they denied that they had beaten the men. At their trial, the men were convicted and sentenced to death. The U.S. Supreme Court overturned the convictions, stating that the men had been held incommunicado even though charges had not formally been filed and that the threat and "haunting fear" of mob violence was all around them. Their confessions, the Court said, were therefore inadmissible.
See also: Brown v. Mississippi.

Chapman, Tracy (b. March 20, 1964, Cleveland, Ohio): Folk and BLUES singer, songwriter, and guitarist. Chapman became known for the powerful social messages of her lyrics as well as her expressive voice. She grew up in Cleveland, OHIO, and was writing songs before she was a teenager. Her parents were divorced, and her mother struggled financially while raising her two daughters. A good student, Chapman won a minority placement scholarship to a Connecticut prep school, Wooster, and then went on to Tufts University in Boston, graduating in 1986. She began per-

Tracy Chapman accepting a Grammy Award in 1989. *(AP/Wide World Photos)*

forming her own songs, playing on an old, battered guitar, while at Wooster and continued during her college years.

Her first album, *Tracy Chapman*, was released in 1988. It contained the surprise hit "Fast Car" and the widely played "Talkin' 'Bout a Revolution." Chapman won 1989 Grammy Awards for best new artist, best female pop vocal performance, and best contemporary folk performance. Also in 1988 she was part of the Amnesty International Human Rights Now! tour. Social concerns formed a major part of Chapman's life and career, and she frequently participated in, and performed at, marches, protest gatherings, and events to benefit nonprofit organizations.

Her second album, *Crossroads* (1989), sold well in spite of receiving little radio play because of its politically oriented content. *Matters of the Heart* (1992) was less successful. However, the 1995 release *New Beginnings* returned Chapman to the limelight; its songs largely concern personal growth and renewal. The album's "Give Me One Reason," a blues song written by Chapman, was a hit and won the 1996 Grammy Award for best song. The song was also recorded by veteran bluesman B. B. KING.

Charles, Ray (Ray Charles Robinson; b. September 23, 1930, Albany, Georgia): Singer, composer, and pianist. Like many black musicians, Ray Charles was exposed to music at his church, where he sang. When Ray was a baby, his parents, Bailey and Areatha Robinson—Ray later dropped the family name to avoid confusion with the boxer Sugar Ray ROBINSON—moved to Greenville, Florida. Ray's father worked for a railroad and as a handyman, and his mother cooked and washed for white families. When Ray was five years old, his brother George drowned while the children were playing in their backyard; Ray's attempts to rescue him were futile. Soon afterward, Ray developed an eye disease that left him completely blind by the time he was seven years old.

Early Education

Charles's mother encouraged him to function independently and insisted that he learn by touch how to contend with daily life. By the time he started boarding school for the blind at St. Augustine's School for Deaf and Blind Children in Orlando, Florida, he knew how to print the alphabet as well as how to play the piano, a skill he acquired through the encouragement of a neighbor, Wiley Pittman.

In Orlando, Charles studied piano and experimented with the saxophone and clarinet, and he learned enough theory to construct band arrangements. When Charles was fifteen years old, however, his mother died of food poisoning; his father died soon afterward, leaving Ray orphaned and without resources. Rather than resort to dependency, he instead began traveling throughout the state, playing in pickup bands and surviving on the meager earnings he could garner. He claims that when he had six hundred dollars saved, he asked a friend to select a city on a map of the United States that was as far away from the South as one could get and still remain within the boundaries of the United States. Thus at the age of almost eighteen, he arrived in Seattle, WASHINGTON.

Building His Career

Charles quickly became acquainted with local Seattle musicians and their haunts. He soon organized a trio of piano, drums, and electric guitar that played in clubs in town. He also liked to frequent after-hours JAZZ clubs where musicians would gather to hold spontaneous sessions; the music of choice owed a great deal to Nat "King" COLE and his version of "cool," which was, in turn, heavily influenced by the BLUES. Among the musicians Charles worked with and influenced at the time was composer and trumpeter Quincy JONES, who became a lifelong friend.

Although Charles's trio had achieved local renown, the center of popular music seemed remote from Seattle, so Charles relocated to LOS ANGELES, CALIFORNIA, an important area for recording jazz and RHYTHM AND BLUES. During the next few years, Charles lived on the road, playing clubs all over the country, and it was during this time that his particular blend of blues and jazz began to emerge. In the process, he helped create a new genre of music, later to be called soul, heavily influenced by the gospel music of the African American churches.

After thousands of miles of traveling across the country, sometimes performing alone (as in his smash performance at HARLEM's famed APOLLO THEATER) and sometimes performing with sidemen unfamiliar to him, he formed a seven-man group in Dallas and went on the road as Ray Charles and His Band. Charles, as composer, arranger, and performer, came into his own with the development of his own brand of music, a combination of rhythm and blues, blues, and gospel, with Charles as vocalist alternately speaking, shouting, and crooning, echoing the idioms of black church music in a unique blend of the sectarian and the secular.

Later Years

Charles sometimes integrated into his arrangements and songs country and western influences as well as the strains of rhythm and blues and gospel. As he toured the country and recorded, he acquired a following that enthusiastically cheered his performances. One song, "This Little Girl of Mine," based on the gospel song "This Little Light of Mine," was a particular favorite. In 1957 he integrated the

Ray Charles during the taping of a television special on his career in 1991. (AP/Wide World Photos)

Raeletts (sometimes spelled the Raylettes) into his act. This group, made up of four or five women backup singers, quickly became essential to the performances.

Charles released his biggest-selling hits between 1959 and 1966, and they included "What'd I Say" (1959), "Hit the Road Jack" (1961), "I Can't Stop Loving You" (1962), and "Crying Time" (1966). Charles won a number of Grammy Awards, beginning in 1960, including one in 1990 for "I'll Be Good to You," a duet with Chaka Khan.

Because Charles became so versatile, so gifted in so many aspects of music, his work is almost impossible to classify. He can correctly be called a composer, singer, pianist, rhythm-and-blues vocalist, blues performer, country singer, saxophonist, and more. Part of the explanation for his worldwide popularity—he toured Europe, South America, and Japan—must lie in his versatility as well as in his ability to appeal to many different kinds of audiences without compromising his musical integrity. Some people were disappointed, particularly in the 1960's, at his reluctance to include political messages or racial protests in his music, but such direct action was not Charles's interest. On the other hand, his rendition of "Georgia on My Mind" (1960), which has come to be known as his signature song (and which was adopted by the state of GEORGIA as its own), manages to communicate the pain of the southern African American experience without expressing it directly.

Overcoming Drug Dependency

During the late 1940's Charles became addicted to heroin. In 1964 he was arrested for drug possession at Boston's Logan Airport. He then checked himself into a clinic and was able to quit using heroin. He regretted his drug usage but did not dwell on it, and because his treatment was successful, the charges against him were eventually dropped.

By the 1980's and 1990's Charles's recordings (among them the albums *Just Between Us*, 1988, and *My World*, 1993) no longer sold huge numbers, but he remained an active and popular touring performer; he performed, for example, at the 1999 Playboy Jazz Festival at the Hollywood Bowl. Charles was given a Kennedy Center Award in 1986 and a National Medal of the Arts in 1993.

—*Jean Gandesbery*

See also: Gospel music and spirituals; Songwriters and composers.

Suggested Readings:

Feather, Leonard. "Ray Charles." In *From Satchmo to Miles*. New York: Stein and Day, 1972.

Lydon, Michael. "Raw Truth and Joy: Ray Charles Cuts Through His Smoothness with Jolts of Musical Pleasure." *The Atlantic* (March, 1991): 120-122.

_____."Ray Charles." In *Boogie Lightning*. New York: Dial Press, 1974.

_____. *Ray Charles: Man and Music*. New York: Riverhead, 1998.

Martin, Guy. "Blue Genius: Brother Ray Charles Sings the Gospel Truth." *Esquire* (May, 1986): 92-100.

Mathis, Sharon Bell. *Ray Charles*. New York: Thomas Y. Crowell, 1973.

Charleston: DANCE popular in the 1920's. The Charleston, which probably had African roots, emerged among southern blacks, who carried it north on their way to HARLEM, New York. The Charleston, which grew out of JAZZ and RAGTIME along with other dances such as the BLACK BOTTOM, big apple, shimmy, and ballin' the jack, expressed a revolt against more restrictive dance forms by separating dance partners, who used free-swinging arms and knees, independent hops, and unconventional posturings while moving to a carefree, pulsing beat.

Charleston, South Carolina, riot: One of the many violent confrontations between blacks and whites during the RED SUMMER OF 1919.

In 1919 African Americans constituted more than half of Charleston's population of eighty thousand. Racial tensions had been exacerbated by the revival of the KU KLUX KLAN in 1915 and the frustrations of African American veterans returning from WORLD WAR I. On Saturday evening, May 10, 1919, an incident involving white sailors from the Charleston naval base and local African Americans sparked a riot that lasted well into Sunday morning, May 11. It turned the downtown Charleston area into a virtual battleground.

Precise details concerning the inciting incident were never settled conclusively, but around 8:30 P.M. on Saturday at least one white sailor and at least one local African American clashed, perhaps in a downtown poolroom, apparently resulting in a mortality on one side or the other. Word of the incident spread quickly, and within hours thousands of white sailors and Charlestonian civilians were roaming the streets looking for African Americans to beat or kill.

A number of African Americans fought back. Shootings, looting, sniper fire from automobiles, beatings, robberies, and destruction of property persisted in spite of the peacekeeping efforts of Marines and city and county police. By the time order had been restored, four people had died and sixty had been treated for injuries. A full-scale naval investigation ultimately indicted three sailors, convicting and imprisoning two of them for their part in the events.

—*Terry Nienhuis*

See also: Race riots.

Charlton, Samuel (c. 1761, New Jersey—1843, New York, New York): Revolutionary war soldier. Born a slave, Charlton was sent to fight in the AMERICAN REVOLUTION at the age of sixteen or seventeen as a substitute for his master. He served at the battles of Brandywine, Germantown, and Monmouth. Charlton returned to his master at the end of the war. When he received his freedom following his master's death, he moved with his wife to NEW YORK CITY.

Chase-Riboud, Barbara (b. June 20, 1939, Philadelphia, Pennsylvania): Sculptor and writer. Chase-Riboud was born into a black middle-class family and began studying art at the Fletcher Art School when she was seven years old. While still in high school, she won a *Seventeen* magazine art prize and sold her first prints to the Museum of Modern Art. Chase-Riboud enrolled in the Tyler College of Art at Temple University and graduated with a B.A. degree in 1957. After receiving a John Hay Whitney Award, she traveled to Rome and Egypt to study sculpture and returned to the United States to complete her M.F.A. degree at Yale University in 1960.

Chase-Riboud returned to Europe after graduating from Yale and traveled extensively with her French photojournalist husband. Over the years, her sculpture incorporated fabrics and symbolic forms inspired by her travels in Africa and in China, along with themes from her experiences during the early Civil Rights movement. Her works have been exhibited in various European museums, as well as the Betty Parsons Gallery in New York, the Massachusetts Institute of Technology, and the University Art Gallery in Berkeley, California.

Also a talented writer, Chase-Riboud published novels and several volumes of poetry. Perhaps her best-known written work is the novel *Sally Hemings* (1979), a portrait of the life of Thomas Jefferson's alleged slave mistress. *See also:* Hemings, Sally; Sculptors.

Chavis, Benjamin Franklin, Jr. (b. January 22, 1948, Oxford, North Carolina): CIVIL RIGHTS activist and cleric. Chavis became famous as a member of the Wilmington Ten. Representing the United Church of Christ, Chavis organized civil rights demonstrations in favor of equal education rights in Wilmington, NORTH CAROLINA. In February, 1971, a local white-owned grocery store was burned down following a racial disturbance. Chavis and nine others were arrested and charged in connection with the violence. A jury of ten whites and two blacks convicted the Wilmington Ten on arson and conspiracy charges, handing down severe sentences, including thirty-four years in prison for Chavis. Chavis insisted on the complete innocence of the Wilmington Ten, charging that they were the victims of racist and political persecution.

Charges Overturned

Allegations surfaced later that the FEDERAL BUREAU OF INVESTIGATION and the Bureau of Alcohol, Tobacco, and Firearms in the Treasury Department had secretly paid witnesses to testify against Chavis so as to guarantee his conviction. The case of the Wilmington Ten soon became internationally notorious because of its alleged violations of human rights and abuses by the state. Amnesty International designated the defendants as political prisoners.

In 1977 a key state witness publicly indicated that he had been pressured into giving damaging testimony. A second witness stated that he was given a minibike and employment at a service station in exchange for his testimony. Defense attorneys moved to overturn the convictions, charging prosecutorial misconduct at the original trial. Despite this, on May 20, 1977, North Carolina Superior Court judge George M. Fountain denied the motion for a retrial of the case. Following two weeks of hearings, he ruled that there had been no substantial denial of the defendants' constitutional rights.

Continuing controversy over the case prompted the governor of North Carolina to intervene in 1978, leading to the parole of Chavis and other members of the Wilmington Ten. On January 24, 1980, fifty-five members of the U.S. House of Representatives implored the state of North Carolina to set aside the charges because the case "raised substantial doubts" about justice in the United States. On December 4, 1980, the U.S. Court of Appeals overturned the original decision, ruling that evidence suggested the denial of a fair trial. The state of North Carolina did not contest the ruling. Chavis went on to direct a civil rights commission in the 1980's.

Executive Director of the NAACP

As executive director of the United Church of Christ's Commission for Racial Justice from 1985 to 1993, Chavis exhibited impressive organizing skills. He accepted the position of executive director of the NATIONAL ASSOCIATION FOR THE ADVANCEMENT OF COLORED PEOPLE (NAACP) in April, 1993. One of the most prominent civil rights organizations in the nation, the NAACP had waned in influence during the 1980's; leaders hoped that the talented Chavis could bring new direction and energy to the organization.

Arguing that the largely middle-class NAACP had lost touch with the concerns of most African Americans and was therefore increasingly irrelevant, Chavis attempted to re-

Benjamin Franklin Chavis, Jr., in April, 1993, immediately after he was named executive director of the NAACP. *(AP/Wide World Photos)*

vive the group's fortunes through increased contacts with radical organizations and street gangs. This strategy troubled NAACP members, many of whom were especially critical of Chavis's close relationship with the leader of the NATION OF ISLAM, Louis FARRAKHAN, whose anti-Semitic remarks generated controversy the NAACP wished to avoid.

Doubts about Chavis's leadership were compounded in June of 1994, when Washington, D.C., attorney Mary E. Stansel filed a sexual harassment suit against Chavis and the NAACP. The organization's board of directors met on August 20, 1994, to discuss the charges and to assess Chavis's leadership. Board members learned that Chavis had promised Stansel a $332,400 settlement without their approval. Critics also charged that Chavis had squandered the organization's money, leaving the NAACP with a debt of more than $2 million. Chavis responded that he had done nothing wrong and had offered Stansel the settlement in order to avoid an embarrassing public lawsuit. He claimed that he had inherited the large debt from his predecessor. Unconvinced by Chavis's defense, the board voted to dismiss him from his position.

After the NAACP

An angry Chavis responded with a denunciation of the board, calling his dismissal "a lynching." He filed a lawsuit against the NAACP claiming that he had been wrongfully fired. Chavis and the NAACP later settled out of court. Chavis contended that the settlement was for far less than he deserved but that he had accepted it because the protracted legal wrangling was unfair to his family.

Chavis turned his efforts to a new civil rights group, the National African American Leadership Summit (NAALS). Organized as summit meetings for black leaders from many different groups, NAALS quickly developed an agenda of its own. The MILLION MAN MARCH, a mass protest meeting held in Washington, D.C., in October of 1995, was planned at an NAALS meeting, and Chavis served as the event's national director. Critics again questioned the close ties between Chavis and Louis Farrakhan, who served as keynote speaker for the march.

—*Updated by Thomas Clarkin*

Checker, Chubby (Ernest Evans; b. October 3, 1941, Philadelphia, Pennsylvania): Singer. Checker is most closely associated with the twist, a popular DANCE of the 1960's that gained international fame. Chubby Checker (the name is a playful twist on the name Fats DOMINO) recorded the song, "The Twist" (1960), that was accompanied by the dance craze of the same name. Hank Ballard had recorded a version of the song as a B side of a single in 1959, but it and the dance received little attention at the time.

The popularity of the twist can be explained in part by the changing times of the 1960's, when Americans were beginning to pay serious attention to new musical strains and attempting to incorporate rhythm and blues into dance music. As a dance, the twist represented a remarkable departure from the more conventional forms of ballroom dancing. Its patterns enabled partners to express themselves in less structured ways and allowed greater freedom of motion and mobility. Strong physical movement and gestures formed the foundations of the dance, accompanied by the throaty, wailing notes of the music.

Checker was never able to diversify enough to cast off his association in popular culture as

Chubby Checker in late 1961, when he was introducing the twist. *(AP/Wide World Photos)*

the icon and articulator of one popular movement. As an indication of how deeply entrenched his identity was with that particular dance, the titles of his albums of the mid-1960's include *Twist* (1962), *Twistin' Around the World* (1962), and *Let's Twist Again* (1962). He attempted to follow up his success as a dance innovator by introducing the Fly and the Pony, danced to his songs "Pony Time" (1961) and "The Fly" (1961). Both songs reached the top ten.

Dr. James Cheek. (*©Roy Lewis Archives*)

Checker married Catharina Lodders, Miss World of 1962, in December, 1963. His hits ended in 1965, but he remained a popular nightclub performer. He continued to record and to perform in rock revival shows. He experimented with disco-tinged music in the early 1980's. For many people, nostalgia for the early 1960's is associated with what some consider to be a more innocent time, an era that includes sock hops, drive-ins, and penny loafers. The music that accompanies this supposedly innocent time is often the dance music of the twist.

Cheek, James (b. December 4, 1932, Roanoke Rapids, North Carolina): Educator and administrator. Facing a threat of total blindness that required numerous surgical operations at age ten, Cheek grew up to be a serious student. He graduated from Shaw University in Raleigh, NORTH CAROLINA, in 1955. An interest in theology resulted in a bachelor's degree in divinity from Colgate University in Hamilton, New York, in 1958. In 1962 he completed his Ph.D. at Drew University in Madison, New Jersey.

Imaginative, innovative, and astute, Cheek became the president of Shaw University in 1963 after several years spent teaching. He saved the institution from academic and financial collapse by gaining the financial support of businesses and foundations and by establishing programs of special interest to African Americans. His success at Shaw did not go unnoticed. In 1969 he was made the fifteenth president of HOWARD UNIVERSITY in Washington, D.C. When he retired in 1989, Cheek had brought stability to the institution, led African American college presidents to the White House to discuss the future of HISTORICALLY BLACK COLLEGES, and steered Howard University into involvement in a variety of noncampus activities. At Tennessee Wesleyan College, where he served as president after leaving Howard University, he began a program of building the college for the future.

Cheek served as a member of the task force on adult education for the Department of Education, member of the President's Commission on Campus Unrest, special consultant to the president on black colleges and universities, and member of the steering committee of the National Urban Coalition. He was honored with doctorates from many American and international institutions. He was also a

1983 recipient of the Presidential Medal of Freedom. Cheek became a trustee, director, or member of numerous professional and civic organizations, including the American Society of Church History, American Academy of Religion, OPERATION PUSH, National Council on Educating the Disadvantaged, Common Cause Policy Council, and the Joint Center for Political Studies.

Cheek, King (b. May 26, 1937, Weldon, North Carolina): Educator and lawyer. Cheek earned degrees in economics and law. Among his numerous administrative positions were posts as president of Shaw University and Morgan State College. A leader in civic and professional organizations as well, Cheek was awarded the Grand Commander of the Order of the Star of Africa in 1971 by President William Tubman of LIBERIA.

Chemists: From agricultural and food chemistry to nuclear and analytical chemistry, from biological to physical chemistry, and from inorganic to organic chemistry, chemists have made substantial contributions to creating and maintaining the quality of American life. Despite the importance of chemistry, most Americans are unlikely to know the names of its leading practitioners. With the exception of George Washington CARVER, few African American chemists who have made valuable scientific contributions are widely known. However, many black chemists have made breakthrough discoveries that have had beneficial results for all Americans.

Educator and Innovator

Born in Missouri to slave parents in 1860, George Washington Carver overcame the shortcomings of his early education and enrolled at Simpson College in Iowa when he was twenty-five years old. In 1891 he transferred to what became Iowa State University and graduated with B.S. and M.S. degrees in agricultural chemistry and botany. It appeared that he would settle down on the school's faculty and carry out a life of academic research. In 1896, however, he accepted a position at Booker T. WASHINGTON's TUSKEGEE INSTITUTE, where he spent the rest of his career doing practical agricultural research instead.

Carver was both a biologist and a chemist, and his endeavors led to the development of

George Washington Carver (second from right) teaching in a Tuskegee Institute chemistry laboratory. *(Library of Congress)*

more than five hundred different products—ranging from instant coffee to ink to shampoo—from products he isolated from peanuts, sweet potatoes, and pecans. Carver's efforts to improve agricultural yields through the application of better fertilizers and techniques such as crop rotation helped rejuvenate southern agriculture and other southern industries.

Food Additives

Lloyd A. HALL, born in Elgin, Illinois, in 1894, began his scientific studies at Northwestern University, where he received his B.S. degree in pharmaceutical chemistry in 1916. After graduation, Hall worked as a chemist for the Chicago Department of Health from 1916 to 1918 and served as assistant chief inspector of powder and explosives for the U.S. Army during WORLD WAR I. After the war, he served as chief chemist for John Morrell Chemical Company (1918-1920) and later for Boyer Chemical Company (1920-1922). During this time, he earned a Ph.D. from the University of Chicago. As director, chief chemist, and later president of the Griffith Chemical Company from 1925 to 1946, Hall was responsible for formulating many preservatives, antioxidants, and

Lloyd A. Hall. *(Koehne)*

flavorings that are added to food in order to keep it fresh and flavorful. Before his efforts in the field of food chemistry, most food additive treatments were haphazard. Hall's systematic approach led him to apply for more than one hundred patents in food chemistry. His expertise created a wide demand for his services as a food consultant by many government agencies before his death in 1971.

Pharmaceutical Applications of Hormone Research

Percy L. JULIAN, born in Montgomery, Alabama, in 1899, studied chemistry at DePauw University, where he graduated in 1920. He then studied organic chemistry at Harvard University and received his M.S. degree in 1923. After completing his studies at Harvard, he accepted a professorship at HOWARD UNIVERSITY, remaining there until he began doctoral studies in Vienna, Austria. In 1931 he received his Ph.D. degree and returned to Howard to serve as chair of its chemistry department. After disagreements with the university's administration forced him to leave Howard and accept a position at DePauw, he synthesized physostigmine, a bean extract used to treat glaucoma.

In 1936 Julian left academia to become director of soybean research at the Glidden Company. During the course of his research, Julian invented soybean-derived "Aero-Foam," used to extinguish fires, and discovered methods for synthesizing male and female hormones from related soybean chemicals. His best known discovery was the development of a soybean-derived form of cortisone, placing this formerly expensive arthritis treatment within the economic reach of the general public.

In 1954 Julian formed Julian Laboratories, which was so successful that he later sold the enterprise to Smith, Kline, and French. During his career, he published more than two hundred papers in scientific journals. He held more than a hundred patents before his death in 1975. The chemistry building at Texas's MacMurray University was later named in his honor.

University Research and Educational Excellence
Two African Americans who advanced chemical research and teaching at HISTORICALLY BLACK COLLEGES were Moddie D. Taylor and Samuel P. Massie. Born in Nymph, Alabama, in 1912, Taylor received his B.S. degree in chemistry from LINCOLN UNIVERSITY in 1935 and earned M.S. and Ph.D. degrees in chemistry from the University of Chicago. While at Chicago, he became involved in research for the Manhattan Project and received a certificate of merit from the U.S. secretary of war in 1945. He left Chicago to join the chemistry faculty at Howard University in 1959. In 1969 he became chairman of the chemistry department at Howard, a post he held until 1976. Taylor received the Annual Manufacturing Chemist's Award in 1972 in recognition of his talents as a teacher.

Samuel Massie was born in Little Rock, Arkansas, in 1919. He earned his B.S. in chemistry at the University of Arkansas at Pine Bluff in 1938 and earned an M.A. at FISK UNIVERSITY and a Ph.D. at Iowa State University in 1946. Afterward, he returned to Fisk, where he became chairman of the chemistry department in 1953. In 1960 he became a program director for the U.S. National Science Foundation. He was named president of North Carolina Central University in 1963 and joined the faculty of the U.S. Naval Academy in 1972. As a professor of chemistry, Massie advanced to department chairman at the academy in 1977.

Commercial Research
Henry A. Hill was born in Saint Joseph, Montana, in 1915, and earned a B.A. in chemistry at Johnson C. Smith University in 1936. Immediately after he earned a Ph.D. at the Massachusetts Institute of Technology in 1942, he was hired as a research chemist by Atlantic Re-

search Associates, where he became vice president in charge of research in 1944. In 1952 he took an administrative position with National Polychemicals. He founded his own Riverside Research Company in 1961. While serving as president of his own firm, he was on the board of directors of the American Chemical Society from 1971 to 1978, was nominated as president in 1972, and became the society's first African American president in 1977.

Nuclear Chemistry
Born in Waco, Texas, in 1932, James A. HARRIS earned his B.S. in chemistry at Texas's Huston-Tillotson College in 1953. After a stint in the U.S. Army, Harris returned to California to work as an industrial chemist. In 1960 he joined the nuclear chemistry division of the Lawrence Radiation Laboratory in Berkeley, California. There he participated in studies leading to the discovery of the unstable chemical elements rutherfordium and hahnium.

African American chemists have made many valuable contributions to the various fields of chemistry, both in teaching and in research. Their example has encouraged young African Americans to pursue the study of chemistry. In 1977 it was estimated that 131 science graduates, or 1.5 percent of students with Ph.D. degrees in all the natural sciences combined, were African Americans. Studies undertaken during the 1990's estimated that between 1.5 and 4.5 percent of students graduating with Ph.D. degrees in the field of chemistry alone were African Americans.

—*Sanford S. Singer*
See also: Science and technology.

Borman, Stu. "Black Chemist Percy Julian Commemorated on Postage Stamp." *Chemical & Engineering News* 71 (February 1, 1993): 9-12.

Brody, James M. *Created Equal: The Lives and Ideas of Black American Innovators.* New York: William Morrow, 1993.

Hamilton, James B. *What a Time to Live: The Autobiography of James B. Hamilton*. East Lansing: Michigan State University, 1995.

Hayden, Robert C. *Seven Black American Scientists*. Reading, Mass.: Addison-Wesley, 1970.

Klein, Aaron E. *The Hidden Contributors: Black Scientists and Inventors in America*. New York: Doubleday, 1971.

Sammons, Vivian O. *Blacks in Science and Medicine*. New York: Hemisphere, 1990.

Van Sertima, Ivan, ed. *Blacks in Science: Ancient and Modern*. New Brunswick, N.J.: Transaction Books, 1991.

Chenault, Kenneth I. (b. June 2, 1951, Hempstead, New York): Corporate executive and attorney. Born the son of Hortenius Chenault, a dentist, and Anne Chenault, a dental hygienist, Kenneth Chenault attended a preparatory school in New York before being accepted to Bowdoin College in Maine. After receiving his bachelor's degree, he went on to earn his J.D. degree from Harvard Law School in 1976. Chenault passed the New York bar examination and joined the corporate law firm of Rogers & Wells. His work in corporate law encouraged Chenault to take a position as a member of the business consulting firm of Bain & Company in Boston. In 1981 Chenault was hired by American Express and moved back to New York City. He worked in the company's merchandise services division, selling a select line of products via direct mail advertising to American Express card customers.

By 1983 Chenault was named vice president of the merchandise services division with additional responsibility for the company's travel-related services division. In 1984 he was promoted to senior vice president and general manager of merchandise services. Chenault was responsible for generating profits from these auxiliary services while maintaining customer trust and satisfaction. Capitalizing

Kenneth I. Chenault in 1997. *(AP/Wide World Photos)*

on the elite status of the card, Chenault oversaw an expansion of the card's direct sales to nearly $400 million by 1986. Continuing to rise within the American Express corporate structure, Chenault was named president of the American Express Consumer Card Group, USA, becoming chief of card operations in North America.

The advent of tougher economic times in the late 1980's and early 1990's forced Chenault to reposition American Express to compete with credit card companies whose customers were allowed to carry unpaid balances on their cards. Merchants were also expressing dissatisfaction with the 3 percent surcharges American Express required them to pay on card purchases. Although the company's new Optima card was initially offered to established American Express cardholders, problems arose with Optima cardholders who defaulted on their debts. The financial crunch of the early 1990's diminished the company's profits and sullied its image on Wall Street.

Chenault dedicated himself to increasing customer service and maintaining merchant loyalty through focusing on the card's wealthiest customers and emphasizing the traditional advantages offered by the American Express card.

His efforts were successful enough that Chenault continued to rise through the top levels of the company, becoming vice chairman of American Express in 1995. He was named president and chief operating officer in 1997 and chief executive officer in 1999.
See also: Business and commerce.

Chenier, Clifton (June 25, 1925, near Opelousas, Louisiana—December 12, 1987, near Opelousas(?), Louisiana): Musician known as the king of ZYDECO. Zydeco is an uptempo,

Zydeco musician Clifton Chenier. *(©Roy Lewis Archives)*

syncopated dance music of Louisiana's CRE-OLE population. Chenier grew up listening to his father play the accordion, zydeco's traditional lead instrument. By the time he reached the age of sixteen, he had become a proficient accordionist himself.

Often accompanied by his brother Cleveland on the frottier, or metal rub board, Chenier began to blend the traditional zydeco sound with the rhythm-and-blues sound popular in the 1940's. The result was a uniquely hybrid zydeco style. By 1946 Clifton and Cleveland Chenier were in Lake Charles, Louisiana, working at the oil refineries by day and in the local clubs by night.

In 1954 Chenier was discovered by J. R. Fulbright, who signed him to his Elko label. Chenier then released the single "Louisiana Stomp," which became a hit along the Gulf Coast. Recording as well for Imperial, Specialty, and Chess, Chenier took to the road with his band, the Zydeco Ramblers. Toward the end of the decade, the band's once discernibly zydeco sound had evolved into one that was predominantly RHYTHM AND BLUES.

After moving to Houston, Texas, in the early 1960's, Chenier was rescued from possible obscurity by Chris Strachwitz, a blues researcher and owner of Arhoolie Records. After his first Arhoolie single, "Ay Ai Ai" backed with "Why Did You Go Last Night?," sold nearly two thousand copies, Chenier went on to become an international star and Arhoolie's best-selling recording artist. He was featured in a 1974 documentary film entitled *Hot Pepper*.

Chenier's son, C. J. Chenier, kept the family name alive with his own zydeco outfit, the Red Hot Louisiana Band. He enjoyed success in a zydeco resurgence in the late twentieth century.

Chennault, Madelyn (b. July 15, 1934, Atlanta, Georgia): Educator and psychologist. Chennault graduated from Morris Brown College in 1957 with a degree in elementary education and psychology and taught elementary education in public schools in Georgia, California, and Michigan. Prompted by professional interests in educational psychology, special education, and mental retardation, she earned a master's degree in educational psychology from the University of Michigan in 1961 and additional degrees from Indiana University during the 1960's. She completed her doctoral internship at the University of Georgia in 1972. One of the few African American women of her generation with a license to practice clinical psychology, Chennault was director of Fort Valley State College's "crisis clinic," an innovative institution designed to offer services to both the college and the local community in Atlanta, Georgia.

As Calloway Professor of Educational Psychology at Fort Valley State College, Chennault taught courses in psychology and mental retardation. Her research and publications focus on peer relations among mentally retarded pupils and on other aspects of special education. She advocated community-based mental health services and special programs for the poor and mentally retarded and served as an educational consultant for public school integration efforts, community mental health centers, state departments of education, HEAD START programs, and other projects. She was the clinical director of the Community Hypertension Intervention Program at Fort Valley State College from 1972 to 1989.

A member of the Association of Black Psychologists and the American Association of University Professors, Chennault helped pave the way for subsequent generations of African American women to advance in the field of psychology.

See also: Health care professionals.

Chesnutt, Charles Waddell (June 20, 1858, Cleveland, Ohio—November 15, 1932, Cleve-

land, Ohio): Author. At the age of eight Chesnutt moved with his parents to Fayetteville, NORTH CAROLINA, where he lived until 1883. During this period, he completed eight years of formal education and became a successful teacher and administrator in FREEDMEN'S BUREAU schools. He also acquired stenographic skills that helped him to achieve financial security.

Chesnutt began a brief residence in NEW YORK CITY in 1883. He moved to Cleveland, OHIO (the Groveland of his fiction), where he spent the remainder of his life. He gave the fictionalized name of Patesville to Fayetteville, North Carolina. Initially, he worked as a clerk and legal stenographer for a corporation lawyer. He passed the Ohio bar examination in 1887. Chesnutt had a burning ambition to

Charles Waddell Chesnutt. *(Cleveland Public Library)*

write, but this goal was superseded by the desire to earn a living as an attorney and stenographer.

Chesnutt's early publishing successes were with sketches and short stories, with his first major publication in 1885. He eventually published two short-story collections. *The Conjure Woman* (1899) contained six stories, of which "The Goophered Grapevine" is the most widely read. *The Wife of His Youth and Other Stories of the Color Line* (1899) contained nine stories, the most famous of which are the title story and "The Sheriff's Children." Some thirty-eight other stories, including "Baxter's Procrustes," were never published in book form. The overwhelming majority of Chesnutt's short stories are concerned with the question of "passing" and the daily problems facing the person of color in American society. The stories are often complex gems. His characterizations are unpredictable and thought provoking.

Chesnutt was the first African American author to publish in a major magazine, joining the *Atlantic Monthly*'s list of distinguished authors. His two best novels are *The House Behind the Cedars* (1900) and *The Marrow of Tradition* (1901). Both are concerned with African American social ills and the rise of the African American middle class. Neither was particularly successful financially. A third novel, *The Colonel's Dream* (1905), examined the theme of life in the New South. Chesnutt also wrote several more novels that were never published.

Over the next twenty-five years, Chesnutt published only a few letters and pamphlet-length materials on issues of race. He was discouraged by the reception of African American LITERATURE. Chesnutt gained an audience only later, but his reputation is secure as a prominent pioneer short-story writer and novelist. Chesnutt emerged as one of the most talented African American short fiction writers of the late nineteenth and early twentieth centuries.

Chicago blues: Type of BLUES music. Chicago blues reflects the changes from country to urban living experienced by musicians settling in CHICAGO during the 1930's. Previous guitar and harmonica accompaniments became augmented by piano, bass, and drums. During the post-World War II era, electric instruments were incorporated, partly to contend with the noisy atmosphere of the clubs in Chicago. The music of HOWLIN' WOLF and Bo DIDDLEY was often in this style.
See also: Rhythm and blues.

Chicago Defender: One the most important African American newspapers in the United States. Founded in 1905, it championed CIVIL RIGHTS and played a prominent role in African American social and political movements throughout the twentieth century.

Robert Sengstacke ABBOTT, a lawyer and journalist who had moved to Chicago from Georgia, started the paper in his landlady's dining room. Circulation grew quickly because Abbott wrote stories that appealed to the majority of blacks in CHICAGO, ILLINOIS, at a time when most other African American newspapers catered to the educated elite.

During WORLD WAR I the *Defender* achieved national recognition. It encouraged African Americans to leave the South by printing stories about southern racism and discrimination alongside stories of black families who had relocated to Chicago and found good lives. The *Defender*'s Chicago offices became a clearinghouse for migrants; the newspaper staff helped many people find jobs and lobbied local government for better housing.

After surviving hard times during the 1930's, the *Defender* moved to the forefront of the civil rights struggle during and after WORLD WAR II. During the war, editors carefully avoided provocation in the interest of national unity, but they also steadily reminded readers that a war for freedom abroad should also achieve equality at home. During the 1960's the paper's editors cheered and championed the Civil Rights movement. However, they criticized the Civil Rights Act of 1964 for failing to address segregated housing and other problems of discrimination in northern cities. The *Defender* continued to champion fair housing, employment, and education for black Americans.

—*Robert E. McFarland*
See also: Black press; National Newspaper Publishers Association.

Chicago, Illinois: Third largest city in the United States, according to the 1990 U.S. census. Census statistics showed that Chicago in 1990 was home to the second-largest African American community in the United States, numbering more than one million and com-posing 39 percent of the city's population. Chicago's South Side boasted the largest contiguous settlement of African Americans.

The city's black history began with Jean Baptiste Pointe Du Sable, who built a trading post at the confluence of the Chicago River and Lake Michigan in the 1780's. For many years, however, there were few African Americans in the area. In 1850 there were only three hundred in an overall population of thirty thousand, and in 1900 less than 2 percent of the city's 1.7 million inhabitants were black. Major change came with World War I, as southern blacks were attracted to Illinois by Chicago's growing need for labor. By 1930 233,000 African Americans lived in Chicago. The Great Migration lasted into the second half of the twentieth century: By 1960, 837,000 African Americans lived in Chicago, and by 1980 the number was about 1.2 million.

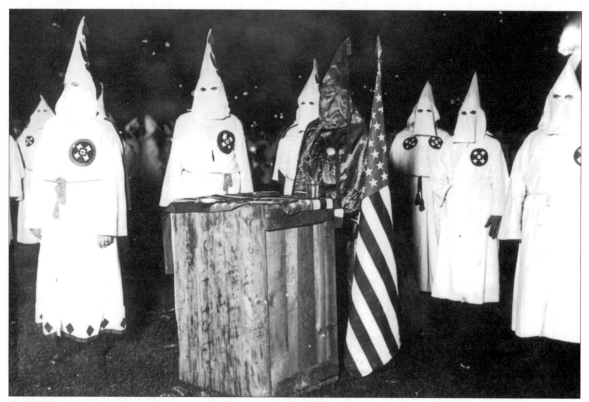

One evidence of racial tensions in Chicago during the early 1920's was the creation of a Chicago branch of the Ku Klux Klan. *(Library of Congress)*

As it grew, Chicago's African American community confronted a highly segregated city. In part as a result of policies adopted by the Chicago Real Estate Board in 1917, residential (and consequently educational) segregation was nearly complete. The city also experienced its share of racial tensions. In 1919 a dispute concerning a Lake Michigan beach led to a major race riot in which fifteen whites and twenty-three African Americans died. In the 1950's and 1960's, sporadic violence accompanied attempts made to integrate housing in the city.

The concentration of African Americans on the city's South Side and, to a lesser extent, on its West Side did, however, make it easier to develop a political base. In 1928 five black aldermen were elected, and Oscar DePriest became the first African American to be elected to Congress from a northern district. African American political power in the city reached a peak with the election of Harold Washington as mayor in 1983.

The city's African American community has been very influential. The Chicago Defender, founded in 1905, has for many years been one of the country's most respected black papers, and Chicago is home to Johnson Publishing Company, the largest black-owned publisher in the world. The city is the home base of Operation PUSH (People United to Save Humanity), founded by Jesse Jackson, as well as of many black artists and writers. *See also:* Urbanization.

Chicago jazz: Style of jazz music. Chicago jazz is generally considered to be derived from New Orleans jazz, first introduced to Chicago by Joe "King" Oliver and his Creole Jazz Band. Chicago jazz featured a two-beat rhythm with stress on the afterbeat, a tenor sax lead, and choppy phrasing. Its influence is clearly seen in Dixieland jazz. Often, each instrument played an individual solo in a song, with the other instruments providing backing.

Lydia Maria Child. *(Library of Congress)*

Child, Lydia Maria (February 11, 1802, Medford, Massachusetts—October 20, 1880, Wayland, Massachusetts): Writer, editor, social reformer, and leader in the Abolitionist movement. For decades a household name because of her children's magazine, fiction, and essays, Child was hailed by Samuel Jackson, an African American abolitionist correspondent, as second only to abolitionist John Brown as a white benefactor of African Americans.

The youngest child of a New England baker, Child had won popular acclaim as a writer and editor by the time she was thirty. In 1833 publication of *An Appeal in Favor of That Class of Americans Called Africans*, the first American book to argue for an end to all forms of Racial discrimination and for immediate emancipation of the slaves, converted many but resulted in her reading public turning against her. Despite social ostracism and lifelong financial hardship, Child persisted in her efforts.

Child edited the *National Anti-Slavery Standard* (1841-1843), wrote abolitionist tracts, helped fugitive slaves, faced angry mobs, and donated what little she could spare to end SLAVERY. During the CIVIL WAR, she edited Harriet Jacobs's *Incidents in the Life of a Slave Girl* (1860), wrote President Abraham Lincoln (1862) urging him not to delay an emancipation proclamation any further, and published *The Freedmen's Book* (1865), a reader including works by African American writers that was of immense practical value in helping emancipated slaves learn to read and adjust to their newfound freedom.

Child helped to turn public opinion against slavery; beyond that she was a staunch advocate of the rights of Native Americans, women, and the poor, and she supported many other progressive reforms.

—*Sue Tarjan*

See also: Children's literature.

Children: African American children emerged as a subject of study in the early 1900's. Theories of child development and methodologies for the study of children did not begin to develop until late in the nineteenth century, and at the time African Americans and their children were considered less than human by many white scholars.

Early Research

The first major studies of African American children were conducted in the late 1940's by Kenneth Clark and Mamie Clark. The results indicated that racism, segregation, and discrimination caused African American children to develop low self-esteem, especially as it related to race. When African American children were asked to choose between a doll with dark skin and a doll with white skin, they said the white doll was prettier and nicer. Moreover, they indicated this was the doll that they wanted to be like and to have as a friend. This research was a major factor in the landmark 1954 U.S. SUPREME COURT case BROWN V. BOARD OF EDUCATION, which declared segregation in public schools to be illegal.

During the 1950's and 1960's, many studies involving African American children were published. The majority of these studies compared the behavior of African American children to that of white children on various measures of personality, aptitude, and achievement. The behavior of the white children was typically used as the standard in such studies; in comparison to this model, African American children were often viewed as deficient or abnormal. African American children were said to have a lesser need for achievement than white children.

Other studies supported the view that African American children were less able to

Early studies of African American children examined young girls' feelings about black and white dolls. *(Hazel Hankin)*

Percentages of Black Families with Children

	Percent Distribution			
	No Children	*One Child*	*Two Children*	*Three or More Children*
1980	38	23	20	18
1985	43	23	20	15
1990	41	25	19	14
1995	42	24	20	14
1997	42	25	20	14

Source: U.S. Bureau of the Census.

delay gratification relative to their white counterparts; they were more likely to choose an immediate small reward rather than a large reward later. Evidence was also given that these children had more external, as opposed to internal, loci of control—that is, African American children were more likely to see events in their world as the result of powerful others, or fate, rather than as the result of their own behavior. Other studies showed African American children to have lower self-esteem, less self-control, and lower intelligence scores. These deficits were said to be the result of inborn deficiencies, disadvantaged environments, poor child rearing, or a combination of these factors.

Later Research

By the 1970's, increasing numbers of African American scholars were questioning the theories, methods, and results of much of the previous research about black children. Issues concerning the cultural bias of tests, the validity of the use of white children as behavioral standards, and the impact of white experimenters and mainstream settings on black test subjects were raised. Much of the research by both African American and white experts during the 1970's refuted previous conclusions about black children.

For example, Curtis Banks and Gregory McQuater showed that although African

American children scored more "externally" than their white counterparts, their scores were not at the external end of the scale but in the middle, while white children scored nearer to the internal end of the scale. The authors interpreted these results as indicating that the African American children realistically viewed the world as sometimes under their control and sometimes not, while the white children probably overestimated their degree of control. Other research indicated that although African American youth may perceive their group as having little control over the political and economic realities of life, they view themselves as having substantial personal control over events in their daily lives.

In other areas, similar results and issues were found. Most studies were not able to duplicate the Clark results when the tests included a wide range of dolls of color or when variations in eye and hair color were considered. Debate arose over whether this meant that there never had been a general black self-esteem problem or whether the BLACK POWER and CIVIL RIGHTS MOVEMENTS of the 1950's and 1960's had raised the self-esteem of African American children. Other studies refuted the research on delay of gratification.

The most controversial area has been that of INTELLIGENCE AND ACHIEVEMENT TESTING: Although African American children on average score fifteen points below their white counterparts on intelligence tests, research on African American children adopted into white homes and research on programs to improve IQ test scores have supported the view that this difference is the result of environmental factors rather than the result of inborn differences. The issue of test bias became so controversial that in

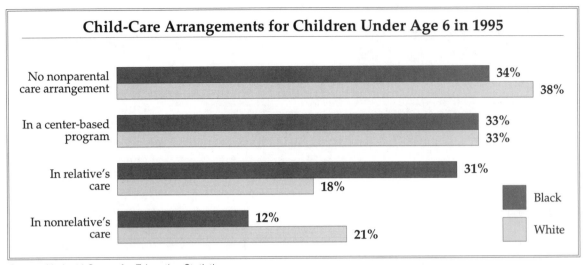

Child-Care Arrangements for Children Under Age 6 in 1995

No nonparental care arrangement
- Black 34%
- White 38%

In a center-based program
- Black 33%
- White 33%

In relative's care
- Black 31%
- White 18%

In nonrelative's care
- Black 12%
- White 21%

Legend: ■ Black ☐ White

Source: National Center for Education Statistics.
Note: Center-based programs include day-care centers, Head Start programs, and preschools.

1977, as a result of a case filed by the Association of Black Psychologists, the California supreme court banned all IQ testing in schools until appropriate steps could be taken to ensure that cultural biases were removed. Many school districts now use IQ testing only for special placements, and numerous precautions are taken to ensure that test scores are not the only determinant of placement and that regular retesting occurs.

Afrocentric Research
In the late 1970's and early 1980's, a new perspective on African American children began to develop. This Afrocentric approach was more proactive and less reactive than the refutational approach discussed above. Emphasis began to be placed on African American children as subjects worthy of study in their own right, without the need for comparison and within an African or African American cultural context. This line of research has focused on the cultural and familial factors that contribute to the cognitions and behaviors of African American children. Their ability to be independent and resilient under adverse circumstances is emphasized. Other concepts examined are the ability to deal with contradiction, a broader concept of family and community, and black children's creativity.

Studies have found that African American children have the same aspirations as their white counterparts but lower expectations of achieving them. *(Hazel Hankin)*

The ability to cope with racism, discrimination, and life in a white world is fundamental for African American children. Studies show that African American children and their families have the same aspirations as their white counterparts but have lower expectations that they will be able to achieve their goals. Other research shows that teachers view African American children differently from white students; teachers have lower expectations of black students and find it harder to see them as intellectually gifted. Many African American children come from homes where nonstandard English, notably BLACK ENGLISH, is spoken, a fact that often leads to perceptual and educational problems. In one court case, the Michigan supreme court recognized that the negative connotations that educational personnel attached to the speaking of nonstandard dialect was harmful to both the self-image and education of African American children, and the court mandated teacher education in nonstandard dialects.

Challenges Facing Young Men

The particular plight of young African American men is a continuing issue. Male African American youths appear to be most vulnerable to the problems plaguing the African American community. Problems such as drugs, crime, and single-parent homes have a disproportionate impact on African American men; a high number of African American children, especially men, have (or are at risk of) numerous physical, psychological, and cognitive disorders. This situation is the result of social factors such as POVERTY, discrimination, poor HEALTH care, and limited informational resources.

For the African American man, the situation is complicated by a society and an educational system that provide him with few role models and perceive him in a stereotypical manner. Research indicates that students model themselves after individuals they perceive as similar to them; school and the behaviors related to school are thus perceived as ap-

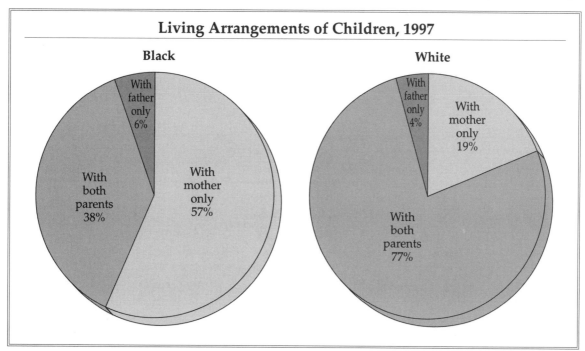

Living Arrangements of Children, 1997

Black

With father only 6%

With both parents 38%

With mother only 57%

White

With father only 4%

With mother only 19%

With both parents 77%

Source: U.S. Bureau of the Census.
Note: Includes only children under 18 living with one or both parents.

propriate for the white women who make up the majority of the role models presented in the schools. African American men would be expected to be least successful in this system, and they are.

—*Rita R. Smith-Wade-El*

See also: Biracial and mixed-race children; Children's Defense Fund; Children's literature; Education; Head Start; Parenting.

Suggested Readings:

Halberstam, David. *The Children*. New York: Random House, 1998.

Hale-Benson, Janice E. *Black Children: Their Roots, Culture and Learning Styles*. Rev. ed. Baltimore: The Johns Hopkins University Press, 1986.

Kunjufu, Jawanza. *Developing Positive Self-Images and Discipline in Black Children*. Chicago: African-American Images, 1984.

Mangum, Garth L., and Stephen F. Seninger. *Coming of Age in the Ghetto: A Dilemma of Youth Unemployment*. Baltimore: The Johns Hopkins University Press, 1978.

Meier, Kenneth J., Joseph Stewart, Jr., and Robert E. England. *Race, Class, and Education: The Politics of Second-Generation Discrimination*. Madison: University of Wisconsin Press, 1989.

Sachar, Emily. *Shut Up and Let the Lady Teach: A Teacher's Year in a Public School*. New York: Poseidon Press, 1991.

Children's Defense Fund: Lobbying organization for CHILDREN and adolescents. An outgrowth of the Washington Research Project, the Children's Defense Fund (CDF) was founded in 1973 in Washington, D.C., by African American lawyer Marian Wright EDELMAN. As an advocacy group for American youth, the organization does research, provides public education, and monitors federal agencies in the areas of child welfare, TEENAGE PREGNANCY prevention, child care and devel-

opment, child health and mental health, and family services.

The fund drafts legislation, engages in litigation, presents testimony, and assists state, local, and community groups. The organization attempts to secure public access to existing services and to create new programs and services as needed. Members ensure that CIVIL RIGHTS laws are enforced, government programs are held accountable, adequate program funding exists, and there is a strong parent and community input related to children and adolescents.

The fund founded several publications: a bimonthly monograph series called Adolescent Pregnancy Prevention Clearinghouse Reports; *Children's Defense Fund Reports*, a monthly newsletter providing information and statistics on relevant topics as well as congressional voting records on children's issues; and *A Vision for America's Future*, an annual report on the status of children, adolescents, and families. Additionally, the fund periodically publishes updated versions of *The Health of America's Children: Maternal and Child Health Data* and other books and pamphlets.

The fund's significant contributions to America's youth, especially low-income African Americans and other low-income youth, are numerous. Its 1975 report on the high rate of school absenteeism spurred new legislation. In 1980 the fund was part of a coalition that resulted in legislation concerning foster care, adoption, and disabled and homeless children as well as abused and neglected children.

The Adolescent Pregnancy Prevention Clearinghouse, begun in 1983, provides assistance to local programs as well as public education through posters and pamphlets. The fund's bilingual immunization publicity program began operating in 1988. By 1990 the work of the fund led the National Academy of Science to advocate that the United States spend ten billion dollars more per year on child care and establish more rigorous regulations concerning child-care centers. In the late 1990's the fund had a staff of more than one hundred and a budget of eighteen million dollars.

In 1996 the fund lobbied unsuccessfully against the sweeping reductions in federal welfare benefits enacted by Congress and supported by the CLINTON ADMINISTRATION. In 1997, however, it won congressional support for the State Children's Health Insurance Program. In 1998 the Children's Defense Fund celebrated its twenty-fifth anniversary in Washington, D.C., at its national conference in Los Angeles. That same year it published *The State of America's Children: A Report from the Children's Defense Fund*.

Children's literature: Children's books published before 1960 generally ignored African Americans and failed to represent American multicultural diversity accurately. By the 1990's, however, the situation had changed dramatically. Children had access to a wide variety of books, including works by African American authors and illustrators, that reflect the rich mosaic of black America's cultural heritage.

Children's Books Before the 1960's
Before 1960 children's literature included few contemporary or realistic black characters. Far more common were portrayals inspired by racist stereotypes. It was not unusual for slaves to be shown as content on a southern plantation or for there to be implications that they could not survive without their benevolent masters.

A particularly controversial representation of black people is Helen Bannerman's *The Story of Little Black Sambo* (1899). Although Bannerman set the story in British-ruled India, American readers generally perceived it as being a story about a black African boy. The classic British tale was widely circulated in the United States. It begins: "Once upon a time there was a little black boy, and his name was Little Black Sambo, his Mother was called Black Mumbo, and his Father was called Black Jumbo." Sambo avoids being eaten by tigers in the jungle by giving them his new clothes. After the predatory animals chase each other in circles, turning into a blur and then into butter, Sambo and his parents enjoy a feast of pancakes slathered with tiger butter.

American editions of *Little Black Sambo* typically contained illustrations that emphasized stereotypical images of blacks. For example, an illustration from a 1932 edition pictures a large mammy figure with huge lips, a kerchief on her head, and an apron. Though set in India, the story still enrages Americans who see Sambo as a racist stereotype. (In 1996 two award-winning African Americans—author Julius Lester and illustrator Jerry Pinkney—adapted the story to a setting in the American South of the 1920's and named it *Sam and the Tigers*. It was a decidedly entertaining and nonracist revision of Bannerman's book.)

Blacks continued to be portrayed into the twentieth century as physically unattractive and unintelligent. *Epaminondas and His Auntie*, by Sara Cone Bryant and illustrated by Inez Hogan (1938), depicts a stereotypical "pickaninny" child who cannot do anything right. Hogan also illustrated the Nicodemus series, which portrayed similar stereotypes. *Little Brown Koko* (1940), written by Blanche Seale Hunt and illustrated by Dorothy Wagstaff, provides another derisive image of African American stereotypical characters: "Once there was a little brown boy named Little Brown Koko. He was the shortest, fattest little Negro you could ever imagine. He had the blackest, little woolly head and great, big, round eyes . . . but he had one bad habit. He was greedy. Why, compared with Little Brown Koko, a pig should be called a well-mannered gentleman."

Negative textual images of African American as uneducated, lazy, poor, menial laborers, dependent upon whites and entrapped in superstitious beliefs, were reinforced with negative visual images of exaggerated facial features, such as large lips and kinky hair. Consequently, African American children found little that engendered pride in their racial heritage. White children suffered too, being misled into thinking that light-skinned people are superior and constitute a majority in the world.

The degree to which pre-1960's books perpetuated unflattering stereotypes of African Americans came into light in 1965 with Nancy Larrick's *Saturday Review* article, "The All-White World of Children's Books." The article also criticized the nearly total exclusion of African Americans in the early 1960's; only four-fifths of 1 percent of the children's books studied offered realistic portrayals of African Americans.

Positive Portrayals

By the late 1960's, more accurate portrayals in both text (including plot, theme, characterization, and language) and illustrations began to appear. With black history being integrated into school curricula, books became available on topics previously ignored: SLAVERY's brutality, the UNDERGROUND RAILROAD, the CIVIL RIGHTS movement, and biographies of heroic African American women and men. This greater diversity heightened sensitivity about racism and led to the removal from libraries and schools of books such as *Nicodemus*, *Little Brown Koko*, and *Little Black Sambo*.

Arguments about what is and is not offensive have continued since the 1960's; some African Americans find books offensive that others see as perfectly acceptable. One controversial book about black culture that came under fire is *Nappy Hair* (1998), a book by African American author Carolivia Herron that celebrates racial differences. After a white ele-

Before the 1960's there were few children's books offering positive portrayals of African American life and cultural diversity. *(CLEO Freelance Photography)*

mentary school teacher read this book to her African American students, some nonwhite parents complained about racial insensitivity. Consequently, the teacher requested reassignment to another school, and the resulting national attention launched the book onto *Publishers Weekly*'s best-seller list.

Many positive portrayals of strong, independent African American children have appeared. An excellent example is the character Grace in Mary Hoffman's *Amazing Grace* (1991), illustrated by Caroline Binch. Grace proves that she can accomplish anything she makes up her mind to do, including playing Peter Pan in the school play even though she is a black girl. In *Boundless Grace* (1995), the sequel to this popular book, the spunky girl travels with her grandmother to the African country of Gambia to visit her father and his new family.

Historical fiction and contemporary realistic fiction explore various facets of the African American experience. Publishers give particular importance to these books, which emphasize respect for the past and pride in ethnicity. They increase the young reader's understanding of social, economic, and personal struggles. Indeed, all children can relate to these stories about situations common to everyone, such as sibling rivalry, problems with parents or grandparents, and peer relationships.

Since the 1970's, a number of outstanding books by African Americans have won the Newbery Award (honoring the best in children's literature), the Caldecott Award (honoring the best illustration), and the Coretta Scott KING Award (honoring the best in African American LITERATURE and illustration since 1969). Angela Johnson's *Heaven* (1998) and Michele Wood's *I See the Rhythm* (1998) won 1999 King Awards.

Folklore Adaptations

Among the best African American FOLKLORE are the Uncle Remus stories, retold in the late nineteenth century by Joel Chandler Harris. Adaptations include Van Dyke Parks's *Jump! The Adventures of Brer Rabbit* (1986) and Julius Lester's series. These tales feature Brer (brother) Rabbit, the supposedly helpless small creature that cleverly outsmarts the more powerful and larger bear and fox. "Brer Rabbit Grossly Deceives Brer Fox," from Parks's collection, ends with Brer Rabbit jumping up, cracking his heels together, and laughing at having triumphed once again.

Another tale, a CREOLE folktale, is Robert D. San Souci's *The Talking Eggs* (1989), illustrated by Jerry Pinkney, an outstanding and prolific African American artist. This African American variant of the Creole tale has a Cinderella motif; goodness and virtue triumph. Pinkney's illustration for *Mirandy and Brother Wind* (1988) won him a Caldecott Honor, as did his artwork for Julius Lester's

John Henry (1994). John Henry, that awesome steel-driving black folk hero, was so strong, he could lift his cradle into the air like a feather; he laughed so loud he scared the sun, and he hammered so hard he beat a steam drill.

Nonfiction and Poetry

A rich assortment of biographies of African Americans and informational books instill pride in African American culture. Among the best nonfiction are Alan Schroeder's *Minty: A Story of Young Harriet Tubman* (1996), illustrated by Jerry Pinkney; James Haskins's *Bayard Rustin: Behind the Scenes of the Civil Rights Movement* (1997); Patricia C. McKISSACK and Frederick L. McKissack's *Christmas in the Big House, Christmas in the Quarters* (1994); and Andrea Davis Pinkney and Brian Pinkney's *Duke Ellington: The Piano Prince and His Orchestra* (1998). This biography describes how jazz encompasses the blues, RAGTIME, folk music, and marches from the African American tradition and how ELLINGTON became the king of piano keys.

Coretta Scott King awards in poetry have gone to *Ashley Bryan's ABC's of African American Poetry* (1997), illustrated by Ashley Bryan; *Soul Looks Back in Wonder: Collection of African American Poets* (1993), illustrated by Tom Feelings; and *In Daddy's Arms I Am Tall: African American Celebrating Fathers* (1997), a collection of poems by various authors illustrated by Javaka Steptoe, son of the Caldecott-winning artist John Steptoe. These intergenerational poems pay tribute to the influence that black fathers have on their children and grandchildren. For example, Dinah Johnson's "My Granddaddy Is My Daddy Too" recounts a child's worship of her hero: "Nobody else's big daddy/ Can carve whistles out of wood," she says, and "Only my grandpa/ Can catch fifteen fish in a day."

Reflecting the large demand for African American children's literature is the Jump at the Sun series from Hyperion Books for

Children. This line of books celebrates black culture by featuring African American children from toddlers to teenagers. These books allow black children to see themselves in many different forms. Even though the books in this series reflect African American people and their culture, they are popular among general readers. To enhance this mainstream cultural image, well-known writers such as Nobel Prize-winning author Toni MORRISON and television star Della Reese have contributed to the series.

Children's literature has made great progress in providing realistic images of African American life and culture. By allowing children to see the diversity of multicultural American society, books both improve the self-esteem of racial and ethnic minorities and heighten the sensitivity and cultural awareness of the majority. The positive presence of African Americans in children's books is important for all American children.

—*Laura M. Zaidman*

See also: Juvenile and young adult fiction; Literature.

Suggested Readings:

Broderick, Dorothy. *The Image of the Black in Children's Fiction*. New York: Bowker, 1973.

Evans, Mari, ed. *Black Women Writers 1950-1980: A Critical Evaluation*. Garden City, N.Y.: Anchor Doubleday, 1984.

Hamilton, Virginia. "On Being a Black Writer in America." *The Lion and the Unicorn* 10, no. 1 (1986): 15-17.

Haskins, Jim. "The Triumph of the Spirit in Nonfiction for Black Children." *Triumphs of the Spirit in Children's Literature*, edited by Francelia Butler and Richard Robert. Hamden, Conn.: Library Professionals Publications, 1986.

Kutzer, M. Daphne, ed. *Writers of Multicultural Fiction for Young Adults: A Bio-critical Sourcebook*. Westport, Conn.: Greenwood, 1996.

MacCann, Donnarae, and Gloria Woodard, eds. *The Black American in Books for Children: Readings in Racism*. 2d ed. Metuchen, N.J.: Scarecrow, 1977.

Norton, Donna E. *Through the Eyes of a Child: An Introduction to Children's Literature*. 5th ed. Upper Saddle River, N.J.: Prentice Hall, 1999.

Sims, Rudine. *Shadow and Substance: Afro-American Experience in Contemporary Children's Fiction*. 2d ed. Chicago: NCTE/MLA, 1982.

Sutherland, Zena. *Children and Books*. 9th ed. New York: Longman, 1997.

Williams, Helen E. *Books by African-American Authors and Illustrators for Children and Young Adults*. Chicago: American Library Association, 1991.

Childress, Alice (October 12, 1920, Charleston, South Carolina—August 14, 1994, New York, New York): Dramatist, novelist, and actor. Known primarily for her contributions to the American THEATER, Alice Childress was also a distinguished novelist and essayist. During her professional career, she produced fourteen plays, four novels, and a substantial number of essays, concerned primarily with African American art and theater history.

At the age of five, Childress moved to New York with her family. She attended HARLEM public schools, completing elementary grades and three years of high school. Childress considered herself largely self-educated, although she recognized her grandmother's dramatic skill in storytelling as a major influence on her creative development. She also gave credit to black poet Paul Laurence DUNBAR, William Shakespeare, and the Bible as sources of inspiration.

Childress's career began in the early 1940's, when she worked as an actor with the original AMERICAN NEGRO THEATRE (ANT) in Harlem. In 1949 the group staged her one-act play *Florence*, which was based on an encounter between two women—one black and the other white—in a waiting room of a segregated train station. Childress continued her association with the theater company for twelve years, during which time she served as drama coach, drama director, member of the board of directors, and personnel director.

While Childress was struggling to make it in the acting and writing worlds, she had to take other work to support herself and a young daughter, the product of an early, failed marriage. She held a number of jobs, such as domestic worker, assistant machinist, photograph retoucher, saleswoman, and insurance agent. Her intimate knowledge of the blue-collar world allowed her to populate her created worlds with everyday working people who are not stereotypical. In 1955 her play *Trouble in Mind* opened to considerable acclaim in New York City. It received the 1956 Obie Award. Another highly acclaimed play, *Wedding Band* (pr. 1966, Ann Arbor, Michigan, and 1972, New York City), had its Broadway option set aside after several years.

By the 1970's and 1980's, Childress had turned her attention to other literary pursuits, producing four novels. Two of these novels were written for adolescent readers: *A Hero Ain't Nothin' but a Sandwich* (1973) and *Rainbow Jordan* (1981). Both these works focused on the difficulties faced by black teenagers growing up in the inner city and reflected Childress's concern with the problems of the urban poor. Although *A Hero Ain't Nothin' but a Sandwich* was made into a film that won numerous awards, including the Black Filmmakers Award for outstanding contribution to the arts, the book was the center of controversy when it was banned from some school libraries because of its frank depiction of the life of a young heroin addict.

In the 1980's, Childress collaborated with her husband, Nathan Woodard, in producing *Gullah* (1984), a musical based on her work *Sea Island Song*, and *Moms* (1987), a play based on the life of the female black comedian Jackie "Moms" MABLEY. At the time of her death from cancer in 1994, Childress was working on a novel about her great-grandmothers—one African, the other Scots-Irish.

Despite Childress's remarkable talent and her prodigious output, her works have not received widespread attention. Rejecting advice to write about people of accomplishment, she insisted upon writing honestly about ordinary black people attempting to cope with the problems of daily existence in the United States—complex problems that a conservative reading and viewing public were often unwilling to confront. Thus the body of work Childress produced was often controversial and frequently went against the tide of popularity.

—*Updated by Gladys J. Washington*

See also: Literature.

Alice Childress in 1991. *(Ray Grist)*

Chisholm, Shirley (b. Shirley St. Hill; November 30, 1924, Brooklyn, New York): NEW YORK politician. Distinguished as an educator, politician, and feminist, Chisholm represented to several generations of Americans of both genders and many ethnicities a model of independence and integrity. The title of her 1970 autobiography, *Unbought and Unbossed*, reflects accurately her nature and presents the qualities that make her a compelling public figure.

Early Years

Chisholm's mother, Ruby Seale, was a native of BARBADOS; her father, Charles St. Hill, was born in British Guiana and grew up in CUBA and Barbados. The two immigrated to New York separately during the early 1920's. Charles and Ruby had not been well acquainted in Barbados, but they became better acquainted in Brooklyn, where there was a sizable colony of Barbadians, and married. Shirley's mother worked as a seamstress, while her father was employed as a baker's helper and factory hand—menial and low-paying jobs. Because of their precarious financial situation, the parents decided to place Shirley and her two sisters with their maternal grand-

Shirley Chisholm in 1971. *(AP/Wide World Photos)*

mother back on the family farm in Barbados. When Shirley was four years old, her mother returned to Barbados to be with her children, who would stay in Barbados until 1934. Such arrangements were common among Barbadians, who stressed education and family stability as values to be cultivated above all others. In her autobiography, Chisholm discussed the immigrants' "drive to achieve," commenting:

> The Barbadians who came to Brooklyn all wanted, and most of them got, the same two things: a brownstone house and a college education for their children.

The three sisters lived on the family farm and were joined by cousins from the United States, making a total of seven children. Because of the heavy British influence on the island, the educational system taught the traditional curriculum of British schools: reading, writing, arithmetic, and British history. Discipline was quick and punitive, but the children were free to roam the island, enjoying the warm waters of the Caribbean, the farm animals, and the villages and their markets and crowds. Thus, the adjustment to urban life when the girls returned to New York in 1934 was a difficult one, for they returned to an unheated four-room flat. Another sister had been born while the girls were still on the island, and even though the Depression had kept the family from acquiring their desired security, the parents saw to it that their daughters were clothed and provided with amenities; the parents even bought a piano, and Shirley took lessons for nine years, a luxury typical of those provided by the parents' many sacrifices.

Exposure to Black Nationalism

Shirley was first introduced to politics by her father, a supporter of the Confectionary and Bakers International Union who became the shop steward at the bakery where he worked.

He was also a follower of Marcus GARVEY, the leader who advocated black separatism and whose ideas were considered radical—even subversive—at the time. Chisholm credits her father with instilling in his children a racial pride that owed much to Garvey and his philosophy.

The St. Hill parents were strict with their daughters. No dating was allowed, and churchgoing was enforced. Although Shirley was offered scholarships to several colleges when she graduated from Girls' High School in Brooklyn, she was prevented from accepting them because her parents did not have the means to supply necessary room-and-board expenses. Instead, she chose to attend Brooklyn College.

Political Education

Chisholm's years at Brooklyn College were marked by a growing activism. At that time, the student enrollment in the city colleges was more than 90 percent white, even though the tuition was free, because of enrollment policies that excluded inadequately prepared ethnic minorities. Chisholm's decision to become a teacher was based on the realities of the time: Very few professions were open to women, especially African American women. She worked as a volunteer in an Urban League settlement house, and she became active in the campus election campaigns of women candidates.

Upon her graduation, with honors, in 1946, she found a job as a teacher's aide at Mt. Calvary Child Care Center in HARLEM, where she worked for seven years. She also began attending Democratic club meetings and was appalled to discover segregated seating there. Chisholm also discovered a system of racial preference in place that operated on a number of levels; blacks depended upon whites for political favors that extended far beyond the voting booth into the economic and social structures of society. Eventually accepted as a volunteer into the Seventeenth District Democratic Club, she led a rebellion of the women members that secured some status for the women by allowing them their own voice, which had previously been unheard and unacknowledged.

In addition to being politically active in the DEMOCRATIC PARTY, Chisholm was working on a graduate degree at Columbia University in early childhood education. She worked with community groups and became identified as someone who questioned time-honored practices. While at Columbia, too, Shirley met Conrad Chisholm, a private investigator, and they were married in 1949. The couple divorced in 1977.

After a painful setback in her local political club, Chisholm joined a group to form a new organization, the Unity Democratic Club. Advocating more civil-service jobs for minorities, the leadership gained the attention of important political figures, including Eleanor Roosevelt. Despite the opposition of some entrenched political leaders, in 1964 she ran for a position in the state assembly, coping often with sexist comments in addition to the expected racial slurs. Because campaign financing traditionally went to male candidates, she managed her campaign on meager funds, and yet she won election to the assembly. As an assemblywoman that year, she was one of eight black representatives, and the only woman.

Elected Legislator

As a member of the assembly, Chisholm sponsored legislation supporting education, day-care centers, and public school spending. Not surprisingly, she was considered a maverick, a genuine foe of political favoritism. The bill that she considered her most important enabled disadvantaged students to attend college by assisting them in their earlier years. Another secured rights for women schoolteachers whose tenure was threatened because of pregnancy; yet another granted unemployment insurance to domestic workers.

Because of redistricting that created the Twelfth Congressional District, Chisholm was able to run for a seat in the U.S. House of Representatives in 1968. She was opposed by James FARMER, a former head of the CONGRESS OF RACIAL EQUALITY (CORE) and leader in the Civil Rights movement. Chisholm was again victorious; in the House, she preferred committee assignments reflecting her commitments to education and minority rights. Her beliefs that African Americans needed and deserved sound vocational education, business counseling, and university training were reflected in the legislation she supported and the causes she advocated.

As a candidate for the 1972 Democratic presidential nomination, Chisholm never received more than a 7 percent share of the vote in any primary, but she did prove that women candidates could be taken seriously. As a highly respected member of Congress, she continued to be heard on a number of issues and became a member of the House Rules Committee and secretary of the House Democratic Caucus. Her criticism of the REAGAN ADMINISTRATION's cutbacks in service programs was especially vociferous.

Political Retirement

In 1982 Chisholm announced her intention to retire from national politics. Despite her departure from national elective office, her voice remained strong and clear, as she continued to be a spokesperson for the oppressed. She was always an advocate of women's issues—in fact, her observation that it was often more difficult to be a woman than to be a black person upset a great many people. Yet part of her strength and effectiveness involved her ability to enrage people, to challenge their time-honored convictions, and, finally, to get them to think.

After retiring from Congress, Chisholm taught college for a few years and worked in New York State politics. In the early 1990's she moved to FLORIDA, where she divided her time between occasional appearances and speeches to reading, relaxing, and engaging in her main hobby, ballroom dancing.

—Jean Gandesbery

See also: Congressional Black Caucus; Congress members; Politics and government.

Suggested Readings:

Brownmiller, Susan. *Shirley Chisholm: A Biography*. Garden City, N.Y.: Doubleday, 1971.

Chisholm, Shirley. *The Good Fight*. New York: Harper & Row, 1973.

_____. *Unbought and Unbossed*. Boston: Houghton Mifflin, 1970.

Davis, Flora. *Moving the Mountain: The Women's Movement in America Since 1960*. New York: Simon & Schuster, 1991.

Duffy, Susan, comp. *Shirley Chisholm: A Bibliography of Writings by and About Her*. Metuchen, N.J.: Scarecrow Press, 1988.

Haskins, James. *Fighting Shirley Chisholm*. New York: Dial Press, 1975.

Christian, Charlie (July 29, 1916, Dallas, Texas—March 2, 1942, New York, New York): JAZZ guitarist. Reared in Oklahoma City, OKLAHOMA, Charles "Charlie" Christian began performing in local venues, playing bass with the Alphonso Trent band. He began his guitar playing at the age of twelve and his professional career at fifteen. Having studied with his blind father, who sang and played guitar, Christian also received early performance exposure in the Jeter-Pillars Orchestra in St. Louis, Missouri. He was one of the first guitarists to become known for his work on amplified acoustic guitar. In 1939, at the urging of John Hammond, he ventured to Los Angeles, where he was auditioned by Benny Goodman.

Christian recorded with the Goodman orchestra and was heard on radio programs. In

1939 he recorded with Goodman and can be heard on *Flying Home* (1939) and *Stardust* (1939). In 1940 he was part of the Goodman recordings *Gone with "What" Wind* (1940) and *Good Enough to Keep* (1941). Christian also can be heard on *Solo Flight: The Genius of Charlie Christian*. He recorded as a leader, producing *Jazz Immortal* (1941) and *The Harlem Jazz Scene* (1941). Christian's phenomenal and meteoric rise resulted in his winning the *Down Beat* poll as best guitarist from 1939 to 1941 as well as the *Metronome* poll in 1941 and 1942.

Christian became a proponent of early bop guitar style and was an influence on future electric guitar players. As a solo performer, he employed single-string melodic lines which were akin to the solo style of bop instrumentalists. He also experimented with the innovative chord progressions characteristic of BEBOP. His solos have been transcribed and published as *Charlie Christian: Harlem Jazz* (1958) and *Charlie Christian: Jazz Improvisation* (1975), which was published in Japan. He participated in jam sessions with seminal figures of bop such as Charlie PARKER and Dizzy GILLESPIE. Part of the uptown HARLEM musical scene at MINTON'S PLAYHOUSE, Christian has been credited by some for creating the name "bebop" because of his habit of humming vocal syllables during performances.

Christian, Spencer (b. July 23, 1947, Newport News, Virginia): Meteorologist, television personality, and writer. Christian began his career in broadcasting as a news reporter in 1971 with television station WWBT in Richmond, VIRGINIA. He took up weathercasting at that station the following year and later served as weatherman for television stations WBAL in BALTIMORE and WABC in NEW YORK CITY.

Christian gained national exposure in 1986 when he became a weather personality, cohost, and interviewer with ABC's weekday morning program *Good Morning America*. He continued with the program through the 1990's while pursuing other interests as well. He hosted a Public Broadcasting Service series called *Tracks Ahead* and hosted the *Triple Threat* game show on BLACK ENTERTAINMENT TELEVISION (BET).

In 1993 Christian was elected to the Virginia Communications Hall of Fame. A wine connoisseur, he started the program *Spencer Christian's Wine Cellar* for the Home and Garden Television cable network in 1995. Christian also embarked on a writing career with such books as *Electing Our Government: Everything You Need to Know to Make Your Vote Really Count* in 1996 and a number of entries in his Spencer Christian's World of Wonder series for children.

Christ's Sanctified Holy Church: PENTECOSTAL religious denomination with headquarters in Jennings, LOUISIANA. The church's name was adopted officially in 1922 when the group, previously part of the Colored Church South, moved to Jennings from West Lake, Louisiana. The church emphasized the idea of a single Lord and stressed sanctification as a gradual experience. Baptism of the Holy Spirit is evidenced by speaking in tongues. Men and women have equal status in the church. Marriage outside the church puts a member on probation; if the marriage partner is not baptized with the Holy Spirit within six months, the member is ejected from the church. In the 1980's the denomination claimed sixty member churches with a total membership of about one thousand.

See also: Pentecostalism; Religion.

Church burnings: Throughout most of U.S. history, African Americans have viewed the burning of black churches as an assault on black culture generally—acts of intimidation

Ruins of Mount Mary Baptist Church, which was burned to the ground in Sasser, Georgia, in 1962. *(AP/Wide World Photos)*

and potent symbols of racism. During the CIVIL RIGHTS movement of the 1960's, many southern black churches were burned by angry white racists. Widely reported church burnings in the 1980's and 1990's, on the other hand, did not seem to demonstrate a clear pattern of racial motivation.

Historically and currently, the church is a social and cultural focal point of many African American communities. It is a major source of support for black families, the chief advocate for black issues, a major organization in black politics, and the center of networks that help empower black individuals and communities. Approximately 70 percent of African American adults are affiliated with black churches. Black churches offer love, caring, and a sense of belonging. For these reasons, black churches have often been targets of racial violence.

History of Church Burning

Many slaveowners encouraged the existence of black churches so that slaves would focus their attention on the promise of an afterlife rather than on the harsh conditions of SLAVERY. Black churches gradually became centers for black culture, the abolition movement, the UNDERGROUND RAILROAD, and the education of slaves in the fundamentals of reading, writing, and mathematics.

The earliest recorded racially motivated church arson occurred in 1822 when the AFRICAN METHODIST EPISCOPAL CHURCH in Charleston, SOUTH CAROLINA, was burned by whites who feared that slaves were meeting there to plan an insurrection. After the Charleston incident, most southern states either outlawed or severely restricted black churches. Restrictions included a North Carolina law requiring five white men to be present at any church meeting that blacks attended and a South Carolina law banning black church meetings between sunset and sunrise.

One of the first waves of black church burnings occurred in the 1890's, a decade when many post-CIVIL WAR laws aimed at aiding and protecting former slaves were being overturned. Church burnings often occurred in association with lynchings, white defense of segregated facilities, and other racial indignities of the JIM CROW era.

The Twentieth Century

In the 1960's, the activities of the Civil Rights movement were promoted and aided by black churches, and a number of civil rights leaders were ministers. This situation made churches targets of hatred and racist attacks, including burnings and bombings. In MISSISSIPPI, thirty-four black churches were burned in three months during the summer of 1964 alone. The burning of black churches was an act of white defiance in reaction to black attempts to obtain—and later, their success in obtaining—basic civil rights.

More than fifteen years later, church burnings peaked again in 1980. Some of these arsons were burnings of black churches, but most involved white churches. Criminologists and sociologists who examined the 1980 arsons generally concluded that most were attributable to frustration and anger caused by the economic hardships of the depression that had begun in the late 1970's.

In the mid-1990's, another rash of church fires erupted in two clusters, one in the Carolinas and the other in Tennessee and Alabama. More than sixty-four church arson fires were reported in 1995 and 1996. The federal and state governments reacted by assigning a large number of federal and state investigators to church arson investigations, doubling the federal penalty for church arson to twenty years in prison, and approving $10 million in loans to help churches rebuild.

The mid-1990's church burnings were initially perceived as a genuine racial threat, a church-burning "epidemic," and they were quickly promoted as such by the media, particularly on television news programs. More careful analysis, however, eventually indicated that the numbers were a statistical aberration and did not warrant fears that the country was sinking into a new period of RACIAL VIOLENCE AND HATRED.

A number of factors, investigators found, had contributed to them misleading numbers. Among them were changes in crime reporting techniques and standards, errors in reporting the racial composition of various church memberships, the withholding of facts,

and incomplete analysis of the statistics by initial investigators. Moreover, the heavy media coverage of church burnings apparently led to copycat arsons that further encouraged the perception of a crisis.

On the other hand, many observers noted that the quick and strong reactions of both the government and the public to the situation provided evidence that Americans were serious about ending acts of racial violence and promoting racial harmony.

Reasons for Church Arson

Both white and black churches are burned each year for a variety of reasons, including insurance fraud, thrill seeking, vandalism, mental derangement, revenge, cover for burglaries, religious hatred, and racial hatred. While the burnings of black churches in the mid-1960's could often be directly linked to racial hatred, church burnings in the 1980's and 1990's did not show a clear pattern of racial motivation. Some church burnings were racially motivated, but many more were acts of vandalism that did not appear to be racially motivated. Arson analysts concluded that

The Reverend W. D. Lewis stands in front of the charred remains of his church in Alabama's Greene County in early 1996. *(AP/Wide World Photos)*

most 1990's church arsons were attributable to juvenile thrill seekers and vandals rather than to the acts of racists and that they were part of an overall temporary increase in arson crimes nationwide.

—*Gordon Neal Diem*

See also: Lynching; Religion.

Suggested Readings:

Bradley, Bill. "Our Unresolved Dilemma: Church Burnings and America's Quest for Healing." *Sojourners* 25 (September/October, 1996): 30-33.

Carter, Carolyn S. "Church Burnings in African American Communities: Implications for Empowerment Practice." *Social Work* 44 (January, 1999): 62-69.

Fumento, Michael. "Politics and Church Burnings." *Commentary* 102 (October, 1996): 57-60.

Heyboer, Kelly. "The 'Epidemic' of Black Church Fires." *American Journalism Review* 18 (September, 1996): 10-12.

Walton, Anthony. "Why Race Is Still a Burning Issue." *U.S. Catholic* 61 (October, 1996): 6-7.

Wilson, Charles Reagan. "Church Burnings and the Christian Community." *Christian Century* 113 (September 25, 1996): 890-896.

Churches of God, Holiness: Religious denomination. The church was organized by K. H. Burruss in Georgia in 1914, and its headquarters was established in ATLANTA, GEORGIA. The denomination claimed about forty churches with a membership of approximately twenty-five thousand in the 1990's.

See also: Religion.

Church of Christ Holiness (U.S.A.): Religious denomination. The church formed after a split in the CHURCH OF GOD IN CHRIST in 1907. A group led by Charles Harrison Mason kept the original name, and Charles Price Jones and his followers adopted the new name. Jones had rejected Mason's doctrine of speaking in tongues.

See also: Religion.

Church of God and Saints of Christ: Religious denomination. William S. CROWDY founded the church in 1896 in Lawrence, KANSAS. Its first annual assembly was held in 1900 in PHILADELPHIA, PENNSYLVANIA. Church doctrine is a mix of Judaism, Christianity, and BLACK NATIONALISM. Members believe that black people are descendants of the ten lost tribes of Israel, and they observe the Jewish Sabbath. A 1990 report claimed 127 churches and 38,127 members.

See also: Religion.

Church of God in Christ: Religious denomination. Organized in 1897 in MEMPHIS, TENNESSEE, by Charles Harrison Mason and Charles Price Jones, this Pentecostal church emphasized experiential dimensions of Christian life. When the two church founders had begun preaching the Holiness doctrine of entire sanctification, or a second experience of grace after conversion that made a Christian holy, Baptists in MISSISSIPPI had objected, prompting Mason and Jones to found their church. In 1907 Jones and his followers split from the church, forming the CHURCH OF CHRIST HOLINESS (U.S.A.). The Church of God in Christ became the largest black Pentecostal denomination, claiming about two million members by 1990.

See also: Religion.

Church of Jesus Christ of Latter-day Saints: Religious body founded in NEW YORK STATE during the early nineteenth century that did not extend full membership privileges to African Americans until 1978.

A native of upstate New York, Joseph Smith, Jr., claimed to have visions during the 1820's that led to his discovery and translation of golden plates containing a history of the early Americas. After he published this account as the Book of Mormon in 1830, he organized the Church of Jesus Christ of Latter-day Saints (LDS) and began an aggressive missionary campaign throughout the Northeast and parts of Western Europe. That missionary campaign eventually became worldwide. By the year 2000, the church—whose members are generally known as Mormons—claimed 10 million members.

Teaching that his church was a restoration of Christ's organization, Smith introduced a lay priesthood and temple ordinances, which he claimed were the keys to receive the full blessings in the afterlife, which is the focus of Mormon theology.

Denial of the Priesthood

Like many other European Americans in the North, early Mormons opposed SLAVERY but believed that blacks were inferior to whites. Nevertheless, at least two black men, Elijah Abel and Walker Lewis, were ordained to the lay priesthood during Smith's lifetime. During the 1840's, however, the church determined that descendants of Africans could not enter the priesthood because they were the descendants ("seed") of Cain and Ham and were thus cursed. This determination was derived from readings of the Bible and exclusively Mormon scriptures, especially the Book of Abraham in the Pearl of Great Price. Another explanation for denial of the priesthood was that blacks had refused to fight in a battle between Satan and Jesus in a pre-Earth life.

These interpretations were never considered to be scriptures themselves. Through more than a century, church leaders reinforced priesthood denial by attributing the ban on black membership in the priesthood to Smith. The basis of this policy was muddied by the

During the lifetime of Joseph Smith, who founded the Church of Jesus Christ of Latter-day Saints, at least two African Americans were ordained into his church's priesthood. *(Library of Congress)*

fact that its key doctrinal support derived from a passage that Smith claimed to have translated from an Egyptian papyrus he purchased from an itinerant trader in Ohio. In contrast to the "golden plates" of the Book of Mormon, which disappeared after Smith "translated" them, the papyrus was a tangible document that could be shown to be unrelated to Smith's purported translation.

In 1949 LDS leaders issued their first official public statement on this subject, explaining that the practice was dictated by God. During the 1960's CIVIL RIGHTS movement, African Americans protested the policy by threatening to demonstrate outside church headquarters and taking other actions against the church. College athletes refused to play, or wore black armbands, in games against church-owned Brigham Young University.

Some LDS members objected as well, by publishing articles. In at least one case, they ordained an African American without church citation. In response, LDS leaders issued statements in 1963 and 1969 confirming priesthood denial but emphasizing equal rights for African Americans. The 1969 statement omitted references to Cain and Ham and a premortal life. It stated that God alone knew the reasons blacks could not hold the priesthood.

Change in Policy

By the late 1970's, protests had died down, so many Mormons were surprised when church president Spencer W. Kimball issued a declaration on June 9, 1978, that men of African descent could henceforth hold the priesthood. Most observers agreed that the proclamation came because of the church's worldwide growth, particularly in Brazil, where determinating individuals' racial backgrounds was often impossible. Moreover, people in Nigeria had been asking for missionaries since 1946 and organizing their own churches using the Book of Mormon.

Until 1978, LDS missionaries avoided African American neighborhoods. Despite priesthood limitation and some discrimination from European American Mormons, a few African Americans joined the church and remained faithful. Indeed, black Mormons were among the first settlers in UTAH in 1847. Former slaves immigrated to Utah, settling in a farming community near Salt Lake City. Other African Americans also accepted the Mormon Church, believing that the priesthood restriction would be eventually resolved. In 1998 some scholars suggested that LDS church leaders should issue a statement apologizing for earlier statements about blacks. Rumors circulated that leaders planned to make such a statement, but the church's public communications division said that no such move was being discussed. The issue of renouncing earlier church prophecies was a potentially explosive one with possible ramifications extending well beyond racial issues.

African American Mormons

Following Kimball's 1978 announcement, missionaries throughout the world, including the United States, started working in black neighborhoods and baptizing converts. Because church records do not list race or color, it is impossible to determine the precise number of African American Mormons. It is clear, however, that African Americans have joined in increasing numbers. Like other Americans and people throughout the world, African Americans have joined the church because it stresses conservative religious and family values, literal interpretation of the scriptures, and a strict moral code. However, many African Americans continue to be distrustful of the many racist passages that remain in church scriptures.

African American Mormons have been ordained to lay priesthood offices, and they have served as missionaries and in other church positions in their local congregations. Brazilian Helvecio Martins became the first member of African descent to become one of the church's "geneal authorities" and served in the so-called Second Quorum of the Seventy from 1990 to 1995.

In some areas of the United States, virtually all-black congregations have been formed. The composition of these congregations seems to have more to do with the residence of their members—which is the primary determinant of Mormon "ward" membership—than with conscious self-segregation. One survey of two hundred African American Mormons found that slightly more than 80 percent said that they "never" wanted to belong to an all-black ward. Only 2.5 percent said they "very often" wanted to worship with only blacks. Most African American Mormons surveyed and interviewed for a Brigham Young University study said that they appreciate the opportunity to worship, share resources, and visit with other Latter-day Saints. However, they also complained about some continuing prejudice and discrimination within the church.

—Jessie L. Embry
—R. Kent Rasmussen

See also: Racial discrimination; Religion.

Suggested Readings:

Bringhurst, Newell G. Saints, Slaves, and Blacks: The Changing Place of Black People Within Mormonism. Westport, Conn.: Greenwood Press, 1981.

Embry, Jessie L. Black Saints in a White Church: Contemporary African American Mormons. Salt Lake City: Signature Books, 1994.

Ostling, Richard N., and Joan K. Ostling. Mormon America: The Power and the Promise. San Francisco: HarperSanFrancisco, 1999.

Church of the Living God: Parent religious denomination to several smaller denominations with the same root name. (It is also known as Christian Workers for Fellowship.) William Christian, a former slave, left the BAPTIST Church to form the denomination in 1889. Church doctrine is trinitarian and rejects the idea of speaking in tongues as evidence of baptism of the Holy Spirit. Members believe that Jesus Christ and biblical saints were black. A 1993 report claimed 170 churches and forty-two thousand members.

See also: Religion.

Cinque, Joseph (c. 1811-c. 1879): Leader of the AMISTAD SLAVE REVOLT. Joseph Cinque was the leader of the fifty-three African slaves aboard the schooner La Amistad who, in the summer of 1839, rose up against their captors and took control of the vessel. Once Cinque and his comrades had taken over the ship, they attempted to sail back to AFRICA. After two months at sea, they anchored at the north-

ern tip of Long Island, New York, where they were boarded and taken into custody by a U.S. coastal survey brig. A group of NEW YORK members of the ABOLITIONIST MOVEMENT came forward to assure their defense in the U.S. courts. Finally, the Africans' case came before the U.S. SUPREME COURT, before which former president John Quincy Adams argued their case. The Court set them free, and the abolitionists who had supported them arranged for their return to Africa.

Capture in Africa

Joseph Cinque was born in Mani in the former kingdom of Mende, about ten days' travel from the west coast of Africa in an area now part of Sierra Leone. "Cinque" was the name his Spanish captors gave him; he pronounced his own name more like "Shinquaw." Consequently, his name has been spelled variously as Cinque, Cinquez, Cingue, Singbe, Jinqua, Singua, and Shinquaw. He lived with his father, who was a principal figure in his village. A rice farmer, he was married and had a son and two daughters. Around March, 1839, while he was traveling along a road, he was seized by four of his own countrymen, taken to the coast, sold into SLAVERY, and put aboard a SLAVE SHIP bound for the Caribbean.

Chained to other captives, Cinque was forced to lie huddled together with them on a lower deck with a four-foot-high ceiling. The captives were kept in that situation day and night, fed a diet of rice with little water to drink, and whipped when they failed to respond suitably to their captors' orders. Many died during the passage. In June, Cinque arrived in Havana, CUBA, where he was sold and put aboard the Amistad with fifty-two other captives to be taken to work in plantations in another part of Cuba.

Shipboard Revolt

Trouble erupted on the ship after four days at sea, when the ship's cook had teased the Africans with the threat that they would be killed and eaten when they arrived at their destination. Cinque rallied his comrades and, with cane knives they found stored on the ship, they attacked their captors. The Africans killed the cook and the ship's captain and wounded one of the Spanish owners. The two crew members fled in a small boat, leaving the two owners, José Ruiz and Pedro Montez, at the mercy of the victors. Cinque immediately took control of the ship and ordered the remaining Spaniards to take them back to Africa by sailing east, toward the rising sun. Montez, having once been master of a vessel, sailed east during the day, trying to make as little headway as possible. At night, however, he turned the ship and sailed west and north by the stars. The result was a zigzag course that eventually brought the schooner off the coast of Long Island, New York.

On August 24, 1839, Cinque had the ship anchored near Culloden Point, Long Island, and led a landing party to search for water and supplies. Soon thereafter, the *Amistad* was approached by the U.S. brig *Washington*. A boarding party from the *Washington* ordered the Africans below at gunpoint. According to some witnesses, Cinque dived into the water but was retaken. Back aboard the *Amistad*, he gathered his comrades around him and encouraged them to resist.

It was apparent to the boarding party that Cinque was the leader and that it would be wise to separate him from the others. The officers of the *Washington*, therefore, removed him in handcuffs to the brig for the night. The next day, Cinque convinced his jailers to return him to the *Amistad* by offering to show them a cache of doubloons. Once again, he gathered the Africans about him and encouraged them to strike out in their own defense, saying that it was better to die than to spend their lives in slavery. The excitement created by his speech resulted in Cinque's seizure and return to the *Washington*. On August 29, a district court convened on board the *Washington* ruled that the Africans should be committed to the New Haven, CONNECTICUT, county jail and charged with the crimes of murder and piracy. The prisoners were ordered to stand trial before the next circuit court at Hartford, Connecticut.

Descriptions of Cinque at the time of his arrest indicate that he was about five feet eight inches tall, erect in stature, well built, and energetic. He appeared to be about twenty-five years old. He was characterized as intelligent, cool, composed, courageous, and decisive, with no suggestion of maliciousness in his demeanor.

Trial in the United States
A circuit court dropped the charges of murder and piracy and referred the matter of whether the Africans should legally be considered to be property to a district court, which convened in New Haven on January 7, 1840. The courtroom was crowded; Yale University had dismissed

Engraving made of Joseph Cinque while he was awaiting trial in Connecticut. *(Library of Congress)*

law classes so that students could attend. Intense public interest drew people from all walks of life. Spectators remained in their seats during the two-hour lunch recesses to ensure themselves a place to sit. At the trial, Cinque was called as a witness. He spoke clearly and with dignity. He demonstrated by action how Ruiz had examined the slaves in Cuba to ascertain their physical condition. By getting down on the floor, he showed how they were packed and chained in the hold of the ship. He described how they were mistreated with beatings and insufficient provisions.

The decision of the court came one week later: The prisoners were not slaves by the laws of Spain itself; they had been kidnapped and illegally enslaved. The court ordered the Africans to be delivered to the president of the United States and transported back to Africa. The U.S. government, however, appealed the case, first to circuit court and finally to the Supreme Court.

The Supreme Court upheld the lower-court rulings, except for the order mandating the Africans' return to Africa. Cinque and his comrades were free, but they had no way to get home. The task of raising the funds for their return and securing their livelihood in the interim fell to the abolitionists who had befriended them.

Return to Africa

At last, nearly three years after he was taken from Africa, Cinque embarked for Sierra Leone with his fellow Africans on November 27, 1841, aboard the ship *Gentleman*. During the two years that the Africans had been in custody in the United States, Cinque remained their leader and inspiration. He helped to raise the funds for their trip home by speaking in churches and before sympathetic audiences. He kept up his compatriots' spirits and generally acted as their spokesman. The long ordeal took a terrible toll, however; only thirty-five of the original fifty-three captives

remained alive to reach Sierra Leone in January, 1842.

A group of African American and white missionaries accompanied the returning Africans for the purpose of starting a mission dedicated to counteracting the SLAVE TRADE on the west coast of Africa. Some of the *Amistad* Africans accompanied the missionaries to the site of the mission and helped with its organization. That mission station, about halfway between Freetown and Monrovia, became an obstacle to those who participated in the slave trade and the intertribal wars that fed it.

Cinque chose not to join the mission group. He instead went into business for himself and even traveled to Jamaica. Later in his life, he returned to the mission, where he became an interpreter. He died around 1879 and was buried at the mission station. His funeral was conducted by an African American missionary, the Reverend Albert President Miller, a graduate of FISK UNIVERSITY.

Senegalese actor Djimon Hounsou played Cinque in the 1997 film *Amistad*, directed by Steven Spielberg.

—*B. Edmon Martin*

Suggested Readings:

The Amistad Case: The Most Celebrated Slave Mutiny of the Nineteenth Century. 2 vols. Reprint. New York: Johnson Reprint, 1968.

Bemis, Samuel F. *John Quincy Adams and the Union*. New York: Alfred A. Knopf, 1970.

Brownlee, Fred L. *New Day Ascending*. Boston: Pilgrim Press, 1946.

Jones, Howard. *Mutiny on the Amistad*. New York: Oxford University Press, 1987.

Martin, B. Edmon. *All We Want Is Make Us Free*. Lanham, Md.: University Press of America, 1986.

Rosen, Gary. "'Amistad' and the Abuse of History." *Commentary* 105 (February, 1998): 46-51.

Wyatt-Brown, Bertram. *Lewis Tappan and the Evangelical War Against Slavery*. New York: Atheneum, 1971.

Citizens' Equal Rights Association: Civil rights organization. The association sent a committee to Washington, D.C., in 1890 to submit an address to the people of the United States adopted by a "convention of Colored Americans" in February, 1890. The address described denial of voting rights, segregation, and discriminatory treatment by the judicial system, among other wrongs done to African Americans. It asked for amendment of laws and for voters to elect only those legislators who supported equal rights.

Citizenship and race: The original document of the U.S. CONSTITUTION, which took effect in 1789, did not define national citizenship, even though citizenship was a requirement for holding office in the new federal government. Persons were simply considered citizens of the United States if they were citizens of one of its states. Article I, section 8, of the Constitution empowered Congress to establish a uniform rule of naturalization (the granting of citizenship to people not born in the United States), and Congress did so through the Naturalization Act of 1790. Reflecting racial biases of the period, the act limited naturalization eligibility to whites, denying Africans and Asians the privilege of becoming U.S. citizens.

Leaving the definition of national citizenship to the interpretation of individual states led to wide differences in the treatment of persons of African descent. Southern slave states did not consider free blacks entitled to become citizens. Northern states, which were gradually ending the institution of SLAVERY, usually permitted free blacks to vote as citizens. However, when states began to eliminate property requirements for voting, racist attitudes in the North led to markedly unequal treatment of blacks. As NEW JERSEY, PENNSYLVANIA, and CONNECTICUT expanded white suffrage, they completely disfranchised blacks who had pre-viously been eligible to vote. When NEW YORK STATE eliminated property requirements for voting by whites, it kept substantial property requirements in effect for blacks. By 1840 only MASSACHUSETTS, NEW HAMPSHIRE, VERMONT, and MAINE allowed blacks to vote on an equal basis with whites.

Slavery Controversy

Issues involving black claims to citizenship inevitably arose during arguments over slavery in the nineteenth century. One contentious issue in the congressional debate over the admission of Missouri to statehood was a clause in the proposed state constitution barring free blacks from entering the state. Northerners objected that this clause violated Article IV, section 2, of the Constitution, which provided that citizens of each state were entitled to all the privileges and immunities of citizens in every state. Southerners argued that blacks could not be considered citizens, claiming that no northern state granted blacks equal civil and political rights with whites. After considerable debate, northerners and southerners agreed to the MISSOURI COMPROMISE of 1820, which eliminated the disputed provision.

The issue of black citizenship arose again in the DRED SCOTT DECISION of 1857. Scott's owner had taken him from the slave state of Missouri to free territory in Illinois and Wisconsin. When Scott returned to Missouri, its state courts refused to accept his claim that he had become free because of his stay in free territory. Scott then appealed his case to the federal courts. The main question before the U.S. SUPREME COURT involved the power of Congress to regulate slavery in the territories. However, another issue was whether Scott was a citizen entitled to sue in the federal courts. Chief Justice Roger B. Taney, in his leading opinion, rejecting Scott's claim to freedom, argued that since no blacks had been citizens of any state when the Constitution was adopted, no black could be a citizen of the United States. The opinion was based on faulty history—during the 1780's Massachusetts, New York, New Jersey, and New Hampshire considered free blacks to be citizens, even though they did not treat them as fully equal to whites. Taney's decision infuriated the REPUBLICAN PARTY, which made reversal of his ruling a major political goal.

Reconstruction

Union victory in the CIVIL WAR, which ended in 1865, permitted the Republican Party to pass the Fourteenth and Fifteenth Amendments to the Constitution, reversing the Supreme Court's ruling on black citizenship. The opening section of the FOURTEENTH AMENDMENT (1868) for the first time defined citizenship, making federal citizenship primary and state citizenship secondary: "All persons born or naturalized in the United States, and subject to the jurisdiction thereof, are citizens of the United States and of the state wherein they reside." Three following clauses prohibited states from abridging the privileges or immunities of citizens, depriving persons of life, liberty, or property without due process of law, and denying any person the equal protection of the laws. The FIFTEENTH AMENDMENT (1870) guaranteed that the right to vote could not be abridged on the basis of race.

Ironically, the Fourteenth Amendment was used more to provide protection for business corporations than to protect African Americans. In the 1880's and 1890's the Supreme Court began to interpret its due process clause in ways that severely limited the ability of the states and the federal government to regulate the activities of businessmen. During the same decades the Court effectively vitiated the equal protection clause by accepting state imposition of rigid racial segregation. Practices such as the unequal application of literacy tests markedly reduced the number of blacks

able to vote and practically annulled the Fifteenth Amendment.

Civil Rights Movement

Black leaders and CIVIL RIGHTS organizations protested the denial of equal citizenship rights to blacks, but they had little success until after WORLD WAR II. In the 1950's, the strategy of the NATIONAL ASSOCIATION FOR THE ADVANCEMENT OF COLORED PEOPLE (NAACP) of suing in federal court to protest segregation began to produce results, especially in decisions affecting education. Nonviolent protests such as the MONTGOMERY BUS BOYCOTT and the SIT-INS of the 1960's attracted national attention to the unequal treatment of black citizens and led to enactment of a series of federal laws designed to reverse civil and political discrimination based on race.

The Voting Rights Act of 1964 (readopted and expanded in 1970, 1975, and 1982) barred arbitrary denial of the right to register to vote and the use of discriminatory literacy tests, and it provided for federal enforcement of voting rights. These voting rights provisions permitted a greater number of blacks to participate in the political process and enabled an increasing number of blacks to be elected to public office. The Civil Rights movement came closer to attaining equality for African Americans than had any previous attempt at citizenship rights reform.

—*Milton Berman*

See also: Reconstruction; Segregation and integration; Voting Rights Act of 1965.

Suggested Readings:

Karst, Kenneth L. *Belonging to America: Equal Citizenship and the Constitution.* New Haven: Yale University Press, 1989.

Kettner, James H. *The Development of American Citizenship, 1608-1870.* Chapel Hill: University of North Carolina Press, 1978.

Smith, Rogers M. *Civic Ideals: Conflicting Vi-*

sions of Citizenship in the United States. New Haven: Yale University Press, 1997.

Spinner, Jeff. *The Boundaries of Citizenship: Race, Ethnicity, and Nationality in the Liberal State*. Baltimore: The Johns Hopkins University Press, 1994.

Civil rights: From the time of emancipation, African Americans have struggled to attain social, economic, political, and civic equality in the United States. The struggle has been a continuous and often successful one against institutional and individual racial discrimination and oppression.

Constitutional Protections

The Thirteenth, Fourteenth, and Fifteenth Amendments to the U.S. Constitution, passed by Congress and ratified by the states in the years immediately following the CIVIL WAR, guaranteed basic civil rights to African Americans. The THIRTEENTH AMENDMENT, passed and ratified in 1865, abolished SLAVERY throughout the United States. The FOURTEENTH AMENDMENT, added to the Constitution in 1867, made African Americans citizens and forbade the states from depriving them of life, liberty, or property without "due process of law." The FIFTEENTH AMENDMENT, passed in 1870, gave African Americans voting rights throughout the United States by prohibiting states from depriving anyone of the right to vote because of "race, color, or condition of previous servitude."

The three Civil War amendments arose from the desire of the REPUBLICAN PARTY majority in Congress to punish the South for its role in the Civil War as well as to give the Republicans power in the South by franchising freedmen, who were expected to vote Republican. As a result of these amendments, African Americans in the South in the years from 1867 to 1877 had significant political power, electing local, state, and federal legislators and

other officials in many southern states. To further back these amendments, Congress passed civil rights laws in 1866, 1870, and 1875 that gave African Americans equal access to jobs, EDUCATION, and public accommodations.

The political power that the freedmen attained in the South during the RECONSTRUCTION era was not accompanied by economic power. Newly freed slaves did not receive land of their own after the war to any great extent and so were obliged to work as farm laborers, tenant farmers, or sharecroppers for their former owners. As a result, the southern white elite could and did neutralize the political power of African Americans through economic intimidation or manipulation.

As for social or civic equality, established patterns of African American exclusion and subordination were left little changed by civil rights laws. White southerners, determined to preserve their supremacy by any means necessary, resorted to terror and fraud to eliminate African Americans from their polity. Racist terror groups such as the KU KLUX KLAN frequently disrupted elections by beating, burning, and killing African American voters and politicians. The federal government by the mid-1870's had adopted a policy of allowing the South to settle its own racial problems. The Supreme Court offered little help in enforcing the spirit of the new federal laws and amendments.

Erosion of Rights

African Americans in the South saw their hard-won freedom erode during the latter part of the nineteenth century. They were excluded from supervisory, skilled, and professional occupations; from decent housing; from public accommodations such as railroads, steamships, streetcars, restaurants, theaters, parks, and hotels; and from most hospitals, orphanages, and mental institutions. Where and when African Americans were not excluded

Before passage of the Civil Rights Act of 1964, African Americans were routinely relegated to segregated seats in balconies. *(Library of Congress)*

from these institutions, they were relegated to grossly inferior versions of them.

African American CHILDREN were strictly segregated from white children, with separate and inferior schools. White southerners believed that African Americans could not be educated to any great extent and that, in any event, they should not share the educational opportunities given to white children. African American children therefore were educated in tumbledown buildings, received secondhand books, went to school for six months of the year instead of nine, and were taught by teachers who had less education and received lower pay than those teaching white children.

Consequently, most southern African Americans lacked the education and the skills needed to compete with whites for social, economic, or political power. Largely confined to farm labor and SHARECROPPING, most African Americans in the nineteenth-century South lived lives of POVERTY and hopelessness.

Formation of a Black Elite
In the midst of this situation, however, a small African American elite developed. Composed of ministers, schoolteachers, small businesspeople, journalists, doctors, and lawyers, this tiny group keenly felt the pain of the erosion of civil rights. Against great odds, they built institutions and organizations to protect their community.

By the 1890's, a small but significant African American infrastructure of churches, colleges, businesses, hospitals, and newspapers had appeared in the South to provide services to the black community and employment for its professionals. African Americans, not yet disfranchised, also rediscovered their voting power and sent black politicians to state legislatures and to Congress. These representatives cooperated with southern white Populists who sought sweeping socioeconomic change.

These trends posed a threat to southern white supremacists, who in response moved to eliminate completely any civil rights African Americans had or thought they had. Social insecurity brought on by the panic of 1893, which devastated the South's economy, helped fuel a wave of racism that swept the world at that time. The result was the creation of a statutory system of racial exclusion and separation in the South that lasted for the first half of the twentieth century and was known as Jim Crow.

The Era of Jim Crow
The first manifestation of JIM CROW LAWS came with the movement by many southern states to rewrite their constitutions to disfranchise African Americans. The techniques used to disfranchise blacks evaded the constraints imposed by the Fifteenth Amendment. Devices such as literacy tests, property require-

ments, and the poll tax were applied almost exclusively to African Americans. This was a result of the GRANDFATHER CLAUSE applied to these voting provisions. This clause stipulated that if a voter, or his father or grandfather, was a registered voter before 1867, then he was automatically registered. Since no African Americans voted in the South before that year, they had to qualify under the various provisions of southern voting laws, provisions designed to exclude them. Consequently, by 1901, African Americans virtually had disappeared from the political affairs of the South.

With African American voting power eliminated by disfranchisement, southern state legislatures enacted laws strictly segregating the races in all areas of public and private life. Schools, hospitals, parks, public buildings, public transportation, hotels, theaters, and restaurants were by law required to segregate the races. Interracial marriages also were banned. These arrangements were given constitutional protection by the Supreme Court, which in 1896 ruled in the PLESSY V. FERGUSON decision that SEPARATE BUT EQUAL accommodations for the races did not violate the Fourteenth Amendment.

Reactions to Segregation

The African American community had two reactions to the South's solidification of racial segregation and exclusion. One response, associated with Booker T. WASHINGTON, was for African Americans to accommodate themselves as best they could to the new realities of DISFRANCHISEMENT, segregation, and exclusion by concentrating on acquiring economic security through ownership of land, businesses, and remunerative skills. Once African Americans met these goals, in Washington's viewpoint, southern whites would respect them and would dismantle their oppressive racial system. The other reaction, associated with W. E. B. Du Bois and many northern African Americans, was to protest Jim Crow laws

through lawsuits, publicity, lobbying—and voting, where possible.

For the first fifteen years of the twentieth century, the African American community was torn between the accommodationist tactics of Booker T. Washington and the protest viewpoint of Du Bois. Because Washington, through his influence with wealthy white philanthropists and the federal government, controlled the flow of white money and power into African American communities, he had the upper hand in this debate. He used his position as a power broker to control or influence African American newspapers, colleges, and businesses, and in doing so he stifled his critics and opponents.

Those, like Du Bois, who favored protest struggled on. They met in Niagara Falls, Ontario, Canada, in 1905 to coordinate anti-Jim Crow strategies. From this meeting came the NIAGARA MOVEMENT, whose goal was to roll back the tide of racism through protest and lawsuits. Although Booker T. Washington privately may have supported the goals of the Niagara Movement (he gave covert support to antidisfranchisement organizations in Maryland and secretly financed railroad discrimination lawsuits), he believed it to be a threat to his hegemony over the African American community.

The NAACP

In 1908 a race riot in Springfield, Illinois, roused some northern white progressives to take action against the nation's worsening racial climate. Washington's accommodationist tactics had proved futile in preventing race riots, lynchings, and the passage of more Jim Crow laws in the South. The Niagara Movement's protest tactics looked newly promising. In 1909 white liberals including Oswald Garrison Villard, the grandson of William Lloyd Garrison and publisher of the *New York World*, along with Du Bois and other prominent black leaders of the Niagara Movement, created the NATIONAL ASSOCIATION FOR THE Advancement of Colored People (NAACP).

The NAACP's goal was to combat local, state, and national racism by challenging the constitutionality of Jim Crow and disfranchisement laws through lawsuits, political lobbying, and publicity. Du Bois ran the organization's research and publications division. In that role, he edited *The Crisis*, the NAACP magazine. The rise of the NAACP coincided with the decline of the accommodationist policies associated with Washington.

Victories in the Courts

For the next fifty years, the NAACP spearheaded the African American drive for civil rights. Slowly, it began to win significant civil rights victories, starting in 1915 with GUINN V. UNITED STATES, in which the U.S. Supreme Court invalidated Oklahoma's grandfather clause regarding voting rights. In 1917 the NAACP successfully argued the BUCHANAN V. WARLEY case before the Supreme Court. The Court in this case invalidated residential segregation laws in Baltimore, Louisville, and New Orleans. Among other decisions advancing civil rights and equality was *Gaines v. Missouri* in 1938, which ordered that state to admit black students to the University of Missouri law school or to establish a black law school of equal quality.

SMITH V. ALLWRIGHT in 1944 invalidated the Texas "white primary." This decision meant that southern states could no longer bar African Americans from voting in DEMOCRATIC PARTY primary elections, which in the one-party South of that era were the only significant elections. Other notable courtroom civil rights victories include SHELLEY V. KRAEMER in 1948, which made racially RESTRICTIVE COVENANTS in housing deeds legally unenforceable. This decision, in theory, opened up new opportunities for African Americans to purchase homes where they chose. The most important civil rights case

won by the NAACP was BROWN V. BOARD OF EDUCATION in 1954.

Brown v. Board of Education

This case was the culmination of years of effort to render public school segregation laws unconstitutional. The NAACP, in the late 1940's and early 1950's, sponsored lawsuits in Clarendon County, South Carolina, Washington, D.C., Topeka, Kansas, and elsewhere against racially segregated public schools. Led by Thurgood MARSHALL, the NAACP's legal team successfully shepherded the Topeka school segregation suit to the Supreme Court in late 1953. This suit, filed by Oliver Brown on behalf of his daughter Linda, contended that Topeka's segregation of students by race was a violation of the Fourteenth Amendment. Using theories advanced by noted African American psychologist Kenneth CLARK, Marshall argued that racially segregated schools damaged the self-esteem of African American children by setting them apart from the mainstream. This stigmatized them, crippling their education. As a result, racially segregated school systems could not provide black children with an equal education and therefore violated the Fourteenth Amendment.

The Supreme Court accepted this argument, and in May of 1954 it ruled unanimously that racial segregation in public education was unconstitutional. This decision, in effect, overturned the 1896 *Plessy v. Ferguson* ruling which had given constitutional protection to racial segregation laws. In doing so, the Supreme Court cast constitutional doubt on all laws infringing on the civil rights of African Americans.

The Great Migration

While the NAACP was struggling in the courtroom to secure the civil rights of African Americans in the first half of the twentieth century, other forces worked against American racism. One major factor was the GREAT

MIGRATION from the South to the North that began in 1915 and lasted until the 1970's. This migration transplanted millions of African Americans from a rural, racially oppressive, and hopeless environment to an urban environment that, though still racist, offered more opportunity.

In the North, African Americans could vote, were not publicly humiliated by Jim Crow laws, and found increased economic and educational opportunity. Although racial segregation existed in jobs, housing, and education, it was informal and less rigid than that in the South. Because blacks could vote in the North, they had considerably more leverage, especially in presidential elections, than their voteless brethren in the South. As a result, northern blacks, their numbers yearly swelled by migrants from the South, began to exert themselves politically and socially.

They did this by providing much of the material support for the NAACP and by electing black politicians to local, state, and national offices. This was true especially in CHICAGO, whose black population began sending black representatives to Congress in 1928, and in NEW YORK CITY. Other examples of the civil rights advocacy of northern blacks were the Garvey movement of the 1920's, which was one of the first mass-based expressions of BLACK NATIONALISM, and a movement in 1941 to hold a massive march on Washington, D.C., to demand civil rights. The threat of such a march pressured President Franklin D. Roosevelt to issue EXECUTIVE ORDER 8802, banning racial discrimination in employment by defense contractors. This movement, led by A. Philip RANDOLPH, the head of the BROTHERHOOD OF SLEEPING CAR PORTERS, a leading African American labor union, also resulted in the establishment of the Fair Employment Practices Commission (FEPC). Although the FEPC lacked the power to desegregate America's defense industries completely during WORLD WAR II, the opportunities it did provide were welcomed by an African American community devastated by the GREAT DEPRESSION. As a result, black workers shared somewhat in the prosperity brought on by World War II and its aftermath.

The Boycott Period

In the postwar period, African Americans were less willing to accept racial caste systems. This militancy expressed itself in direct action against racial segregation. This action at first involved various southern African American communities boycotting institutions that mistreated them, particularly bus companies. In the early 1950's, black communities in Baton Rouge, LOUISIANA, and Jacksonville, FLORIDA, boycotted the local transit companies to secure more equitable treatment on the buses. The most successful of these boycotts took place in MONTGOMERY, ALABAMA, in 1955 and 1956. There, an African American community chafing under a Jim Crow system and emboldened by the *Brown v. Board of Education* decision ended racial segregation on Montgomery's buses.

The MONTGOMERY BUS BOYCOTT was set off by the arrest on December 1, 1955, of Rosa PARKS, a respected member of the black community, for violating Montgomery's bus segregation ordinance by sitting at the first empty seat she found rather than standing in the overcrowded "colored" section of the bus. Her defiance was not totally spontaneous, as such an action had been contemplated for quite some time by Montgomery's black leaders. An ad hoc organization, the Montgomery Improvement Association (MIA), soon formed to organize a boycott of Montgomery's buses.

Though initially led by E. D. Nixon and other respected members of the community, the MIA called on a newly arrived Baptist minister, Martin Luther KING, Jr., to be its leader and spokesperson. King was highly educated, with a Ph.D. from Boston University; he was articulate and cultured but still able to relate to the grass roots. The leaders of the boycott effort thought that he would be an effective spokesperson. Also, as a newcomer to the city, King was believed to be more likely to unite Montgomery's somewhat fractious black community than would a leader with established local political ties.

Because of the organization and determination of Montgomery's black community, the bus boycott was a success, culminating in a 1956 Supreme Court decision invalidating Montgomery's bus segregation ordinance. By that time, the Montgomery bus company was close to bankruptcy as a result of the loss of its black patronage. The boycott's success brought to the forefront the inspirational leadership of King, who soon became the leading spokesperson for the Civil Rights movement.

The success of the Montgomery bus boycott made King and his tactics of mass nonviolent direct action predominant in the Civil Rights movement. This fact did not mean that the legalistic approach favored by the NAACP was superseded. That organization provided legal support for nonviolent protesters, defending them in southern courts and, in the case of Montgomery, taking their case all the way to the Supreme Court. Although there was some competitiveness between the NAACP and King and his associates, their approaches to the civil rights struggle were complementary.

Governmental Support for Civil Rights

The federal government finally began to take more interest in advancing the civil rights of African Americans. The Supreme Court had weighed in with the *Brown v. Board of Education* decision in 1954. In 1957 President Dwight D. Eisenhower supported the black struggle by sending U.S. Army units to Little Rock, Arkansas, during the LITTLE ROCK CRISIS to enforce a federal court order admitting nine African American students to that city's Central High School. That same year, Congress passed the first civil rights legislation in more than eighty years. The Civil Rights Bill of 1957 had more symbolic than real value, as it was watered down considerably in its passage through Congress. However, it did establish the U.S. Civil Rights Commission to investigate civil rights abuses and provided for the Justice Department to investigate voting rights abuses in the South.

The Sit-In Movement

By 1960 the Civil Rights movement had made only limited progress. African Americans in the South still were refused service by most stores, restaurants, lunch counters, and theaters. On February 1, 1960, four African American students from North Carolina Agricultural and Technical College, tired of their humiliating exclusion from the restaurants and lunch counters of Greensboro, North Carolina, decided to do something about that situation. They sat at the local five and dime store's lunch counter until they were served. The next day, Ezell Blair, Joseph McNeill, Franklin McClain, and David Richmond were joined in their SIT-IN by more students from North Carolina A&T.

In succeeding weeks, more and more students joined in the protest in Greensboro. Eventually, the lunch counters and restaurants, hurt by the bad publicity, gave in and started serving blacks. The sit-in movement spread throughout the South as African American students in Durham, Nashville, Charlotte, Chattanooga, and Atlanta, among other cities, took direct action, often involving the deliberate disobeyance of racial segregation laws, to end Jim Crow in the South. These students were inspired by Indian nationalist leader Mohandas Gandhi's principles of nonviolence put forth by King, but his organization, the SOUTHERN CHRISTIAN LEADERSHIP CONFERENCE (SCLC), already had become too bureaucratic and conservative for the taste of the young militants who spearheaded the sit-

Ronald Martin, Robert Patterson, and Mark Martin helped pioneer the sit-in tactic in Greensboro, North Carolina, in February, 1960. *(Library of Congress)*

The Freedom Rides

In 1961 a new front was opened in the battle for civil rights. To test recent court rulings invalidating racial segregation in interstate bus-station waiting rooms, the CONGRESS OF RACIAL EQUALITY (CORE) organized inter-racial groups to ride buses throughout the South, sitting where they chose, including in "white" waiting rooms. These demonstrations, called FREEDOM RIDES, generated a considerable amount of violence, especially in the Deep South, where white mobs in Alabama dragged freedom riders off their buses and beat them unmercifully.

in movement. This was even more true of the NAACP. Therefore, leaders of the sit-in movement started the STUDENT NONVIOLENT COORDINATING COMMITTEE (SNCC) to organize the sit-in movement sweeping the South.

Many northern whites, especially young people, sympathized with the protests, especially since they were carried out in a peaceful and dignified manner. The South responded with puzzled fury. Some localities quickly and peacefully gave in to the protesters' demand for desegregated public accommodations. Others responded with arrests, police brutality, and mob violence. The televised sight of well-dressed and composed young black people being dragged from lunch counters and beaten by police or civilian mobs emphasized to blacks and sympathetic whites as never before the brutality inherent in the southern racial order. As a result, the southern system of race relations found itself under relentless scrutiny and attack.

The freedom rides added more energy to the Civil Rights movement and roused the federal government to intervene in southern race relations. President John F. Kennedy, though sympathetic to African American concerns, initially was more concerned with placating the South, which he counted as part of his electoral coalition, than in helping to end its racial segregation. The violence the South inflicted on the freedom riders, however, could not be ignored: Kennedy sent Justice Department officials and federal marshals to Alabama to defuse the situation. The freedom ride movement spread throughout the South. In 1962 the Interstate Commerce Commission forbade interstate bus companies from using racially segregated bus stations.

The Civil Rights movement moved forward on many fronts. By the beginning of 1963, most public accommodations in the upper South and border states had been desegregated. The Deep South, however, was as insistent as ever in maintaining its racial order. A glaring example of this intransigence was the bloody admission of James MEREDITH to the University of Mississippi in the fall of 1962. Although ordered by a federal court to admit Meredith, Mississippi officials, led by Governor Ross Barnett, at first defied the court order. They eventually admitted Meredith, but not before encouraging a campus riot that left two dead. To ensure Meredith's protection, President Kennedy sent U.S. Army units to Oxford to restore order. Meredith was admitted to the university and eventually graduated.

Birmingham Demonstrations

In an attempt to destroy the Deep South's resistance to civil rights, King and the SCLC, at the behest of local African American leaders, decided to force Birmingham, Alabama, to desegregate its public accommodations. This effort, which took place during the spring of 1963, consisted of massive nonviolent disruption of Birmingham's daily life with mass marches, sit-ins, and picket lines. Protesters hoped to provoke local authorities into reactions that would discredit them in the eyes of the American people, thereby generating na-

tionwide support for civil rights. This hope was fulfilled as Eugene "Bull" Connor, Birmingham's police chief, unleashed attack dogs, police officers wielding billy clubs, and fire fighters with powerful hoses. The excessive force and violence used to put down the demonstrations discredited Birmingham's white power structure and brought national condemnation. As a result, in May of 1963 Birmingham's city government concluded an agreement with King and his followers that effectively desegregated public accommodations in the city.

The BIRMINGHAM DEMONSTRATIONS OF 1963 accelerated the African American community's struggle for civil rights. Hundreds of demonstrations similar to those in Birmingham were staged in various southern and northern cities. Wherever it existed, by law in the South or by custom in the North, racial discrimination and segregation were battled by militant blacks and sympathetic whites.

March on Washington

These efforts culminated in the MARCH ON WASHINGTON on August 28, 1963, when more than 250,000 black and white Americans converged on the nation's capital to express their desire for civil rights for all. President John F. KENNEDY had at first tried to discourage the march but came to see it as a useful lobbying tool for his civil rights proposals before Congress. The march proceeded peacefully to the Lincoln Memorial, where the marchers were addressed by various white and black dignitaries. King solidified his place as the leader of the Civil Rights movement with his legendary "I Have a Dream" speech, in which he eloquently expressed the necessity of a society free of racism.

At the height of the Birmingham demonstrations, city firefighters were ordered to turn high-powered hoses on the demonstrators. *(AP/Wide World Photos)*

Voter Registration

Many observers view the March on Washington as the culmination of the Civil Rights movement, but there was still much to be done. Removing the barriers to African American voting in the South was the next struggle. This effort concentrated on Mississippi and Alabama. In the summer of 1964, hundreds of black and white students went south under the auspices of the Student Nonviolent Coordinating Committee to register black VOTERS. Many whites viewed these volunteers as "outside agitators" bent on destroying the South's way of life and responded to them with violence and intimidation. The worst example of this came in June, 1964, when three civil rights workers—James Chaney, Andrew Goodman, and Michael Schwerner—were kidnapped and murdered by Ku Klux Klansmen in Neshoba County, Mississippi. Among those implicated in the murders were the county sheriff and his deputy. The difficulty of regis-

tering black voters in an atmosphere of constant violence and intimidation made it clear to civil rights leaders that federal intervention was needed.

The assassination of John F. Kennedy brought Lyndon B. JOHNSON to the presidency. He was more inclined to act decisively on civil rights than his predecessor. Using the memory of Kennedy as a prod, Johnson pushed the landmark Civil Rights Bill of 1964 through Congress. This legislation, the most sweeping since Reconstruction, banned racial discrimination in public accommodations, hiring practices, and education.

In the spring of 1965, King, by then a Nobel Peace Prize winner, and the SCLC decided to join SNCC in pressing for voting rights in the South. They picked Selma, Alabama, a notoriously racist city, to register black voters. As in Birmingham, the goal was to concentrate national attention on southern racial abuses to encourage federal intervention and legislation.

This time, the legislation desired was a federal voting rights bill that would remove all literacy tests and other impediments to voting and would take voter registration in the South out of local hands, thereby preventing the traditional subterfuges used to discourage black voting. This goal was achieved as Congress, prodded by Johnson and incensed by the violence that Selma's white citizens inflicted on those protesting disfranchisement, passed the VOTING RIGHTS ACT OF 1965.

The burned-out car used by James Chaney, Andrew Goodman, and Michael Schwerner before they were murdered by opponents to their voter registration work. *(AP/Wide World Photos)*

Later Efforts

The large-scale struggle for civil rights embodied in the Civil Rights movement had

In April, 1964, residents of Kansas City, Missouri, voted on a referendum to outlaw racial discrimination in public accommodations. Broader protections were soon legislated by the U.S. Congress. *(AP/Wide World Photos)*

faded by 1970. The primary reason was simply that, through legislation from 1964 to 1968 (the Civil Rights Act of 1968 banned racial discrimination in housing), racial discrimination had been made illegal and basic civil rights had therefore been reiterated by law. Particularly in the late 1960's and 1970's, the EQUAL EMPLOYMENT OPPORTUNITY COMMISSION (EEOC), established by the Civil Rights Act of 1964, served as a reminder that the federal government would prosecute discrimination cases.

Other reasons included the fact that black leadership was not unified, having divided into mainstream liberal and radical factions. Moreover, the violence of urban uprisings by blacks in the last half of the 1960's alienated and confused many whites. Black leaders realized that the struggle for civil rights would continue in the form of struggles against subtle types of discrimination that were not easily dealt with by law.

In the late 1960's, King and others had realized that economic parity for African Americans was just as important as civil rights. However, King was assassinated in 1968 before he could mobilize the black and white communities in an effort to work toward such parity. Social and economic gains by African Americans were slowed during the 1980's by the more conservative philosophy of the federal government. Many in the government had come to believe that AFFIRMATIVE ACTION efforts to bring about equality for blacks constituted REVERSE DISCRIMINATION—discrimination against whites. The last major civil rights legislation of the twentieth century, the Civil Rights Act of 1991, was designed to reverse Supreme Court decisions in the 1980's that had made it harder to contest job bias.

A crucial aspect of civil rights issues from the 1970's through the 1990's was the fact that the civil rights battlefield had expanded. First the struggle of women for equal rights, then issues concerning guaranteed rights for people with disabilities and for gays and lesbians often took center stage. These groups did not achieve equal results, but one landmark piece of legislation was the 1990 Americans with Disabilities Act, which guaranteed people with disabilities access to public buildings.

—*Hayward Farrar*

See also: Accommodation; Constitution, U.S.; Housing discrimination; Race riots; Racial discrimination; Segregation and integration.

Suggested Readings:

Albert, Peter J., and Ronald Hoffman, eds. *We Shall Overcome: Martin Luther King and the Black Freedom Struggle.* New York: Pantheon Books, 1990.

Bradley, David, and Shelley Fisher Fishkin, eds. *The Encyclopedia of Civil Rights in America.* New York: M. E. Sharpe, 1998.

Branch, Taylor. *Pillar of Fire: America in the King Years, 1963-1965*. New York: Simon & Schuster, 1998.

Davis, Townsend. *Weary Feet, Rested Souls: A Guided History of the Civil Rights Movement*. New York: W. W. Norton, 1998.

Graham, Hugh D. *The Civil Rights Era*. New York: Oxford University Press, 1990.

Kasher, Steven. *The Civil Rights Movement: A Photographic History, 1954-1968*. New York: Abbeville Press, 1996.

Levy, Peter B. *The Civil Rights Movement*. Westport, Conn.: Greenwood Press, 1998.

Lowery, Charles D., and John F. Marszalek, eds. *Encyclopedia of African-American Civil Rights: From Emancipation to the Present*. New York: Greenwood Press, 1992.

Marable, Manning. *Race, Reform, and Rebellion*. 2d ed. Jackson: University Press of Mississippi, 1991.

Marsh, Charles. *God's Long Summer: Stories of Faith and Civil Rights*. Princeton, N.J.: Princeton University Press, 1997.

Morris, Aldon D. *The Origins of the Civil Rights Movement: Black Communities Organizing for Change*. New York: Free Press, 1984.

Riches, William T. M. *The Civil Rights Movement: Struggle and Resistance*. New York: St. Martin's Press, 1997.

Salmond, John A. *"My Mind Set On Freedom": A History of the Civil Rights Movement, 1954-1968*. Chicago: Ivan R. Dee, 1997.

Young, Andrew. *An Easy Burden: The Civil Rights Movement and the Transformation of America*. New York: HarperCollins, 1996.

Civil rights and congressional legislation: The original U.S. Constitution as written in 1787 contained no explicit statement of citizens' rights. The framers of the Constitution assumed at first that the newly created system of federation constrained the national government to act only with its specifically delegated powers. The existence of SLAVERY, which de-nied the principles of human dignity and equality set forth in the country's founding documents, was another reason for the reluctance of the Founders to adopt a formal bill of rights. Thus, the Constitution was believed to be both a source of political power for the national government and a restraint on that power.

Civil liberties, however, remained a cause of concern for those who were suspicious of the new Constitution. Some states, beginning with Pennsylvania, made the ratification of the new document conditional upon the inclusion of formal guarantees of civil liberties for citizens. The concessions thus obtained meant that the first task of the newly created Congress in 1789 was to agree on the first amendments to the Constitution. When adopted in 1791, those ten amendments became known as the Bill of Rights; the words of those first ten amendments have been treated as sacred and never amended.

The CIVIL RIGHTS and civil liberties of American citizens are guaranteed in the Bill of Rights. Civil liberties constitute an area of personal freedom with which governments are constrained from interfering. Civil rights, on the other hand, are legal or moral claims that citizens are entitled to force the government to take affirmative steps to secure. Cumulatively, the Bill of Rights guarantees the freedoms of speech, religion, and the press; the right to bear arms; the right to due process of law; and rights afforded to criminal suspects. The Ninth and Tenth Amendments create an additional, undefined area of liberty for the people.

The Bill of Rights became a source of inspiration for a number of countries around the world. The equal extension of these rights to every American citizen, however, has been the result of a long historical struggle marked by intense controversy and conflict over constitutional interpretation. The Bill of Rights originally bound only the federal government; the nationalization of these rights and their uniform application to all states did not become a reality until the twentieth century, and the process was not completed until the 1960's.

Congress and the Supreme Court
In addition to the Bill of Rights, congressional laws, executive orders, and state statutes are the main sources of protection for individual rights and liberties. Congressional legislation has served to strengthen and supplement constitutionally guaranteed civil rights. Congress has also initiated major constitutional amendments in this direction. On the other hand, the U.S. SUPREME COURT derived for itself in the early years of the United States the power of judicial review. The Supreme Court thus acts as the guardian of the Constitution, including its formal amendments. Although Congress has the lawmaking powers, any act of Congress that violates the words or spirit of the Constitution can be declared invalid by the Supreme Court.

Before the CIVIL WAR, the American political system operated on the principle of duality of citizenship for American citizens. Each U.S. resident was considered a citizen of both the United States and of the state in which the person resided. The doctrines of the Bill of Rights, however, were not extended to the states; in other words, if a state did not protect a right guaranteed in the Bill of Rights, a resident of that state could not claim such a right on the basis of the Bill of Rights. The Bill of Rights did not apply to laws of the states or procedures of the states.

The Reconstruction Era
The original Constitution of the United States did not ban slavery. During the Civil War, the EMANCIPATION PROCLAMATION of 1863 de-clared all slaves within areas of rebellion free. Subsequently, the THIRTEENTH AMENDMENT to the Constitution, which declared slavery to be illegal, was passed by Congress in January, 1865, and was ratified by the requisite number of states in December of the same year. Congress proposed the FOURTEENTH AMENDMENT in June, 1866; the amendment, which was ratified in July, 1868, was designed to provide "equal protection of laws" to freed blacks. Moreover, the FOURTEENTH AMENDMENT clearly established the principle of national citizenship, emphasizing that "no State shall make or enforce any law which shall abridge the privileges or immunities of citizens of the United States." Congress proposed the FIFTEENTH AMENDMENT in February, 1869, to protect the right of blacks to vote; the Fifteenth Amendment was ratified in March, 1870. Once again, states were barred from denying a constitutionally guaranteed right to any citizen "on account of race, color, or previous condition of servitude."

Congress passed the Civil Rights Act of 1875 to protect blacks from discrimination by proprietors of hotels, theaters, railways, and other public accommodations; such discrimination was widespread in the segregated

Crowd gathered at the Capitol Building responds to the House's passage of the Civil Rights Act of 1866. *(Library of Congress)*

southern states. The implementation of the "equal protection" clauses of the new amendments and other new legislation, however, put Congress and the Supreme Court on a collision course.

In the 1883 *Civil Rights Cases*, the Supreme Court declared the Civil Rights Act of 1875 unconstitutional on the ground that the Fourteenth Amendment applied only to discriminatory actions of state officials "operating under cover of law" and not to the discriminatory actions of individuals or companies offering service to the public. The language of the Fourteenth and Fifteenth Amendments appears to be an effort to extend the Bill of Rights to all citizens in every state, but this was not the Supreme Court's interpretation for another hundred years. In 1873 the Supreme Court gave its judgment in the *Slaughterhouse Cases* that the Fourteenth Amendment did not impose the uniform application of the entire Bill of Rights to all citizens but was intended to protect only blacks as a class. Finally, in 1896, in PLESSY v. FERGUSON, the Supreme Court upheld the legality of racial separation, noting in its opinion that SEPARATE BUT EQUAL public facilities were constitutional. Thus, the Fourteenth Amendment remained ineffective.

Between 1925 and 1937, a slow process of nationalizing the civil liberties guaranteed by the First Amendment began when the Supreme Court held that the freedom of speech, and later the freedoms of press and assembly, were protected from infringement by the states. In 1937 the Supreme Court took a step backward in *Palko v. Connecticut*, in which the Court held that not all rights, but only those which were implicit in the concept of "ordered liberty," were for national application.

Civil Rights Era

Following WORLD WAR II, with the changing international political climate and the mounting pressure of democratic challenge at home and abroad during the height of the Cold War, the movement for expansion of democratic rights began to gain momentum under the leadership of black organizations. President Harry S Truman's decision to desegregate the Army following World War II was a step in that direction. In 1954, in the historic case BROWN v. BOARD OF EDUCATION, the Supreme Court declared separate educational facilities for black children to be "inherently unequal"; the *Brown* decision reversed the *Plessy v. Ferguson* ruling and gave a severe blow to the practice of segregation. The judgment in *Brown* ushered in a new era for civil rights by conveying the revolutionary message that radical change in race relations was possible through the formal institutions of government.

The Civil Rights movement spearheaded by African Americans, which was to flower in the 1960's under the leadership of Martin Luther KING, Jr., had as its prime target the legal and political segregation and racial discrimination in the South. Later, in the late 1960's and the early 1970's, the movement expanded to other parts of the United States, where RACIAL DISCRIMINATION often did not have the patronage of local and state laws but was nevertheless widespread; such discrimination was often subtle and informal.

Congress responded to the changing political situation in the country as the Civil Rights movement began to gain strength. Thus the Civil Rights Act of 1957 was passed making it a federal crime to intimidate a voter or to prevent a person from voting. The act also established the COMMISSION ON CIVIL RIGHTS to monitor progress in civil rights. The Civil Rights Act of 1960 was intended to increase penalties for obstruction of voting; the 1960 act declared it a crime to destroy any voting records within twenty-two months of an election and established federal power to appoint referees to register voters wherever a pattern of discrimination was found by a federal court. The resistance in southern states to the federal pressure was stiff and violent.

President Lyndon B. Johnson signs the Civil Rights Act of 1964, as Vice President Hubert Humphrey (behind Johnson) and congressional leaders look on. *(AP/Wide World Photos)*

The Civil Rights movement, though originating with the black cause, raised the consciousness of numerous other deprived groups, many of which began to organize themselves around the issue of rights. A number of other minority groups—Asian Americans, Hispanic Americans, Native Americans, gay and lesbian groups, people with disabilities, the homeless, and others—began to demand equal rights and the equal protection of laws.

Congress passed the Equal Pay Act of 1963 to ban wage discrimination on the basis of sex in jobs requiring equal skill, effort, and responsibility. The Civil Rights Act of 1964, a landmark piece of legislation, became the Magna Carta of racial minorities and other deprived groups. The provisions of the 1964 Act outlawed discrimination in private commerce, authorized the attorney general to sue for desegregation of public schools, and recommended the withholding of federal aid to segregated schools. Title VII of the act outlawed discrimination in a variety of employment practices on the basis of race, religion, and sex. The act also established the EQUAL EMPLOYMENT OPPORTUNITY COMMISSION (EEOC) to enforce the law; however, the act had application only to the private sector. The subsequent passage of the Equal Employment Opportunity Act of 1972 was an attempt to correct this imbalance by extending such protection to the public sector as well. In 1978 Congress further amended the Civil Rights Act of 1964 to include protection for pregnant employees by requiring that pregnancy be treated as a disability that entitled pregnant workers to medical and liability insurance benefits.

The VOTING RIGHTS ACT OF 1965 was passed to ensure the principle of universal adult suffrage for the first time in American history. The 1965 act dealt a final blow to such discriminatory practices as the use of literacy tests, property taxes, or poll taxes as conditions for voter qualification. The act also provided for affirmative intervention by the federal government to increase voter registration in areas of low voter turnout. Amendments to the Voting Rights Act were enacted by Congress in 1970, 1975, and 1982; the amendments extended the act's application to states outside the South, provided for the printing of ballots in languages other than English, and strengthened the provisions of the original act. The Civil Rights Act of 1968 outlawed discrimination in the rental or sale of property on the basis of religion or race.

Post-Civil Rights Movement Era
By the early 1970's, through congressional legislation, the process of extending legal guarantees of civil rights to all U.S. citizens had been largely completed. The political equality of all citizens had been ensured for the first time in American history through the affirmative efforts of the government. Legal segregation in the southern states was to become a piece of history, and many of the goals of the Civil Rights movement had been accomplished. Yet the extension of the process of integration to the nonsouthern states, where racial discrimination was less blatant but nevertheless present, brought about violent racial confrontations.

The decline of the Civil Rights movement was hastened by the emergence of the BLACK POWER MOVEMENT in the late 1960's. The African American community was split by the two very different forms of activism, as were the multiracial ranks of civil rights activists. The use of AFFIRMATIVE ACTION in employment practices, which at times meant the establishment of quotas for minority hiring and promotion, was attacked by conservatives and by many liberals as well. At the base of the controversy was the nature of American civil rights, which were guaranteed to individuals and not to groups. Moreover, the adoption of policies of group preference could be considered to lead to REVERSE DISCRIMINATION.

The principle of liberty and the principle of equality often seemed to be competing with each other.

The election of Ronald Reagan to the presidency signified a conservative trend in federal enforcement of civil rights laws. The first signals of the new attitude were the drastic financial cutbacks and staff reductions the REAGAN ADMINISTRATION ordered at the Commission on Civil Rights, the Equal Employment Opportunity Commission, and other federal agencies dealing with civil rights implementation. Next came the appointment of conservative justices to the Supreme Court and the appointment of arch-conservative William Rehnquist as chief justice. The number of federally filed discrimination suits fell during the Reagan years, and the burden of proof in discrimination cases shifted from the employer to the employee.

Nevertheless, the basic progress made in the extension and protection of civil rights in the United States during the latter half of the twentieth century seems to be irreversible, even under conservative governments. A proof of this was the passage of the Civil Rights Act of 1991, which reinforced existing laws forbidding racial and sexual discrimination and added provisions outlawing age and handicap discrimination. The 1991 act was designed in part to reverse the effects of the Supreme Court's decisions of the 1980's that had shifted the burden of proof to the complainant in discrimination cases.

The original bill was sponsored by Democratic legislators in 1989 and was pushed through Congress despite President George Bush's threat to veto it. Both the DEMOCRATIC PARTY and the REPUBLICAN PARTY accused each other of being enemies of equal rights. In November, 1991, a compromise version of the bill sponsored by moderate Republicans was passed by both houses of Congress and became law upon Bush's signing. The conservative allies of the president accused him of capitulating to proponents of a "quota bill," while Bush's liberal opponents attacked him as acting as an opportunist. Despite such political bickerings and partisan contests, Congress in the 1990's generally retained its role as a supporter of civil rights. Moreover, as the 1991 act indicated, even conservative presidential administrations felt the necessity for the adoption of civil rights measures.

—*Indu Vohra*

See also: Congressional Black Caucus; Congress members; Constitution, U.S.; Housing discrimination; Politics and government; Racial discrimination; Segregation and integration.

Suggested Readings:

Belknap, Michal R., ed. *Securing the Enactment of Civil Rights Legislation, 1965-1968.* Vol. 14 in *Civil Rights, the White House, and the Justice Department, 1945-1968.* New York: Garland, 1991.

Berry, Mary F. *Black Resistance, White Law: A History of Constitutional Racism in America.* New York: Penguin Books, 1994.

Franklin, John H., and Genna R. McNeil, eds. *African Americans and the Living Constitution.* Washington, D.C.: Smithsonian Institution Press, 1995.

Howard, John R. *The Shifting Wind: The Supreme Court and Civil Rights from Reconstruction to Brown.* Albany: State University of New York Press, 1999.

Loevy, Robert D., ed. *The Civil Rights Act of 1964: The Passage of the Law That Ended Racial Segregation.* Albany: State University of New York Press, 1997.

_____. *To End All Segregation: The Politics of the Passage of the Civil Rights Act of 1964.* Lanham, Md.: University Press of America, 1990.

Ritz, Susan. *The Civil Rights Act of 1991: Its Impact on Employment Discrimination Litigation.* New York: Practicing Law Institute, 1992.

Schwemm, Robert G., ed. *The Fair Housing Act After Twenty Years.* New Haven, Conn.: Yale Law School, 1989.

Warren, Gorham & Lamont, Inc. *Analysis of the Civil Rights Act of 1991.* Boston: Warren, Gorham & Lamont, 1991.

Whalen, Charles W., and Barbara Whalen. *The Longest Debate: A Legislative History of the 1964 Civil Rights Act.* Washington, D.C.: Seven Locks Press, 1985.

Civil rights court cases: Historically, race has been the most significant factor in the development of constitutional CIVIL RIGHTS law. A review of civil rights cases involving African Americans thus highlights the tortuous and tumultuous process of making the U.S. Constitution a living reality for all American citizens.

Civil Rights

In the aftermath of the CIVIL WAR, Congress ratified the THIRTEENTH AMENDMENT (1865), prohibiting slavery and involuntary servitude; the FOURTEENTH AMENDMENT (1868), guaranteeing equal protection against discrimination to all citizens; and the FIFTEENTH AMENDMENT (1870), prohibiting discrimination in voting on the basis of race, color, or previous condition of servitude. Congress also passed the Civil Rights Act of 1866, which explicitly declared that all persons born in the United States were citizens and were entitled to equality of treatment before the law. The Civil Rights Act of 1875 extended protection for African Americans by outlawing discrimination in public accommodations. The flurry of post-Civil War legislation set the stage for more than a century of struggle over many of these principles.

The denial of equality has been profound and devastating to African American citizens. The lack of equal access to public accommodations, housing, education, voting, employment, and the criminal justice system has affected virtually every African American. In these areas, the passage of major civil rights laws has resulted in radical changes in constitutional interpretations of equality and consequently transformed the United States into a significantly more democratic society.

Early Supreme Court Decisions
Prior to the 1950's, the U.S. SUPREME COURT was not especially responsive to the plight of African Americans or the poor. The first major civil rights case before the Supreme Court, *Dred Scott v. Sandford* (1857, commonly called the DRED SCOTT DECISION), declared that African Americans were not protected by the Constitution. The ratification of the Thirteenth, Fourteenth and Fifteenth Amendments and the passing of the Civil Right Acts of 1866 and 1875 invalidated the Dred Scott decision.

The *Civil Rights Cases* (1883) were the first cases to come before the Supreme Court to test the applicability of the Thirteenth and Fourteenth Amendments and the two Civil Rights Acts. These five cases, heard together by the Court, raised the issue of whether the denial of accommodation in hotels and theaters to people of color violated the constitutional guarantees of the Thirteenth and Fourteenth Amendments. The Court's decision was a significant blow to African American rights.

It held that such denial did not violate the Constitution, saying that the Thirteenth Amendment was intended to protect specific narrow legal rights but not to extend to the "social rights of men and races in the community." It also found that the Civil Rights Act of 1875 prohibiting discrimination in public accommodations was unconstitutional, stating that Congress did not have the authority to prohibit discrimination by the owners of public accommodations (such as inns, theaters, and transportation).

Thirteen years later, in an even greater setback for African Americans, the Court's decision in PLESSY V. FERGUSON (1896) denied equality before the law to African Americans. The Court ruled that the maintenance of segregated facilities for train passengers did not violate the equal protection clause of the Fourteenth Amendment so long as the segregated facilities were SEPARATE BUT EQUAL. In practice, facilities provided for blacks in such cases were routinely inferior, and the effect of the decision was to subject African Americans to legalized discrimination in almost every area of life.

Emerging Equality
In 1954 the Supreme Court made perhaps the most significant constitutional decision of the twentieth century. The Court was asked to reconsider the separate but equal doctrine established in *Plessy v. Ferguson*. In 1954 a unanimous Court ruled in BROWN V. BOARD OF EDUCATION that racial segregation in public schools denied equal protection to blacks. This precedent served as the legal principle behind major civil rights cases and laws that led to a tremendous expansion in civil rights over the next two decades.

Education and Equality
In a nation where education is vital to opportunity and success, African Americans suffered profoundly from segregated school systems. Public expenditures for white schools long exceeded the expenditures for African American schools. After invalidating the constitutionality of separate but equal schools in the *Brown* decision, the Court in 1955, in *Brown II*, ordered that schools must be desegregated with "all deliberate speed."

In a series of decisions over the next two decades, the Court was to address a range of issues and questions relevant to the elimination of unequal educational opportunity at all levels. Voluntary student-transfer plans based on race were invalidated in *Goss v. Board of Education* (1963). In *Griffin v. Prince Edward County*

A year after winning the *Brown v. Board of Education* decision at the Supreme Court, NAACP lawyers Louis J. Redding (left) and Thurgood Marshall returned to the Court to press for full implementation of its desegregation order. *(Library of Congress)*

School Board (1964), an effort to close integrated public schools and provide public support for white children to attend private schools was found to be unconstitutional. In GREEN V. COUNTY SCHOOL BOARD OF NEW KENT COUNTY (1968), freedom-of-choice attendance plans that produced little desegregation were ruled invalid. In ALEXANDER V. HOLMES COUNTY BOARD OF EDUCATION (1969), the Court stated that the "all deliberate speed" directive was no longer permissible: All schools were obligated to end dual schools at once and to operate only integrated schools.

In SWANN V. CHARLOTTE-MECKLENBURG BOARD OF EDUCATION (1971), the Court approved racial quotas, the rearrangement of school districts and attendance zones, and the use of transportation, particularly busing, as remedial measures to desegregate schools. In *Runyon v. McCrary* (1976), the Court held that private commercial schools that excluded qualified children solely on the basis of race were unconstitutional. Despite this impressive movement toward equality, during the 1980's a notable retrenchment took place among the executive and judiciary branches against further desegregation.

In the 1978 case *Regents of the University of California v. Allan Bakke*, widely known simply as the BAKKE CASE, the Supreme Court ruled that the medical school of the University of California at Davis could not legally reserve a certain number of places for minority students. However, the Court also upheld some types of AFFIRMATIVE ACTION in its ruling by saying that race could be considered as a factor in admissions policies in order to "remedy disadvantages cast on minorities by past racial prejudice."

In 1991 the Supreme Court's *Oklahoma Board of Education v. Dowell* decision held that a school district may have a desegregation order lifted after good-faith efforts at desegregation have been made and vestiges of past discrimination have been eliminated as much as can reasonably be expected.

Although not a U.S. Supreme Court decision, the case HOPWOOD V. UNIVERSITY OF TEXAS (1996) set an important precedent. The U.S. Court of Appeals, Fifth Circuit, held that the University of Texas law school's affirmative action program was unconstitutional. The court stated that the consideration of race to promote diversity among the student body contradicts "the aims of equal protection." (The Fifth Circuit's area includes Texas, Louisiana, and Mississippi; because the school changed its policy after the court's decision, the case was not heard by the Supreme Court.)

Voting and Equality

A citizen's right to vote is essential if a society is to be a representative democracy. Until the 1960's, African Americans were excluded from voting by such tactics as physical and economic harassment and intimidation, the use of literacy tests, poll taxes, racial GERRY-MANDERING, and the denial of access to registration. In a series of cases, the Supreme Court forbade these practices on constitutional grounds. In GOMILLION V. LIGHTFOOT (1960), racial gerrymandering was ruled unconstitutional. In BAKER V. CARR (1962), the Court established that the federal judiciary had the authority to intervene in reapportionment issues because reapportionment touched on the question of equal protection. In *Reynolds v. Sims* (1964), the Court ruled that Alabama had to reapportion voting districts to conform to the "one man, one vote" principle. In 1965 Congress passed the VOTING RIGHTS ACTS OF 1965, which prohibited the establishment of any voting qualifications or procedures that would deny or abridge a person's right to vote because of race, color, or inclusion in a minority group. In *Presley v. Etowah County Commission* (1992), however, the Court narrowed the protection of the Voting Rights Act when it approved the practice by white incumbents of transferring a successful African American candidate's authority to other elected or appointed white officials.

In 1995, in *Miller v. Johnson*, the Supreme Court held that states were in violation of the Constitution's equal protection clause if they drew state congressional districts in such a way as to purposely include a majority of African American residents.

Equality and Employment

Title VII of the Civil Rights Act of 1964 contained broad prohibitions against discrimina-tion in employment. In 1965 Executive Order 11246 required that government contractors must engage in affirmative action to eliminate discrimination.

In *Griggs v. Duke Power Company* (1971), the Court enumerated the standards that were to control employment discrimination cases for the next decade; in its decision, the Court declared that job-qualification standards must be related to job performance. In UNITED STEELWORKERS OF AMERICA V. WEBER (1979, also known as *Kaiser Aluminum and Chemical Corporation v. Weber*), the Court approved the use of voluntary affirmative action programs by private employers. In *Fullilove v. Klutznick* (1980), the setting aside of a percentage of federal funds for minority-owned businesses in public works projects was approved.

In its 1988-1989 session, a more conservative Court handed down a series of rulings that overturned some major equal-employment rulings. In *Wards Cove Packing Company v. Atonio* (1989), the Court shifted the burden of proof from the employer to the plaintiff, who was required to show that an employer's practice was discriminatory. The decision also limited the use of statistical evidence as proof of discrimination. In *Patterson v. McLean Credit Union* (1989), the Court severely restricted the coverage of the Civil Rights Act of 1966 to cover only hiring decisions; any discrimination that occurred after an employee was hired, the Court stated, was not covered by the act. In *Richmond v. J. A. Croson Company* (1989), the set-aside principle established by the *Fullilove* case was overturned. Congress, though, passed the Civil Rights Act of 1991, which rejected the Court's new interpretations and—with the exception of the *Croson* decision—restored the law to the standards that had existed before the 1988-1989 Supreme Court term.

In *Adarand Constructors v. Peña* (1995), the Court ruled that a broad affirmative action program requiring firms doing business with the federal Department of Transportation to give a certain percentage of their contracts to minority businesses was unconstitutional. The Court held that the use of affirmative action to right past wrongs must pass the "strict scrutiny" test and must promote a compelling state interest.

Equality and Housing

In SHELLEY V. KRAEMER (1948), the Court declared that state judicial enforcement of RESTRICTIVE COVENANTS aimed at preventing blacks from purchasing property in white neighborhoods violated the Fourteenth Amendment. In *Reitman v. Mulkey* (1967), a law that would have allowed discrimination in the sale or leasing of housing was deemed unconstitutional. In *Jones v. Alfred H. Mayer Company* (1968), the Court prohibited private racial discrimination in the sale or rental of real or personal property. Congress passed Title VIII of the 1968 Civil Rights Act, which contains these principles and other broad prohibitions against discrimination in housing.

Matters of Family

Until the 1950's, a majority of states had MISCEGENATION statutes that prohibited interracial dating and marriage. In LOVING V. VIRGINIA (1967), the Court held that miscegenation statues violate the equal protection clause. In *Levy v. Louisiana* (1968), the Court addressed the legal status of illegitimate children. The case involved an African American woman who had died allegedly as the result of medical malpractice; the Court ruled that her illegitimate children had the full protection of the equal protection clause of the Constitution. In *Shapiro v. Thompson* (1969), the Court ruled that a citizen could not be denied welfare benefits because of a residency requirement.

Administration of Justice

The federal judiciary has been reluctant to intervene in criminal cases that fall within the jurisdiction of states. Consequently, white people have not often been convicted of crimes against African Americans. In UNITED STATES V. PRICE (1966), the Court decided that the white citizens who were accused of murdering three civil rights workers in Mississippi could be tried under a federal statute. In *Pierson v. Ray* (1967), the Court established the right of demonstrators to challenge illegal laws through affirmative civil suits for false arrests, even when the demonstrators had deliberately allowed themselves to be arrested in order to make the challenge.

In SWAIN V. ALABAMA (1965), the Court upheld the right of prosecutors to use peremptory challenges to remove African Americans from juries; in *Batson v. Kentucky* (1986), the Court reversed this ruling and declared that prosecutors had to demonstrate that the removal of any African American juror was based on nonracial grounds. In VASQUEZ V. HILLERY (1986), the Court condemned racial discrimination in the selection of grand juries. In *McCleskey v. Kemp* (1987), however, the Court voted to permit CAPITAL PUNISHMENT even though statistical data showed that African Americans were more likely to be executed than Anglo-Americans were.

—*Richard Hudson*

See also: Civil rights and congressional legislation; Constitution, U.S.

Suggested Readings:

Altschiller, Donald, ed. *Affirmative Action.* New York: H. W. Wilson, 1991.

Baum, Lawrence. *The Supreme Court.* 4th ed. Washington, D.C.: Congressional Quarterly Press, 1992.

Bender, Leslie. *Power, Privilege and Law: A Civil Rights Reader.* St. Paul, Minn.: West, 1995.

Bradley, David, and Shelley Fisher Fishkin, eds. *The Encyclopedia of Civil Rights in America.* New York: M. E. Sharpe, 1998.

Brooks, Roy L, Gilbert P. Carrasco, and Gordon A. Marin. *Civil Rights Litigation:*

Cases and Perspectives. Durham, N.C.: Carolina Academic Press, 1995.

Domino, John C. *Civil Rights and Liberties: Toward the Twenty-first Century*. New York: HarperCollins College Publishers, 1994.

Eisenberg, Theodore. *Civil Rights Legislation: Cases and Materials*. 4th ed. Charlottesville, Va.: Michie, 1996.

Ginger, Ann F. *The Law, the Supreme Court and the People's Rights*. Rev. ed. Woodbury, N.Y.: Barron's, 1977.

Mendelson, Wallace. *The American Constitution and the Judicial Process*. Homewood, Ill.: Dorsey Press, 1980.

Schwartz, Bernard, and Alan M. Dershowitz. *Behind Bakke: Affirmative Action and the Supreme Court*. Rev. ed. New York: Notable Trials Library, 1995.

Tatalovich, Raymond, and Byron W. Daynes, eds. *Moral Controversies in American Politics: Cases in Social Regulatory Policy*. Armonk, N.Y.: M. E. Sharpe, 1998.

Thomas, Brook, ed. *Plessy v. Ferguson: A Brief History with Documents*. Boston: Bedford Books, 1997.

Civil War: Also known as the War Between the States, a protracted conflict in which the Northern states fought to prevent eleven Southern states from seceding from the Union. The war began in April, 1861, after the southern states began seceding from the United States. The secessionists were unhappy with Republican Abraham Lincoln's election as president, partly because of the REPUBLICAN PARTY's opposition to the spread of SLAVERY to new western territories. The first seven states to secede proclaimed the formation of a new country, the Confederate States of America, or the CONFEDERACY, in February of 1861. In the following months, four more states seceded. Lincoln believed fervently that the full union of the United States must be preserved.

Fighting began in April, 1861. Lincoln had ordered that supplies and reinforcements be sent to Fort Sumter, in the Charleston, SOUTH CAROLINA, harbor. The fort was the main Union outpost remaining in the South. South Carolina heard that reinforcements were coming, and on April 12-13, 1861, South Carolina troops attacked the fort before they could arrive. This engagement marked the beginning of the war. The war raged for almost four years, until the South's official surrender at Appomattox on April 9, 1865. The struggle was bloody and bitter, dividing communities and even families.

On the eve of the war, the population of blacks in the United States exceeded four million. Though a distinct minority, American blacks were to play a crucial role in the Civil War. Free blacks, who resided mostly in the northern states, constituted a formidable part of the ABOLITIONIST MOVEMENT. Many were wealthy, law-abiding, and taxpaying but denied citizenship and the franchise (the right to vote). They were, therefore, very active in advocating reform.

Black Response to the War
On the outbreak of war, free blacks overwhelmingly supported the Republican Party and the Union cause. However, neither the party nor Abraham Lincoln had any intention of interfering with slavery. In his inaugural address on March 4, Lincoln even pledged his commitment to the FUGITIVE SLAVE LAW.

Blacks—slaves and free—saw things differently, and they quickly linked the war to slavery. Since the war was a confrontation between the free North and slave South, blacks saw it as nothing but a war against slavery. It thus had a special significance to them, and they were determined to be active participants. Slaves became restive, deserting their plantations to join the Union. Free blacks began insisting on active black participation in the war effort. Initially, those slaves who crossed to the Union lines were turned back.

Drummer boy named Taylor, who served in the 78th Regiment of the U.S. Colored Infantry. *(National Archives)*

This policy, however, could not stem the tide of refugees, and what began as a trickle became a flood. On May 24, 1861, Union general Benjamin Butler decreed that fugitive slaves were "contraband of war" and would no longer be returned. As their numbers increased, they were organized into camps and engaged in building fortifications and other tasks required by the Union army. At the same time, various philanthropic organizations became involved in relief efforts.

Blacks were not satisfied with being sidelined into relief camps. The war meant much more to them, and they were not willing to sit idly while others fought against slavery. They quickly offered their services to the Union army. In several northern cities, blacks formed military companies and started drilling in anticipation of service. Leading blacks volunteered to raise troops.

Exclusion
The government, however, turned down black offers. Many able-bodied African Americans were, at the very best, employed as laborers. Many were simply turned away. There were many reasons for this initial rejection of black volunteers. The preservation of the Union, not the destruction of slavery, was considered the main objective of the war, and many Republicans thought it would be possible to restore and preserve the Union without tampering with the system of slavery. Many, too, were scared of the prospect of slave insurrection, and some argued that slaves were inferior and accustomed to bondage and, therefore, would make poor soldiers. Some, moreover, objected on the grounds that white officers would not fight alongside blacks.

Though the government continued its exclusionary policy, ignoring blacks who wished to serve became increasingly difficult. Frederick DOUGLASS and Martin DELANY persistently urged the government to reconsider its policy. They drew attention to the crippling effect black enlistment would have on the rebellion.

First Black Troops
Throughout 1862, President Lincoln, Congress, and the military debated the issue of black enlistment. Meanwhile, the black influx to Union lines increased, and blacks continued to be engaged in both the army and navy as laborers. Finally, on August 25, 1862, the first authorization for the enlistment of blacks as soldiers was sent to General Rufus Saxton. Military necessity forced the abandonment of

exclusion. Even before official authorization, Union commanders in the field had been compelled by manpower shortages to enlist blacks as soldiers. The need for more men became apparent as thousands of white soldiers were scheduled for discharge in the fall of 1863, and white volunteers could not meet the ever-increasing demand. Perhaps the most compelling factors were the defeats Union forces experienced at Fredericksburg and Vicksburg.

Manpower shortages and the prospect of losing the war finally forced the government to recognize the critical importance of the slavery issue. With the EMANCIPATION PROCLAMATION, in January, 1863, which announced that slaves in the rebellious states were free, Lincoln officially made slavery a war issue and opened the doors to black soldiers. Following the proclamation, Secretary of War Edwin Stanton authorized the formation of four black infantry regiments and a battalion of six companies. A BUREAU OF COLORED TROOPS was established, and black enlistment began in several states. Blacks welcomed this turn of events, and within a short time several black regiments were filled. On July 30, 1863, the first U.S. Colored Troop was mustered into federal service.

Blacks in the Confederacy

The Confederate states also confronted the difficult question of what to do with blacks, especially the millions of slaves. Ironically, blacks also volunteered to fight for the Confederacy, though on a much smaller scale. In Nashville, New Orleans, and Richmond, for

When General Nathan Bedford Forrest took Fort Pillow in Tennessee on April 12, 1864, he made good on the Confederacy's promise to kill all captured African American soldiers serving the Union. *(Library of Congress)*

example, blacks offered their services in defense of the rebellion. Many of these blacks were property owners—some even owned slaves—who saw the North as a threat. Though these blacks were wealthy and eager to protect their property, their support of the Confederacy was also a result of the strength of anti-Union propaganda. They were told that the "Yankees" would subject them to a worse form of slavery. Several Confederate states welcomed these volunteers and passed bills authorizing their enlistment as laborers. Also during the early days of the war, some black volunteers were received into the fighting forces of the rebels.

The Confederate government was also reluctant to embrace black support. First, there was the risk involved in arming slaves. Second, many leaders also felt that fighting was the occupation of the "superior" white race and that blacks were better suited for menial jobs. Third, some saw the inherent contradiction in enlisting the support of slaves. There were also many who found arming blacks revolting to the southern sense of pride and honor. While the Confederate government dragged its feet, Confederate generals in the field began to feel the pressures of war. By February, 1865, General Robert E. Lee was in favor of black enrollment with the promise of freedom to all who enlisted and their families. On March 13, 1865, the Confederate congress authorized the enlistment of blacks. Thousands of blacks were enlisted, but there is no evidence that they took part in battle. By this time the war was in its final weeks.

Blacks did fight in major battles on the Union side. They displayed courage and bravery, and they won the admiration and commendation of their superior officers. Of the Congressional Medals of Honor given to men who distinguished themselves in the war, twenty went to blacks. It has been estimated that more than 178,000 blacks served in the Union army during the war; these soldiers saw combat in more than two hundred engagements.

Many black women, too, are among the unsung heroes of the Civil War; their contributions were unacknowledged for years. Yet the war could have been much more difficult without them. Harriet TUBMAN, the legendary UNDERground Railroad conductor, risked her life to spy for and guide Union forces. She also nursed the wounded. The same was true of Sojourner TRUTH, who also spied for the Union army and nursed the sick and wounded at Freedmen's Hospital in Washington, D.C., Mary Elizabeth Bowser was the leader of the Union supporters in Richmond. Her job as a servant of Confederate president Jefferson Davis exposed her to sensitive and classified military information, which she passed on to the Union side.

By participating in the war, African Americans made a strong case for citizenship and equality. Black problems and issues became major factors in the peace settlement and during RECONSTRUCTION. The Emancipation Proclamation had freed thousands of slaves in the Deep South, and the THIRTEENTH AMENDMENT (1865) abolished slavery completely. Blacks thus contributed to striking the final blow against slavery.

—*Tunde Adeleke*

See also: Fifty-fourth Massachusetts Colored Infantry.

Suggested Readings:

Barrow, Charles K., J. H. Segars, and R. B. Rosenburg, eds. *Forgotten Confederates: An Anthology About Black Southerners.* Atlanta, Ga.: Southern Heritage Press, 1995.

Berlin, Ira. *Free at Last: A Documentary History of Slavery, Freedom, and the Civil War.* New York: The New Press, 1992.

Berlin, Ira, Joseph P. Reidy, and Leslie S. Rowland, eds. *Freedom's Soldiers: The Black Military Experience in the Civil War.* New

The assault of the 54th Massachusetts Colored Infantry on South Carolina's Fort Wagner in July, 1863, was dramatized in the 1989 film *Glory. (Tri-Star Pictures, Inc.)*

York: Cambridge University Press, 1998.

Berry, Mary F. *Military Necessity and Civil Rights Policy: Black Citizenship and the Constitution, 1861-1868*. Port Washington, N.Y.: Kennikat Press, 1978.

Burchard, Peter. *"We'll Stand by the Union": Robert Gould Shaw and the Massachusetts Regiment*. New York: Facts on File, 1993.

Drinkard, Dorothy L. *Illinois Freedom Fighters: A Civil War Saga of the 29th Infantry, United States Colored Troops*. Needham Heights, Mass.: Simon & Schuster, 1998.

Durden, Robert. *The Gray and the Black: The Confederate Debate on Emancipation*. Baton Rouge: Louisiana State University Press, 1972.

Higginson, Thomas W. *Army Life in a Black Regiment*. Boston: Fields, Osgood, 1870. Reprint. Alexandria, Va.: Time-Life Books, 1982.

Lanning, Michael L. *The African American Soldier from Crispus Attucks to Colin Powell*. Seacaucus, N.J.: Birch Lane Press, 1997.

Nieman, Donald G., ed. *The Day of the Jubilee: The Civil War Experience of Black Southerners*. New York: Garland, 1994.

Westwood, Howard C. *Black Troops, White Commanders, and Freedmen During the Civil War*. Carbondale: Southern Illinois University Press, 1992.

Clark, Joe Louis (b. May 7, 1939, Rochelle, Georgia): Educator and educational administrator. Clark was hired as a principal at Eastside High School in Paterson, NEW JERSEY, in 1982. The 1989 motion picture *Lean on Me* is a dramatized version of Clark's battle to rid the high school of drugs and violence. Because of his successful efforts at Eastside, Clark was honored for academic and disciplinary excellence at a White House ceremony by President Ronald Reagan in 1985. Clark received the Principal of Leadership Award in 1986 from the National School Safety Center and re-

Joe Clark in 1987. *(AP/Wide World Photos)*

ceived the Humanitarian Award from the National Black Policeman's Association in 1988.

Clark, Kenneth Bancroft (b. July 24, 1914, Panama Canal Zone): Psychologist and educator. Kenneth Clark was born in Panama in the U.S. Canal Zone to Miriam Hanson Clark and Arthur Bancroft Clark, an agent of the United Fruit Company. Clark credited his mother with being a major factor in his intellectual and social development. Against her husband's wishes, she immigrated with the couple's two children, four-year-old Kenneth and his two-year-old sister Beulah, to the United States. The family settled in HARLEM, New York; Clark's mother became a seamstress in a sweatshop in the garment district of Manhattan and later became a union organizer.

Education
Clark attended neighborhood public schools. Though he displayed a keen intellect and achieved excellent grades, a junior high school counselor advised him to attend a vocational secondary school to prepare him for the man-

ual trades; at the time, many educators still advocated industrial education for African Americans. A letter from the counselor to Clark's mother in which the counselor reiterated his advice that Clark should attend a vocational high school prompted her to demand an appointment with the counselor. Clark's mother informed the school official that, though she did not care where he sent his own son, hers was not going to a vocational school. Clark went instead to George Washington High School, which had a college preparatory program.

After his graduation from high school in 1931, Clark enrolled at HOWARD UNIVERSITY, where he earned a bachelor's degree in psychology in 1935 and a master's degree in 1936. He received a Ph.D. in experimental psychology from Columbia University in 1940. Two children, Kate Miriam and Hilton Bancroft, resulted from his April 14, 1938, marriage to Mamie Phipps, a classmate at Howard who also earned a Ph.D. in psychology from Columbia.

Clark also credited teachers and mentors for assisting in his intellectual development and professional orientation. Exposure to and interactions with Howard scholars such as English professor Sterling BROWN, political scientist Ralph BUNCHE, economist Abram Harris, philosopher Alain LOCKE, and, most of all, psychologist Francis Cecil Sumner molded Clark's thinking and shaped his career. Clark noted that his Howard professors were "tutors, models, and friends" who "made their students into instruments of change." He went to Howard as a premedical student intending to become a physician, but a psychology class his sophomore year with Sumner altered his aspirations. Largely to continue his association with Sumner, Clark taught at Howard for a year after he obtained his master's degree; later, on Sumner's recommendation, he left Howard to pursue a Ph.D. in experimental psychology at Columbia.

Professional Life

With his degree, Clark joined the small but expanding community of African Americans with degrees from prominent educational institutions who, in spite of their attainments, found it difficult to gain employment commensurate with their training. On graduation from Columbia, Clark became a fellow of the Julius Rosenwald Fund and an assistant professor of psychology at HAMPTON INSTITUTE in Virginia. Only a year later, he resigned when the college's president said that his "brand of psychology was not helping students to adjust to the realities of American racism." A historically black college, Hampton was the alma mater of Booker T. WASHINGTON, the apostle of industrial education for African Americans and the leading exponent of the philosophy of ACCOMMODATION, which sanctioned second-class status for blacks. Hampton's leaders, desirous of maintaining the support of local and state leaders, saw Clark's notions as potential threats to local social and political norms and, more significant, to the economic well-being of the institution.

Between 1941 and 1942, Clark served on the research staff of the Office of War Information as an assistant social science analyst; his primary task was to assess the morale of the African American population. In 1942 he began a thirty-three-year career at the City College of New York with his appointment as an instructor in the school's Department of Psychology. In 1960 he became the first African American to be granted tenure in any of the constituent colleges of the city university. On retirement in 1975, City College elevated Clark to the emeritus rank. He served as visiting professor at Columbia University (1955), at the University of California at Berkeley (1958), and at Harvard University (1965).

In 1946 Clark and his wife established the Northside Testing and Consultation Center to treat African American children with personality and learning problems. (The center became the Northside Center for Child Development in 1948.) In creating the center, the Clarks asserted that the application of psychology could be used to contribute to a more stable family life for blacks, since many problems that afflicted blacks had psychological origins. They also maintained that applied psychology could improve race relations as well as the self-esteem of residents of black communities. In 1949 the Clarks opened the center to children regardless of ethnicity.

National Impact

Clark was a key member of the team of social scientists that worked with lawyers in the educational desegregation cases of the 1950's. In 1950 he issued a psychological study that demonstrated that school segregation retarded the development of both black and white children. The next year, the NATIONAL ASSOCIATION FOR THE ADVANCEMENT OF

Kenneth B. Clark in 1970. *(AP/Wide World Photos)*

COLORED PEOPLE (NAACP) invoked his theory and used him as an expert witness at a federal court hearing a school desegregation case in Charleston, South Carolina. Two years later, in 1954, the U.S. SUPREME COURT cited his studies on the effects of segregation on the development of children in the pivotal decision of BROWN V. BOARD OF EDUCATION, in which the Court held that the operation of "separate but equal" school facilities for blacks and whites was unconstitutional.

Also in 1954, Clark reproved the New York City Board of Education for fostering DE FACTO SEGREGATION in some of its schools. He asserted that "it is no longer necessary to have specific techniques for excluding Negro children from academic and other specialized schools." Paralleling his assertions about legally segregated school systems, he held that black children in the city's schools "not only feel inferior but are inferior in achievements" and that many schools were without proper instructional, counseling, and guidance programs because of segregation.

Though high-ranking administrators rejected Clark's conclusions, an investigation later confirmed them and generated wide-ranging reforms in the school system. In 1956 Clark chaired a subcommission on educational standards and curriculum for the board of education's commission on integration in the schools. The subcommission's report asserted that environmental factors, and not innate racial differences, determined differences in intellectual ability. The report recommended the provision of adequate facilities in minority neighborhoods, smaller classes, and an enriched curriculum.

In 1964 Clark founded and became the director of Harlem Youth Opportunities (HARYOU), an organization seeking to increase participation of low-income groups in decisions on education, economic development, employment, training, and housing. HARYOU became a national prototype for community development programs. Clark won the SPINGARN MEDAL in 1961, the Sidney Hillman Book Award and the Kurt Lewin Award in 1965, the College Board Medal for Distinguished Service to Education in 1980, and the Franklin Delano Roosevelt Four Freedoms Award in 1985.

Clark's service was varied. In the years after 1950 he was a social science consultant to the legal and educational division of the NAACP, a consultant to the personnel division of the U.S. State Department, and a member of the New York State Board of Regents. He served as a member of the New York City Board of Education, the advisory committee of the division of intercultural relations in education of the New York State Department of Education, and the New York State Youth Commission. He served as president of the Metropolitan Research Center from 1967 to 1975 and as president of the American Psychological Association for 1970-1971. He was made a fellow of the American Psychological Association and was a member of numerous boards of directors, including those of Howard University, the University of Chicago, and the Woodrow Wilson International Center for Scholars.

Publications

Clark's many publications include *Desegregation: An Appraisal of the Evidence* (1953), *Prejudice and Your Child* (1955), *Dark Ghetto: Dilemmas of Social Power* (1965), *How Relevant Is Education in America Today?* (with Alex C. Sherriffs, 1970), *A Possible Reality: A Design for the Attainment of High Academic Achievement for Inner-City Students* (1972), *Pathos of Power* (1974), and, with John Hope Franklin, *The Nineteen Eighties: Prologue and Prospect* (1981).

—*Ashton Wesley Welch*

Suggested Readings:

Clark, Kenneth B., and Kate C. Harris. "What Do Blacks Really Want?" *Ebony* (January, 1985): 108.

"Contribution by a Psychologist in the Public Interest Gold Medal Award." *American Psychologist* 43 (April, 1988): 263-264.

Keppel, Ben. *The Work of Democracy: Ralph Bunche, Kenneth B. Clark, Lorraine Hansberry, and the Cultural Politics of Race*. Cambridge, Mass.: Harvard University Press, 1995.

Markowitz, Gerald E., and Davis Rosner. *Children, Race, and Power: Kenneth and Mamie Clark's Northside Center*. Charlottesville: University Press of Virginia, 1996.

Sammons, Vivian O. *Blacks in Science and Medicine*. New York: Hemisphere, 1990.

Tushnet, Mark V. *The NAACP's Legal Strategy Against Segregated Education, 1925-1950*. Chapel Hill: University of North Carolina Press, 1987.

Clark, Mark (1952, Peoria, Illinois—December 4, 1969, Chicago, Illinois): Member of the BLACK PANTHER PARTY. An elite unit of the CHICAGO police, working in collaboration with the FEDERAL BUREAU OF INVESTIGATION (FBI), raided the residence of Chicago Black Panther leader Fred HAMPTON on December 4, 1969. Several Black Panthers, including Clark, were spending the night. Clark apparently was sleeping on watch duty and was armed with a shotgun. After police kicked in Hampton's apartment door, Clark was shot point blank in the chest and was killed instantly.

Clark, Septima Poinsette (May 3, 1898, Charleston, South Carolina—December 15, 1987, Charleston, South Carolina): SOUTH CAROLINA civil rights activist. Clark, in 1955, was fired from a teaching job in Charleston for refusing to give up her membership in the NATIONAL ASSOCIATION FOR THE ADVANCEMENT OF COLORED PEOPLE (NAACP). She began working for the SOUTHERN CHRISTIAN LEADERSHIP CONFERENCE (SCLC), setting up literacy and voter registration schools for semiliterate adults. Her schools transformed hundreds of barely literate adults into teachers serving their own communities. They also trained college students to work as citizenship educators throughout the South. She published two autobiographies, *Echo in My Soul* (1962) and *Ready from Within: Septima Clark and the Civil Rights Movement* (1986).

Clarke, John Henrik (January 1, 1915, Union Springs, Alabama—July 16, 1998, New York, New York): Historian, journalist, editor, anthologist, teacher, poet, writer of fiction, community activist, and lecturer. Clarke was born in Union Springs, ALABAMA, but spent his childhood and young adulthood in Columbus, GEORGIA. One of nine children of a SHARECROPPER father and mother who took in laundry, he was the first of the family's children to learn to read. With that ability came responsibility, and he became a Sunday school teacher at his Baptist church when he was only ten years old; he read stories in the Bible to other children.

As a result of his Bible study, Clarke became interested in stories about black people in ancient history; he had found his life's work while still a child. Seeking information, he asked a lawyer about the history of African peoples and was told that his people had no history. Clarke did not believe the answer; later, when in high school, he began to find some of the answers to his questions after reading a seminal essay by black bibliophile and book collector Arthur SCHOMBURG entitled "The Negro Digs Up His Past."

Beginnings of the Harlem Experience
Determined to pursue writing as a career, Clarke arrived in NEW YORK CITY in 1933, just as the HARLEM RENAISSANCE was coming to a close. Shortly after his arrival, he met Schomburg at the branch of the New York

Public Library that housed Schomburg's collection of materials on African peoples (later called the SCHOMBURG CENTER FOR RESEARCH IN BLACK CULTURE). Schomburg instructed the young Clarke that he would have to know the history of the world before he could understand African and black history, which he said were "the missing pages" of history. Clarke named Schomburg; Willis N. Huggins, the founder of the Harlem History Club; and noted HOWARD UNIVERSITY Africanist William Leo Hansberry among his principal teachers. The first historian he had come in contact with, however, was his own grandmother, nicknamed Mom Mary, who had been a slave. Clarke's first studies in history were oral testimonies about his family and how it had resisted the servitude into which it had been thrust.

Early Career and Historical Training
From 1941 to 1945, Clarke was in the quartermaster's unit of the U.S. Army Air Force, in which he earned the rank of sergeant major. After the war, he studied at New York University from 1948 to 1952 and at the New School for Social Research from 1956 to 1958, concentrating in history and world literature. He linked his interest in Africans in world history to his own search for identity. During his search, he joined several leftist organizations, including the National League of Negro Youth, the Young Communist League, and the Harlem Writers Guild. He became, however, in his words "a socialist, a pan-Africanist and an African World Nationalist."

Clarke's formal training later included time at the University of Ibadan in Nigeria and at the University of Ghana in Accra. His study was also profoundly influenced by Huggins's Harlem History Club, which became known as the Blyden Society, after Liberian pan-Africanist Edward Wilmot Blyden. Clarke called the latter an "informal university," in which the likes of Kwame Nkrumah, later the

Historian John Henrik Clarke.

first president of independent Ghana, studied. Clarke received an honorary doctorate from the University of Denver.

Teaching, Research, and Journalism
The HARLEM community's informal scholarly and educational associations, meeting often in community centers and church buildings, created the historian Clarke, and for more than two decades, he was a teacher in these same community-based institutions. As a result, his early teaching career was irregular. In 1964 as director of the federal antipoverty program's Heritage Teaching Program, he had his first permanent position, which lasted for five years. Through this program and subsequent teaching, he sought to show young black people how to use history for their own liberation and, through history, how to gain self-confidence and pride in African peoples and their contributions to human civilization.

In 1967 Clarke became a professor of African and world history at Hunter College in New York City. During his tenure, he served as chairman of the department. He retired from full-time teaching in 1988; afterward he served the college as a professor emeritus of the Department of Africana and Puerto Rican Studies.

Through the years Clarke worked for several publications. He was a cofounder and associate editor of *The Harlem Quarterly* (1949-1950), a feature writer for the PITTSBURGH COURIER (1957-1958), and an associate editor of *Freedomways* magazine (1962-1982). He also wrote and edited more than twenty books, including a volume of poetry and an anthology of African American short stories. His published work includes *Malcolm X: The Man and His Times* (1969), *Marcus Garvey and the Vision of Africa* (1974), and *William Styron's Nat Turner: Ten Black Writers Respond* (1968).

Harlem as His Home
The black community of Harlem, New York, was always home to Clarke and his family, and Clarke was involved in many of the area's political events. During the 1930's, he joined Marcus GARVEY's movement. Clarke also protested against white Harlem storeowners who would not employ blacks, and he helped launch Adam Clayton POWELL, Jr.'s controversial political career as Harlem's U.S. congressman. He took part in protests at the new Schomburg Center for Research in Black Culture when New York Public Library officials tried to replace black employees who had held library positions for years. Harlem provided him with resources, library and archival, for his research and teaching, and with black scholars and intellectuals who were in the forefront of developments in African, African American, and black history not only in Harlem and the United States but also throughout the world.

Foreign Travel
Clarke went to AFRICA on the first of many trips in 1958. He visited newly independent

Ghana. Upon his return home, he decided to focus his career on learning, writing, and teaching about the African continent and Africans there and throughout the world. During this visit, he also worked as a reporter for Ghanaian president Kwame Nkrumah's newspaper. Later, on a trip to Dakar, Senegal, to attend the Second International Congress of Africanists, he met Cheikh Anta Diop, the Senegalese scientist and historian whose historical studies were seminal in African historiography from an African perspective. Clarke remained a close colleague of Diop until the latter's death in 1986. Clarke himself was responsible for the U.S. publication of Diop's landmark *Precolonial Black Africa: A Comparative Study of the Political and Social Systems of Europe and Black Africa, from Antiquity to the Formation of Modern States* (1987).

African Heritage Studies Association
The year 1968 was an important one for African scholarship by African and African American academics and writers. That year, at a convention of the African Studies Association (ASA) in Los Angeles, Clarke and other members of the association's black caucus complained about the influence of Eurocentric scholarship in American college and university teaching about Africa. The caucus contended that this influence reflected negatively not only on scholarship but also on the lives of African-descended scholars and peoples. The complaints seemed to fall on deaf ears, however.

At the ASA's Montreal meeting in 1969, the black caucus formed an independent association, the African Heritage Studies Association (AHSA). Clarke was chosen as the organization's first president. He articulated the ideological framework of the AHSA in 1970, stating that its purpose was "to effect a world union of African peoples, committed to the preservation, interpretation, and creative presentation of the historical and cultural heritage of African people, both on the ancestral soil of Africa and in diaspora in the Americas and throughout the world."

—*Nancy Elizabeth Fitch*
See also: Afrocentricity; Diaspora, African; Historiography; Pan-Africanism.

Suggested Readings:

Boyd, Herb. "In Memoriam: Dr. John Henrik Clarke (1915-1998)." *The Black Scholar* 28 (Fall/Winter, 1998): 50-52.

_____. "John Henrik Clarke." *American Visions* 13 (October/November, 1998): 30-31.

Clarke, John Henrik. "The Origin and Growth of Afro-American Literature." In *Black Voices: An Anthology of Afro-American Literature*. Edited by Abraham Chapman. New York: Mentor Books, 1968.

Cruse, Harold. *The Crisis of the Negro Intellectual*. New York: Quill, 1984.

Ford, Nick A. *Black Studies: Threat or Challenge?* Port Washington, N.Y.: Kennikat Press, 1973.

Harris, Joseph E., ed. *Global Dimensions of the African Diaspora*. Washington, D.C.: Howard University Press, 1982.

Kinshasa, Kwando M. *Emigration vs. Assimilation*. Jefferson, N.C.: McFarland, 1988.

Classical and operatic music: Scholarly attention has been paid to African American musical contributions in folk and religious traditions (for example, GOSPEL MUSIC AND SPIRITUALS) and in popular MUSIC traditions (for example, in BLUES and JAZZ). However, African Americans also have a significant legacy in classical music—one that has been largely overlooked.

Early Composers, Conductors, and Instrumentalists
Colonial journals and chronicles document the presence of African American instrumentalists (mostly violinists and flutists). Nontra-

ditional sources, such as notices for SLAVE RUNAWAYS in which a fugitive's musical background or instrumental proficiencies were described, also document the musical talents of colonial blacks. The first American classical music composer of African ancestry to gain an international reputation was Louis Moreau Gottschalk (1829-1869). The NEW ORLEANS-born virtuoso not only was hailed as a preeminent pianist throughout Europe but also was distinguished as the composer of works such as *Bamboula*, *The Banjo*, *The Union*, and *Night in the Tropics*.

As a center of diverse musical activity throughout much of the nineteenth century, New Orleans produced several African American art-music composers and musicians. During the 1830's, more than a hundred blacks formed the Negro Philharmonic Society, which presented many concerts. One of the principal music directors of the orchestra was Richard Lambert, a distinguished musician and teacher. His sons, Lucien and Sidney Lambert, both had major careers as musicians and composers in Europe. Among Lucien's compositions were *La Bresiliana*, *L'Americaine*, and *La Juive*. Sidney, who also taught piano in Paris, composed several works, including *L'Africaine* and *Anna Bolean*.

PHILADELPHIA also boasted its share of African American composers and musicians, including guitarist-composer Justin Holland (1819-1886), violinist Edward Hill, and bandleaders and composers Aaron J. R. Conner, James Hemmenway, and Isaac Hazzard. The most prestigious and internationally acclaimed musician of nineteenth-century Philadelphia was composer and bandleader Francis "Frank" Johnson (1792-1844). Johnson is believed to have been the first American bandleader to have led a successful European tour, which he did in 1837; he also toured widely in the United States. Johnson was a skilled horn player and violinist, and his nearly two hundred compositions

were frequently performed by other bands during his lifetime. His works include marches, songs, quadrilles, and compositions in many other genres. He was one of the best-known composers of the period.

Throughout the nineteenth century, several African American classical composers and instrumentalists gained reputations in other regions of the country. One of the more celebrated, Georgia-born pianist Thomas "Blind Tom" BETHUNE (1849-1908), was enslaved as a child. After his exceptional musical talent came to the attention of his owner, Colonel Bethune, Thomas began playing for local audiences; eventually, he toured throughout the United States and in Europe. He was also the composer of several songs. In St. Louis, the earliest known African American composer was Joseph William Postlewaite (1837-1889). Like Bethune, he was enslaved as a child, but he began having his compositions published before he gained his freedom in 1850.

Twentieth-Century Musicians and Composers
In the first few decades of the twentieth century, several art-music composers and all-black orchestras emerged. In Philadelphia, for example, there was the Philadelphia Concert Orchestra, founded in 1905, and the Philadelphia Orchestra Association, founded in 1907; in Washington, the Colombian and Invincible Orchestra was founded circa 1900; the Victorian Concert Orchestra in Boston was founded in 1906; the Coleridge Taylor Concert Orchestra in Pittsburgh formed around 1930; and similar ensembles formed in other parts of the country.

As director of the National Conservatory of Music in New York during the mid-1890's, the European composer Antonín Dvořák encouraged the talent of several African American musicians and composers. Among them was Harry T. Burleigh, who arranged many spirituals as art songs for solo voice. Other compos-

(continued on page 527)

Notable Classical and Operatic Musicians and Performers

Addison, Adele (b. July 24, 1925, New York, N.Y.). Soprano opera singer. Addison is considered to be a specialist in baroque music as well as an important advocate of contemporary music. She debuted in Boston in 1948, establishing a career that included engagements with major American orchestras and opera companies.

Allen, Betty Lou (b. Mar. 17, 1930, Campbell, Ohio). Mezzo-soprano. In 1952 Allen sang in Virgil Thomson's *Four Saints in Three Acts* as St. Theresa II, and in 1954 as Queenie in *Show Boat*, with the New York City Opera. In 1975 she sang the role of Monisha in Scott JOPLIN's *Treemonisha* with the Houston Grand Opera and in 1979 she became the executive director of the Harlem School of the Arts.

Anderson, Marian. *See main text entry.*

Anderson, Thomas Jefferson (b. Aug. 17, 1928, Coatesville, Pa.). Composer. Anderson's principal works are *Symphony in Three Movements* (1964), *Squares* (1965), *Connections* (1966), *Personals* (1966), *Rotations* (1967), and *Chamber Symphony* (1968). His orchestration of Scott Joplin's *Treemonisha* premiered in 1972.

Arroyo, Martina (b. Feb. 2, 1937?, New York, N.Y.). Soprano opera singer. Arroyo won the national Metropolitan Opera audition in 1959 and debuted in the performance of Samuel Barber's *Andromache's Farewell* with the New York Philharmonic in 1963. She performed at the White House in 1977.

Battle, Kathleen. *See main text entry.*

Bonds, Margaret Allison (Mar. 3, 1913, Chicago, Ill.—Apr. 26, 1972, Los Angeles, Calif.). Pianist and composer. In 1930 Bonds established the Allied Arts Academy for ballet and music in CHICAGO. Her principal works include *Mass in D Minor*, a ballet entitled *Migration*, and two musicals, *Romey and Julie* and *Shakespeare in Harlem*.

Bryant, Joyce (b. 1928, San Francisco, Calif.). Opera soprano and nightclub singer. In 1960 Bryant made her first appearance as a concert soprano. She subsequently gave solo recitals, appeared as a guest artist with symphony orchestras, and sang at the New York City Opera for three years. Bryant was best known for her 1961 performance as Bess in the company's production of *Porgy and Bess*.

Bumbry, Grace Ann (b. Jan. 4, 1937, St. Louis, Mo.). Opera singer. Bumbry made her European debut in 1960 and became a mainstay at New York's Metropolitan Opera after her debut there in 1965. Bumbry sung at the White House and garnered many awards, including a 1979 Grammy Award.

Burleigh, Harry T. (Dec. 2, 1866, Erie, Pa.—Sept. 12, 1949, Stamford, Conn.). Composer and arranger. Burleigh was both a student of and an influence on European composer Antonin Dvorak. He was the first African American to receive a scholarship to the National Conservatory of Music. He came to national prominence as a composer of art music based on spirituals. His arrangements of spirituals, including "Swing Low, Sweet Chariot," have proved enduring.

Associated Publishers, Inc.

Conrad, Barbara (b. Aug. 11, 1945, Pittsburgh, Pa.). Opera singer. A powerful mezzo-soprano, Conrad began performing at the Metropolitan Opera in 1982 and appeared in such roles as Annina in *Der Rosenkavalier* and Maria in *Porgy and Bess*.

Cordero, Roque (b. Aug. 16, 1917, Panama City, Panama). Composer and conductor. Cordero's *Obertura Panameña no. 2* was premiered by the Minnesota Symphony Orchestra. He received the Kennedy Center award in 1978. Principal works include *Capricho interiorano* (1939) and *Rapsodia campesina* (1953).

DePriest, James (b. Nov. 21, 1936, Philadelphia, Pa.). Conductor and music director. DePriest led orchestras all over the world. He was assistant conductor for Leonard Bernstein and the New York Philharmonic (1965-1966) and associate conductor of the National Symphony Orchestra in Washington, D.C. (1971-1975). After serving as music director of

L'Orchestre Symphonique de Que, he became conductor of the Oregon Symphony in 1980.

Dett, Robert Nathaniel. *See main text entry.*

Dixon, Dean (Jan. 10, 1915, New York, N.Y.—Nov. 3, 1976, Zurich, Switzerland). Conductor. Dixon became the first African American conductor of the New York Philharmonic Orchestra in 1941, and was also the youngest person to conduct that orchestra. He founded the Dean Dixon Symphony Orchestra and the Dean Dixon Choral Society in New York.

Dobbs, Mattiwilda (b. July 11, 1925, Atlanta, Ga.). Opera soprano. She made her debut in France and became the first African American to perform at La Scala Theatre in Milan, Italy, in 1952. She made a tour of the United States in 1954 and performed before the British monarch. She debuted with the New York Metropolitan Opera in 1956.

Metropolitan Opera Association

Estes, Simon (b. Feb. 2, 1938, Centerville, Iowa). Opera singer and recitalist. In 1965 Estes debuted at the Deutsche Oper in West Berlin, singing Ramfis in Giuseppe Verdi's *Aida*. Estes sang in other operas during his stay in Germany, including *Salome, Don Carlos,* and *Moses and Aaron*. In 1966 he won a bronze medal in the Tchaikovsky Vocal Competition in Moscow. In 1978 he was the first African American male to sing a lead at Bayreuth, the opera house built by Richard Wagner. In 1982 he made his formal Metropolitan Opera debut as the Langrave in Wagner's *Tannhauser*. He sang Porgy in the first performance ever of Gershwin's *Porgy and Bess* at the Met.

Evanti, Lillian. *See main text entry.*

Gottschalk, Louis Moreau (May 8, 1829, New Orleans, La.—Dec. 18, 1869, Rio de Janeiro, Brazil). Composer and pianist. After extensive study of piano and music composition in Paris, Gottschalk performed to great acclaim throughout Europe, often playing his own works, which became known as "CREOLE" compositions. His work is heralded as a precursor of RAGTIME and JAZZ.

Graves, Denyse. Mezzo-soprano. Hailed as the "voice of the twenty-first century," Graves made her debut at the Metropolitan Opera in the 1995-1996 season. She became known for her portrayal of Carmen, though she played many roles in the top opera houses. Graves performed at the Nobel Prize ceremony in December, 1999.

Greenfield, Elizabeth Taylor. *See main text entry.*

Grist, Reri (b. c. 1934, New York, N.Y.). Opera singer. Grist's operatic debut occurred in 1959. She soon was offered sought-after soprano roles in major operas in the United States and in Europe. She gave frequent concerts and recorded with many leading orchestras.

Metropolitan Opera Association

Harris, Margaret R. (b. Sept. 15, 1943, Chicago, Ill.). Conductor, pianist, and composer. In 1971 Harris took over as musical director of the musical *Hair*. He subsequently conducted the St. Louis, Los Angeles, and Chicago symphony orchestras.

Hayes, Roland. *See main text entry.*

Hendricks, Barbara (b. Nov. 20, 1948, Stephens, Ark.). Opera singer. Hendricks made her debut with the San Francisco Spring Opera in its production of *Ormindo* in 1974. She made numerous recordings, and she performed in the 1988 film version of *La Bohème*.

Hyers Sisters. *See main text entry.*

Jackson, Isaiah Allen (b. Jan. 22, 1945, Richmond, Va.). Orchestra conductor. Jackson founded the Juilliard String Ensemble and served as the group's conductor. He also served as an assistant to Leopold Stowkowski with the American Symphony Orchestra and held the position of music director with the New York Youth Symphony from 1969 to 1973. He became the first American to hold a major post at Britain's Covent Garden when he was appointed to serve as principal conductor and later as music director of the Royal Ballet.

(continued)

Johnson, J. Rosamond. *See main text entry.*

Jones, Sissieretta. *See main text entry.*

Kay, Ulysses (b. Jan. 7, 1917, Tucson, Ariz.). Musician and composer. Kay composed such works as *A Short Overture* (1947), *The Boor* (1955), *Concerto for Orchestra* (1953), *Serenade for Orchestra* (1945), and *Sinfonia in E* (1951).

Maynor, Dorothy. *See main text entry.*

McFerrin, Robert, Sr. (b. Mar. 19, 1921, Marianna, Ark.). Opera singer. McFerrin debuted with the Metropolitan Opera in 1955, playing the role of Amonasro in *Aida*. He has performed major roles in many operas.

Mitchell, Leona Pearl (b. Oct. 13, 1949, Enid, Okla.). Soprano opera singer. Mitchell is well known for several appearances in a variety of films and for her performances for President Gerald Ford (1976) and President Jimmy Carter (1978 and 1979).

Mitchell, Nellie E. Brown. *See main text entry.*

Morgan, Michael (b. 1957, Washington, D.C.). Conductor. In 1980 Morgan won first prize in the Hans Swarowsky International Conductors Competition. He later won first prize in the Gino Marrinuzzi International Conductors Competition. Morgan became the affiliate artist conductor of the Chicago Symphony Orchestra in 1987.

Norman, Jessye. *See main text entry.*

Perkinson, Coleridge-Taylor (b. June 14, 1932, New York, N.Y.). Composer and conductor. Between 1959 and 1962, Perkinson served as the conductor for the Brooklyn Community Orchestra. In 1967 he was appointed as the first composer-in-residence of the Negro Ensemble Company. He served as the music director for Jerome Robbins's American Theater Laboratory (1966-1967), and in 1969 he became the conductor of the Alvin AILEY American Dance Theater

at the Brooklyn Academy of Music. His best known works include *Sinfonietta for Strings* (1953), *Concerto for Viola and Orchestra* (1954), *Attitudes* (1964), *A Warm December* (1972), and *Freedom Road* (1979).

Perry, Julia (Mar. 25, 1924, Lexington, Ky.—Apr. 24, 1979, Akron, Ohio). Composer. Perry moved to Europe in 1951 and studied with Luigi Dallapiccola in Florence and Nadia Boulanger in Paris. Perry's major works include *Stabat Mater* (1951), *Homunculus, C. F.* (1969), *Children's Symphony* (1978), and an opera, *The Cask of Amontillado* (1954).

Pratt, Awadagin (b. Mar. 3, 1966, Pittsburgh, Pa.). Classical pianist. Awadagin Pratt was the first student at Baltimore's Peabody Conservatory in 137 years to complete majors in piano, violin, and conducting. In 1992 he was the first African American to win the Naumburg International Piano Competition. His first album, *A Long Way From Normal* (1994), was followed by *Beethoven Piano Sonatas* in 1996. He made his New York professional debut in 1995 as a guest performer with the New York Philharmonic Orchestra.

Price, Leontyne. *See main text entry.*

Robeson, Paul. *See main text entry.*

Schuyler, Philippa Duke. *See main text entry.*

Selika, Marie. *See main text entry.*

Shirley, George (b. Apr. 18, 1934, Indianapolis, Ind.). Opera lead tenor. Shirley was the first African American male to perform leading roles with the New York Metropolitan Opera Company. He won international fame with his performances in *Die Fledermaus, The Magic Flute, La Bohème*, and *Madame Butterfly*.  Shirley encouraged other opera singers to record their performances, as he had done, and initiated a radio program on African Americans in classical music.

Smith, Hale (b. June 29, 1925, Cleveland, Ohio). Composer. Smith's works include *Epicedial Variations* (1956), *Contours for Orchestra* (1962), and *By Yearnings and by Beautiful* (1961). He also arranged and wrote works for such prominent jazz artists as Quincy JONES, Ahmad Jamal, and Eric DOLPHY.

Still, William Grant. *See main text entry.*

Swanson, Howard (Aug. 18, 1907, Atlanta, Ga.—Nov. 12, 1978, New York, N.Y.). Composer. Swanson gained national recognition in 1949 with the performance of his song "The Negro Speaks of Rivers." In 1950 his *Short Symphony* was performed by the New York Philharmonic Orchestra. Other works include *Night Music* (1950), *Music for Strings* (1952), *Vista No. II* (1969).

Verrett, Shirley (b. May 31, 1933, New Orleans, La.). Mezzo-soprano opera singer. One of the most successful African Americans in opera, Verrett made her debut at the Metropolitan Opera House in 1968

in the role of Carmen. During the 1976-1977 season alone, she sang seventeen performances at the Met, including the opening night in *Il Travatore*. She also performed in European opera houses, including Covent Garden (London) and Teatro Licero (Barcelona).

Warfield, William. *See main text entry.*

Watts, Andre (b. June 20, 1946, Nuremberg, Germany). Concert pianist. Watts came to national prominence at age sixteen when he played with the New York Philharmonic under conductor Leonard Bernstein. He performed at President Richard Nixon's inaugural in 1969.

Wilson, Olly (b. Sept. 7, 1937, St. Louis, Mo.). Composer. In 1968 Wilson's electronic music composition *Cetus* (1967) won first prize in the first International Electronic Music Competition. In 1970 he became a professor at the University of California at Berkeley. His major works include *Structure for Orchestra*

ers in the tradition of Burleigh were Clarence Cameron White, Harry Lawrence Freeman, Will Marion Cook, and Robert Nathaniel DETT, whose oratorio *The Ordering of Moses* (1937) was hailed as a significant choral work. By the 1930's, William Grant STILL had inspired a new generation of art-music composers with his works such as *Afro-American Symphony* (1930), which incorporated blues and other popular musical idioms. In this "nationalist" tradition, Still's contemporaries, including William Dawson, Hall Johnson, John Wesley Work, and Florence Price, composed large-scale symphonic works, operas, choral works, and art songs.

By the mid-1950's, yet another generation of African American classical composers emerged, including George WALKER, Howard Swanson, Julia Perry, and Ulysses Kay. A more difficult challenge was faced by several black orchestra conductors of the period, including Dean Dixon (1915-1976), who left the United States in 1948 because of the discrimination

that black conductors faced. He established a reputation in Europe and Australia before returning as guest conductor of several major U.S. orchestras until his death in the mid-1970's.

In 1968 a group of African American classical composers formed the Society of Black Composers. Its membership included Olly Wilson, Noel DaCosta, T. J. Anderson, Dorothy Moore, Carman Moore, Wendell Logan, and Frederick Tillis. One of the conductors who overcame enormous obstacles was Henry Lewis. In 1968 he became the first black permanent music director of a major U.S. orchestra when he was chosen to direct the New Jersey Symphony. Other distinguished conductors were Isiah Jackson, Everett Lee, James Frazier, James DePriest, and Paul Freeman.

Early Concert Singers

Although there was no shortage of African American singers during the pre- and post-CIVIL WAR eras, they performed largely on the minstrel stage, especially after the war. There was, however, a classically trained singer, Elizabeth Taylor GREENFIELD, who had an established reputation as an operatic singer before the mid-nineteenth century. She was promoted as the "black swan," a play on the nickname of the renowned Swedish soprano Jenny Lind, who was known as the "white swan." Greenfield sang extensively in the United States and in England, including a command performance before Queen Victoria in 1854.

While most of the prominent nineteenth-century African American concert singers were women, there were at least two well-known male singers. Philadelphia tenor Thomas Bowers (1826-1885) was celebrated as the "American Mario." Specializing in operatic and oratorio arias, Bowers apparently refused to sing MINSTREL songs, which were popular throughout the century. Like his teacher, Greenfield, Bowers also sang at antislavery meetings. The other celebrated tenor of the period was Sidney Woodward (1860-1924) of Boston, who was hailed as the "greatest tenor of the race." Harry T. Burleigh made a name as a renowned concert baritone and as a composer.

In his celebrated book *Music and Some Highly Musical People* (1878), James Monroe Trotter commented on the promising career of soprano Nellie E. Brown MITCHELL. She studied voice at the New England Conservatory and made a successful New York debut in 1874. She later toured with her own company. By the mid-1880's, she was hailed as one of America's greatest singers of African descent. Brown was one of several major female concert singers on the scene during the last quarter of the nineteenth century. The others were Marie SELIKA, known as the "queen of staccato"; Flora Batson Bergen (1864-1906), known as the "doubled-voice queen of song"; and Matilda Sissieretta JONES, the celebrated "black Patti" (the nickname was the result of comparisons made between Jones and the white soprano Adelina Patti). Jones's first major engagement was at the White House in 1892, when she sang for President Benjamin Harrison. By the mid-1890's, she had sung in Europe, Asia, and Africa. After a decline in public interest in African American prima donnas, Jones became the leader of a VAUDE-VILLE touring group called Black Patti's Troubadours.

Early Twentieth-Century Singers
By the end of the nineteenth century, performing engagements had become sparse for African American female concert singers, but it was—and has since been—more difficult for male singers. The first African American male singer to gain renown in the twentieth century (aside from Harry T. Burleigh) was Roland Hayes. He was born in Georgia and reared in Tennessee, where, in 1911, he toured with the FISK JUBILEE SINGERS. In 1920 he went to London for further study and sang for Britain's King George V in 1921. From the 1920's to the 1940's, Hayes was one of the world's leading concert singers. He sang with the world's major orchestras and was a sought-after recitalist. In 1962 he came out of retirement at age seventy-five to give a Carnegie Hall benefit concert for black colleges. The renowned singer, actor, and scholar Paul ROBESON was a contemporary of Hayes, although he devoted a large part of his career to musical theater and film rather than to the concert stage.

The leading female artist of the period was Marian ANDERSON, who was born in Philadelphia. After extensive study, she made her Town Hall debut in New York at the age of twenty. During the 1930's, Anderson toured extensively and was well received in Europe, but she was at the center of a national embarrassment when the Daughters of the American Revolution (DAR) refused her permission to sing in Constitution Hall in 1939 because of her color. First Lady Eleanor Roosevelt, after

Contralto Marian Anderson performing for service men and women during World War II. *(National Archives)*

resigning from the DAR, arranged for Anderson to sing at the Lincoln Memorial for an audience of seventy-five thousand. Anderson again made history in 1955 when she became the first African American to sing at the Metropolitan Opera House.

A growing number of classical singers were following and extending the path that Anderson and Roland Hayes had made. Soprano Dorothy MAYNOR, a contemporary of Anderson, was another major star. Following Anderson at the Metropolitan Opera were baritone Robert McFerrin and soprano Mattiwilda Dobbs. The New York City Opera had become the first major U.S. opera company to engage African American singers. The first African American to debut there, in 1945, was Todd DUNCAN, who had created the title role in George Gershwin's *Porgy and Bess* (1935) a decade earlier. Duncan was followed

at the New York City Opera by soprano Camilla Williams (b. 1922), who won media acclaim for her lead role in a 1946 production of Giacomo Puccini's *Madame Butterfly* (1904).

Civil Rights Era and Beyond

Leontyne PRICE's career was gaining momentum in the late 1950's as Anderson was approaching retirement. By the mid-1960's, Price had become one of the world's greatest opera stars. She debuted at the Metropolitan Opera in 1961 in Guiseppe Verdi's *Il Trovatore* (1852) but had already sung at major opera companies in Europe and the United States. In 1966 she performed at the opening of the New Metropolitan Opera House at Lincoln Center, singing the title role of Samuel Barber's *Antony and Cleopatra*. Price retired from opera in 1985 but maintained a busy schedule as a recitalist. Several renowned African American di-

Shirley Verrett (left) and Grace Bumbry rehearsing for the Metropolitan Opera in early 1982. *(AP/Wide World Photos)*

then include Vinson Cole, Philip Creech, Set McCoy, Dorceal Duncan, Willard White, and Donnie Ray Albert.

By the late 1980's, bass-baritone Simon Estes had become the most prominent African American male singer on the operatic stage. Among female singers, sopranos Jessye Norman and Kathleen Battle were at the pinnacle of the opera. Norman established herself as a leading recitalist before turning to opera. In her triumphant Metropolitan Opera debut during the 1983-1984 season, she sang the roles of both Cassandra and Dido in Hector Berlioz's 1855 *Les Troyens* (a feat that had been first accomplished by Shirley Verrett in the same production a decade earlier). Other major black female singers include Florence Quivar, Barbara Hendricks, Roberta Alexander, Gwendolyn Bradley, and Priscilla Baskerville.

—*Christopher Brooks*

vas emerged after Price during the 1960's and 1970's, most notably Shirley Verrett and Grace Ann Bumbry. Other distinguished talents of the period included Martina Arroyo, Clamma Dale, Christiane Eda-Pierre, Reri Grist, Felicia Weathers, Betty Allen, Carmen Bathrop, Gwendolyn Killibrew, Esther Hinds, and Leona Mitchell.

The road for male concert singers continued to be more difficult. One singer who overcame obstacles was tenor George Shirley, who sang many leading roles at the Metropolitan Opera and New York City Opera during the 1960's and 1970's. Other major singers since

Suggested Readings:

Abdul, Raoul. *Blacks in Classical Music*. New York: Dodd, Mead, 1977.

Brooks, Tilford. *America's Black Musical Heritage*. Englewood Cliffs, N.J.: Prentice-Hall, 1984.

Cheatham, Wallace. *Dialogues on Opera and the African-American Experience*. Lanham, Md.: Scarecrow Press, 1997.

Cuney-Hare, Maud. *Negro Musicians and Their Music*. Washington, D.C.: Associated Publishers, 1936.

De Lerma, Dominique-Rene. *Reflections on*

Afro-American Music. Kent, Ohio: Kent State University Press, 1973.

Handy, D. Antoinette. *Black Conductors*. Metuchen, N.J.: Scarecrow Press, 1995.

Trotter, James. *Music and Some Highly Musical People*. Boston: Lee and Shepard, 1878. Reprint. New York: Johnson Reprint, 1968.

Smith, Eric L. *Blacks in Opera: An Encyclopedia of People and Companies, 1873-1993*. Jefferson, N.C.: McFarland, 1995.

Southern, Eileen. *The Music of Black Americans*. 2d ed. New York: W. W. Norton, 1983.

Story, Rosalyn M. *And So I Sing: African American Divas of Opera and Concert*. New York: Warner Books, 1990.

Class structure: Term applying to social systems in which people are ranked hierarchically along some dimensions of inequality, such as income, wealth, power, prestige, and privilege. A class structure consists of several strata of people who share common lifestyles, life-chances, and communal identity. People in the United States are roughly divided into "upper class," "upper-middle class," "middle-middle class," "lower-middle class (working class)," and "lower class." The twentieth century saw dynamic changes in the class structure because of generational upward mobility and technological development.

Social Inequality

In spite of the economic and industrial development and technological innovations in science and medical fields during the twentieth century, American society continued to suffer from unequal distributions of social wealth. In 1995, according to that year's report by the Joint Economic Committee of the U.S. Congress, about 17,000 Americans declared more than 1 million dollars in annual income, while the median family income of Americans was only about $36,000. The same report found that the richest 10 percent, roughly, of all Americans owned 70 percent of the nation's wealth. Furthermore, 0.5 percent of Americans owned almost 35 percent of all American wealth. About 15 percent of Americans were living under the POVERTY line, and about one-fourth of all the children under the age of six were living in poverty.

This class structure, with its great degree of inequality of income and wealth distribution, is a major social problem of American society. People in the upper and upper-middle classes certainly enjoy more comfortable lifestyles and have greater life-chances than those in lower classes. These factors lead to better educational and occupational opportunities and further accumulation of wealth. In contrast, people in the lower class suffer from a lesser share of life-chances and a lack of educational and occupational opportunities. Children of families living under the poverty line experience lack of upward mobility unless they receive educational and welfare support from the government.

Theoretical Explanations of Class Structure

Karl Marx, Max Weber, and Gerhard Lenski are the most frequently cited scholars who attempted to explain the emergence and persistence of social class. Marx, who observed human inequality in nineteenth-century Europe, analyzed class structure related to the emergence of capitalism after the Industrial Revolution. He argued that a society consisted of "haves," who owned the means of production, and "have-nots." Capitalists owned all the means of production, such as land, factories, resources, and capital. What they did not own was labor. Those who did not own means of production exchanged their labor for wages. However, manufacturing done with machines produced "surplus value," which was returned to capitalists, not given to laborers. According to Marx, the most important source of inequality was related to ownership of the economic system. Those who owned means of production were also called the bourgeoisie, and those who did not were called the proletariat (the working class). Marx also argued that the economic system had great impact on other social systems, such as politics, religion, education, family, and the military.

In contrast to Marx's economic determinism, Weber analyzed social class using a multidimensional model of inequality. He argued that there were three sources of inequality: class, status, and party. Weber's usage of the term "class" is similar to that of Marx: Social inequality is derived from economic inequality, which is frequently measured by income and wealth. The second term, "status," refers to prestige or honor of different groups, such as family lineage and lifestyles. People in the same stratum of the status hierarchy exhibit common consumption patterns, club memberships, and residential areas, as well as endogamy (marriage within the group). The third term, "party," refers to political power, the ability to have impact on the decision-making processes of society. Besides political parties, labor unions, consumer groups, and racial organizations also have political impact on societal decision making in modern society.

In the mid-1960's, Gerhard Lenski developed a model that described a class structure of the distributive system. Lenski's model combined the Marxian class system and the Weberian multidimensional model of social inequality. Lenski argued that a society consists of several class hierarchies across different social systems, such as political, property, occupational, and ethnic systems. One who ranks high in the ethnic dimension does not necessarily rank high in the property dimension. Similarly, one who ranks high in the occupational dimension does not necessarily rank high in the ethnic dimension. Class structure is the "distributive system" of individuals who hold different positions in the hierarchies in the various dimensions.

What is common among these three scholars is that class structure is related to differential distribution of power, which in turn determines differential distribution of wealth, education, occupation, and prestige. American society is not only stratified into several social classes but also characterized by inequality in several dimensions.

Class Structure and Race

In American society there exists an intersection of one's racial and ethnic background and one's class position. Racial and ethnic minority groups are frequently and systematically ranked low in the hierarchies of several dimensions, and they receive lesser shares of wealth, education, political power, and life-chances, thus creating racial and ethnic inequality in society.

Although racial and ethnic inequality has existed since the founding of the United States, the degree of inequality that each group experiences has changed. Native Americans were deprived not only of their land by European colonizers but also of political power and autonomy. Lack of education, unemployment, and poverty on many reservations in the twentieth century were the results of differential power distribution between Native Americans and the dominant group. African Americans also continued to experience social inequality long after the ending of SLAVERY.

Although other minority groups, such as Hispanic Americans and Asian Americans, immigrated to the U.S. voluntarily, they have also experienced discrimination in EDUCATION, occupation, housing, and marriage. Similarly, white ethnic groups, such as Italian and Irish immigrants, have experienced social inequality in varying degrees. Jews experienced hardships caused by religious discrimination. As Gerhard Lenski noted, one's position in the occupational system does not necessarily parallel one's position in the racial system. Nonetheless, individuals with racial and ethnic minority backgrounds are likely to enjoy a lesser share of social wealth and power.

Although the wealth and power gaps between the dominant group (whites) and racial minority groups have narrowed somewhat in postindustrial society, the intersection of class structure and race continues to exist. Racial inequality exists not only because of individual discrimination against racial minority groups but also because of "institutionalized discrimination," which has a great and persistent impact on social inequality. Although institutionalized discrimination is unintentional, it creates a pattern of unequal treatment of individuals based on group membership (race, ethnicity, and gender) that is built into the educational, economic, political, and justice systems. The educational system provides one of the best examples of this type of discrimination. The gap between African Americans and whites in educational achievement narrowed in the last few decades of the twentieth century, with the median years of formal schooling for whites and African Americans both a little over twelve years. Yet 25 percent of whites hold college degrees as opposed to 12 percent of African Americans.

This persistent gap in education is partly attributable to de facto residential segregation in American society. The quality of education in inner cities, where many African Americans and Hispanics live, is poorer than that in middle-class residential areas, where most of the families are whites. Inner-city schoolchildren are automatically placed at a disadvantage in qualifying for well-paid jobs, and they are not well prepared to compete against children from the middle class for entrance to prestigious colleges, thus creating further inequality in occupational opportunities.

In the dimension of occupation, a larger proportion of African American men are classified as semiskilled and skilled labor (33 percent and 20 percent respectively) than white

men (19 percent and 16 percent respectively), and a smaller proportion of them occupy technical and professional positions (17 percent and 13 percent respectively) than whites (20 percent and 27 percent respectively). A similar pattern exists between African American women and white women. Occupational inequality is further reflected in income. According to a report by the U.S. Department of Commerce in 1994, the median annual earnings of white men and those of African American men were $31,012 and $22,369 respectively. The median earnings of white women and African American women were $21,659 and $19,819 respectively. When white men were used as a reference group (100 percent), African American men, white women, and African American women were earning about 72 percent, 70 percent, and 64 percent of white men's earnings respectively.

Between 1940 and the early 1970's, the African American middle class grew rapidly. The percentage of African American households with earnings at least twice the poverty line grew from 1 percent to 39 percent during this period. The U.S. Bureau of the Census reported in 1990 that 47 percent of African American households and 74 percent of white households were categorized as middle class. However, while about one-tenth of whites were living under the poverty line, about one-third of African Americans were. These data indicate that the income gap between whites and African Americans narrowed in the last decades of the twentieth century. Yet they also show that class inequality exists between these two groups and that African Americans have become more polarized in the income and occupational hierarchies.

In *The Declining Significance of Race* (1978), sociologist William WILSON wrote that "class has become more important than race in determining black life-chances in the modern industrial period."

Wilson noted that occupational upward

mobility was increasingly based upon education, thus restricting the job opportunities of inner-city youths. On one hand, the changes in the economic system that American society experienced in the twentieth century created a large proportion of African Americans in the middle class. On the other hand, they also contributed to the perpetuation of what has been called an "underclass" in inner cities.

The issues of welfare and HEALTH became focal points of the intersection of class structure and race in the late twentieth century. In the 1990's, studies showed a wide gap between African Americans and whites in INFANT MORTALITY rates (deaths per 1,000 live births)—18.2 and 8.5 respectively, according to the National Center for Health Statistics in 1993. Many risk factors help account for this gap, such as maternal age, maternal education, availability of health and medical services, and environmental quality, and these risk factors are closely related to socioeconomic status. Similarly, African Americans have more than their share of other diseases, such as CANCER, heart disease, stroke, and diabetes. Furthermore, some diseases are related to environmental pollution caused by hazardous waste, garbage dumps, and chemical plants—which are likely to be located in or near poor communities. Robert Bullard, in his 1993 article "Waste and Racism: A Stacked Deck?," argued that African Americans and other minority groups are unfairly treated in decisions about such environmental issues.

—*Hisako Matsuo*

See also: De facto segregation; Environmental hazards and discrimination.

Suggested Readings:

Bullard, Robert. "Waste and Racism: A Stacked Deck?" *Forum: For Applied Research and Public Policy* 8, no. 1 (1993): 29-35.

Thomas, Gail E. *Race and Ethnicity in America.* Bristol, Pa.: Taylor & Francis, 1995.

Wilson, Julius William. *The Declining Significance of Race: Blacks and Changing American Institutions.* Chicago: University of Chicago Press, 1978.

Clayatt v. United States: U.S. SUPREME COURT case in 1905 that invalidated state peonage laws. The Court upheld congressional legislation invalidating peonage; the decision was based on the THIRTEENTH AMENDMENT (1865), which had made SLAVERY unconstitutional. Peonage laws, under which debtors worked off their debts, were seen by the Court as maintaining a form of slavery.

Cleage, Albert Buford, Jr. (b. June 13, 1911, Indianapolis, Indiana): Theologian, author, CIVIL RIGHTS activist, and pastor best known for his outspoken advocacy of black Christian nationalism and for his classic study in black theology entitled *The Black Messiah* (1968).

Early in his career, Cleage worked as a welfare advocate and was pastor for churches in several states before joining DETROIT's Shrine of the Black Madonna in 1952. His political involvements include board work for the NATIONAL ASSOCIATION FOR THE ADVANCEMENT OF COLORED PEOPLE (NAACP) as well as work training young ministers in the activist theology of black Christian nationalism. Cleage taught and lectured extensively on black theology and liberation politics.

Beginning with *The Black Messiah*, and following four years later with his second book, *Black Christian Nationalism: New Directions for the Black Church* (1972), Cleage was instrumental in posing a radical challenge to white-dominated Christian theologies. Continuing a tradition begun in the nineteenth century by religious black nationalist writers such as Robert Young (*The Ethiopian Manifesto: Issued in Defense of the Black Man's Rights in the Scale of Universal Freedom*, 1829), Cleage expanded and deepened a theology that locates authentic Christianity within the black community and then extends that claim to a call for political action.

Cleage's version of black Christian nationalism is deeply confrontational, both with the institutions of the white church and with what he calls the white power establishment. Cleage's theology claims Jesus as the Black Messiah, a revolutionary leader sent by God to liberate the sanctified Black Nation of Israel. Cleage sees black Christians as having a sacred duty to work for the liberation of all black peoples, thus expressing the will of God in human history. Cleage's nationalistic politics include an essentially separatist stance and a call for black nationalists to renounce individualism in favor of a commitment to the welfare of the black nation. His Black Messiah movement was founded in Detroit, Michigan, in the 1960's.

See also: Black nationalism.

Albert Buford Cleage, Jr., in 1973. *(AP/Wide World Photos)*

Cleaver, Eldridge (August 31, 1935, Wabbaseka, Arkansas—May 1, 1998, Pomona, California): Radical leader, writer, and member of the BLACK PANTHER PARTY. Leroy Eldridge Cleaver was the third child and oldest son born to Leroy Cleaver and his wife, Thelma Robinson Cleaver. Cleaver's parents struggled to make ends meet, and the family moved to Phoenix and eventually to Los Angeles in search of a better life. Cleaver grew up in Rose Hill, an East Los Angeles neighborhood, and learned to speak Spanish with his young Chicano friends. Domestic squabbles between his parents led to his estrangement from his father, and he turned to criminal activities to vent his anger. According to his autobiography, *Soul on Fire* (1978), he was first arrested in 1947 and was sent to reform school in Whittier in 1949. He was sent to a second reform school in 1952.

Prison Life

Cleaver was convicted of possessing marijuana and was sentenced to serve time in prison in Soledad, California, in 1954. After being paroled in 1957, his criminal activities escalated. He was arrested for the attempted rape of a nurse, was convicted of assault with intent to kill, and began to serve a fourteen-year sentence at California's San Quentin Penitentiary in 1958. He was later transferred to Folsom prison and then to Soledad. While in prison, Cleaver earned his high school diploma and was inspired by the charismatic leadership of MALCOLM X to join the NATION OF ISLAM (the Black Muslim faith). After the schism in the Nation of Islam between Malcolm X and Elijah MUHAMMAD, Cleaver sided with Malcolm X and renounced the teachings of Elijah MUHAMMAD. During his time in prison, Cleaver began to write letters and essays.

Militant Black Panther

Cleaver was paroled from Soledad in 1966 after serving nine years of his sentence, and he settled in the Haight-Ashbury section of San Francisco. Almost immediately, he became involved in the newly formed Black Panther Party and became a staff writer for *Ramparts*, a glossy San Francisco-based radical magazine. Cleaver met Black Panther leaders Huey NEWTON and Bobby SEALE at a 1967 meeting to plan a memorial service honoring Malcolm X. As a journalist, Cleaver contacted the STUDENT NONVIOLENT COORDINATING COMMITTEE (SNCC) in order to observe its campus programs. Cleaver met his future wife, Kathleen Neal, on a visit to SNCC headquarters in Nashville, Tennessee, and they were married in December of 1967. Although leaders of SNCC and the Black Panther Party announced a merger of their organizations, the two groups never actually became one. Many SNCC members and other civil rights and liberal groups became supporters of the Black Panther Party and provided financial assistance for the party's efforts.

After joining the party, Cleaver became the Black Panthers' minister of information. As such, he was responsible for preparing public speeches for Newton and Seale, for generating editorial material for the party newspaper, and for providing press releases and public information on the party's activities to the media. Gradually, Cleaver was called upon to deliver public lectures himself, especially in the wake of his enormous celebrity after the publication of his prison essays and observations about black life in *Soul on Ice* (1968). In April of 1968, Cleaver was wounded and fellow Panther Bobby Hutton was killed during an armed confrontation with Oakland police. Cleaver was incarcerated at Vacaville prison for violating the terms of his parole as a result of his participation in the shoot-out. He was released in

Eldridge Cleaver at a rally in Washington, D.C., in 1968. *(Library of Congress)*

June on $50,000 bail and traveled extensively, lecturing at various college campuses.

Flight and Exile

In November of 1968, Cleaver fled the country to avoid appearing at a parole hearing that would inevitably send him back to prison. With royalties from *Soul on Ice*, he was able to finance his escape and sought refuge in CUBA. For the next four years, he and his wife traveled under false passports between Cuba, the Soviet Union, and China. In May of 1969, they arrived in Algeria, where their son Maceo was born. In 1970 the family visited China, North Vietnam, and North Korea, where their daughter Joju was born, before the family returned to Algeria.

In 1971 Black Panther Party leadership split, and Cleaver and his supporters—who formed the international section of the party—were expelled. After disputes with the Algerian government over the disposition of ransom money obtained by International Panther skyjackers, Cleaver fled to France in 1972 and settled in Paris, where his family joined him in 1973. After spending two years in relative seclusion, Cleaver determined that he would surrender to authorities to be extradited to the United States.

Born-Again Christian

Cleaver surrendered to American authorities in Paris and in November of 1975 was flown to New York, where he was officially arrested and extradited to California. He was incarcerated in San Diego before being transferred to Alameda County Jail in January, 1976, to face his original parole violation charges. Cleaver was visited by Christian Fundamentalist ministers in prison and became a born-again Christian. A wealthy Christian businessman posted the necessary securities to meet Cleaver's $100,000 bail, and Cleaver was released in August of 1976. Upon his release, he attended a Billy Graham crusade in San Diego and decided to become an evangelist minister.

Cleaver and his family moved back to San Francisco, where Cleaver founded a prison ministry, the Eldridge Cleaver Crusades. He became a popular campus speaker and published a Christian-influenced memoir entitled *Soul on Fire* (1978).

Cleaver soon abandoned Christian Fundamentalism in favor of a new faith he called "Christlam," a fusion of Islamic and Christian teachings. During the early 1980's, Cleaver also became involved with the Unification Church of Reverend Sun Myung Moon and later briefly converted to the Church of Jesus Christ of Latter-day Saints (Mormons) some time in 1982.

Conservative Activist

After his prison ministry folded and an entrepreneurial effort to market a line of men's clothing failed, Cleaver turned his interest to conservative electoral politics. During the 1980's he endorsed Ronald Reagan, became a conservative independent candidate for Congress in 1984 in an attempt to oust Democrat Ronald DELLUMS, and campaigned for the Republican nomination to run against Senator Alan Cranston in 1986. His failed political career coincided with the breakup of his marriage, resulting in divorce in 1988, and with a series of arrests for drug possession and burglary in 1987 and 1988.

Cleaver began using crack, and he developed an addiction in the early 1990's. In 1994 he was hospitalized after another addict struck him on the head. After that incident, he stopped using drugs. He moved to Florida for a time to teach at the Daniel Iverson Center for Christian Studies and preached in Berkeley, California. Later he moved to Southern California and became involved with the New Vision Center, Church of Religious Science, in Fontana.

Eldridge Cleaver's career, along with those of his Black Panther colleagues Huey Newton and Bobby Seale, reflected the turbu-

Emanuel Cleaver II at an election rally in 1991. *(AP/Wide World Photos)*

lence of the times in which he lived as well as the hardships faced by African Americans during those times. While the facts of Cleaver's life can be outlined, the impulses that propelled him to abandon the violence and self-destructive life of a criminal in the 1950's for the militant radicalism of the Black Panther Party in the 1960's, and then to leave the confusion and poverty of self-exile in the 1970's for the Christian Fundamentalism and ultra-conservative activism of the 1980's, remain enigmatic.

—*Ellyn West*

Suggested Readings:

Cleaver, Eldridge. *Soul on Fire*. Waco, Tex.: Word Books, 1978.

_____. *Soul on Ice*. New York: Dell, 1968.

Hubbard, Kim, and Meg Grant. "Free at Last; Ex-fugitive, Ex-addict, Eldridge Cleaver Speaks Out Now for the Lord." *People Weekly* (April 15, 1996): 79-80.

Lockwood, Lee. *Conversation with Eldridge Cleaver*. New York: McGraw-Hill, 1970.

Parks, Gordon. "What Became of the Prophets of Rage?" *Life* special issue (Spring, 1988): 32.

Rout, Kathleen. *Eldridge Cleaver*. Boston: G. K. Hall, 1991.

"Whatever Happened to . . . Eldridge Cleaver?" *Ebony* (March, 1988): 66-68.

Cleaver, Emanuel, II (b. October 26, 1944, Waxahachie, Texas): Politician, pastor, and CIVIL RIGHTS activist. The second of four children born to Lucky and Marie Cleaver, Emanuel Cleaver II descends from a long line of clergymen, who include his great-grandfather and grandfather, as well as various cousins and uncles. Cleaver's father, however, ran a cleaning establishment and worked in construction. The family of six lived in a former slave cabin which had two bedrooms and a kitchen but no indoor toilet. On weekends, Cleaver and his sisters picked cotton to help supplement the family income. When Cleaver was in second grade, his family moved to Wichita Falls, Texas. His father then worked as a maitre d' at a downtown club for white professional men, and his mother worked as a secretary.

After graduating from Booker T. Washington High School, Cleaver attended Murray State College in southern OKLAHOMA for one year. He later transferred to Prairie View A&M, a HISTORICALLY BLACK COLLEGE near HOUSTON, TEXAS. Active in the Civil Rights movement, he led a nonviolent demonstration outside three segregated motion picture theaters in Wichita Falls while he was a high school student. Throughout his college career, he actively supported the SOUTHERN CHRISTIAN LEADERSHIP CONFERENCE (SCLC) and eventually became regional vice president of the organization. He took part in the MARCH ON WASHINGTON in 1963 and walked in the famous 1965 SELMA TO MONTGOMERY MARCH led by Martin Luther King, Jr.

In 1968 Cleaver received his bachelor's degree and moved to Kansas City, MISSOURI, to work at Bendix Corporation. After he left Bendix, he worked first for Catholic Family and Community Services, and later for the Young Men's Christian Association (YMCA). During his first years in Kansas City, Cleaver continued his civil rights activities. In 1972 he founded the Kansas City chapter of the SCLC; later that same year, he planned a poor people's encampment near the Country Club Plaza in Kansas City. The city stopped the poor people's protest, but Cleaver became well known as a political activist.

In 1970 Cleaver married Dianne Donaldson, a Kansas City native with whom he had four children. In 1972 he began studying at St. Paul Theological Seminary, where he received a master of divinity degree in 1976. One year later, he was ordained a METHODIST minister. Cleaver was named the pastor of St. James United Methodist Church, whose membership grew greatly during his pastorate.

Cleaver launched his political career in 1970, when he made an unsuccessful bid for the Missouri statehouse. In 1975 he made another attempt for office in his campaign against incumbent councilman Bruce R. Watkins of Kansas City. In 1979 Cleaver was elected to Kansas City's city council; he was reelected in 1983 and 1987. On the council, Cleaver abandoned his overt militancy in favor of forming coalitions to effect change. While he was member of the city council, Cleaver continued to preach and perform his pastoral duties at St. James Methodist Church.

In 1991 Cleaver was elected mayor of Kansas City, becoming the first African American to hold this office. He was reelected in 1995. During his terms as mayor, Cleaver appointed the first female mayor pro tem of Kansas City and appointed many African American men and women to serve on city boards and commissions.

See also: Mayors; Selma to Montgomery march.

Cleveland, James (December 5, 1931, Chicago, Illinois—February 9, 1991, Los Angeles, California): Gospel singer, pianist, composer, arranger, producer, and church pastor. Cleveland received much of his musical training at Pilgrim Baptist Church under gospel great Thomas A. DORSEY, musical director of that church. In 1949 the Reverend C. L. FRANKLIN invited Cleveland to DETROIT, MICHIGAN, and hired him as director of his New Bethel Baptist Church choir. There, Cleveland taught the reverend's nine-year-old daughter, Aretha FRANKLIN, to sing gospel. His instruction had a lingering influence on her musical career. He was to have tremendous influence on other aspiring gospel singers as well.

Cleveland later founded the Cornerstone Institutional Baptist Church in LOS ANGELES, CALIFORNIA, and organized his own gospel group, the Cleveland Singers. With his own place of operation and singing group, he went on to astounding achievements in the world of gospel music. In the 1960's, he fathered the modern gospel sound with his innovative arrangements. In 1968 he founded the annual week-long Gospel Music Workshop of America, which grew to twenty-five thousand members. He wrote more than four hundred songs and recorded more than one hundred albums, winning four Grammys and earning sixteen gold records. Among the many songs he composed are "Everything Will Be All Right," "Peace Be Still," "The Love of God," "The Backslider—Where Is Your Faith," "Lord, Help Me to Hold Out," "I've Been in the Storm Too Long," and "Walk Around Heaven All Day."

One of Cleveland's most highly recognized achievements was the 1972 coarrangement and coproduction of Aretha Franklin's historic and celebrated album *Amazing Grace* at New Temple Missionary Baptist Church in Los Angeles. Franklin was the lead vocalist, but Cleveland assisted with the music and arrangements. He joined Franklin in one song, "Precious Memories." He also directed the Southern California Community Choir, which backed Franklin. The recording was done over two consecutive nights, before the congregation, and brought together famous persons who had influenced Franklin's life—the Reverend C. L. Franklin, Clara Ward, and John Hammond. The album was a smashing success, achieving gold status and winning a Grammy Award for Franklin.

See also: Gospel music and spirituals.

Cliff, Michelle (b. November 2, 1946, Kingston, Jamaica): Writer. Cliff's novels, poems, and short stories provide a voice for the oppressed, particularly those of JAMAICAN heritage. They are concerned with social and political issues related to colonialism and racism. Cliff's writing uncovers the shame of SLAVERY in order to help others reclaim their history; it undermines the languages of the oppressors who relied on the servitude of others. In doing so, it retells the history of her people in a subversive manner. Rather than focusing on the development of individual identity, her autobiographical writings show a preoccupation with re-creating a collective identity that is proud of its heritage.

Cliff's first novel, *Abeng* (1984), shows the complex and compromised relationship between a light-skinned girl (based to some extent on Cliff's own experience) and a girl with darker skin. They eventually are split apart by a violent incident. Cliff's other works include the novel *No Telephone to Heaven* (1987) and a book of short stories, *Bodies of Water* (1990), as well as a book of poems, *The Land of Look Behind* (1985). The novel *Free Enterprise* (1993) focuses on the resistance that the slave trade engendered, continuing Cliff's interest in portraying the dignity of colonized people.

—*Holly L. Norton*

See also: Literature.

Clinton, George Wylie (March 28, 1859, Cedar Creek, South Carolina—1921): EPISCOPAL cleric, bishop of the AFRICAN METHODIST EPISCOPAL CHURCH. He was among the first African Americans to study at the University of South Carolina. Clinton was licensed as a local preacher in 1879 and became a bishop in 1896. He remained a bishop until 1920. Clinton edited *African-American Spokesman* and founded *The AME Zion Quarterly Review.* He also served as editor of *Star of Zion* and wrote *Christianity Under the Searchlight* (1909).

Clinton administration: The relationship of the administration of President Bill Clinton— who took office in 1993—to the African American community was complex. African American politicians and voters were among the strongest supporters of the DEMOCRATIC PARTY and President Clinton for years, but they seemingly received little in return for their support. The proper understanding of this complexity goes to the heart of American politics in the 1990's. It helps explains why the REPUBLICAN PARTY gained and held control of both congressional houses while Clinton himself was becoming increasingly popular, even as he achieved fewer objectives and became mired in scandals. The African Americans' attitude toward Clinton reflected their larger relationship to American politics generally toward the end of the century.

African American Support for Clinton

At the height of both the House of Representatives Judiciary Committee's impeachment hearings and the Senate's impeachment trial of Clinton in early 1999, there were no more vocal supporters of Clinton than African Americans. This was true in both open committee sessions and on television talk shows. In each of Clinton's two election campaigns for the presidency, in 1992 and 1996, the percentage of African Americans who voted for him exceeded that of any other demographic group, and the African American voter turnout was generally heavy. African Americans were a significant part of the plurality that helped Clinton become the first elected Democratic president to be reelected since Franklin D. Roosevelt in 1944. At the same time, African Americans contributed to the Democratic Party's victory in picking up congressional seats in the same reelection campaign—for the first time since the reelection of President Woodrow Wilson (1913-1921) in 1916.

More significantly, during 1998, the critical sixth year of the Clinton presidency, when

President Clinton's many African American appointees included Franklin Raines, whom he named to head the Office of Management and Budget in April, 1996. *(AP/Wide World Photos)*

most two-term presidents find that their party loses approximately sixty-five seats in off-year elections, the Clinton administration actually gained five house seats. This was due largely to the extraordinary effort by the African American community to turn out their voters in key congressional districts. What might have turned into a disaster for the Clinton administration and the Democrats instead turned into a rousing victory. It had been 160 years since the party of any second-term president had gained congressional seats an in off-year election.

Despite this remarkable support, the Clinton administration had delivered little of real substance to the African American community. Clinton did appoint a number of African Americans to prominent positions in his cabinet, the bureaucracy, and the federal judiciary. However, these were mostly symbolic gains that did not necessarily benefit rank-and-file voters. Moreover, Clinton did not in-

Notable African American Appointees in the Clinton Administration

Jesse Brown	Secretary of Veterans Affairs
Lee Patrick Brown	Director of the Office of National Drug Control Policy
Ron Brown	Secretary of Commerce
Joycelyn Elders	U.S. surgeon general
Mike Espy	Secretary of Agriculture
Hazel O'Leary	Secretary of Energy
Mary Frances Berry	Chair of the U.S. Civil Rights Commission
Walter D. Broadnax	Deputy secretary of Health and Human Services
Drew S. Days III	Solicitor general
Clarence R. Duvernay	Deputy secretary of the Department of Housing and Urban Development (HUD)
Marian Wright Edelman	U.S. representative to the United Nations International Children's Education Fund (UNICEF)
Larry Irving	Assistant secretary for communications and information (Department of Commerce)
Bob J. Nash	Undersecretary for small community and rural development (Department of Agriculture)
Emmett Paige, Jr.	Assistant secretary for command, control, communications, and intelligence (Department of Defense)
Rodney E. Slater	Administrator of the Federal Highway Administration (Department of Transportation)
Togo D. West, Jr.	Secretary of the Army (Department of Defense)
Clifton Reginald Wharton, Jr.	Deputy secretary of state

clude an African American in his first two appointments to the Supreme Court. Clinton also showed only limited loyalty to his other appointees and dropped his support of several African American political leaders when their appointments or nominations ran into any kind of trouble. For example, he withdrew the nomination of Lani Guinier for a Justice Department post when her somewhat unconventional, but legally defensible, views on racial GERRYMANDERING became known. Clinton forced Jocelyn Elders, the first African American woman to serve as U.S. surgeon general, to resign after her stands on a series of medical and social problems proved embarrassing to the White House.

Symbolic Gains

Clinton made other symbolic gestures for the black community. For example, in 1999 he announced a major race initiative and dialogue, which allowed discussion of problems of African Americans to receive some prominence. He seemed willing to issue a national apology for SLAVERY and SEGREGATION in the past but was unwilling to support any proposals for REPARATIONS for the damage done by those policies to African Americans. Most disappointing to many African Americans was Clinton's support of Republican-led welfare reform initiatives containing provisions to the long-range disadvantage of many low-income African Americans and whites. Clinton expressed sympathy for a number of African American policy concerns, but the budget constraints kept him from undertaking any initiatives that required substantial budget outlays.

Despite Clinton's lack of support for African American policy issues, African Americans apparently accepted the political difficulties he and his Democratic Party faced and believed that if impeachment brought him down, they would be left in a worse predicament. African Americans have found federal and state prosecutors contrary to the interests of most African Americans, so that a federal prosecutor, such as Kenneth Starr—who amassed the impeachment trial evidence—was a natural target for their animosity. The all-white Republican composition of the House Judiciary Committee and the all-white contingent of House impeachment managers in the Senate impeachment trial only reinforced the sense that the Republican Party did not have best interests of the African American community at heart.

Superficially, Clinton pursued a political strategy of appearing to be a moderate beset by extremists from both the Left and the Right. This strategy of appearing to hold the middle ground had been used before, by Democratic President Harry S Truman (1945-1953) in his 1948 presidential election campaign and by Republican President Dwight Eisenhower (1953-1961) throughout his administration. However, the Clinton strategy was more than a simple compromise position in the middle; it deliberately sought to provoke animosity between the extremists in an attempt to make whatever position Clinton adopted the only reasonable position in the national debate. Clinton's strategy, called "triangulation" by his former political adviser, Dick Morris, depended on liberal groups, including African Americans, to take a leadership role in carrying the fight against conservative forces on the Right, particularly on the Religious Right. Clinton then would be in triangular relationship opposed to both groups. While such a strategy made sense for Clinton's administration, it is hard to see why African Americans acquiesced to it.

Redistricting and Republican Control of Congress

One explanation for the strong African American support for Clinton turns on the explanation of why the Republicans gained control of the House of Representatives in 1994. The conventional answer was that Republican pre-1994 policies were more popular than Clinton administration initiatives. In 1993 Republican House minority leader Newt Gingrich developed a program called "Contract with America." It included a number of legislative initiatives he promised the Republicans would pass if they gained control of the Congress in the 1994 midterm elections. Most Republican candidates pledged that they would join in this effort. After the Republicans won, the supposition was that a clear majority of Americans favored this new program.

This conventional explanation had a problem. The Republicans passed nearly all their proposed legislation and then became so unpopular they lost the presidential election in 1996. The answer is more complicated. It is certainly true that the Democratic presidential and congressional leadership did not look capable as they headed into the 1994 election. The Democrats had controlled both houses of Congress and the White House but had passed little legislation. Nevertheless, it was normal for parties holding the White House to lose seats in off-year elections, and Democrats had lost seats before without losing control.

The real answer to the Republican control of Congress lies in the impact of REDISTRICTING after the 1990 CENSUS. As the result of the reapportionment decisions of BAKER V. CARR (1962), REYNOLDS V. SIMS (1964), WESBERRY V. SANDERS (1964), and *Kirkpatrick v. Preisler* (1969), states almost universally adopted single-member, single-election districts for congressional, state legislative, and local governing bodies under the so-called "one person, one vote" principle. Such districts significantly improved the chances for success of many otherwise unelectable minority individuals over alternative districting systems, coupled with the VOTING RIGHTS ACT OF 1965. African

Americans gradually won thousands of offices. Nevertheless, the percentage of African American officeholders remained below the percentage of African Americans in the overall population.

Some then proposed a form of AFFIRMATIVE ACTION in which congressional district lines would be drawn specifically to favor the election of African American congresspersons. Oddly shaped districts were drawn to join small areas with majority African American populations together. While this trend meant that African Americans would be elected in increasing numbers, other districts from which African American areas were removed were more difficult for the Democratic Party to hold. Nationally, when the 1990 census impact on redistricting cycle had been completed in 1994, the Republicans were already due for large gains. Coupled with the normal decline in the party strength in midterm elections for the party holding the White House, the Republicans were able to gain control of Congress for the first time since 1954.

African American membership increased in the Congress, but overall Democrats declined to the point of losing control. The decision to draw such racially determined legislative district lines had created a curious alliance between African Americans and Republicans—both of which gained at the expense of white Democratic candidates. Nonetheless political factors were such that Democrats could not easily oppose the creation of these new racially motivated districts, even though it was to their political disadvantage, without seeming to be returning to the white segregationist origins of the southern Democratic Party. Both African American and white Democratic Party members endorsed these new districts, but it ultimately worked to the disadvantage of both.

In 1995 African Americans recognized the difficulty. Naturally, this was a consequence of patterns of political conduct that had pre-

vailed since the 1960's. The Supreme Court had mandated that legislative districts be equal in size under the one-person, one-vote principle, but it had never set any meaningful standards that prohibited gerrymandering. While gerrymandering implies redrawing lines for partisan political advantage, the actual practice had been for Democrats and Republicans to agree on a bipartisan gerrymander of the districts resulting in an increase in one-party seats for members of both parties. With the addition of the normal incumbency advantage, almost every congressperson in both parties acquired a safe seat. After that, a circular process occurred in which the large campaign contributions went to those most likely to win, and those most likely to win were those who had the extra money with which to campaign. The specially drawn new districts with African Americans majorities tipped the balance of this old arrangement just enough to give Republicans control of Congress.

Ironically, the Supreme Court, with an overwhelming number of Republican appointees, concluded that the odd shapes of many newly drawn African American majority districts were constitutionally suspect in *Shaw v. Reno* (1993) and sent them back to lower courts for reconsideration. The Supreme Court's view may have meant that there would be fewer such districts after the 2000 census, but that would not aid the Democrats in the short term. The long-term benefits for both African American and white Democrats seemed to lie in their working together rather than African Americans pressing for whatever symbolic gains come from an increasing number of African Americans holding seats in legislative bodies at the expense of substantive representation.

—*Richard L. Wilson*

See also: Civil rights and congressional legislation; Electoral politics; Politics and government.

Suggested Readings:

Birnbaum, Jeffrey. *The Madhouse.* New York: Times Books, 1996.

Campbell, Colin, and Bert Rockman. *The Clinton Presidency: First Appraisals.* Chatham, N.J.: Chatham House, 1996.

Ceaser, James W., and Andrew E. Busch. *Losing to Win: The 1996 Elections and American Politics.* Lanham, Md.: Rowman and Littlefield, 1997.

Drew, Elizabeth. *Showdown: The Struggle Between the Gingrich Congress and the Clinton White House.* New York: Simon and Schuster, 1996.

Maraniss, David. *First in His Class.* New York: Simon and Schuster, 1994.

Morris, Dick. *Behind the Oval Office.* New York: Random House, 1997.

Woodward, Bob. *The Agenda: Inside the Clinton White House.* New York: Simon and Schuster, 1994.

Clyburn, James E. (b. July 21, 1940, Sumter, South Carolina): SOUTH CAROLINA politician. After receiving his undergraduate degree from South Carolina State College in 1962, Clyburn worked as a high school history teacher until 1965. A committed CIVIL RIGHTS activist, Clyburn became involved in various community and labor organizations, serving as a counselor with the South Carolina Employee Security Commission (1965-1968), as director of the Neighborhood Youth Corps (1966-1968), and as executive director of the state's Commission for Farm Workers (1968-1971). While attending the University of South Carolina Law School from 1972 to 1974, Clyburn served as a special assistant to Governor John C. West for human resource development.

Clyburn went on to serve for nearly twenty years as South Carolina's Human Affairs Commissioner. Defeating opponent John

James E. Clyburn (left) confers with fellow Congressional Black Caucus members Maxine Waters and William Clay in June, 1998. *(AP/Wide World Photos)*

Chase in 1992, Clyburn was elected to Congress from South Carolina's Sixth Congressional District; he won reelection in 1994. Clyburn was the first African American representative elected to Congress from South Carolina since 1897. Upon taking office in 1993, Clyburn was appointed to serve on the House Committee on Veterans' Affairs and on the House Committee on Public Works and Transportation. Reelected throughout the 1990's, in 1999 he assumed leadership of the CONGRESSIONAL BLACK CAUCUS, taking over the chair from Maxine WATERS.

See also: Congress members; Politics and government.

Coachman, Alice (b. November 29, 1923, Albany, Georgia): Athlete. Coachman was the first black woman to win an Olympic gold medal in track and field. Coachman set an Olympic record for the high jump at five feet, six and one-quarter inches in London in 1948. She was known for her unusual technique, which combined the western roll and straight jumping. In addition to her 1948 medal, she won twenty-five Amateur Athletic Union national titles, was national high jump champion for twelve consecutive years, and was voted into the National Track and Field Hall of Fame in 1975.

See also: Olympic gold medal winners.

Coalition Against Blaxploitation: Interest group within the FILM industry in the early 1970's. The coalition was formed after several hundred African American artists met in the early 1970's to discuss the image of black people that was being presented in films. Coalition members met with studio and film industry union leaders to find ways to improve the screen image of African Americans and to improve working conditions for African Americans in the film industry. The trend

toward violent, action-filled, and often sexually oriented BLAXPLOITATION films to which the coalition objected had died out by the mid-1970's.

Cobb, William Montague (b. October 12, 1904, Washington, D.C.): Physician, scholar, and CIVIL RIGHTS activist. Cobb received his medical degree from HOWARD UNIVERSITY (1929) and a Ph.D. in anatomy from Western Reserve University (1932). Cobb served on the faculty at Howard's medical college beginning in 1928 and was named professor emeritus in 1973. He was also active in the NATIONAL ASSOCIATION FOR THE ADVANCEMENT OF COLORED PEOPLE (NAACP) and was a member of its national board of directors. Cobb wrote several articles on African American anatomy and is well respected for his writings on the history of blacks in MEDICINE.

Cochran, Johnnie L., Jr. (b. October 2, 1937, Shreveport, Louisiana): Attorney. When Cochran was six years old, his family moved to California, where they lived in a middle-class neighborhood. His father worked for many years as an executive for the Golden State Mutual Life Insurance, the largest black-owned business in the United States. Johnnie, Jr., was reared by loving, religious parents who encouraged his education. He attended Los Angeles High School, where most of his classmates were upper-middle-class whites. He graduated in 1959 from the University of California at Los Angeles and earned his J.D. degree in 1962 from the Loyola University School of Law.

Cochran began his law career in the Los Angeles city attorney's office from 1963 to 1965. He later became the first African American to work in the Los Angeles district attorney's office, from 1978 to 1980. He became best known, however, as a defense attorney in private practice, working with celebrity clients such as Michael JACKSON and O. J. SIMPSON. He also represented Reginald O. Denny, a white truck driver who was severely beaten during the 1992 LOS ANGELES RIOTS. Cochran represented such large organizations as the Automobile Club of Southern California, University of Southern California, and Atlantic Richfield Company (ARCO).

Cochran located his corporate office on Los Angeles's Wilshire Boulevard, and his firm became known for the predominance of mi-

Johnnie L. Cochran, Jr. (right) with former Black Panther leader Geronimo Pratt, whom he was still representing in 1998. *(AP/Wide World Photos)*

norities among its staff members. Cochran was named trial attorney of the year in 1982 by the John M. Langston Bar Association; he was named attorney of the year in 1990 by the Los Angeles Trial Association. A religious man, Cochran began attending the Second Baptist Church regularly as a young man; through the years he donated a considerable amount of money to the church.

An influential member of Los Angeles's black community with a net worth estimated at $5 million as a result of his successful legal practice, Cochran committed himself to giving back to the community and improving other people's lives. Among his charitable contributions, Cochran gave $250,000 to help finance ten units of low-income housing in Southwest Los Angeles, known as the Cochran Villas. He also donated a $50,000 scholarship fund (named after his father) to assist African Americans attending UCLA and contributed $100,000 to the same school's Tom Bradley International Center.

At the 1995 O. J. Simpson murder trial, Cochran was a highly outspoken member of

Simpson's team of defense attorneys. He drew most of the publicity and most of the media criticism for the conduct of the Simpson legal defense. Some critics accused him of playing the RACE CARD to convince jurors to set aside the assertions of the prosecution; others asserted that he effectively used the history of police brutality and racism in Los Angeles to persuade jurors in his closing arguments. Considered by many to be the key architect of the defense team's strategy, Cochran earned the lion's share of the credit for Simpson's acquittal in October of 1995. Buoyed by his success, Cochran announced in 1996 that he intended to file a writ of *habeas corpus* to reopen the case against Geronimo Pratt, a former member of the BLACK PANTHER PARTY who was convicted of murdering a schoolteacher in 1970. In 1997 the court agreed to reconsider Pratt's case. Cochran published a memoir, *Journey to Justice*, in 1996, that devoted as much space to his interest in the Pratt case as it did to the Simpson trial.

Among Cochran's numerous clients after the Simpson victory were victims of the 1995 bombing of the federal building in Oklahoma City. He also became involved in a number of New York City area cases involving alleged police misconduct, including representing Abner Louima in his brutality suit against the New York police. In the late 1990's Cochran began, then discontinued, a weeknight program for the Court TV cable network called *Johnnie Cochran Tonight*. In 1999 he announced plans to combine his firm with the New York firm Schneider, Kleinick, Weitz, Damashek, and Shoot.

See also: Legal professions.

Coker, Daniel (Isaac Wright; 1780, Frederick County or Baltimore County, Maryland—1846, Freetown, Sierra Leone): Educator and missionary. Coker was one of the founders of the AFRICAN METHODIST EPISCOPAL ZION CHURCH. He also founded Bethel Charity School for Negroes, in 1816. Coker is best known for his missionary work in Sierra Leone, a British colony in West Africa originally founded as a haven for freed slaves, and for his book *Journal of Daniel Coker* (1820), a chronicle of his trip to AFRICA.

Cole, Johnnetta Betsch (b. October 19, 1936, Jacksonville, Florida): University administrator. Trained as an anthropologist, Cole was the first African American woman president of SPELMAN COLLEGE in ATLANTA, GEORGIA.

At fifteen, Cole entered FISK UNIVERSITY in Nashville, TENNESSEE, as a participant in an early admissions program. She transferred to OBERLIN COLLEGE in OHIO, where she earned her undergraduate degree. Cole was later awarded the master's and doctorate in anthropology from Northwestern University in Evanston, Illinois.

Cole began her career as an assistant professor of anthropology and director of black studies at Washington State University. During her thirteen years with the University of Massachusetts at Amherst, she rose from assistant to full professor in the department of anthropology. She also served two years as assistant provost for undergraduate studies. After teaching anthropology for a year as a visiting professor at Hunter College of the City University of New York, she became a professor of anthropology and director of the Latin American and Caribbean studies program at Hunter. In 1987 she left to become president of Spelman College.

Founded in 1881 by two white Baptist female missionaries, Spelman is the nation's oldest HISTORICALLY BLACK COLLEGE for women. Cole became its seventh president. During her tenure, the school was named in *U.S. News and World Report*'s list of the best colleges in the United States. In 1989 Spelman ranked second in a listing of the South's best liberal arts colleges. Under Cole's leadership, the school's student body of close to eighteen hundred women included students from almost every state and from twelve countries. Spelman's incoming students had the highest combined Scholastic Aptitude Test scores of freshmen at any historically black college or university. Cole served as president of the college until 1997.

Cole received several honorary degrees from institutions of higher learning, including Fisk, Yale, and Princeton Universities and Bates and Williams Colleges. She also received awards for her achievements. She was a recipient of Northwestern's Alumni Merit Award and an Achievement Award from the American Association of University Women. She was director of President George Bush's Points of Light Foundation. Cole published the book *Conversations: Straight Talk with America's Sister President* in 1993.

Cole, Nat "King" (Nathaniel Adams Coles; March 17, 1919, Montgomery, Alabama—February 15, 1965, Santa Monica, California): Singer and pianist. Originally an innovative JAZZ pianist whose work inspired pianists such as Art TATUM and Oscar PETERSON, Cole became the first male African American jazz singer after Louis ARMSTRONG to achieve worldwide fame.

Cole began his career as a pianist by emulating the distinctive piano style of Earl "Fatha" HINES. He eventually developed a unique style and became one of the most respected jazz artists of his day. The only other jazz pianists of his time who were his peers in terms of harmonic sophistication were Duke ELLINGTON and Art Tatum—both of whom are regarded by many musicians and scholars as the greatest pianists in the history of jazz. When he began singing in order to provide some variety in his performances, Cole became popular. His velvet voice and straightforward, unaffected singing style made him an instant success. He went on to become one of the most popular singers in the world, although he had to contend with racism throughout his career. He was the first African American male singer to be accepted by white listeners as a singer of ballads. Before he achieved his great success, it was considered unacceptable for black men to perform love songs for a mixed audience.

Born Nathaniel Coles (he later dropped the "s"), Cole was one of six children of the Reverend James Coles and Perlina Adams Coles, a music teacher. His birthdate is usually given as 1919; however, some sources list it as 1916. (Cole himself gave two or three different birth years at different times.) His parents, like many other African American southerners, moved to CHICAGO in search of a better life; Cole was four at the time. Like all his siblings, he exhibited musical talent at an early age, playing tunes by ear.

Although his strict BAPTIST parents frowned on secular music, Cole fell under the spell of the popular artists of the day, and the great pi-anist Earl Hines became his idol. While still in high school, Cole formed his own big band, Nat Cole and His Rogues of Rhythm, which had twelve to fourteen members. The group rapidly became successful, and on one occasion, when Cole was still in high school, he and the Rogues beat Hines's group in a battle of the bands at the SAVOY BALLROOM. Cole's brother Eddie, who was playing in New York with the band of Noble Sissle and Eubie BLAKE, returned to Chicago when he heard of Nat's success. The two formed a new band, Eddie Cole's Solid Swingers. It was at that time that the brothers dropped the "s" from their last name for good.

In 1937 Nat and Eddie Cole went on tour with a revival of the musical *Shuffle Along*, the first all-black show to achieve success on Broadway. While on tour, Nat married Nadine Robinson, a beautiful dancer ten years his senior. The show ended in Long Beach, California, where the Coles found themselves stranded. Urged on by Nadine, who believed

Nat "King" Cole. *(AP/Wide World Photos)*

in his talent more than he did, Cole eked out a living in LOS ANGELES by playing one-night stands, doing occasional studio work, and playing in shows. During that time, he developed a unique piano style that combined a flawless technique with a remarkable harmonic sophistication. In 1939 he was asked to organize a quartet to play at the Swanee Club. He did so, but when the drummer backed out at the last minute, the group played as a trio.

Guitarist Oscar Moore and bassist Wesley Prince formed a perfect musical match for Cole, and the three continued to play together even though a trio of that instrumentation was unheard of at the time. The King Cole Trio, as they became known after Cole's name was linked with the hero of the nursery rhyme "Old King Cole" as a marketing ploy, developed a group style in which the musical interplay was almost telepathic, and in their vocal features they developed a three-part unison singing style that was unusual and very popular.

Cole was an untrained singer, but he had a compelling vocal style. His baritone voice was smooth, his diction was excellent, he sang with virtually no vibrato, and he focused on the lyrics he was singing rather than on vocal effects and embellishments. He seemed absolutely honest and believable, and his listeners could identify with the emotions he expressed. Although he sometimes sang slightly flat during the early part of his career, that characteristic seemed only to increase the charm of his singing.

Cole's first great success came after he recorded "Straighten Up and Fly Right," a song of his own that he had sold outright when he was struggling in Los Angeles. His singing, combined with the remarkable playing of the trio, made the song a hit. He continued to record and tour, and he had the biggest hit of his life when he recorded "The Christmas Song" in 1946. From that moment, Cole added other instruments to the trio when he recorded. He

disbanded the trio in 1951, focusing on singing rather than playing, to the chagrin of many jazz fans. His singing, however, got even better after he gave up the piano.

In 1946 Cole met singer Maria Ellington while on tour. Smitten with her beauty and sophistication, he divorced Nadine to marry her. Maria craved success in all its forms, and she set about to improve her husband's diction, teach him how to dress better, and advise him regarding his career. Although Maria earned the resentment of many of those who worked with Cole, her influence on her husband was mostly beneficial.

In addition to recording such hits as "Nature Boy," "Mona Lisa," and "Unforgettable," Cole worked on radio, on television, and in films. His was the first black jazz group to have a sponsored radio show, and he had his own television show from 1956 to 1957. The show ultimately was taken off the air because too many sponsors were afraid to support an African American television show. Cole acted or sang in a number of movies, including *St. Louis Blues*, in which he played W. C. Handy.

Cole remained popular until the time of his death. A lifelong smoker, he developed lung cancer and died at Santa Monica Hospital in 1965. His daughter Natalie, herself a fine singer, won a Grammy Award for her recording of "Unforgettable," which, through the creative use of recording technology, combined her singing with her father's.

—*Shawn Woodyard*

See also: Music.

Suggested Readings:

Gourse, Leslie. *Unforgettable: The Life and Mystique of Nat King Cole.* New York: St. Martin's Press, 1991.

Haskins, James, with Kathleen Benson. *Nat King Cole: A Personal and Professional Biography.* New York: Stein and Day, 1984.

Ruuth, Marianne. *Nat King Cole.* New York: Holloway House, 1992.

Teubig, Klaus. *Straighten Up and Fly Right.* Westport, Conn.: Greenwood Press, 1994.

Cole, Rebecca J. (1846—1922): Medical doctor. Cole followed Rebecca Lee CRUMPLER to become the second African American woman to earn a medical degree in the United States. She may have been the first African American woman actually to practice MEDICINE, however, as it is said that she did so before she had formal certification. She received her degree from the Woman's Medical College of Pennsylvania in 1867. Cole was appointed "sanitary visitor" at Elizabeth Blackwell's Hospital in New York City and practiced medicine in Columbia, SOUTH CAROLINA, before settling in WASHINGTON, D.C., where her race and sex prevented her from practicing to her potential. She served as physician to the Home for Dependent Colored Women and Children.

Cole, Thomas W., Jr. (b. January 11, 1941, Vernon, Texas): Educational administrator. Cole was the first president (1989) of Clark Atlanta University, formed by the merger of Clark College and ATLANTA UNIVERSITY. He previously had been a professor of chemistry and served as provost at Atlanta University as well as teaching at other universities. He was president of West Virginia State College (1982-1986) and on the West Virginia Board of Regents immediately prior to taking the Clark Atlanta post.
See also: Higher education.

Coleman, Bessie (January 26, 1893, Atlanta, Texas—April 30, 1926, Jacksonville, Florida): Pilot. Coleman learned to fly in Europe because there was nowhere in the United States for an African American woman to learn. She was the first black woman, and one of the first women, to earn an international pilot's li-

While barnstorming through the United States during the 1920's, Bessie Coleman earned the nickname "Brave Bessie" because of her daredevil flying feats. *(Arkent Archive)*

cense. She planned to teach young black men to fly but died in a plane crash before realizing that ambition. During the 1990's Coleman was honored by the U.S. Postal Service by being depicted in the Black Heritage postage stamp series.
See also: Aviators and astronauts.

Coleman, Ornette (b. March 19, 1930, Fort Worth, Texas): JAZZ saxophonist. Ornette Coleman was in the forefront of the "free jazz" movement of the late 1950's and early 1960's, and he drew both high praise and fierce criticism for his experimental work. He was nota-

Saxophonist Ornette Coleman in 1985. *(AP/Wide World Photos)*

as, occasionally, trumpet and violin. Coleman's popularity, and the quality of his music, went up and down through the years. A later quartet featured Dewey Redman, Charlie Haden, and Ed Blackwell. In 1972 Coleman's orchestral work *Skies of America* was premiered at the Newport Jazz Festival. His recordings include *Town Hall Concert* (1962), *Forms and Sounds* (1967), *New York Is Now* (1968), and *Ornette and Prime Time: Opening the Caravan of Dreams* (1985).

Coleman, William Thaddeus, Jr. (b. July 7, 1920, Germantown, Pennsylvania): Attorney and government official. Coleman graduated from the University of Pennsylvania (1941) and Harvard University Law School (LL.B., 1946). He served as legal secretary to SUPREME COURT Justice Felix Frankfurter and was appointed as secretary of transportation by President Gerald Ford. Coleman also served as president of the NATIONAL ASSOCIATION FOR THE ADVANCEMENT OF COLORED PEOPLE Legal Defense and Educational Fund.

bly influenced by Charlie PARKER. His first album, *Something Else!!!* was released in 1958, *The Shape of Jazz to Come* in 1959, and the landmark *Free Jazz* in 1960. Trumpeter Don Cherry, bassist Charlie Haden, and drummer Billy Higgins played on much of Coleman's work at this time. Free jazz frequently avoided preconceived song structure altogether, simply allowing a group of players to improvise collectively. Some audiences found this approach exhilarating; others found it unlistenable.

Coleman performed primarily on alto saxophone, but also on tenor saxophone as well

Coles, Honi (1911, Philadelphia, Pennsylvania—November 12, 1992, New York, New York): Tap dancer. At the age of twelve, Charles "Honi" Coles competed in amateur nights at local PHILADELPHIA, PENNSYLVANIA, theaters, winning often. At one of these events, Honi (a nickname given to him by his mother) befriended George and Danny Miller. Calling themselves the Three Millers, they opened at the Lafayette Theater in HARLEM in 1931. When the show folded, Coles went home to Philadelphia to devote the year to practice.

Upon his return to New York in 1932, he was said to have the fastest feet in the business. He danced in the Harlem Opera House and the APOLLO THEATER and became one of the more recognized members of the Hoofers Club. From 1934 to 1940, he toured the United States and Europe with the Lucky Seven Trio and a comedy acted called Howell and Coles.

As a solo dancer traveling with Cab CALLOWAY and his band from 1940 to 1943, Coles met tapper Cholly ATKINS. During WORLD WAR II, Atkins and Coles went into the Army. Upon their discharge in 1945, Coles and Atkins were immediately booked by the Apollo Theater as a "class act." Their trademark became the slow soft shoe, with identical steps executed with absolute precision. During the late 1940's, they danced with a series of big bands including those of Cab Calloway, Louis ARMSTRONG, Charlie Barnet, Lionel HAMPTON, Billy ECKSTINE, and Count BASIE.

Coles and Atkins opened on Broadway in *Gentlemen Prefer Blondes* (1949). Their early 1950's work included *Kiss Me Kate* and *Girl Crazy* in summer stock, a European tour with Count Basie, and two films—*Rock 'n' Roll Revue* (1952) and *Harlem Variety Revue* (1955). After performances in Las Vegas and with Pearl BAILEY, Coles and Atkins split up.

In the 1960's, Coles became production manager at the Apollo Theater and president of the Negro Actors Guild. In 1976 he appeared in the Broadway show *Bubbling Brown Sugar*. Subsequent shows were *Black Broadway* (1980) and *My One and Only* (1983), for which he won a Tony Award. Additional appearances included educational television, special shows on dance, and jazz festivals. In May, 1988, Coles became the recipient of the Thirty-ninth Annual Capezio Dance Award.

Colescott, Robert (b. August 26, 1925, Oakland, California): Painter and arts educator. Colescott is best known for humorously adapting the subjects of famous paintings in a way that draws attention to African American concerns. The humor he injects into depictions of these serious concerns allows a diverse public to appreciate minority problems more freely and fully.

Colescott's art education began at the University of California at Berkeley, where he graduated in 1949. He went on to study painting with Fernand Leger in Paris and later taught at the University of Arizona. After leaving Paris, he lived in Cairo, Egypt, whose non-Western culture affected him deeply and led him to compare black and white cultures through painting. Ultimately, his experiences impelled him to create art that interjects blacks into the predominantly white world of art history.

In many of his works, he personalizes the position of black culture within the dominant white one by painting himself—usually with white hair and dark-rimmed glasses—as one of the subjects in the painting. His most frequently used device is transforming white subjects in paintings into BLACKFACE. For example, by reversing race in a well-known Renaissance composition, *Arnolfini Wedding* by Jan van Eyck, he creates a work that urges the viewer to consider where blacks were then and to imagine what were they doing.

Colescott's technique is neo-expressionist, emphasizing loose, brushy strokes with intense, thickly applied color. His compositions often combine several ideas and produce a collage-like effect. Colescott has influenced many postmodern artists, both white and black.

—*Ann Stewart Balakier*
See also: Painters and illustrators.

Collectibles: Items created before 1970 that were written by or about, or depict images of, black persons. These items are also sometimes called black Americana, black memorabilia, and ethnic collectibles. People who disapprove of the marketing and collecting of items that portray African Americans in negative, degrading ways regard many of these items as contemptible and racist artifacts.

A wide range of items are considered black collectibles. Relatively common examples include sheet music with cartoonish depictions of blacks on the cover, "mammy" cookie jars and kitchenware, and folk art from the 1960's. Examples of rarer pieces are slave folk art, nineteenth-century and early twentieth-century toys and games, and JIM CROW segregation signs from the South. Beginning in the mid-1980's, the field of collecting black collectibles became so popular that almost any item that relates to African American history is considered

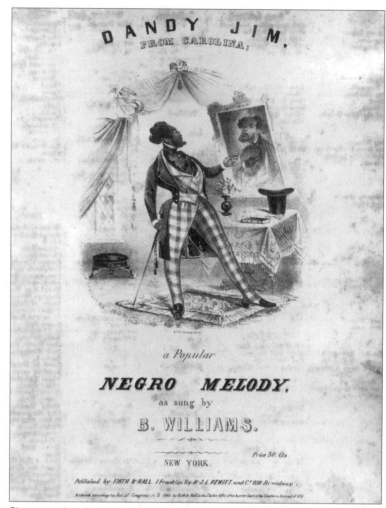

Sheet music with depictions of black stereotypes, such as the minstrel figure "Dandy Jim," have become valuable African American collectibles. *(Library of Congress)*

valuable. Although the images found in black collectibles can be either positive or negative, the greatest demand is for those articles that portray blacks in a degrading manner.

What Black Collectibles Reveal

An examination of black collectibles reveals a great deal about the history of race relations in the United States and about attitudes that were held by whites toward blacks. First, they indicate that racist images permeated American culture. Companies manufactured pencils, lighters, fishing lures, banks, handker-

chiefs, toys, letter openers, postcards, perfume bottles, can openers, and countless other products that caricatured and stereotyped blacks or black culture. Second, these racist products buttressed the racial hierarchy in the United States by reinforcing racial stereotypes and thereby helping justify RACIAL DISCRIMINATION.

Third, racist collectibles were a part of the American socialization process. Little children, white and black, read books such as *Little Pickaninnies*, *Coon Yarns*, and *Ten Little Nigger Boys*. A number of demeaning stereotypes evolved that perpetuated white racist perceptions of blacks, among them the Sambo, the mammy, the jigger, and the pickaninny. The so-called Sambo, the "loyal servant," was often portrayed as a chicken thief. Mammy, the supposed nurturer and protector of the white household, was routinely portrayed as illiterate, dirty, ugly, and immodest. Jiggers were seen as irresponsible, overly flamboyant, and obsessed with dancing and drinking. Even children—labeled pickaninnies—felt the sting. The young black girls depicted on the packaging of Trixy Molasses and Picaninny Freeze ice cream are both so caricatured that they resemble Halloween monsters more than people. A 1916 advertisement by the Morris & Bendien Company, for example, showed a slightly caricatured black baby drinking from a bottle of ink; the caption read "Nigger Milk."

Finally, racist products helped legitimize violence against blacks. A mechanical bank with the label "Always Did 'Spise a Mule" features a black man who is thrown from a mule when a coin is placed in his mouth. The board game called "Hit the Dodger! Knock Him Out!" required the player to swing a ball on a string toward the face of Sambo. Milton Bradley manufactured the "Jolly Darkie Target Game," the object of which was to throw objects into the face of a black man. A 1920's rattle shows a white boy punching a black boy's face. One of the most disturbing things about such racist items is the fact that a large number of racist collectibles are currently being reproduced.

The Collectors

The estimated fifty thousand or more American collectors of black collectibles fall into four general categories. Nostalgic collectors buy black collectibles because it makes them think of a happier, simpler time. The majority of these collectors are white. Liberator collectors purchase racist collectibles because they find them offensive and wish to remove them from the public eye. There are both black and white members of this category, and they often destroy the items they buy. These collectors were common in the 1960's and 1970's; the high price of black collectibles in the 1990's prohibited all but the most wealthy individuals from buying every offensive piece that was publicly displayed.

Heritage collectors are blacks who believe that all black collectibles, even derogatory pieces, have a historical importance that should be preserved. Jeanette Carson and Malinda Saunders promoted the first black collectibles show in 1984, which attracted about six hundred (mostly white) customers. At their ninth annual show in 1993, more than seven thousand people attended. More than 90 percent of those in attendance were African Americans, many of them heritage collectors.

Investors are the final category of collectors of black collectibles. Beginning around 1985, the prices of black collectibles began to skyrocket. For example, mammy jars that sold for six to eight dollars in 1985 commanded from forty to sixty dollars by 1990. This sellers' market brought in a wave of profit-seeking entrepreneurs, primarily dealers with private collections. Most of the members of this category are white, but a growing percentage of black collectors were starting to sell parts of their collections at a significant profit by the late 1990's.

Examples of Collectibles

A society's values and beliefs are both reflected in and shaped by what sociologists call its "material culture"—its physical objects. An American living in the South in the 1940's and 1950's saw "White Only" and "Colored Only" signs. Equally insidious, Americans everywhere saw Golliwogg perfume bottles, Little Black Sambo books and records, black lawn jockeys, Ten Little Darkies greeting cards, and countless other reminders that blacks were second-class citizens. These images reinforced

and undergirded several oppressive caricatures of African Americans, including the pickaninny, mammy, Sambo, uncle, and jigger.

Pickaninnies

Pickaninny was a pejorative word used to describe black children. The pickaninny image
suggests that black children are ugly, stupid,
poor, and have stereotypical physical traits.
Shabbily dressed black children, with very
dark skin, huge eyes, and large, cherry-red
lips, grinning and eating watermelon, are recurring characters in black collectibles. These
pickaninnies do not seem fully human. They
speak to animals as equals, for example; a
postcard shows a black boy saying to a pig,
"Whose Baby is OO?" Many postcards and
trade cards used animal names, such as the
common "coon," to describe black children.
For example, on one a black boy carries a tree
branch that contains eight raccoons; the caption reads: "Nine Coons, Count 'Em."

A second aspect of pickaninnies is that they
lacked modesty. Some of the trade cards produced for Fairbanks Soaps featuring the "Fairbanks Twins" (they later became the Gold
Dust Twins) showed two naked black boys
bathing. Bisque outhouse figurines made and
distributed in the 1940's often had naked or
near-naked black children sitting on toilets.
These items included such captions as "One
Moment Please," "Quit Yo Peakin'," and
"Next." The "Naughty Goose" ashtrays and
novelty items showed a goose biting the geni-
tals of a young black boy. This was an often-
repeated theme in novelty items. On postcards, black children were often presented
urinating, naked, or with their buttocks exposed; the cards had captions such as "Black-
out" or "Cheek to Cheek." The black child was
also used in racial polemics. In the 1950's, the
Asheville (North Carolina) Post Card Company distributed a series of "I'se Happy Down
South" postcards, partly in response to the
growing CIVIL RIGHTS movement.

Mammies

Until the 1960's, mammy was the predominant depiction of black women in the popular
culture. The image of the obese, dark-skinned
mammy in head rags, often rolling her eyes in
humorous exasperation, was personified in
films by actors such as Hattie McDANIEL, who
starred in Gone with the Wind (1939). Born during SLAVERY, the mammy idea was not com-
mercialized until the late nineteenth century.
Around 1875 the mammylike character "Aunt
Sally" appeared on cans of a baking powder. In 1893 the most famous mammy, Aunt
Jemima—wide-mouthed and rag-headed—
was created to sell pancakes. She was a commercial success. She soon acquired a husband, Uncle Mose, and two children, Diana
and Wade. Various black women, including
Nancy Green and Edith Wilson, were hired to
travel from town to town cooking pancakes as
Aunt Jemima. Her slogan was "I'se in town,
honey."

In the twentieth century, the mammy image was also used to sell Luzianne coffee, Fun-
To-Wash detergent, Mammy oranges, Long-
wood Plantation syrup, and a host of other
foods and household products. Mammy figures are most prevalent in "kitchen collectibles" such as salt and pepper shakers, cookie
jars, grocery-list holders, creamers, teapots,
wall plaques, tablecloths, potholder hangers,
dish towels, and cookbooks. All these items
have become prized collectibles. The Nelson
McCoy Pottery Company specialized in
mammy cookie jars. The ubiquitous mammy
image was also found on clocks, dolls, string
holders, ashtrays, pin cushions, cast iron
banks, bottle openers, paperweights, wall
lamps, and various novelty items.

The mammy image had an enduring appeal
for many decades. From slavery through the
Jim Crow era, mammy represented to whites
a loyal, contented, simpler black American—
unlike the blacks engaging in SIT-INS and other
civil rights demonstrations by the 1950's and

One of the most enduring African American stereotypes is that of the "mammy." *(Library of Congress)*

natural servant, cheerful and obedient. Sambo was born on the plantation but survived into the middle of the twentieth century.

The mammy myth found a human (and commercial) face with Aunt Jemima, but there was no single dominant Sambo character. Instead, there were literally thousands of images of black male butlers, chefs, porters, chauffeurs, valets, and shoe shiners who cheerfully and humbly accommodated themselves to a life of servitude. One of the most repellant uses of the Sambo image was employed by the Coon Chicken Inn restaurant chain. These diners were popular in the Northwest in the 1930's and 1940's. The restaurant's logo was a very dark-skinned porter, with a sneer, a winking eye, and exaggerated red lips. The porter's head also served as an entrance to the restaurant: Customers entered through his teeth.

1960's. She was the distant cousin of the "happy slave," representing the perfect blend of natural cheerfulness and obsequiousness.

Sambos

Like the mammy construct, the idea of Sambo arose in the minds of slave masters. It was probably created to soothe fears of slave revolts. Sambo was a sad medley of contradictory traits. He was an adult and a perpetual child, humble yet deceitful, infantile but wise, and responsible though dependent. Like the mammy creation, Sambo was believed to be a

Many Sambos used to advertise products were caricatured: coal-black skin, oversized red or orange lips, a toothy smile, and a bald head or unkempt hair. This was especially true for local or regional products. This portrayal is on the packaging of Mason's Challenge Blacking (for boots), Sharpoint Wire Cobbler Nails, and many other products. National companies tended to have Sambos with lighter skin color, less pronounced lips, combed hair or a clean hat, and laundered clothing. An example of this "softer" Sambo is Rastus, the Cream of Wheat chef.

This sheet music published in 1869 evokes the "Sambo" image. *(Library of Congress)*

Beginning around 1907, the Rastus character became the central advertising representative of Cream of Wheat. By the 1920's, the smiling black chef was appearing in *National Geographic*, *Etude*, *Needlecraft*, and dozens of other magazines. Racist attitudes often were a part of the advertisements. In a 1921 advertisement that appeared in *Needlecraft* magazine, his lips were tinted red, and he held a small blackboard that stated "Maybe Cream of Wheat ain't got no vitamines. I dont know what them things is. If they's bugs they aint none in Cream of Wheat but she's sho' good to eat and cheap. Costs 'bout 1¢ fo' a great big dish. Rastus."

Uncles

Another recurring character in the Cream of Wheat advertisements is an elderly black man, called simply "Uncle." In a 1921 advertisement that appeared in numerous magazines, a little white boy sits in a Cream of Wheat rickshaw. The boy has a whip drawn to lash the back of an elderly black man who is lighting his cigarette instead of pulling the cart. The words at the bottom of the advertisement are "Giddap, Uncle."

The uncle image, in fact, has its own place in black collectibles. In many ways the uncle was similar to the Sambo, especially the slavery-era Sambo image. Like all black caricatures, they were subservient and inferior to whites. Both were portrayed as ugly, ignorant, perpetual children, but the uncle was older and less likely to be employed. An 1892 advertisement for Dixon's Carburet of Iron Stove Polish features "Uncle Obadiah" and ten pickaninnies. The uncle is old, and his clothes are patched. A modern, sanitized version is the image on Uncle Ben's Rice. Like Aunt Jemima, he has gradually been updated through the years, acquiring lighter skin and softer features.

Jiggers

The image of the fun-loving, work-hating black man known as the jigger was not especially beneficial for food advertisers, but it sold toys, banks, songs, sheet music, postcards, posters, and novelty items. Sheet music with jigger images on the cover had titles such as "Rastus Rag," "Koonville Koonlets," "How Come You Do Me Like You Do," and "The Parade of the Darktown Wangdoodles." Interestingly, the jiggers (sometimes called coons) were often presented as brown-skinned rather than black, though they retained the exaggerated lips of the Sambo, mammy, and other caricatures. For example, the sheet music for "There's a Dark Man Coming with a Bundle" shows an extravagantly dressed brown-skinned man. The jigger was also a favorite theme in mechanical toys. The Tomb Alabama Coon Jigger is typical. It shows a slim, dark-brown, gaudily dressed figure. When wound, the figure does a tap dance.

—David Pilgrim

See also: Advertising.

Suggested Readings:

Bogle, Donald. *Toms, Coons, Mulattoes, Mammies, and Bucks: An Interpretive History of Blacks in American Film.* 3d ed. New York: Continuum, 1994.

Congdon-Martin, Douglas. *Images in Black: 150 Years of Black Collectibles.* West Chester, Pa.: Schiffer, 1990.

Goings, Kenneth W. *Mammy and Uncle Mose: Black Collectibles and American Stereotyping.* Bloomington: Indiana University Press, 1994.

Kisch, John, and Edward Mapp. *A Separate Cinema: Fifty Years of Black-Cast Posters.* New York: Farrar, Straus & Giroux, 1992.

Reno, Dawn E. *Collecting Black Americana.* New York: Crown, 1986.

Turner, Patricia A. *Ceramic Uncles and Celluloid Mammies: Black Images and Their Influence on Culture.* New York: Anchor Books, 1994.

Young, Jackie. *Black Collectibles: Mammy and Her Friends.* West Chester, Pa.: Schiffer, 1988.

College fraternities and sororities: American college fraternities and sororities were established to help college men and women learn to live together socially. They create a social life for undergraduate students who are their members. They have their own club songs, stories, and rituals. Two or three Greek letters name the societies; only inducted members know their full meaning and symbolic importance. There are rivalries on some college campuses, and to compete for new pledges, clubs hold "rush parties." The National Pan-Hellenic Council (NPHC) lists member fraternities and sororities, which include Greek letter societies founded by African American men and women.

The first intercollegiate Greek letter fraternity in the United States founded by African American college men was Alpha Phi Alpha. A chapter was established at Cornell University, in Ithaca, New York, during 1906. Alpha Phi Alpha has grown to maintain headquarters on Martin Luther King Drive in CHICAGO; it is interracial, and in the 1990's it had over 250 active undergraduate chapters. Two other fraternities were founded at HOWARD UNIVERSITY, Washington D.C., in the early 1900's to benefit male African American students. They are Omega Psi Phi, founded in 1911, and Phi Beta Sigma, founded in 1914.

The first African American women's college sorority, Alpha Kappa Alpha, was established at Howard University in 1908. Two other sororities joined this one on the Howard University campus. The NATIONAL COUNCIL OF NEGRO WOMEN established Delta Sigma Theta in 1913 for women pursuing the teaching profession. Sorority sisters volunteered with organizations such as the Young Women's Christian Association (YWCA), NATIONAL ASSOCIATION FOR THE ADVANCEMENT

OF COLORED PEOPLE, NATIONAL URBAN LEAGUE, Girl Scouts, and Red Cross. A sister sorority, Zeta Phi Beta, was established in 1920 to complement the men's fraternity Phi Beta Sigma.

The first college men's society, Phi Beta Kappa, was founded in 1776, at the College of William and Mary in Williamsburg, Virginia. The focus of this organization is on promoting one's mental capacities. In 1877 George Washington Henderson was the first black member elected to Phi Beta Kappa. Henderson graduated at the top of his class from the University of Vermont. Henderson went on to Yale Divinity School and became a minister and a professor. Paul ROBESON was elected to Phi Beta Kappa at Rutgers College in New Brunswick, New Jersey. He became an acclaimed actor and singer.

Not all universities had Phi Beta Kappa chapters. In 1949 an article in *The Saturday Evening Post* pointed out that Howard University did not have one. In the furor that followed, three prominent black universities applied for and were accepted to establish chapters of Phi Beta Kappa: FISK UNIVERSITY in 1952, Howard in 1953, and Morehouse College in 1967.

—*Betsy L. Nichols*

See also: Fraternal societies; Historically black colleges.

Collins, Marva (b. August 31, 1936, Monroeville, Alabama): Educator. Collins founded a private school, Westside Preparatory School, in Chicago. In the late 1970's and 1980's the media called Collins a miracle worker because of the impressive results she achieved teaching students labeled as unteachable by the public EDUCATION system.

Beginnings
Marva Collins was born to Henry Knight and Bessie May (Nettles) Knight. Her father was a successful businessman who owned a cattle ranch, a grocery store, and a funeral parlor.

Her book *Marva Collins' Way* (1990) traces her desire to learn, her strong sense of herself, and her determination to live up to examples her father set for her when she was growing up.

Collins learned to read before she went to school. Her formal education began in Monroeville, ALABAMA, in a simple school building in which the primary grades were taught with two grades to a classroom. Since African Americans were not allowed in the libraries in Monroeville, Collins eagerly waited for books she received from her father and other relatives as gifts. She read such books as the Nancy Drew mysteries, Richard WRIGHT's *Black Boy* (1945), and Erskine Caldwell's *God's Little Acre* (1933).

In 1953 Collins graduated from Escambia County Training School, an all-black high school, and enrolled at Clark College, an all-black women's liberal arts school in ATLANTA, GEORGIA. At Clark she majored in secretarial science and took education courses. In 1957 she received her bachelor of arts degree in secretarial sciences and returned to Alabama. Unable to find a secretarial position, she found a job teaching typing, shorthand, bookkeeping, and business law at Monroe County Training School. After two years of teaching, Collins moved to CHICAGO in 1959. There she went to work as a medical secretary at Mount Sinai Hospital. During this time she met Clarence Collins, a drafter with the Sunbeam Corporation, and they were married in 1960.

Chicago Public School System
Collins began teaching in the Chicago public school system at Calhoun South Elementary School in September, 1960. She taught as a full-time substitute without seniority or permanent placement because she lacked enough education credits to qualify for a teaching certificate.

Over the next fourteen years, Collins taught at inner-city schools in Chicago's public school system. Collins felt that many of the teachers working in the inner-city schools were poorly trained and apathetic about teaching. Collins approached her classrooms with innovative ideas. She expected her students to perform to the best of their abilities, and she taught her students more than the required curriculum. Her students read classical literature, performed plays, and learned the Latin roots of words.

While Collins taught at Delano Elementary School, she became increasingly disillusioned with the public school system. In 1975, at age thirty-nine, she quit her job. At the request of a group of parents, Collins agreed to start a private school. With $5,000 from her retirement money, some textbooks that she found in a school trash bin, and space in the basement of Daniel Hale Williams University, Collins began the Daniel Hale Williams Westside Preparatory School with four students.

Westside Preparatory School

To gain greater independence, Collins moved the school into the second floor of her home, a brownstone in West Garfield Park. With the aid of her husband's carpentry skill, Collins converted the second-floor apartment into classrooms. At the same time, she shortened the school's name to Westside Preparatory School. In September, 1980, the school was moved into the second floor of the National Bank of Commerce Building on Madison Street. A year later, in September, 1981, Collins's school moved into two one-story brick buildings on Chicago Avenue.

Westside Preparatory School established a schedule with no recess breaks or gym periods. Students were to spend their days reading, writing, and studying mathematics. Students at all grade levels were to read such writers as William Shakespeare, Plato, Ralph Waldo Emerson, Fyodor Dostoevski, and Dante Alighieri. Each day, students were to write a composition and memorize a quotation of their own choosing. Every two weeks,

each student was expected to read a new book and give an oral or written presentation on it.

In 1979 Westside was featured on the television show *60 Minutes* and in newspapers and magazines across the country. In 1980 President Ronald Reagan asked Collins to become U.S. secretary of education, but she turned down the position to continue her work at Westside. In 1981 *The Marva Collins Story*, a made-for-television film starring Cicely Tyson, was made about Collins and her school.

Westside did accept federal funds but depended on student tuition of $150-$200 a month per student and on donations for its survival. Many celebrities made financial contributions to Westside. Recording artist Prince donated $500,000 to Collins's National Teacher Training Institute, designed to train teachers from across the country in Collins's teaching methods. Actor Mr. T donated $17,000 to sponsor sixty students from a public housing project for a summer reading-and-writing program. In addition, Collins used money she earns from her speaking engagements to support the school.

Criticism

Collins's achievements at Westside were not spared criticism. In 1982 a series of critical news stories questioned her credentials and her claims about her students' achievements. The stories alleged that a résumé for Collins given to students' parents contained a nonexistent degree from Northwestern University, that Collins had refused to let students off the school bus if their tuition had not been paid, that she had inflated students' test scores to make it appear that they had made large educational gains while at Westside, and that she had placed her name on a test that had been copyrighted by C. H. Schutter, the deceased principal of Delano Elementary School, where Collins had once taught.

Collins answered many of the charges

against her on a two-part episode of a television talk show. She insisted that someone had altered her résumé without her knowledge. Collins also admitted that she had once prevented some students from leaving a school bus because their parents had not paid their tuition bill. In reply to the charge of stealing the test, Collins stated that she and Schutter had created the test together. Other charges went unanswered. This criticism of Collins by the media, a few parents, and several past employees did not tarnish Westside's reputation. Its reputation led Kevin Ross, a former Creighton University basketball player, to enroll in the school at age twenty-three in order to improve his basic academic skills. By the end of the school year, Ross's math scores had doubled, and his reading scores had tripled.

Honors and Awards

Collins served on the President's Commission on White House Fellowships and on the National Advisory Board of Private Education. HOWARD UNIVERSITY, Dartmouth College, Chicago State University, and Amherst College awarded her honorary degrees. Her other honors include the Sojourner Truth National Award, Phi Delta Kappa and Chicago Urban League teacher of the year awards, and an award from the American Institute for Public Service.

—*Demetrice A. Worley*

Suggested Readings:

Adler, Jerry, and Donna Foote. "The Marva Collins Story." *Newsweek* (March 8, 1982): 64-65.

Collins, Marva. *"Ordinary" Children, Extraordinary Teachers.* Norfolk, Va.: Hampton Roads, 1992.

Collins, Marva, and Civia Tamarkin. *Marva Collins' Way.* Los Angeles: Jeremy P. Tarcher, 1990.

Davis, Marianna W., ed. *Civil Rights, Politics and Government, Education, Medicine, Science.* Vol. 2 in *Contributions of Black Women to America.* Columbia, S.C.: Kenday Press, 1982.

Kinnon, Joy B. "Marva Collins: The Collins Creed." *Ebony* (December 1996): 122-126.

"Marva Collins." In *Contemporary Heroes and Heroines,* edited by Ray B. Browne. Detroit: Gale Research, 1990.

"Marva Collins." In *What We Know So Far: Wisdom Among Women,* edited by Beth Benatovich. New York: St. Martin's Press, 1995.

Reed, S. "Marva Collins: 'I Take the Kids No One Else Wants!'" *Instructor* 91 (January, 1982): 18-19.

Collins, Robert Frederick (b. January 27, 1931, New Orleans, Louisiana): Federal JUDGE. Collins graduated cum laude from Dillard University with his B.A. degree in 1951. He earned his J.D. degree in 1954 from Louisiana State University. Collins served in the U.S. Army from 1954 to 1956 before beginning his legal career. He became a partner in the firm of Augustine, Collins, Smith and Warren in NEW ORLEANS and worked there from 1956 to 1959. He returned to academia in 1959, when he took a position as law instructor at Southern University Law School. He stayed on the school's faculty until 1961. He became senior partner in Collins, Douglas, and Elie in New Orleans in 1960 and remained with the firm until 1972.

Collins's political career began in the late 1960's. He served as an assistant city attorney and legal adviser in New Orleans from 1967 to 1969 and concurrently served as judge ad hoc of the traffic court of New Orleans. From 1971 to 1972, he served as attorney for the New Orleans Housing Authority.

Collins received his first judgeship in 1972, when he became judge magistrate to the Criminal District Court of Orleans Parish in LOUISIANA. In preparation for his work, Collins attended the University of Nevada National Judge College and graduated in 1973. Presi-

Robert Frederick Collins (center) leaving courthouse after being convicted of accepting a bribe in 1991. *(AP/Wide World Photos)*

can life developed. Among these was the colonization movement, whose members advocated sending FREE BLACKS in the United States to colonies in Africa. The American Society for Colonizing the Free People of Color in the United States, commonly known as the AMERICAN COLONIZATION SOCIETY, was founded in 1816 to further this goal. It counted among its members such prominent national figures as Speaker of the House Henry Clay, U.S. Chief Justice John Marshall, and former president James Madison. A number of its principal figures were southerners.

Foundations of the Movement
The number of free African Americans increased dramatically after the AMERICAN REVOLUTION—from some sixty thousand in 1790 to a quarter of a million by 1820. Many were denied civil and political liberties and lived in POVERTY. In response to these problems, Robert Finley, a PRESBYTERIAN minister in NEW JERSEY, worked to found a colonization society—an organization that would send free black Americans to colonize Africa. Finley argued that colonization would bring three benefits: It would help resolve racial conflicts within the United States, it would allow free blacks to improve their lives free of racial discrimination, and it would create a Christian outpost in Africa from which Christianity would spread across the continent.

Finley also believed that colonization provided a solution to the growing tensions over

dent Jimmy Carter appointed Collins to the post of U.S. district judge for the Eastern District of Louisiana in 1978.

Collins's distinguished career was destroyed in 1991 when he was convicted of taking a bribe from a drug smuggler. The conviction gave him the unfortunate distinction of being the first federal judge to be found guilty of taking a bribe.

Colonization movement: Nineteenth-century effort to relocate free African Americans to colonies in AFRICA. During the early decades of the nineteenth century, a number of reform movements that intended to improve Ameri-

SLAVERY. Slaveholders who opposed freeing slaves because they feared the presence of free blacks in their midst would no longer reject emancipation, he reasoned, because the newly freed slaves would not remain in the United States. Because the slavery issue was so contentious, other members of the colonization society chose to avoid discussion of the relationship between emancipation and colonization. Thus the American Colonization Society was not part of the ABOLITIONIST MOVEMENT. It did not condemn slavery or slaveholders. Although the society sought to improve the lives of free African Americans, it was nonetheless racist in its outlook, seeking to create an all-white United States (except for slaves) by removing members of a race that the society's supporters considered to be inferior.

Thomas Jefferson, who had advocated a colonization plan as early as 1784, appreciated the society's goal. While Jefferson had little interest in the advancement of Christianity in Africa, he hoped that the free black colony would lead to the economic and social development of the continent. Jefferson perceived this benefit as a partial repayment for the havoc and misery that the slave trade had brought to Africans over the centuries. Eventually, however, Jefferson dismissed the colonization society's plans as impossible to achieve. Jefferson pointed out that the cost of transporting free blacks to Africa and establishing the colonies made the project untenable.

Opposition

An 1817 meeting of PHILADELPHIA's free blacks revealed strong African American opposition to colonization. Many African Americans objected to the movement as an insult to members of their race. They also pointed out that the United States was their home and declared that they had no desire to travel to Africa. At another meeting held later that year, the Philadelphia group argued that enslaved blacks would suffer even greater degradation if free blacks left the United States. This objection was echoed by some white abolitionists who came to believe that slaveholders had fostered the colonization program in an attempt to lessen opposition to slavery.

Liberia and Emigration

Despite such objections, the American Colonization Society founded the colony of LIBERIA on the western coast of Africa in 1821. Over the next four decades, some twelve thousand free blacks journeyed to Liberia. The colony survived but did not thrive, in part because the colonization society lacked sufficient funds. The heated debate over whether slavery should be allowed in the new state of MISSOURI in 1820 had destroyed southern support for colonization, which slaveholders began to suspect was a first step toward emancipation. In the North, growing calls for abolition weakened the colonization movement. The society's reputation was further damaged in the 1830's when several of its prominent members repudiated colonization and instead devoted their energies to the antislavery movement.

The 1840's did not see an improvement in the American Colonization Society's fortunes. Unable to raise funds, the group was in considerable debt. Liberia had proved to be unmanageable, and the American press carried stories about the internal problems of the colony. In 1846 the society abandoned control over the colony, calling upon colony leaders to declare Liberia an independent state. With this act, the American Colonization Society became an emigration organization, sponsoring the voluntary migration of free blacks to Liberia rather than advocating any large-scale forced colonization program. In this capacity it had greater success, receiving increased funding and sponsoring the emigration of some four thousand emigrants between 1846 and 1854.

The Civil War and After

Colonization again became an issue during the CIVIL WAR, when many northerners feared that thousands of slaves would seek freedom and refuge in the northern states. In 1862 Congress appropriated funds to colonize former slaves living in Washington, D.C. President Abraham Lincoln approved a plan to establish a colony in Haiti. When this scheme's promoters proved to be crooked, Lincoln had to send a ship to rescue the starving colonists. Although Lincoln remained interested in colonization, events in the war outstripped efforts to send free blacks abroad, and the plans came to naught.

After the Civil War, some black leaders such as Henry McNeal TURNER and Alfred Sam called for African Americans to move to Africa as a remedy to the discrimination that they encountered in American society. However, these efforts are more properly considered emigration rather than colonization movements. The American Colonization Society remained in existence during this period, a tiny group apparently committed to remembering the past rather than actively promoting colonization or emigration.

—*Thomas Clarkin*

Suggested Readings:

Griffith, Cyril E. *The African Dream: Martin R. Delany and the Emergence of Pan-African Thought.* University Park: Pennsylvania State University Press, 1975.

Kinsasha, Kwando M. *Emigration vs. Assimilation: The Debate in the African American Press, 1827-1861.* Jefferson, N.C.: McFarland, 1988.

Staudenraus, P. J. *The African Colonization Movement, 1816-1865.* New York: Columbia University Press, 1961.

Colorado: Colorado has one of the largest African American populations in the intermountain West, and African Americans have played prominent roles in state and local communities. Its 1997 African American population of about 168,000 represented slightly more than 4 percent of the state's total population of 3.9 million.

African Americans—slaves and freed—were among the first settlers at the Pike's Peak gold fields in the 1850's. Only forty-six free African Americans were listed in the 1860 census, and European Americans refused blacks suffrage in 1861 and 1865 and excluded African Americans from the school systems. Congress rejected the territory's 1867 application for statehood, and there were those who believed the rejection occurred because by then blacks had been given suffrage. Blacks maintained the right to vote, schools were integrated, and blacks could be officers and jurors, although segregated housing continued for ninety years. African Americans Barney FORD and William Jefferson Hardin, who supported statehood, were members of the territorial legislature.

New mining opportunities and the arrival of the railroad brought more African Americans to Colorado. Blacks also came to homestead and form colonies. By 1890 there were 3,780 blacks, and Denver had a successful black community; many African Americans elsewhere in the state, however, faced significant discrimination. Despite CIVIL RIGHTS legislation, many blacks were forced to live in GHETTO areas, had limited employment opportunities, were barred from some businesses, and were bothered by the police.

WORLD WAR II brought increased employment opportunities and more blacks to Colorado. In 1969 the Denver School Board adopted a busing program to integrate Denver's schools; some white parents attempted to block the program, but the U.S. SUPREME COURT ruled in favor of the school district in 1973.

Through the years African Americans have developed a strong community and held important leadership positions in Colorado.

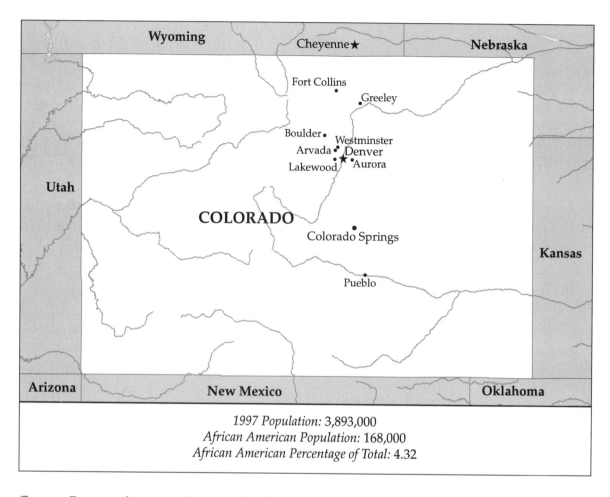

1997 Population: 3,893,000
African American Population: 168,000
African American Percentage of Total: 4.32

George BROWN, for example, was the first black state senator, and he was elected state lieutenant governor in 1973. That same year Penfield Tate became mayor of Boulder, and Wellington Webb was elected to the state legislature. In 1991 Webb became Denver's first black MAYOR.

—*Jessie L. Embry*

Color consciousness: Awareness of racial differences. For most people, colors serve as a form of expression and provide opportunities for creativity. Early in life, individuals learn to prefer certain colors in clothing, toys, or other personal possessions. Color takes on meaning that goes far beyond preference when it is used to describe people. For those individuals who have come to be known as "people of color," skin tone carries an identity and determines a way of life as well as the quality of that life.

With the exception of gender, no other inherited or achieved characteristic so defines an individual life from birth to death as does color. Therefore, it is not surprising that African Americans, reflecting the importance assigned to color by contemporary society, have come to identify themselves primarily in terms of color. In this context, color has long expressed or implied a value judgment: White is better than black, brown, or almond. Skin color is linked to such personal qualities as character, intelligence, honesty, and ambition. Even if these messages are not verbalized, they are implied by the behavior of individuals and groups and by the rewards and advantages of everyday life, particularly as experienced through schools, churches, jobs, and political positions. The United States is by no means the only society in the modern world that is highly color conscious. It is, however, one of the longest-surviving color hierarchies.

African Americans have been known by different labels at different times in history: "Negroes," "coloreds," "blacks," "people of color," "Afro-Americans," and "African Americans." Most of these terms are labels denoting color. "Negro," for example, comes from Spanish *negro*, for black. For many years, "colored" was the term used by some whites

to show a degree of respect for some African Americans. It was most likely to be used in polite exchanges or in the delicate balancing act maintained between employees and employers who knew that they needed each other. "Colored" was also used by whites to acknowledge that some African Americans were different (meaning more acceptable) than others. In personal interaction, "colored" served as protection against that slip of the tongue when whites would "misspeak," using the derogatory but familiar "nigger" instead of Negro.

In the 1960's, African Americans took the very thing used to define their daily exis-

An exhibit titled "African American Identity and American Culture" at the Strong Museum in Rochester, New York, addressed such issues as how names such as "Colored" and "Negro" arose. *(Don Franklin)*

tence—their color—and attempted to transform it into a positive identity. Asserting that they were known for color above all, they began to identify themselves as "black" people. "Black" became part of daily language and part of a cultural revolution represented by slogans such as "Black Is Beautiful" and the popular James BROWN song "Say It Loud, I'm Black and I'm Proud." It was a symbolic revolution driven by African Americans' determination to cultivate group pride, especially in their children. The term "African American" began to be used interchangeably with "black" in the 1980's. Thus the primary term of identification was related to continent of origin (of one's forebears) rather than color.

Even in a social climate that is much improved from that experienced by earlier generations, some groups are still defined, and their daily lives largely determined, by color. Several reasons may be advanced to explain this situation. First, color determines the opportunities to which individuals have access as well as those which they are denied in life. Second, the preference for light or near-white skin color over darker shades serves to divide and fracture groups that need to stand together. African Americans have suffered the most in this respect because of the varying shades of color clearly manifest among them. Finally, color as defined in the United States is assigned such importance that it serves to shape what individuals think of themselves, in terms of self-esteem as well as group pride or heritage.

Color and Opportunity

U.S. culture and society have long shown a preference for groups whose physical characteristics resemble those found among the peoples of Western Europe. The more so-called white characteristics that a person possesses, the more opportunities—economic, educational, and social—are afforded to him or her. Since the days of SLAVERY, color has been a good predictor of privilege in the United States.

During the era of slavery, many free people of color were the illegitimate offspring of white slave masters and black slave mothers. Known as MULATTOES, these mixed-race offspring were often provided a rudimentary education and a job skill and were set free. Freedom was granted not so much out of paternal love as it was to remove these children from the household, especially from the view of the white mistress. Such advantages may have been provided out of a sense of guilt, yet they afforded mulattoes a much-needed boost in securing employment, in founding small businesses, and in pursuing skilled professions. Even if the mixed-race offspring (usually light-skinned) were not set free and "sent away," they frequently were given some of the most desirable jobs available. Jobs as servants in the "big house" or as craftspeople (blacksmiths, carpenters, and other skilled workers) were preferable to working in the fields. The darker the skin, the further from the "big house" an individual was likely to be during the slave period. As an added advantage, house servants were sometimes taught to read and write (even though illegal for slaves) or learned from the master's white children.

There is strong evidence that color in individuals or groups has traditionally been associated with certain advantages or disadvantages. This association is referred to in the black community with the phrase "light at the top." Sociologists Elisabeth Mullins and Paul Sites studied the origins of contemporary eminent black Americans (*American Sociological Review*, 1984). Among other things, what these persons had in common was that they tended to rank toward the lighter end of the color continuum.

Bart Landry's book *The New Black Middle Class* (1987) documents the close association between color and economic success and social acceptance for blacks. According to Landry, it was not until about 1915 or 1920 that the criteria for membership in the black upper classes began to shift from color to achievement (education, business success, and so forth). The economic advantage of color, however, is not totally a thing of the past. In their 1990 study published in the journal *Social Forces*, sociologists Michael G. Hughes and Bradley R. Hertel found that "the significance of color remains." For example, light-skinned blacks were reported to be better off than those of darker skin color in earnings, in education, and in job level. In a 1995 issue of *The Chronicle of Higher Education*, James Johnson, Jr., and Walter C. Farrell, Jr., reported that in Chicago, "race and skin tone play a major role in who works and who does not." Being African American and dark was found to reduce the odds of working by 52 percent.

Many modern observers argue that the problems remaining for African Americans are economic in nature, that racism as an oppressive force is largely a thing of the past. It is true that money, talent, and special abilities— all of which are evident in the entertainment world and in sports—cut across racial barriers. Yet even well-known African Americans may find themselves in situations in which they are treated as just another black face, and almost any middle-class or professional African American has had such experiences. In his book *Race Matters* (1993), author Cornel WEST described his painful failure to secure a cab in New York City. Black professional women have been stopped in the halls of luxury hotels and asked to provide maid service. Middle- and upper-class African Americans may experience racism less frequently than their poorer brothers and sisters, but

such experiences can nonetheless be personally devastating. Color remains a constant obstacle to be overcome.

Divided by Color

Color is not a topic that African Americans generally discuss openly with whites. Color consciousness has been called the "dirty little secret" that blacks guard, knowing that it divides them as a people, as a community, and even as families. Perhaps the saddest legacy of racism in the United States is the attention

NATIONAL BESTSELLER

Race Matters

"As moving as any of the sermons of the Rev. Martin Luther King, as profound as W.E.B. Du Bois's *The Souls of Black Folk*, as exhilarating in their offering of liberation as James Baldwin's early essays."
—*Washington Post Book World*

Cornel West

In *Race Matters*, Cornel West picks up W. E. B. Du Bois's argument that the "problem of the twentieth century is the problem of the color line."

given to differences in skin color within the black community. Since the days of the elite "blue vein" societies for light-skinned southern blacks, African Americans have seemingly accepted, at least partially, white society's color hierarchy.

Persons at both ends of the color continuum have been (and still are) the target of hostility from other blacks. It is evident that light-skinned members of the black community have traditionally enjoyed certain opportunities that were denied to their darker peers. At the same time, however, they have been subjected to prejudiced attitudes within their own group held by individuals who resent or even envy their color. Persons with light skin experience mixed messages in response to their color; to be "light" is to be envied by some and hated by others. MALCOLM X enjoyed some social advantages because he was light in color and had green eyes and reddish-brown hair. Yet he recalled in his autobiography that he came to "hate every drop of the white rapist's blood" that was in him as a result of his mother's ancestry.

The African American community has its own language to communicate different skin tones and attitudes toward them. For example, if one is "color-struck," he or she is known for taking great pride in being light-skinned or for associations with those who are light in color. To be "partial to color" is to show a preference for those of light color. Light skin tones have many different labels: "half white," "light," "bright," "fair," "brown-skinned," "red-bone," "high yellow," or "yellow," to name some of the most common. Persons who are dark in color are frequently referred to as "chocolate," "dark," "ink spot," "blue black," "ink black," "shiny black," "coal black," or "tarbaby"; other descriptions gauge their color in reference to something else: "black as a hoot owl," "black as the ace of spades." In 1946 Charles H. Parrish reported in the *Journal of Negro Education* that he had found 145 differ-

ent terms to describe skin color in the vocabulary of African American teenagers.

In the nineteenth century, whites became so obsessed with preserving their genetic traits that they began to use (and even to legalize) what was known as the "one-drop rule." Any known African ancestry, regardless of how remote, required one to be identified as "Negro" or "colored." In the black community, however, it was skin color rather than proportion of ancestry that made the difference.

Whites who become aware of color discrimination within the black community often use such knowledge to rationalize their own behavior and thinking. For this reason, cases such as that of Tracy Morrow Walker are not usually made public. Walker, a light-skinned African American, knew that her dark-skinned supervisor discriminated against her and believed that this discrimination was caused by her color. She filed a formal complaint under Title VII of the Civil Rights Act of 1964, a provision that prohibits discrimination on the basis of color as well as race, sex, religion, or national origin. Her case eventually became a federal lawsuit that was decided on appeal in Walker's favor in 1990.

A Question of Identity

The primary reason for the growing Afrocentricism in the United States may well be that it offers a history and a heritage that precedes and is separated from slavery, segregation, and racism. People of African ancestry living in the United States would like the ideal of Africa to serve the same purpose for them that Israel does for Jews. Yet Africa is a continent, an enormous land mass with numerous subgroups of people who possess diverse cultural traditions. Personal or group identification with an entity such as Africa is more intellectual than emotional. Identification with specific states, or tribes, or even regions is difficult for most African Americans to establish given the effective destruction of their slave ancestors' knowledge of their African origins upon arriving in the United States. Nevertheless, African Americans are working to forge a renewed identity and cultural heritage from their African roots.

Perhaps the most dramatic evidence of the importance of color in the formation of personal identity and sense of self-worth is found in the "doll studies" first reported by Kenneth and Mamie Clark in "The Development of Consciousness of Self and the Emergence of Racial Identification in Negro Preschool Children," published in the *Journal of Social Psychology* in 1939. Children as young as three consistently showed a preference for white dolls over black or colored dolls. Their explanations were that the white doll looked "prettier," "nicer," or "smarter."

In *The Color Complex* (1992), authors Kathy Russell, Midge Wilson, and Ronald Hall summarized later doll studies. Some studies conducted in the 1980's produced results similar to the Clarks' original findings; others did not. Russell, Wilson, and Hall show that the negative identities and color associations can be unlearned or overcome by consistent use of positive messages associated with differences such as skin color. Positive identity messages must also come from many different sources. Although it is not totally sufficient, it is especially important that parents give their children positive messages about themselves, their race, and their heritage. These messages, however, must be reinforced by schools, by churches, by government, and especially by the media.

In child rearing, parents are expected to follow a pattern that will successfully prepare or socialize their children for life as productive, law-abiding citizens and as functional, emotionally fulfilled family members. The parents of African American children have an added responsibility in preparing their children to live in a society that will devalue and perhaps damage them because of their color. For example, among an ethnically diverse group of parents discussing strategies for training their children and preparing them for life outside the family, the African Americans in the group, without exception (and without having conferred in advance) all mentioned two things that set them apart from other parents. First, they believed it was necessary to teach their children how to respond the first time somebody called them a "nigger." Second, they needed to teach their sons how to act (and how to survive) when stopped by white law enforcement officers.

In a world that remains highly color conscious, the racial self-identity of children is truly a matter of survival. There is little doubt that those who will survive to become emotionally healthy adults are those who were taught not only the harsh realities of a racial society but also a healthy sense of self born of family and group pride. Color is merely a perceived difference. It is people, beginning with the black community itself, who make it into a positive or a negative experience.

—*Joyce E. Williams*

See also: Passing; Race, racism, and race relations; Racial discrimination.

Suggested Readings:

Appiah, Anthony, and Amy Gutmann. *Color Conscious: The Political Morality of Race.* Princeton, N.J.: Princeton University Press, 1996.

Cose, Ellis. *The Rage of a Privileged Class.* New York: HarperCollins, 1993.

Evans, Gaynelle. "Color-Coded Hearts: Color Consciousness Among Blacks." *Black Issues in Higher Education* 13 (July 11, 1996): 42-43.

Feagin, Joe R., and Melvin P. Sikes. *Living with Racism: The Black Middle-Class Experience.* Boston: Beacon Press, 1994.

Hughes, Michael G., and Bradley R. Hertel. "The Significance of Color Remains: A Study of Life Chances, Mate Selection, and Ethnic

Consciousness Among Black Americans."
Social Forces 68, no. 4 (1990): 1105-1120.

Johnson, James H., Jr. and Walter C. Farrell, Jr. "Race Still Matters." *The Chronicle of Higher Education* 40 (July 7, 1995): A48.

Landry, Bart. *The New Black Middle Class.* Berkeley: University of California Press, 1987.

Russell, Kathy, Midge Wilson, and Ronald Hall. *The Color Complex: The Politics of Skin Color Among African Americans.* New York: Harcourt Brace Jovanovich, 1992.

West, Cornel. *Race Matters.* Boston: Beacon Press, 1993.

Colored American Opera Company: First African American opera company established in the United States. It began in WASHINGTON, D.C., in 1872, featuring several local artists. Its roster included Agnes Gray Smallwood, soprano; Lena Miller and Mary A. Coakley, contraltos; Henry Grant and Richard Tompkins, tenors; William T. Benjamin and George Jackson, baritones; and Thomas H. Williams, bass. The music director was John Esputa, and the business manager was Henry Donohoe. There was also a chorus of about thirty voices.

The only documented performances of the company came the year after its formation, in 1873. The work performed was Julius Eichberg's *Doctor of Alcantara.* The company performed the work at Lincoln Hall in Washington, D.C., in February of that year. It repeated the performance later that month at the Agricultural Hall in Philadelphia, Pennsylvania. The performances received very favorable reviews in the African American press. There is no record of other performances by the company.

The Colored American Opera Company was the forerunner of several African American opera companies that formed in the twentieth century, including the Drury Opera Company (New York, 1900-1930's), Aeolian Opera Association (New York, 1934), Detroit Negro Opera (1938), National Negro Opera Company (Pittsburgh, 1941-1962), American Negro Opera Company (1944), Opera Ebony (Philadelphia, started in 1974), and Opera South (Jackson, Mississippi, started in 1970). *See also:* Classical and operatic music.

Colored Farmers' Alliance: Social, economic, and political organization formed in 1886. The POPULIST MOVEMENT of the 1890's was composed primarily of farmers in the American Midwest and South who banded together in organizations called alliances to put political pressure on local, state, and federal government to alleviate their problems. These problems included low prices for cotton, corn, and wheat; unfair freight charges; difficulty in borrowing; and foreclosures. These alliances coalesced into the Populist Party, which was to represent farm and labor interests nationwide.

In the South, black farmers formed the Colored Farmers' Alliance in 1886 to represent their interests. Patterned on the Midwest Alliance and the Southern Alliance, the Colored Farmers' Alliance worked with these groups on issues common to white and black farmers. For a short while in the 1890's, it looked as though poor white and black farmers in the South, through their respective alliances, would at last unite against their common enemies—owners of large PLANTATIONS, the railroads, and the industrialists of the "New South."

The grand coalition was not to be. Those ruling the South in the 1890's skillfully played on the racial fears, prejudices, and insecurities of poor white farmers to separate them from poor African Americans. By the mid-1890's, white farmers viewed their black counterparts as enemies and supported attempts to remove African Americans from the South's political and civic system. Hostilities were heightened by a call by the Colored Farmers' Alliance for a strike by cotton pickers. In the wake of white indifference and hostility, the Colored Farmers' Alliance collapsed, taking with it the best chance for interracial cooperation in the South during the nineteenth century. The destruction of the alliance helped cripple the Populist movement in the South, as many white Populists became vociferous racists who blamed African Americans for their problems.

See also: Agriculture; Sharecropping; Southern Tenant Farmers' Union.

Coltrane, Alice (Turiya Sagittinanda; b. August 27, 1937, Detroit, Michigan): JAZZ musician. Trained in the classics, Coltrane learned to perform on piano, organ, and harp. She studied jazz piano with noted jazz player Bud Powell. In 1966 she married tenor saxophonist John COLTRANE. Among the artists with whom she performed are Coltrane (she replaced McCoy TYNER in his quartet), Kenny

Alice Coltrane in 1976. *(AP/Wide World Photos)*

Burrell, Lucky Thompson, Yusef Lateef, and Johnny Griffin. She also worked with her own ensemble. She founded the Vedantic Center in California in 1972. Her recordings *Ptah the El Daoud* (1970) and *Transfiguration* (1978) reflect her spirituality.

Coltrane, John (September 23, 1926, Hamlet, North Carolina—July 17, 1967, Huntington, New York): JAZZ saxophonist. John William Coltrane was born in Hamlet, NORTH CAROLINA, and grew up in nearby High Point. He was reared in the home of his grandfather, Walter Blair, the pastor of St. Stephen's AFRICAN METHODIST EPISCOPAL ZION CHURCH. Early musical influences on John included his father, who played violin and ukelele, and his mother, who played piano. His elementary musical education came in a community band, where he learned to play clarinet, and in the William Penn High School Band, where he took up the alto saxophone. His first commitment was to playing the alto saxophone, and he was influenced by the playing style of Johnny HODGES of the Duke ELLINGTON Orchestra.

Early Professional Career

After he completed high school, Coltrane moved to PHILADELPHIA, where, while working as a laborer in a sugar refinery, he studied music at the Ornstein School of Music. By 1945 he was drafted for military service, and he completed his tour of duty as a clarinetist in a Navy band. He returned to Philadelphia in June of 1946 and was able to obtain work as a backup musician for a variety of rhythm-and-blues performers. During this time, he played for King Colax, Joe Webb, Shirley Scott, Jimmy SMITH, and Big Maybelle, among others. He obtained his first extended professional musical employment with Eddie "Cleanhead" Vinson's band in 1947. Vinson was himself an alto player, so Coltrane was forced to take up the tenor saxophone, the horn he would play for most of his career. This band toured cross-country in 1947 and 1948, and Coltrane was heavily influenced by his bandleader. He also came into contact with the playing styles of Coleman HAWKINS and Charlie "Bird" PARKER.

After leaving Vinson in mid-1947, Coltrane played with groups headed by Jimmy Heath and Howard McGhee before joining Dizzy GILLESPIE's big band in mid-1949. Gillespie was trying to tour with a large band that played predominantly BEBOP-influenced tunes. It was with Gillespie that Coltrane had his first recording experience in 1949. In this band, he also came into contact with Yusef Lateef, who first stimulated his interest in Eastern religious traditions.

Coltrane left the Gillespie group (which was by then a sextet) in early 1951 and re-turned to Philadelphia. He once again took up a more formal musical education and enrolled in the Granoff School of Music, where he came under the tutelage of Dennis Sandole and Matthew Rastelli. While at Granoff, Coltrane was introduced to the European art-music tradition; he was especially interested in the work of Claude Debussy, Maurice Ravel, Béla Bartok, and Igor Stravinsky.

Professional work in the early to mid-1950's included stints with the bands of Earl Bostic and Johnny Hodges. It was his association with Miles DAVIS, begun in the spring of 1955, however, that launched Coltrane into the upper echelon of American jazz performers. Coltrane was an essential part of such mid-decade classic jazz albums as 'Round About Midnight and Cookin' that helped to negotiate the transition from the cool to hard-bop style and were prophetic of future challenges. He also began a friendship with fellow tenor player Sonny ROLLINS that resulted in the seminal Tenor Madness; during this period, Coltrane picked up the nickname "Trane." On October 3, 1955, Coltrane married Juanita Grubbs, better known as Naima.

Inconsistent and unreliable performance, likely the result of a serious drug addiction, led to Coltrane's being dropped from the Davis group. In the early spring of 1957, Coltrane had a "conversion": He kicked his drug and alcohol habits and emerged with a new spiritual consciousness. Thelonious MONK invited him to join his group that same year. It was an association which, like that with Davis, would challenge and change Coltrane's conception of jazz. This positive collaboration

Saxophonist John Coltrane. *(Library of Congress)*

led to Coltrane's being offered his own exclusive recording contract with Prestige Records, also in 1957.

Experimental Music

Coltrane reunited with Davis and recorded *Kind of Blue* in October of 1958. That recording, along with his own *Giant Steps*, in April, 1959, and new works by Ornette Coleman and others, signaled the beginnings of a new direction for jazz. Labeled by some "free jazz" (or, more pejoratively, "antijazz"), this new music moved away from the restrictions of the Western song form and experimented with melody, harmonic progression, and non-Western scales and rhythms. It is important to note, however, that the new movement was itself extremely diverse.

Coltrane's contribution to this new music would be most fully worked out within the John Coltrane Quartet, formed in April of 1960. The group's original personnel included Steve Kuhn (piano), Steve Davis (bass), Pete LaRoca (drums), and Coltrane on tenor saxophone. Personnel changes included participation by Reggie Workman (bass) and Billy Higgins (drums) before the emergence of the classic John Coltrane Quartet, which was McCoy TYNER (piano), Jimmy Garrison (bass), and Elvin Jones (drums). In this context, Coltrane began experimenting with the soprano saxophone as well as his traditional tenor.

My Favorite Things, from September of 1960, was an unprecedented success. The highlight of this album was Coltrane's interpretation of the classic show tune from the 1959 musical *The Sound of Music*. The large sales of that album assured Coltrane of a broad following and a steady income throughout the remainder of his career. By 1961 Coltrane was recording for Impulse Records, which released many of his 1960's classics: *Africa Brass* (which featured investigations of African and Indian music), *A Love Supreme* (a profoundly religious recording stemming from Coltrane's 1957 conversion), *Ascension*, and *Meditations*. He also participated in a successful collaboration with Duke Ellington and regularly released (at the urging of producer Bob Thiele) more conservative, ballad-oriented albums.

Personal and Professional Turbulence

Coltrane left Naima, with whom he had three children, in mid-1963, and married Alice McCleod, an accomplished jazz pianist and harpist from Detroit, in 1966. Alice COLTRANE eventually replaced McCoy Tyner at the piano in December of 1965; Tyner left to pursue solo projects. The mid-1960's were a volatile period for American culture generally and for Coltrane personally. His extended musical experiments were subject to much hostile criticism, and his experiments in instrumentation led to difficulties with the members of his band. Eric Dolphy, a flute player who had been a regular contributor to Coltrane recordings and concerts and who was also a close friend, died in 1964. The introduction of a second drummer, Rashied Ali, into the group led to extended conflicts with Elvin Jones.

Coltrane's following, however, was broad and committed. European tours in 1961 and 1963 and a tour of Japan in 1966 brought Coltrane wide international recognition. He regularly finished at or near the top of *Playboy* and *Downtown* magazine jazz polls, and he was named to the *Down Beat* Hall of Fame in October of 1965.

Continual medical problems, perhaps the result of earlier drug and alcohol problems, began to take their toll. John Coltrane died July 17, 1967, of liver failure. Memorial services were held throughout the country.

Musical Accomplishment

One way of understanding Coltrane's contribution is to consider his use of rhythm. Coltrane attempted to further subdivide rhythmic accent into a sharp sixteenth-note pattern. As Louis ARMSTRONG and Charlie Parker before him took the predominant musical style of the day and quickened it, so did Coltrane. A popular description of his musical style in the late 1950's was "sheets of sound." He also investigated music in a cross-cultural context and was deeply influenced by East Indian Ravi Shankar and Nigerian drummer Olatunji.

Coltrane's most challenging work of the 1960's attempted to investigate the possibilities for music outside the traditional Western diatonic scale. Often, the results were long solos by Coltrane and members of his group that made use of repetitive modal patterns. For the nonspecialist, it is probably best to think about Coltrane's accomplishment as one of dynamic experimentation. He was rarely satisfied with the direction of his musical performance and composition and was willing to investigate all avenues. Most important, he was a master of the tenor saxophone, revived interest in the soprano saxophone, and provided the inspiration for a whole generation of imitators. His performances generated powerful responses from his audience and sparked challenging critical debates.

Cultural Impact

Coltrane's spiritual and artistic intensity often gave his compositions and performances the character of a religious ceremony. Such compositions as "Alabama" (a response to the 1963 Birmingham church bombing) spoke eloquently to issues being dealt with in American and African American culture. Because of his intensity and topicality, he tended to inspire a powerful devotion among members of his audience. *A Love Supreme* is both a musical and cultural monument. A "devotional text," it celebrates his spiritual conversion and 1957 victory over drugs. In an era that appreciated such spiritual investigation, Coltrane stood out as a major figure.

As a central figure in the "new black music," or musical avant-garde, Coltrane helped to define an African American art form little concerned with mainstream critical acceptance. His ability to move easily from challenging long works to interpretations of popular ballads helped to develop an audience for the avant-garde. While he eschewed politics, many commentators and followers found political implications within his work. The celebration of musical freedom was, for many, a clear commentary upon the realities of American race politics and the challenges of the Civil Rights movement. Coltrane and his work have provided inspiration for artists in other fields such as poets Michael S. HARPER and Amiri BARAKA and choreographer Alvin AILEY, among many others.

—*James C. Hall*

Suggested Readings:

Budds, Michael J. *Jazz in the Sixties*. Iowa City: University of Iowa Press, 1990.

Fraim, John. *Spirit Catcher: The Life and Art of John Coltrane*. West Liberty, Ohio: GreatHouse, 1996.

Fujioka, Yasuhiro, Lewis Porter, and Yoh-ichi Hamada, eds. *John Coltrane: A Discography and Musical Biography*. Metuchen, N.J.: Scarecrow Press, 1995.

Hester, Karlton E. *The Melodic and Polyrhythmic Development of John Coltrane's Spontaneous Composition in a Racist Society*. Lewiston, N.Y.: Edwin Mellen Press, 1997.

Kofsky, Frank. *John Coltrane and the Jazz Revolution of the 1960's*. 2d ed. New York: Pathfinder, 1998.

Litweiler, John. *The Freedom Principle: Jazz After 1958*. New York: William Morrow, 1984.

Nisenson, Eric. *Ascension: John Coltrane and His Quest*. New York: St. Martin's Press, 1993.

Porter, Lewis. *John Coltrane: His Life and Music*. Ann Arbor: University of Michigan Press, 1998.

Simpkins, Cuthbert O. *Coltrane: A Biography*. Baltimore: Black Classic Press, 1989.

Thomas, J. C. *Chasin' the Trane: The Music and Mystique of John Coltrane*. Garden City, N.Y.: Doubleday, 1975.

Williams, Martin. "John Coltrane: A Man in the Middle." In *The Jazz Tradition*. New York: Oxford University Press, 1983.

Woideck, Carl, ed. *The John Coltrane Companion: Five Decades of Commentary*. New York: Schirmer Books, 1998.

Columnists: Writers of regular features in PRINT JOURNALISM. Among the great, even legendary, African American columnists of the past are Ida B. WELLS, Ethel PAYNE, Martin DELANY, Frederick DOUGLASS, Samuel Ringgold WARD, Langston HUGHES, Benjamin MAYS, and W. E. B. DU BOIS. Modern African American newspaper columnists continue to write in a tradition that emphasizes social justice.

Speaking or writing for African Americans has never been easy, and it was particularly problematic in the early years of the twentieth century. Spanning the era of the HARLEM RE-

NAISSANCE, the crusading journalism career of Ida B. Wells stands as a journalistic marker of militancy, courage, and determination. Decades later, beginning in the early 1970's, many of the nation's best black columnists, molded in the Wells tradition, could be read in major daily newspapers from coast to coast; among them were Michael Cottman of *Newsday*, Brenda Payton of the *Oakland Tribune*, Dorothy GILLIAM of the *Washington Post*, and DeWayne Wickham of *USA Today*.

Among the nationally known columnists writing in the nation's more than two hundred African American newspapers from the 1970's to the 1990's were Marian Wright EDELMAN (children's rights advocacy), Ron Daniels (political commentary), Sam Lacy (sports), James E. Booker (politics in Washington, D.C.), Barbara REYNOLDS (social commentary), Conrad Worrill (BLACK NATIONALISM), Armstrong Williams (conservative black politics), Earl Ofari Hutchinson (liberal social commen-

Columnist Sam Lacy, seen here in 1991, became the first black sports writer admitted to the Baseball Writer's Association in 1948. *(AP/Wide World Photos)*

tary), Julianne Malveaux (economics and feminism), Lenora Fulani (independent and third-party politics), Carl ROWAN (moderate liberal politics), Chuck Stone (social commentary), Keith Orlando Hilton (HIGHER EDUCATION and media theory), and Manning MARABLE (radical leftist politics). Perhaps the most widely known are Edelman, Rowan, and Marable; Marable's column appeared in about 350 newspapers worldwide in the 1990's.

The very first editorial on the front page of the nation's first black newspaper, FREEDOM's JOURNAL (1827), set the tone and charge for African American newspaper columnists for the ages when it boldly pronounced, "We wish to plead our own cause. Too long have others spoken for us." The newspaper's copublishers, Samuel Eli CORNISH and John RUSSWURM, were arguably philosophically very similar to the consistent positions of Chuck Stone and Conrad Worrill, respectively.

Earl Conrad, a white journalist who worked for the black press in the 1940's, wrote in his 1947 book, *Jim Crow America*, that the African American newspaper press of the 1830-1860 period could be considered the spiritual ancestor of the nation's modern labor and radical press. Often black columnists were leading the charge and raising the banner.

Modern African American columnists offer a spectrum of opinions, and they frequently disagree with one another. Within their writings, readers are privy to lively exchanges, humor, social satire, ideas, and opinions that debate such issues as race-based scholarships in higher education, AFFIRMATIVE ACTION, the economic status of black America, and questions such as "What about Africa in the twenty-first century?"

It is perhaps via columnists' opinions, editorials, and letters to the editor that the African American public agenda is most consistently mapped out. If history is an indicator, the pens of black columnists will continue to be called upon to articulate African America's public agenda—and, equally important, to lead the fight against racism and discrimination.

—*Keith Orlando Hilton*

See also: Black press.

Comedy and humor: African American humor has influenced the nature of popular culture since the beginnings of American society. The eclectic nature of this expression reaches beyond ethnic and cultural boundaries, rooting itself in the very essence of American entertainment.

Origins and History

In tracing the origins of African American humor, one must first acknowledge the contributions of the West African culture that was brought to American shores. When the first Africans arrived in the New World through the slave trade, they brought with them a history and culture that embodied a different sense of time and space. In music, the drum and its polyrhythms dominated social customs and religious rituals derived from the people's experience in West AFRICA.

DANCE forms emerged from tribal traditions and shuffle beats; songs were created from the cries and shouts of nature. The wit and humor derived from the oral traditions of West African *griots* were shaped by the oppressive conditions of an enslaved existence. Comic humor aided the first Africans in coping with the alienation that resulted from being transported through the Middle Passage to a new and strange world. Forged in the crucible of the slave experience, the ability to entertain one's self and others enabled African Americans to deal with hardships and cope with an uncertain future.

Minstrels and Minstrel Shows

The black comic tradition evolved out of the MINSTREL traditions of the 1820's. Popular minstrel shows provided sporadic opportunities for black entertainers prior to the CIVIL WAR. While some were allowed to perform as minstrels without darkening their faces with cork, few black performers were allowed to travel in road shows or appear on stages reserved for white performers. Whites who corked their faces presented stereotyped simulations of the slave experience on southern PLANTATIONS. These performances amused and pacified white audiences into believing that black slaves were an inferior subspecies incapable of competing with or being treated as equal to European immigrants.

The minstrel shows of the 1820's through 1840's featured troupes of singers, musicians, comedians, and other performers. Black minstrels such as Signor Corneali and Jon Picayune Butler influenced the most popular white minstrels of the time. One of the most famous of the antebellum minstrel entertainers was William Henry "Master Juba" LANE, an urban saloon dancer who performed with prominent white minstrel troupes. His authenticated routines were adopted from both European and African dance forms. His body movements and hand-slapping gestures created a performance style that was later copied, modified, and perfected by such notable African American dancers as Bill "Bojangles" ROBINSON, Charles "Honi" COLES, Sammy DAVIS, Jr., and Gregory HINES. The hand jive and early shuffles that gave rise to the tap dancing tradition became a permanent feature on the American stage.

As all-black minstrel shows emerged, their acts were billed as "authentic" versions of black life during the plantation days. In reality, most of these performances by black minstrels were not intended to present any semblance of reality. Rather, they were constructed facsimiles designed to draw supportive black audiences who recognized the satiric elements involved as well as naïve white audiences who had little direct contact with African Americans.

During the period from 1850 to 1890, many black-operated and black-owned minstrel troupes emerged to compete with already established white minstrel shows. These minstrel shows traveled extensively throughout the South and Midwest. The most popular venues were in the Northeast and in Europe, where many black minstrels achieved celebrity status. A few black performers had left white-controlled troupes to start their own, such as Charles Hicks's Georgia Minstrels, William McCabe's Georgia Troubadours, Pat Chappelle's Rabbit Foot Company, and Lew Johnson's black-owned Plantation Minstrels.

Some individual minstrel stars, such as James Bland, wrote well-known songs about plantation life although they had no firsthand experience of it. Performer Ernest Hogan popularized the "coon" songs—a genre that helped expand opportunities in the music industry for black entertainers. Many female BLUES singers, including Gertrude "Ma" RAINEY, Ethel WATERS, and Bessie SMITH, and the comedy team of Butter Beans and Susie, worked in the minstrel shows.

African American performers Bob Height and Billy Kersands were among the most notable comics of the era. They created extravaganzas with all-black casts and used advertising techniques and marketing strategies to draw their audiences. Often these minstrel shows produced exaggerated stereotypes bordering on the eccentric. Kersands distinguished himself by perfecting facial distortions that popularized the "coon" character—establishing an archetype and stereotype imitated in and perpetuated by many early silent films and VAUDEVILLE shows of the early twentieth century. The stylized and satirical contortions that Kersands incorporated provoked peals of laughter in his audiences.

The larger the shows and the more eccentric the tricks and illusions they incorporated, the more popular they became. The team of George WALKER and Egbert (Bert) WILLIAMS moved from traveling road shows to minstrel shows to vaudeville. They became the most popular comedy team of their time. After Walker died, Bert Williams signed on to perform with the Ziegfeld Follies. In addition to writing many popular songs, Williams is credited with introducing the CAKEWALK to white audiences. Black audiences accepted and embraced these satiric spectacles and identified with black performers. Many white audiences, however, took these performances to be truthful portrayals, so such performenaces reinforced their skewed perception of black life.

As black comic entertainers gained fame through their performances, some parlayed their wealth into theaters to showcase their talents. The development of the black vaudeville circuit led to the formation of the THEATRE OWNERS BOOKING ASSOCIATION (TOBA), which provided an outlet for these performers to secure work for themselves. The craving for comic entertainment by both black and white audiences extended the interest in BLACKFACE performances, but demand for such comedy eventually diminished.

Linguistic Expression

The wealth of oral tradition found in African American folklore was eventually synthesized into a comedic language. The African American community had developed special bonds forged by their ability to survive the brutality of a slave existence. In this context, humor served several purposes: It allowed African Americans to maintain and secure their identity through the coding of complex social and cultural values, to cope with the alienation of being cut off from family, friends, and traditions, and to poke fun at each other in an attempt to reinforce common attributes they had developed as a result of their status. Laughter was used as armor against impending danger, outside intruders, and adopted values and social mores imposed by the slave master.

This humor was perfected in the form of coded language found in jokes, songs, and folklore. The use of physical gestures, such as facial expressions, body movements, and other mannerisms, aided in the creation of a visual form of communication that could be understood by those who possessed the keys to translating these messages. Vernacular language developed in various forms known as "signifying." The act of "playing the DOZENS" involved one form of self-definition through using quick verbal skills. This verbal competition had its origins in the notion that mothers codify and mold the experience of their male offspring by weakening them to the point of defenselessness. The mother becomes the brunt of most of these verbal jokes, thereby testing competitors' ability to cross the line from verbal challenges to open confrontation.

Other forms of signifying include "jiving" or "jive talk," a form of telling ingenuous statements to avoid detection; "shucking," the act of pretense; "testifying," a way of telling a story for the benefit of documentation and support; "DISSING," a form of humiliation directed against adversaries; and "slamming," a combination of all of these forms within a musical context, particularly in RAP music. These forms are part of a common set of values and attitudes that have transcended time. For example, the popular variety show *In Living Color* (1990-1994), created a stir among middle-class blacks and some confusion among conservative whites as it poked fun at all segments of black life.

The use of exaggerated language, proverbs, punning, and bragging, as well as the religious tradition of call and response—all contributed to the use of language as a pictorial reference point in which the instigator finds some visual aspect of his opponent to exaggerate and develops rhymed verses and word sequences to poke fun. Rhyming and repetition as employed by comedians eventually became

(continued on page 583)

Notable Comedians

Anderson, Eddie "Rochester." *See main text entry.*

Allen, Byron (b. Apr. 22, 1961, Detroit, Mich.). Allen cohosted the television series *Real People* from 1979 to 1984 and hosted *The Byron Allen Show* (1989-1992) and the television special *Jammin'* in 1992. He also guest-hosted on *The Tonight Show* and wrote comedy material for such performers as Jimmie Walker and Freddie Prinze.

Berry, Bertice (b. 1960, Wilmington, Del.). A former Kent State University professor, Berry performed stand-up comedy at various clubs throughout the eastern United States before hosting her own television talk show, *The Bertice Berry Show*, during the 1993-1994 season. Berry then turned to stand-up performances and books, including her autobiography, *Bertice: The World According to Me* (1996), *Straight from the Ghetto: You Know You're Ghetto If . . .* (1996), and *I'm on My Way but Your Foot Is on My Head: A Black Woman's Story of Getting over Life's Hurdles* (1997).

Brown, Ernest "Brownie." A dancer by training, Ernest Brown achieved recognition as a member of the tap team Cook and Brown, which blended tumbling and acrobatics with comedy, satire, and dance. Brown and Charles "Cookie" Cook opened at the COTTON CLUB in Harlem in 1934 and were featured in a number of films, including *52nd Street* (1937), *Toot That Trumpet* (1941), and the short film *Chatter* (1943). The pair also appeared in the Broadway musical *Kiss Me Kate* in 1948. In the 1960's, Brown took part in a tap dance revival at the Newport Jazz Festival.

Cosby, Bill. *See main text entry.*

Fetchit, Stepin. *See main text entry.*

Fletcher, Dusty (d. March 15, 1954). Fletcher toured theaters and clubs across the United States from the 1920's through the 1940's, typically playing a drunk in BLACKFACE, baggy pants, floppy shoes, and a battered tophat. He would attempt unsuccessfully to climb a ladder, finally singing for Richard to open the door. The song "Open the Door, Richard," written by Fletcher and another blackface comic, John Mason, became a hit. His films include *Open the Door,*

Richard (1945), *Hi-de-Ho* (1947), *Killer Diller* (1948), and *Boarding House Blues* (1948).

Foxx, Jamie (Eric Bishop; b. Dec. 13, 1967, Terrell, Texas). A stand-up COMIC, Foxx got his start on the Fox television series *In Living Color*, appearing from 1991 to 1994. In 1996 he began to star in and produce his own television program, *The Jamie Foxx Show*. His film credits include *The Great White Hype* (1996), *Booty Call* (1997), and *The Players Club* (1998).

Foxx, Redd. *See main text entry.*

Goldberg, Whoopi. *See main text entry.*

Gregory, Dick. *See main text entry.*

Hall, Arsenio (b. Feb. 12, 1956, Cleveland, Ohio). During the 1980's, Hall did stand-up comedy on *The Tonight Show* and on *Late Night with David Letterman*. While hosting his own talk show, *The Arsenio Hall Show* (January, 1989—May, 1994), he received three Emmy Award nominations. His films include *Coming to America* (1988) and *Harlem Nights* (1989).

Paramount Pictures Corp.

In 1993 he produced *Bopha!*, a drama about South Africa. Two years later, he hosted *Soul Train's 25th Anniversary Hall of Fame Special*. He starred in the short-lived situation comedy *Arsenio* in 1997 and appeared on the series *Martial Law* beginning in 1998.

Harvey, Steve (b. 1957, Welch, W. Va.). In 1993 Harvey opened Steve Harvey's Comedy House in DALLAS, TEXAS. His first major role was as Steve Tower in the television comedy series *Me and the Boys* (1994-1995). Harvey also starred in an HBO

(continued)

comedy special and hosted an episode of HBO's *Def Comedy Jam* in the 1990's. Beginning in 1996, he starred in his own television comedy series, *The Steve Harvey Show*.

Hughley, D. L. (b. Los Angeles, Calif.). Hughley first gained notice with a stand-up comedy appearance on HBO's *Def Comedy Jam*. He was chosen as the first host of BLACK ENTERTAINMENT TELEVISION's *Comic View*. He filmed three comedy specials for HBO in the 1990's. In 1998 he starred in an ABC situation comedy, *The Hughleys*.

Hunter, Eddie (Feb. 4, 1888, New York, N.Y.—Feb. 14, 1980, New York, N.Y.). Hunter was known during his early VAUDEVILLE career as the "Fighting Comedian." After leaving school in 1903, he began to write vaudeville sketches. He eventually wrote and performed in all-black Broadway musicals, including *How Come* (1923) and *My Magnolia* (1926), the latter written with Alex Rogers.

Lawrence, Martin (b. Apr. 16, 1965, Frankfurt, West Germany). In the 1980's, Lawrence's earthy street humor won him the role of master of ceremonies on *Def Comedy Jam* for HBO. His situation comedy *Martin* aired on Fox from 1992 to 1997. His 1994 concert film *You So Crazy* received an adults-only NC-17 rating, and many theaters would not show it. Films include *Bad Boys* (1995, with Will Smith), *A Thin Line Between Love and Hate* (1996), *Nothing to Lose* (1997), *Life* (1999), and *Blue Streak* (1999).

Mabley, Moms. *See main text entry.*

Markham, Pigmeat. *See main text entry.*

Murphy, Eddie. *See main text entry.*

Pryor, Richard. *See main text entry.*

Rock, Chris (b. 1968, Brooklyn, N.Y.). Known for his edgy, streetwise stand-up comedy, Rock won national attention on *Saturday Night Live* (1990-1993). His first film role was in *Beverly Hills Cop II* (1987). Other films include *I'm Gonna*  *Git You Sucka* (1988), *New Jack City* (1991), *Boomerang* (1992), *CB4* (1993), and *Lethal Weapon 4* (1998). Rock starred in HBO comedy specials in 1993, 1996, and 1999. In 1997 his CD *Roll with the New* won a Grammy Award and his book *Rock This!* became a best-seller. Beginning in 1996, Rock starred in his own show, *The Chris Rock Show*, on HBO.

Russell, Nipsey (b. Oct. 13, 1923, Atlanta, Ga.). Noted for his humorous poetry, Russell began performing at the age of four. After touring as a stand-up comic with Billy Eckstine, Russell made numerous appearances in nightclubs and on television. He was a regular on *The Dean Martin Show* from 1972 to 1973. Of his film roles, he was best known for his portrayal of the Tin Man in *The Wiz* (1978). In 1961-1962 he played Officer Anderson in the television series *Car 54, Where Are You?*, and in 1994, he appeared in the film version of the show.

Sinbad (David Atkins; b. 1957, Benton Harbor, Mich.). Sinbad's stint as a warm-up comedian for studio audiences watching the taping of *The Cosby Show* in New York led to his television debut as a member of the ensemble cast of the show's spin-off series *A Different World* (1987-1991). Known for his outrageous yet family-oriented comedy, Sinbad starred in his own short-lived situation comedy on the Fox network, *The Sinbad Show* (1994-1995). From 1997 to 1998, he hosted the television series *Vibe*.

Walker, Jimmie (b. June 25, 1947, New York). Walker was cast in the role of J. J. Evans, a jive-talking teen who was fond of the phrase "Dyn-o-mite," on the CBS comedy series *Good Times* (1974-1979). *Time* magazine named Walker comedian of the decade. After the series was canceled, Walker returned to stand-up comedy, touring the United States and making appearances on *The Late Show with David Letterman*, *Politically Incorrect*, and *The Tonight Show with Jay Leno*. He also hosted political and issue-oriented radio talk shows on stations around the nation.

Wallace, George. Wallace's club appearances included Caroline's in 1983 and Happy Days at Kew Gardens in 1985. Television appearances include *The Mike Douglas Show* in 1980, *Late Night with David Letterman* in 1983 and 1985, the *Tonight Show* in 1986, *The Fresh Prince of Bel-Air* in 1990, and *Seinfeld* in 1990.

Warfield, Marsha (b. Mar. 5, 1955, Chicago, Ill.). From 1986 to 1991, Warfield played bailiff Roz Russell on the popular television situation comedy *Night Court*. Because of the raunchiness of her stand-up comedy act, her routines most often have been televised on cable outlets on such specials as *Comic Relief* (1987), *Just for Laughs* (1987), and *On Location* (1987). In 1990 she hosted her own celebrity morning talk show, *The Marsha Warfield Show*, on NBC. From 1993 to 1995, she appeared on the situation comedy *Empty Nest* and in 1997 on the series *Smart Guy*. Her films include *The Marva Collins Story* (1981), *Mask* (1985), *D.C. Cab* (1985), *Caddyshack II* (1988), and *Doomsday Rock* (1997).

AP/Wide World Photos

Wayans, Damon (b. Sept. 4, 1960, New York). Wayans, the brother of Keenen Ivory Wayans, was in the original cast of Fox television's *In Living Color* (1990-1992). He also appeared on *Saturday Night Live* in 1985 and 1986. Wayans starred in the 1998 television series *Damon*. Film appearances include roles in *Beverly Hills Cop* (1984), *The Last Boy Scout* (1991), *Mo' Money* (1992), *Major Payne* (1995), *Bulletproof* (1996), *Harlem Aria* (1999), and *Goosed* (1999).

White, Slappy (1921, Baltimore, Md.–Nov. 7, 1995). A comedy partner of Redd Foxx during the 1950's, White was a popular performer live and on the big and small screens. He appeared on television shows such as *Sanford and Son* in 1972 and *Redd Foxx* in 1977. Films include *Amazing Grace* (1974), *Amazon Women on the Moon* (1987), and *Mr. Saturday Night* (1992). White also recorded comedy albums.

Wilson, Flip. *See main text entry.*

Wiltshire, George. Wiltshire was known for his work as a straight man for other comedians from the 1920's through the 1950's. Wiltshire and comedian Dewey "Pigmeat" Markham played the Alhambra Theater in the late 1920's and the APOLLO THEATER beginning in the 1930's. Wiltshire and Markham were featured with singer Edith Wilson in the Broadway cast of *Hot Rhythm* (1930). Films include *It Happened in Harlem* (1945), *Midnight Menace*, (1946), *Junction 88* (1947), *Hi-de-Ho*, (1947), and *Killer Diller* (1948).

---

significant elements in the delivery of oral presentations of other public figures, including clergy, politicians, and blues musicians.

Film and Television
By the early 1900's, the motion picture screen had become the visual outlet for the comic minstrel image. These images left a lasting impression on American viewers. The earliest silent films of the 1890's, particularly small independent films made by European and American filmmakers, experimented with the image of African Americans on screen. In 1903 a film adaptation of a stage version of *Uncle Tom's Cabin*, made with white actors in blackface, was opened in film theaters and claimed to present authentic images of plantation life. Subsequent versions presented in 1914 and 1927 featured African American actors Sam Lukas and James B. Lowe, respectively, in the lead role.

Despite the positive images their screen presence conveyed, these actors could not counteract the negative stereotypes presented in D. W. Griffith's 1915 film *The Birth of a Nation*. As portrayed by white actors in blackface, this film's villainous black characters prompted vigorous protests from the NATIONAL ASSOCIATION FOR THE ADVANCEMENT OF COLORED PEOPLE (NAACP). While these films were not comedies, they did focus attention on the problems associated with the presentation of African Americans on the motion picture screen. In an attempt to counteract harmful negative images, Hollywood offered its audiences a more benign look at black life. The stock characters of the docile servant and the inferior "darky" and "coon," while providing scope for comedy, ultimately became enduring stereotypes in motion pictures.

In these stock parts, African American actors were often expected to provide comic relief in dramatic films. Comedy was used as an effective device in fostering goodwill toward blacks among white audiences, who viewed these comic images as harmless entertainment. Actors such as Stepin FETCHIT, Mantan Moreland, Willie Best, Hattie McDANIEL, Butterfly McQUEEN, Louise BEAVERS, and others became popular comedic mainstays in Hollywood films. Their performances were so humorous that they would often steal attention away from white headliner stars.

The impact of the black comic stereotype through the 1940's established the prototype for both film and television. The cinematic success of the *Our Gang* series of the 1930's, which featured juvenile black actors in the roles of Sunshine Sammy and Buckwheat, set the tone for films such as Walt Disney's *Song of the South* (1946) and the Rastus films, which highlighted a character type sometimes known as the Sambo stereotype. With exaggerated facial grimaces and wild-eyed glances, the black adult and child actors in these films created comic images that reinforced the old minstrel stereotypes of the 1800's.

Stage and screen musicals with all-black casts served as another vehicle for introducing popular comic performers. The vaudeville team of Flournoy Miller and Aubrey Lyles had performed on the theater circuit in the early 1900's and found success on Broadway in the all-black musical comedy *Shuffle Along*, produced by Noble Sissle and Eubie BLAKE in 1921. Lyles died in 1932, but Miller re-created one of their favorite comedy routines with the help of Johnny Lee in the 1943 film *Stormy Weather*. Miller and Lee appeared in a cameo comedy skit referred to as "indefinite talk," in which the two men engaged in a dialogue that continued without a break in the flow of speech, with each participant immediately

understanding what the other was about to say before it was stated aloud. Another performer who made a transition to film was the popular comedian Eddie "Rochester" ANDERSON, known for his recurring role opposite Jack Benny on radio in the 1940's and 1950's, who was featured as a romantic lead opposite Ethel WATERS and Lena HORNE in the all-black feature film *Cabin in the Sky* (1943).

These comedians paved the way for notable black comedies of the 1970's, showcasing the comic talents of actors such as Godfrey Cambridge (*Watermelon Man*, 1970), Bill COSBY (*Uptown Saturday Night*, 1974), and Jimmie Walker (*Let's Do It Again*, 1975). Appearing as black comic leads in largely white ensemble casts, actors Cleavon Little (*Blazing Saddles*, 1974) and Richard PRYOR (*Silver Streak*, 1976) also satirized white assumptions and preconceptions about black culture. Situation comedies that aired on television during the 1970's provided another venue for talented comic performers, including Redd Foxx of *Sanford and Son*; Jimmie Walker of *Good Times*; and Sherman Hemsley, Isabel Sanford, and Marla Gibbs of *The Jeffersons*.

In the 1980's, *Saturday Night Live* comedian Eddie MURPHY made a successful transition to the screen with popular films such as *48 HRS* (1982), *Beverly Hills Cop* (1984), and their sequels. Murphy's popularity continued in the next decade, as he starred in films such as *Vampire in Brooklyn* (1995), *The Nutty Professor* (1996, a remake of a Jerry Lewis film), *Dr. Doolittle* (1998), and *Bowfinger* (1999, with Steve Martin).

Comedian Robert Townsend skewered stereotypes with the release of *Hollywood Shuffle* (1987). During this same period, stand-up COMIC Whoopi GOLDBERG launched a successful film career, first with a dramatic role in the 1985 film adaptation of Alice Walker's *The Color Purple* and later with comedic roles in films including *Ghost* (1990) and *Sister Act* (1994). Popular situation comedies on television during the 1980's also showcased talented black performers. In addition to the hit NBC series *The Cosby Show*, Marsha Warfield was seen on *Night Court*, Jackée Harry performed as part of a black ensemble cast on *227*, and Sinbad headed the cast of *A Different World*.

During the 1990's a number of African American comedians who got their start on the Fox network's *In Living Color* (which featured a comedy troupe assembled by Keenen Ivory Wayans), BET's *Comic View*, or HBO's *Def Comedy Jam*, went on to star in or host their own television series. Martin Lawrence's situation comedy *Martin* appeared from 1992 to 1997 on Fox. The popular comedian and actor also starred in motion pictures such as *Bad Boys* (1995, with Will Smith) and *Blue Streak* (1999).

In 1996 Steve Harvey launched his television series *The Steve Harvey Show* on the WB network, Chris Rock first starred in the HBO series *The Chris Rock Show*, and Jamie Foxx appeared in the series *The Jamie Foxx Show*. D. L. Hughley added his name to the list of television stars with his ABC situation comedy *The Hughleys* in 1998. More established comedians also had their own television series. Robert Townsend launched *The Parent 'Hood* on the WB network in 1995. Bill Cosby starred in a new show, CBS's *Cosby*, beginning in 1996, and he hosted *Kids Say the Darndest Things*, based on the show featuring Art Linkletter, beginning in 1998.

Black comedic style got another boost on the Hollywood screen with the advent of several young African American film directors. Hailed as a brilliant satire of black male-female relationships, Spike LEE's independent film *She's Gotta Have It* (1986) was followed by the mainstream studio release of *School Daze* (1988), a satiric look at student antics on a black college campus. In 1991 brothers Reginald and Warrington Hudlin produced and

A versatile comic and actor, Sinbad has built his career around family-oriented humor. *(AP/Wide World Photos)*

directed *House Party*, a comedic look at HIP-HOP culture and the rap phenomenon in the black community based on Reginald's Academy Award-winning short film, first submitted as a school thesis. The Hudlins followed their *House Party* success with *Boomerang* (1992), a romantic comedy starring Eddie Murphy, and Reginald Hudlin appeared in *The Great White Hype* (1996).

By the end of the 1990's, the themes and characterizations found in comedy and humor as performed by African Americans had come full circle. The exploitive nature of the stereotypical situations and characters found in the early minstrel shows of the 1800's had been modified into an acceptable set of comic conventions. Black performers found themselves in demand to explore a full range of comic characters, whether on stage, screen, or television. The popular nature of comedy, with its liberating ability to poke fun at pretensions and stereotypes within the black community—as well as those in the white American mainstream—provided comic performers with the latitude necessary to preserve old traditions and build new ones despite the complex rules and regulations of the entertainment industry.

—James G. Pappas
See also: *Amos 'n' Andy*; *Cosby Show, The*; *Film*; *Minstrels*; *Television series*.

Suggested Readings:

Bogle, Donald. *Toms, Coons, Mulattoes, Mammies, and Bucks: An Interpretive History of Blacks in American Film*. 3d ed. New York: Continuum, 1994.

Boskin, Joseph. *Sambo: The Rise and Demise of an American Jester*. New York: Oxford University Press, 1986.

Charters, Ann. *Nobody: The Story of Bert Williams*. New York: Macmillan, 1970.

Cripps, Thomas. *Slow Fade to Black: The Negro in American Film, 1900-1942*. New York: Oxford University Press, 1977.

Dance, Daryl C. *Shuckin' and Jivin': Folklore from Contemporary Black Americans*. Bloomington: Indiana University Press, 1978.

Foxx, Redd, and Norman Miller. *Redd Foxx Encyclopedia of Black Humor*. Pasadena, Calif.: Ward Ritchie Press, 1977.

Means Coleman, Robin R. *African American Viewers and the Black Situation Comedy: Situating Racial Humor*. New York: Garland, 1998.

Schechter, William. *The History of Negro Humor in America*. New York: Fleet Press, 1970.

Toll, Robert C. *Blacking Up: The Minstrel Show in Nineteenth-Century America*. New York: Oxford University Press, 194.

Watkins, Mel. *On the Real Side: Laughing, Lynching, and Signifying, the Underground Tradition of African American Humor That Transformed American Culture, from Slavery to Richard Pryor*. New York: Simon & Schuster, 1994.

Comer, James Pierpont (b. September 25, 1934, East Chicago, Indiana): Educator and child psychiatrist. Comer was one of five children born to a steelworker and his wife. Having felt the harsh brunt of discrimination because of their race and their limited education, Comer's parents instilled in him and his siblings a strong sense of self-esteem and encouraged them to achieve their full potential. Comer received his A.B. degree from Indiana University in 1956 and moved to WASHINGTON, D.C., where he enrolled in HOWARD UNIVERSITY's College of Medicine. Comer graduated with his M.D. degree in 1960. After interning at St. Catherine Hospital in East Chicago for one year, Comer returned to Washington to serve on the staff of the U.S. Public Health Service from 1961 to 1963. In 1964 Comer completed his master's degree in public health from the University of Michigan School of Public Health and joined the staff of the National Institute of Mental Health, where he served for four years.

James Comer in 1988. *(AP/Wide World Photos)*

Comer's first academic appointment came when he accepted a post as assistant professor at Yale University's Child Study Center in 1968. In 1969 he was appointed associate dean of the Yale School of Medicine and continued to hold a joint professorship at the Child Study Center. Comer was named director of Yale's School Development Program in 1973 and was appointed to the Maurice Falk Chair as professor of child psychiatry in 1976.

During his tenure at Yale, Comer developed an educational approach that became known informally as the Comer method. Officially established in 1968, it was promulgated by the School Development Program at Yale. Comer's theory held that children's self-esteem, regardless of their race, was vital to their educational success. Rather than focusing on remedial skills training to improve

the academic achievement of black students, Comer developed a social skills training program in which teachers set challenging yet attainable goals for black children, encouraging them to reach beyond society's expectations for them.

Although critics argued that Comer slighted the effects of such factors as POVERTY, FAMILY LIFE, and other social conditions that affect black children's academic performance, his theories produced evidence of their utility. The Comer method was adopted in the New Haven, Connecticut, school system and produced dramatic academic gains among the district's inner-city black children. In 1990 Comer won the McGraw Prize in Education, and the Rockefeller Foundation agreed to fund a five-year, fifteen-million-dollar program to implement the School Development Program at eight schools throughout the United States. The Ford Foundation continued to help fund the program through the 1990's. By 1999 the program was in use at more than seven hundred schools in the United States and other countries. In 1998 the thirtieth anniversary of the School Development Program was celebrated with a tribute and symposium at Yale.

See also: Education.

Comics, stand-up: Comedy in which a single performer speaks directly to the audience has its roots in the monologues performed by comedians as part of VAUDEVILLE shows. However, most of the comedy performed by

African Americans in vaudeville shows took the form of skits and dialogues because many people in white audiences, especially in the South, were displeased if black comics addressed them directly. Perhaps as a result, the monologues that were performed by blacks tended to feature portrayals of interesting characters or to concentrate on storytelling.

The first African American stand-up comic may have been Allen Drew, who performed mostly in black clubs from the 1920's through the 1950's. Eventually known as the "black Milton Berle," he fired off a succession of one-liners, some of which were suggestive. The blue nature of his humor kept him out of many theaters, including those on the THEATRE OWNERS BOOKING ASSOCIATION (TOBA) circuit. ("Blue" humor contains vulgar or obscene language or explicit references to sex or bodily functions.) Among the TOBA comedians who performed monologues were Boot Hope, who specialized in telling tall tales; Pigmeat MARKHAM, best known for his "Here come de judge" routine (later adopted by Sammy DAVIS, Jr.); Dusty Fletcher, who played a drunk and became known for his "Open the door, Richard" routine; and Moms MABLEY, who played a slightly lecherous older woman.

Moms Mabley was one of the first African American comedians to turn to monologues for most of her humor. Her stage persona was that of an older woman constantly in search of a young man. She appeared on stage wearing strange-looking hats and battered cotton dresses. She shuffled, sang parodies, and told stories as part of her act and was known for her suggestive, irreverent humor. In the 1930's and 1940's, she played largely in clubs and at such venues as the APOLLO THEATRE in HARLEM.

Transitions

In the 1940's and 1950's, Slappy White and Nipsey Russell were among the first black stand-up comics to perform before largely white audiences. They cultivated dignified topical humor, delivered in standard English, that avoided the outlandish costumes, dialect, and indirect satire of traditional African American comedy. The sexual references and explicit language favored by performers such as Mabley and Redd Foxx were largely absent. Their success helped other African American stand-up comics, including Dick GREGORY and Bill COSBY, reach mainstream, mixed-race audiences.

Gregory, who had been doing stand-up comedy in small black clubs in the 1950's, jump-started his career with an appearance at the Playboy Club in Chicago in 1961. Using standard speech and avoiding blue language, he created a somewhat cerebral form of satire. By the mid-1960's, influenced by the CIVIL RIGHTS movement, Gregory's humor had became harsher, and he gradually became more activist than comic.

Bill Cosby, who got his start in 1962 in Greenwich Village, was basically a folksy monologist who built his humor around tales of his childhood and family life. His "colorless" brand of comedy eventually led to a successful career as an actor in long-running situation comedies on television.

The wide popularity of Gregory and Cosby led audiences to an appreciation of racier forms of black humor, and the careers of Mabley and Foxx grew in the 1960's. Another comic who got his start in the 1960's was Flip WILSON, whose early television appearances on *The Tonight Show* and *Rowan and Martin's Laugh-in* led to his own television show, *The Flip Wilson Show*, beginning in 1970. Although Wilson avoided profanity and explicit sexual references, he used black street language and portrayed humorous but positive characters.

"In-Your-Face" Humor

Another stand-up comic who got his start during the 1960's was Richard PRYOR. Although his act was considerably "blacker" than Cosby's, containing more black language, character-based humor, biting satire, and jokes about race relations, he was immensely popular with both white and black audiences. He released a number of successful comedy albums, including *That Nigger's Crazy* (1974), and appeared in a series of films, including *Silver Streak* (1976).

The beginning of the 1980's saw a surge in the popularity of stand-up comedy, and many new black stand-up comics emerged, performing in the numerous comedy clubs around the country. Many of them rose to stardom through appearances on comedy and variety television shows such as *Saturday Night Live*, *In Living Color*, and *The Tonight Show*. Others were featured in specials produced by cable television networks, including Home Box Office (HBO) and in shows filmed at comedy clubs such as *A&E's an Evening at the Improv*. Some of the better known comedians to emerge in the early 1980's included Eddie MURPHY, Whoopi GOLDBERG, Arsenio Hall, Robert Townsend, Keenen Ivory Wayans, Sinbad, and Damon Wayans.

Many of these comics, including Murphy in *Eddie Murphy Raw* (1987), went beyond Gregory and Pryor and developed an in-your-face type of humor that did not hesitate to use profanity and explicit sexual references. Wide exposure of this type of humor was made possible by venues such as comedy clubs and cable television networks. Murphy also used physical humor such as exaggerated expressions and body movements and created numerous comic characters such as "Little Richard Simmons," a combination of black musician Little Richard and white fitness-and-diet guru Richard Simmons. Murphy was also a trend-setter in that he parlayed his success as a stand-up comic into a career as a film star.

During the 1980's and 1990's, films and television programs starring African Americans became more common. Like Murphy, many stand-up comics—while continuing to produce comedy CDs and appear on HBO specials—began starring in comedy and action films and even in dramas. Whoopi Goldberg, who first made her name as a stand-up comic and was featured in a popular HBO special, preferred to be known as an actor and concentrated most of her efforts in this area. Other stand-up comics went on to star in situation comedies.

The Hip-Hop Comics
A number of stand-up comics who emerged in the late 1980's and the 1990's also moved from clubs to television specials to situation comedies and films. Martin Lawrence, known for an irreverent, sexually explicit type of humor, starred in his own television series, *Martin* (1992-1997), a situation comedy, then went on to star in action-adventure films such as *Blue Streak* (1999). Chris Rock, a *Saturday Night Live* regular from 1990 to 1993, starred in an HBO special, then became the host of HBO's *The Chris Rock Show*, a talk show, in 1996. Other stand-up comics such as Jamie Foxx, Steve Harvey, and D. L. Hughley became the stars of television situation comedies. These comics were following the pattern created by Murphy and Goldberg in that they moved from stand-up to television or film, but their humor was more directed toward black audiences. The white audience became a secondary consideration—if it enjoyed the humor, fine, but the comics were no longer tailoring their humor to suit white audiences.

—*Rowena Wildin*
See also: Comedy and humor; Television series.

Suggested Readings:

Foxx, Redd, and Norman Miller. *Redd Foxx Encyclopedia of Black Humor*. Pasadena, Calif.: Ward Ritchie Press, 1977.

Means Coleman, Robin R. *African American Viewers and the Black Situation Comedy: Situating Racial Humor*. New York: Garland, 1998.

Schechter, William. *The History of Negro Humor*

in America. New York: Fleet Press, 1970.

Watkins, Mel. *On the Real Side: Laughing, Lying, and Signifying: The Underground Tradition of African-American Humor that Transformed American Culture, from Slavery to Richard Pryor.* New York: Simon & Schuster, 1994.

Zook, Kristal Brent. *Color by Fox: The Fox Network and the Revolution in Black Television.* New York: Oxford University Press, 1999.

Commission on Civil Rights: Federal commission established by the Civil Rights Act of 1957. The charge of the U.S. Commission on Civil Rights (sometimes called the Civil Rights Commission) was to gather facts, from written records and witnesses' testimony, about voting rights violations and economic coercion used to keep African Americans from voting. Further, the commission was charged with trying to educate the public about race relations. The commission held hearings in Washington, D.C., and in many of the southern states and issued periodic reports to the president of the United States. It also cooperated with the new CIVIL RIGHTS division in the Justice Department.

By 1961 the commissioners had collected enough information on attempts to stop African Americans from voting in the South to pressure newly inaugurated President John F. Kennedy to take strong action, a course he resisted. The commission continued to supply the Justice Department with information. By 1962 the commission had investigated conditions in MISSISSIPPI, one of the nation's worst violators of voting rights. That year saw major white protests across the state as well as violence at the University of Mississippi when James MEREDITH, an African American, tried to enroll. Although Kennedy generally disapproved of, and reportedly tried to obstruct, the commission's work, it eventually did submit reports on the Mississippi troubles and those of other southern states.

By late 1963, the commission had collected so much information that President Kennedy had to act. After the murder of Medgar EVERS in Jackson, Mississippi, the president sent a civil rights bill to Congress. After Kennedy was assassinated, Lyndon B. Johnson made passage of that bill his highest priority. Johnson's forces eventually broke a filibuster in the Senate, and the historic Civil Rights Act of 1964 became law. The next year, a voter registration act firmly protected the African American community's right to vote. In the entire process, the U.S. Commission on Civil Rights played a large role with its fact-finding and educational mission.

The commission remained active, but when the Civil Rights movement began its decline in the late 1960's, it lost its high profile. The commission was reestablished by the U.S. Commission on Civil Rights Act of 1983. It continued in its role as a fact-finding agency, also evaluating laws and the effectiveness of federal programs.

See also: Civil rights and congressional legislation; Equal Employment Opportunity Commission (EEOC); Politics and government.

Communist Party: The American Communist Party began in 1919. It never grew very large, peaking at about 100,000 members in 1943. Efforts to recruit black communists had limited success, and the relationship between blacks and communists mirrored the relationship between blacks and white Americans in general.

Early Years, 1919-1938

The Communist Party did little to recruit black Americans during its first ten years. Then the sixth meeting of the Communist International in 1928 ordered an intensive recruitment campaign among blacks utilizing the twin themes of equal rights and self-determination.

The SCOTTSBORO CASES that began in 1931

gave communists high visibility among black Americans. These young black men were accused of raping two white girls in ALABAMA. The communists began a nationwide campaign to publicize the case. The Scottsboro boys were eventually acquitted, but many observers concluded that party lawyers were more interested in exploiting the trial for the party's own publicity than in achieving justice. Throughout the South, party membership remained small in the 1930's. In no southern state were there more than a thousand members. That would change in 1939, when the party turned away from direct action to front organizations.

Success and Setbacks, 1939-1947

Frustrated by their meager gains and upstaged by the New Deal, Communist Party leaders sought to expand party influence through front organizations headed by a cadre of secret party members. The Southern Negro Youth Congress and the Southern Congress for Human Welfare were two of the most successful front organizations. Meanwhile, in New York City, blacks rallied around the leadership of the black communist Ben Davis. Davis was elected to the New York City Council in 1943. His campaign included rallies that drew eight thousand to thirty thousand people. His supporters in-

In 1948 the federal government arrested ten officers of the Communist Party on charges of plotting to overthrow the government. Among the arrested were Henry Winston (center rear) and Benjamin J. Davis (front right). *(Library of Congress)*

cluded black celebrities such as boxer Joe Louis and musician Count Basie. The party lavished publicity on Davis.

During these same years, however, the party made a serious mistake by doing everything it could to stifle the movement for a march on Washington. Mainstream CIVIL RIGHTS and labor unions planned a march on Washington to urge speedy resolution of racial issues. The Communist Party sabotaged plans for the meeting and lost considerable support in doing so. After WORLD WAR II ended in 1945, government persecution of communists and the party's own rigid doctrines cost the party black support. By 1947 many observers predicted that the Communist Party would be declared illegal in the near future.

Decline, 1947-1969

FEDERAL BUREAU OF INVESTIGATION (FBI) programs of the 1950's exploited black-Jewish rifts in the party. Front organizations collapsed or withered. Blacks who refused to renounce the party, such as W. E. B. Du Bois and Paul ROBESON, paid dearly. The party was no longer in the vanguard of civil rights groups. When Angela DAVIS, a fiery black intellectual, joined the Communist Party in 1969, a revival of black interest seemed possible. However, black militant groups and Maoist organizations undercut the party's appeal. By the late twentieth century, the party was a shell of what it once had been, and it had virtually no support from black Americans.

The Communist Party had supported civil rights long before such opinions were popular, but the dogmatic policies and erratic tactics of the party prevented it from gaining lasting support among black Americans.

—*Michael Polley*

Suggested Readings:

Gates, John. *The Story of an American Communist*. New York: Thomas Nelson, 1958.

Horne, Gerald. *The Red and the Black*. New York: Monthly Review Press, 1993.

Klehr, Harvey. *The Heyday of American Communism*. New York: Basic Books, 1984.

Record, Wilson. *Race and Radicalism*. Cornell University Press, 1964.

In 1976 the Communist Party's candidate for vice president was African American Jarvis Tyner. *(Library of Congress)*